EESL

Deputy Manager / Assistant Engineer

Latest Edition
Practice Kit

10 Tests
10 Mock Test

Based On Real Exam Pattern

✓ Thoroughly Revised and Updated

✓ Detailed Analysis of all MCQs

<table>
<tr><td>Title</td><td>: EESL Deputy Manager / Assistant Engineer</td></tr>
<tr><td>Author Name</td><td>: Mr. Rohit Manglik</td></tr>
<tr><td>Published By</td><td>: EduGorilla Community Pvt. Ltd.</td></tr>
<tr><td>Publishers Address</td><td>: 12/651, First Floor Opp. Arvindo Park, Near Jama Masjid,
Indira Nagar, Lucknow, Uttar Pradesh-226016, India</td></tr>
</table>

Copyright EduGorilla

Disclaimer EduGorilla

Although the author and publisher have made every effort to ensure the accuracy of information in this book, we do not assume any responsibility to errors and hereby disclaim any liability to any party for any loss, damage, or disruption caused by errors or omissions, whether such errors or omissions result from negligence, accident, or any other cause.

Compiled and created by EduGorilla Community Pvt. Ltd

Printed By EduGorilla Community Pvt. Ltd.

ROHIT MANGLIK
CEO, EduGorilla

Dear Applicants,

People say *"Success comes to those who work hard."* But I've seen people working hard for their exams day in and day out for marginal success. While others succeed in their examinations by putting in just half the work. So are they God Gifted? No! I believe that it's because they work *smart* and not just *hard*. Similarly, for your exams, you should strategize your preparation so as to increase the likelihood of success. Well with EduGorilla get ready to increase your *chances of selection* in your exam by *16x*.

EduGorilla helps you in not only working *hard* but also working in a *smart and strategic* manner. With EduGorilla's preparation package, you get a chance to make your exam preparation easy, and a fun learning path towards selection. Finding the right path to your preparations can be difficult if you don't know in which direction to head. Don't worry, we have you covered! EduGorilla will be your guide to success in your journey. With our Preparation Package, you can prepare strategically and beat the exam in just one attempt.

EduGorilla's Preparation Package includes-

• **Test Series**   • **Books**

Our preparation package is handcrafted as per the latest changes, expert opinions, and students' discretion. Thus, enabling you to get through each stage of the selection process for your exam.

Our Books are designed by the teachers and experts of the respective exam with a combined 150+ years of experience; to provide you with easy, efficient, and effective learning. Our books are smart, in the sense that not only do they give you the answers to the questions but also provide similar questions for practice.

EduGorilla's competent Test Series gives you real-time experience and confidence through which you can clear your offline or online exam in just one attempt. We currently host 83,000+ mock tests for 1,440+ competitive and academic exams.

Thus, EduGorilla misses no chance to assist you in your preparation and covers all stages of the exam, so that you don't have to look anywhere else.

We provide complete preparation packages for defense, banking, teaching, and other National & State-Level exams. Hence, it doesn't matter which exam you aspire to because you will reach your success.

ALL THE BEST !
Let EduGorilla be your Guide to Success.

Rohit Manglik,
Founder and CEO, EduGorilla

INTRODUCTION

EduGorilla focuses on guiding students to succeed in their examinations. With that in mind, our book, titled "EESL : Deputy Manager / Assistant Engineer", has been drafted through the collective efforts of our distinguished experts with 150+ years of combined experience. This book consists of questions that are created following the latest changes in the syllabus and exam pattern. We compiled the book on the basis of questions that are most likely to appear in the EESL - Deputy Manager / Assistant Engineer. Through EduGorilla's "EESL : Deputy Manager / Assistant Engineer" your chances of success will increase 16x.

EduGorilla does this through our Complete Preparation Package. This package consists of well-conceptualized and structured content in the form of questions that are tailor-made according to your needs and will help you practice for exams in a smart way by pinpointing all the necessary information. It also provides hints and solutions, along with a smart answer sheet for your self-evaluation. You can assess your shortcomings and work accordingly on areas that may require more of your attention.

EduGorilla promises to help you succeed in your examination and accomplish your dream goals. We believe in our aspirants and see them at the top of the merit list. And the first step towards the top is to start preparing with us. EduGorilla's "EESL : Deputy Manager / Assistant Engineer" includes the following attributes.

➤ Well-Researched Content

➤ Top-Notch Quality

➤ Detailed Answers and Analysis

➤ Smart Answer Sheet

➤ Exam Relevant Questions

Therefore, EduGorilla fortifies your preparation and makes it durable enough to help you stand tall and beat the examination.

EESL - Deputy Manager / Assistant Engineer
Scan QR code for Eligibility, Exam Pattern, Syllabus and more.

Book ID: 0232

TABLE OF CONTENTS

Part - I

Q.1 The method of soil conservation in which bare ground between plants is covered with layer of organic matter like straw is called?

A. Mulching   **B.** Contour barriers

C. Rockdam   **D.** Terrace farming

Q.2 _________ is the wearing away of the landscape by different agents like water, wind and ice.

A. Weathering   **B.** Attrition

C. Erosion   **D.** Abrasion

Q.3 In Microsoft Word, ______ allows us to change the color of selected text.

A. Font Color   **B.** Text Color

C. Change Color   **D.** Background Color

Q.4 ________ is the largest phylum of Animalia which includes insects.

A. Annelida   **B.** Chordata

C. Arthropoda   **D.** Platyhelminthes

Q.5 According to the categories of land mentioned in the Chola inscriptions _________ was known as the land gifted to Brahmanas?

A. Vellanvagai   **B.** Brahmadeya

C. Shalabhoga   **D.** Devadana

Q.6 Prithviraja III (1168-1192) was a best known _________ ruler.

A. Chahamana   **B.** Gahadavala

C. Chalukya   **D.** Brahmana

Q.7 Who discovered Insulin?

A. Sir Alexander Fleming

B. Frederick Banting

C. James Watt

D. Sir F.G . Hopkins

Q.8 In 2016, which company lost high profile legal battles with HP and Google?

A. Oracle   **B.** Apple

C. Microsoft   **D.** Intel

Ques (9-12):Direction: Study the following graph carefully to answer the question that follows:

Q.9

What is the difference between the total sale of English newspapers and the sale of Hindi newspapers in all the localities together?

A. 6000   **B.** 8500   **C.** 7000   **D.** 7500

Q.10 The sale of English Newspaper in locality A is approximately what percent of the total sale of English Newspaper in all the localities together?

A. 527%   **B.** 25%   **C.** 111%   **D.** 19%

Q.11 What is the ratio of the sale of Hindi Newspapers in locality A to the sale of Hindi newspapers in locality D?

A. 11: 19   **B.** 6: 5   **C.** 5: 6   **D.** 19: 11

Q.12 The sale of English Newspapers in locality B and D together is approximately what percent of the sale of English Newspapers in locality A, C, and E together?

A. 162%   **B.** 84%   **C.** 70%   **D.** 121%

Q.13 Directions:Study the graph and answer the questions:

Expenditure(in lakhs) of three different Company in five Different year

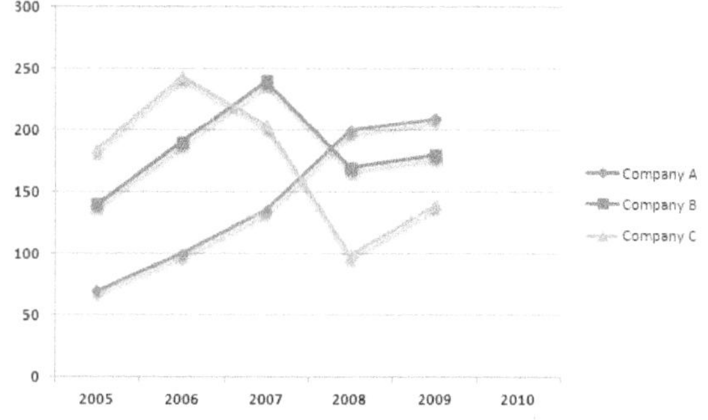

What was the overall average expenditure of Company C in all the years together?

A. Rs. 190 lakhs
B. Rs. 120 lakhs
C. Rs. 180 lakhs
D. Rs. 150 lakhs

Q.14 Directions:Study the graph and answer the questions:

Expenditure(in lakhs) of three different Company in five Different year

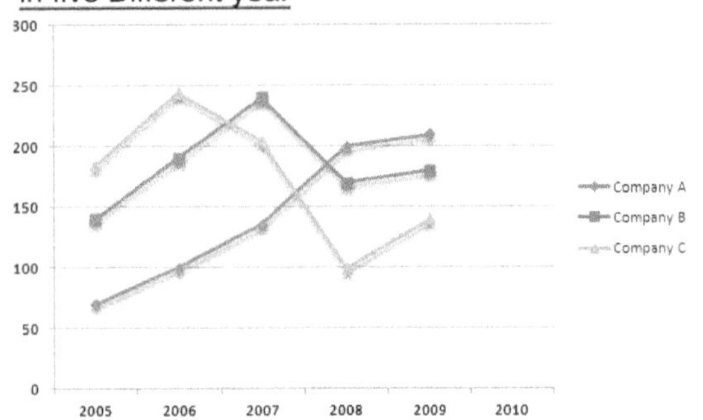

What was the difference between the total expenditure of company B in the year 2006 and 2008 together and the total expenditure of company C in the year 2007 and 2009 together?

A. Rs. 1000000
B. Rs. 100000
C. Rs. 10000000
D. Rs. 100000000

Q.15 Directions:Study the graph and answer the questions:

Expenditure(in lakhs) of three different Company in five Different year

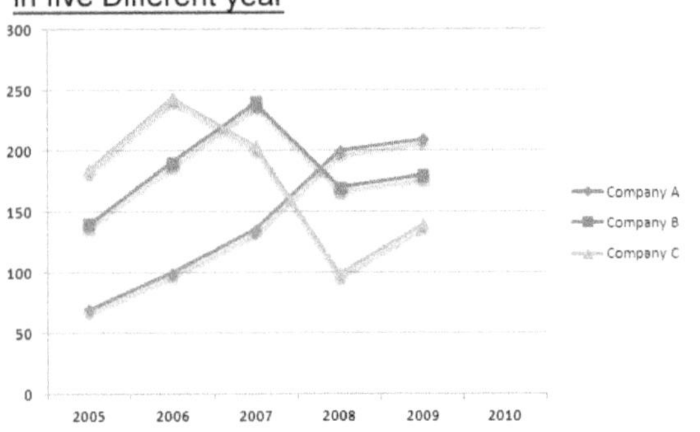

What was the respective ratio between the expenditure of company A in the year 2009 and expenditure of company B in the year 2005?

A. 5:3 B. 3:4 C. 3:5 D. 3:2

Q.16 Directions:Study the graph and answer the questions:

Expenditure(in lakhs) of three different Company in five Different year

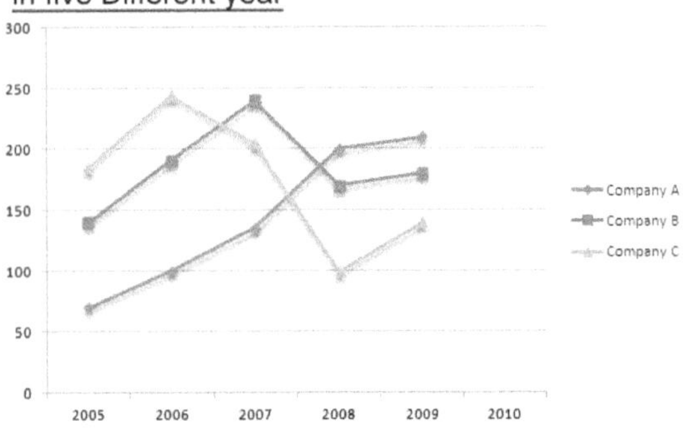

In which year was the total expenditure by all three Companies together second highest?

A. 2005 B. 2006 C. 2007 D. 2008

Q.17 A wholesaler sells a good to a retailer at a profit of 5% and the retailer sells it to a customer at a profit of 10%. If the customer pays Rs. 2,000, what had it cost (in Rs.) to the wholesaler?

A. 1,731.6 B. 3,210.6 C. 1,931.6 D. 2,310.6

Q.18 What least number must be subtracted from 518, so that the sum is completely divisible by 13?

A. 11 B. 10 C. 9 D. 12

Q.19 What is the value of $\tan 45° + \dfrac{1}{3}\cosec 60°$?

A. $\sqrt{3} + 2$ B. $\dfrac{(9+2\sqrt{3})}{9}$ C. $\sqrt{3}$ D. $\dfrac{(2\sqrt{2}+3)}{\sqrt{6}}$

Q.20 If $\cot\theta = \dfrac{21}{20}$, then what is the value of $\sec\theta$?

A. $\dfrac{29}{21}$ B. $\dfrac{21}{29}$ C. $\dfrac{29}{20}$ D. $\dfrac{20}{29}$

Q.21 A Survey was conducted to find what genre of movies people liked the most. 1200 people answered the survey. The pie chart shows the results of that survey. The numbers in the pie chart are the ratios. 15% do not like any of the movies. Study the diagram and answer the followings questions.

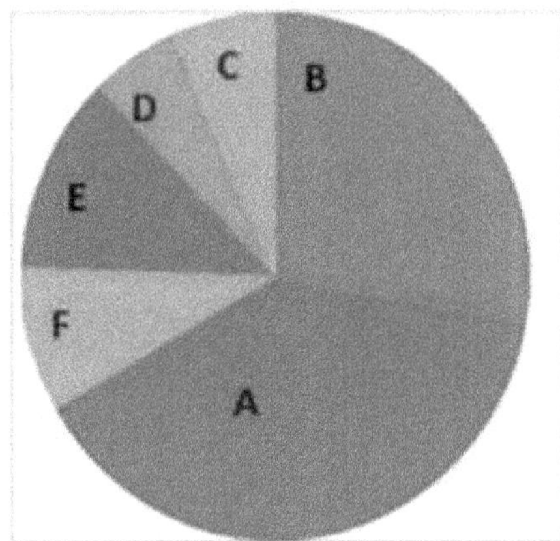

A. Comedy – 35 B. Action – 25
C. Historical – 6 D. Fiction – 5
E. Drama – 11 F. Romance – 3

Which two genres of movies were liked the least?

A. Fiction and Romance
B. Fiction and Drama
C. Drama and Historical
D. Drama and Romance

Q.22 A Survey was conducted to find what genre of movies people liked the most. 1200 people answered the survey. The pie chart shows the results of that survey. The numbers in the pie chart are the ratios. 15% do not like any of the movies. Study the diagram and answer the followings questions.

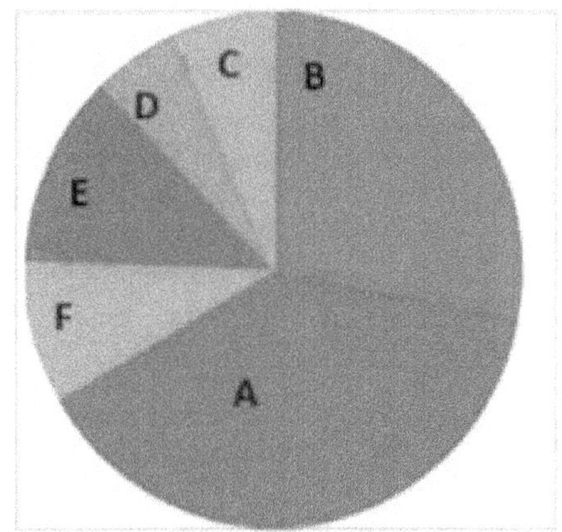

A. Comedy – 35   B. Action – 25
C. Historical – 6   D. Fiction – 5
E. Drama – 11   F. Romance – 3

How many under survey said they liked Historical movies?

A. 6   **B.** 72   **C.** 80   **D.** 60

Q.23 A Survey was conducted to find what genre of movies people liked the most. 1200 people answered the survey. The pie chart shows the results of that survey. The numbers in the pie chart are the ratios. 15% do not like any of the movies. Study the diagram and answer the followings questions.

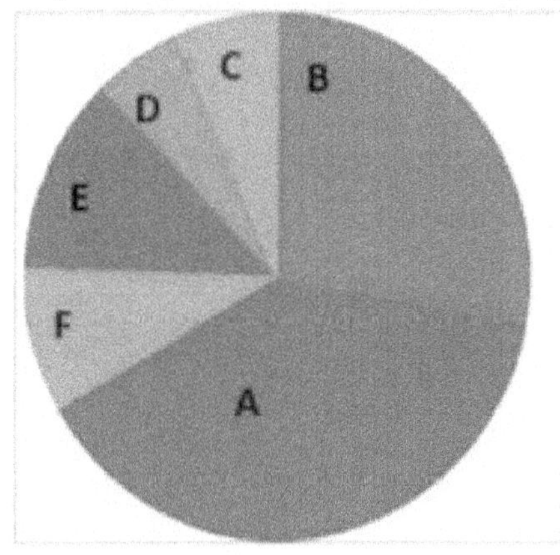

A. Comedy – 35   B. Action – 25
C. Historical – 6   D. Fiction – 5
E. Drama – 11   F. Romance – 3

How many more people under survey like Drama movies than those who like Romance movies?

A. 3   **B.** 96   **C.** 40   **D.** 30

Q.24 A Survey was conducted to find what genre of movies people liked the most. 1200 people answered the survey. The pie chart shows the results of that survey. The numbers in the pie chart are the ratios. 15% do not like any of the movies. Study the diagram and answer the followings questions.

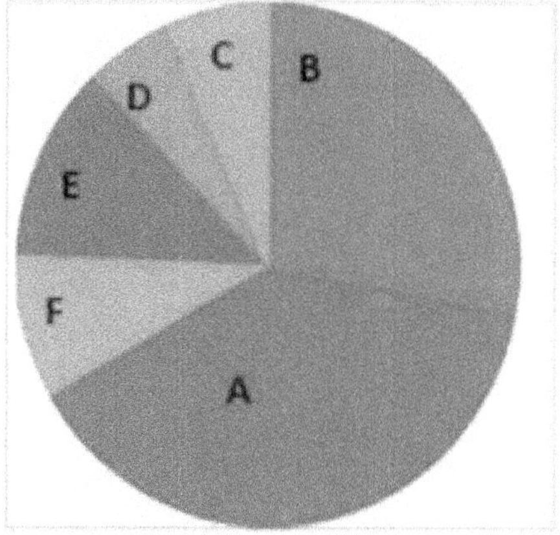

A. Comedy – 35   B. Action – 25
C. Historical – 6   D. Fiction – 5
E. Drama – 11   F. Romance – 3

24% of people who were mailed the survey questionnaire answered the survey. The survey questionnaire was mailed to how many people?

A. 5000   **B.** 10000   **C.** 1200   **D.** 288

Q.25 Where was a joint India-New Development Bank workshop held in September 2019?

A. Hyderabad   **B.** Pune
C. New Delhi   **D.** Jaipur

Q.26 Where is a four-day international symposium on buckwheat being organised in September 2019?

A. Manipur   **B.** Nagaland
C. Meghalaya   **D.** Assam

Q.27 In September 2019, ______ dethroned India captain Virat Kohli to reclaim the top spot in ICC Test rankings.

A. David Warner   **B.** Steve Smith
C. Kane Williamson   **D.** Joe Root

Q.28 Where did the CBI Director Rishi Kumar Shukla inaugurate the 1st National Conference on Cyber Crime Investigation and Cyber Forensics in September 2019?

A. Pune   **B.** Jaipur
C. Bathinda   **D.** New Delhi

Q.29 With which bank has ECL Finance Limited, a subsidiary of Edelweiss Financial Services Limited signed a co-origination agreement in September 2019?

A.   State Bank of India and Central Bank Of India
B.   ICICI Bank and Central Bank Of India
C.   State Bank of India and Canara Bank
D.   Union Bank of India and Central Bank Of India

Q.30 In September 2019, who among the following have been given knighthoods by Theresa May in her resignation honours list?

A.   Geoffrey Boycott and Ian Botham
B.   Geoffrey Boycott and Andrew Strauss
C.   Graham Gooch and Andrew Strauss
D.   Graham Gooch and Geoffrey Boycott

Q.31 In September 2019, who was conferred the 'Lamp of Peace of Saint Francis ' award by the Vatican for his contribution towards establishing peace and harmony?
A. Iqbal Quadir
B. Amartya Sen
C. Muhammad Yunus
D. Mohamed ElBaradei

Q.32 Who has been appointed as the Chair of the Redeployment Coordination Committee (RCC) and head of the UNMHA in September 2019?
A. V. D. Vogra
B. R. Sreenivas
C. Abhijit Guha
D. Jiwesh Nandan

Q.33 In the following question, a sentence has been given in Direct/Indirect speech. Out of the four alternatives suggested, select the one which best expresses the same sentence in Indirect/Direct speech.
"How old is your grandmother?", Navneet asked her.
A. Navne et asked her how old her grandmother is.
B. Navneet asked her how old her grandmother has been.
C. Navneet asked her how old her grandmother was.
D. Navneet asked her how old is her grandmother.

Q.34 In the following question, some part of the sentence may have errors. Find out which part of the sentence has an error and select the appropriate option. If a sentence is free from error, select 'No Error'.
The lady was knocked down (1)/by a speeding car (2)/upon crossing the road.(3)/No Error (4)
A. 1
B. 2
C. 3
D. 4

Q.35 In the following question, out of the four alternatives, select the alternative which is the best substitute of the words/sentence.
Having or involving an extreme or irrational fear of or aversion to something.
A. Valiant
B. Stout
C. Phobic
D. Foolhardy

Q.36 In the following question, out of the four alternatives, select the alternative which will improve the bracketed part of the sentence. In case no improvement is needed, select "no improvement".
I gave up (drinks) many years ago.
A. to drink
B. drink
C. drinking
D. no improvement

Q.37 In the following question, out of the four alternatives, select the word similar in meaning to the word given.
Stupor
A. Sensibility
B. Slumber
C. Liveliness
D. Consciousness

Q.38 In the following question, out of the four alternatives, select the alternative which will improve the bracketed part of the sentence. In case no improvement is needed, select "no improvement".
Rahul went out without (saying) good bye.
A. say even
B. even said
C. say
D. no improvement

Q.39 In the following question, some part of the sentence may have errors. Find out which part of the sentence has an error and select the appropriate option. If a sentence is free from error, select 'No Error'.
Grandfather led (1)/a peaceful life after his (2)/retirement from the army.(3)/No Error (4)
A. 1
B. 2
C. 3
D. 4

Q.40 In the following question, four words are given out of which one word is correctly spelt. Select the correctly spelt word.
A. bereaving
B. bereaveing
C. bereving
D. bireaving

Part - II

Q.41 Advantage of synchronous sequential circuit over asynchronous ones is:
A. Faster operation
B. Case of avoiding problem
C. Lower hardware requirement due to hazards
D. Better noise immunity

Q.42 Synchronous motors are to be used in situations where
A. The load in constant
B. The load is required to be driven at very high speeds
C. The load is to be driven at constant speed
D. The starting torque requirement of the load is very high

Q.43 A pony motor is basically a
A. small induction motor
B. D.C. series motor
C. D.C. shunt motor
D. double winding A.C./D.C. motor

Q.44 The merit of the synchronous motor over induction motor is that
A. it runs at a constant speed
B. it can run over a wide range of power factors both lagging and leading
C. its torque is less sensitive to change in supply frequency
D. all of these

Q.45 The reciprocal of resistance is:
A. Conductance
B. Resistivity
C. Conductivity
D. Drift velocity

Q.46 Mostly, synchronous motors are of
A. alternator type machines
B. induction type machines
C. salient pole type machines
D. smooth cylindrical type machines

Q.47 A synchronous motor can operate at_____.
A. Leading power factor only
B. Lagging power factor only
C. Unity power factor only

D. Lagging, leading and unity power factors

Q.48 Which among the following expressions relate charge, voltage and capacitance of a capacitor?

A. $Q = \frac{c}{v}$ **B.** $Q = \frac{v}{c}$

C. $Q = CV$ **D.** $C = Q^2V$

Q.49 The change of D.C. excitation of a synchronous motor changes

A. Motor speed
B. Applied voltage of the motor
C. Power factor
D. All option are correct

Q.50 According to Maximum Power Transfer Theorem, maximum power is transferred from an AC network to a load when _______.

A. Load impedance (Z_L) must be equivalent to Z_{TH} (complex conjugate of corresponding circuit impedance)

B. Load current (I_L) is equal to short circuit current (I_{SC}) multiplied by the internal resistance of the circuit (R_{int})

C. Load impedance (Z_L) must be equivalent to the inverse of Z_{TH} (complex conjugate of corresponding circuit impedance)

D. Load current (I_L) is equal to short circuit current (I_{SC}) divided by internal resistance of the circuit (R_{int})

Q.51 The superposition theorem can be applied to solve networks when the network contains:

A. two or more than two voltage sources and no current source

B. two or more than two current sources and no voltage source

C. only one source of any type

D. two or more than two sources of anyone, or both types

Q.52 Which of the following theorems can be applied to any network- linear or non-linear, active or passive, time-variant or time-invariant?

A. Thevenin theorem
B. Norton theorem
C. Tellegen theorem
D. superposition theorem

Q.53 A source vs(t) = Vcos100 πt has an internal impedance of (6 + j8) Ω. If a purely resistive load connected to this source has to extract the maximum power out of the source, find its value

A. 6 Ω **B.** 8 Ω **C.** 10 Ω **D.** 14 Ω

Q.54 The device which directly converts solar energy into electric energy is called

A. solar cooker **B.** solar furnace
C. solar cell **D.** none of these

Q.55 The circuit which satisfies Reciprocity Theorem is called?

A. Short circuit **B.** Open circuit
C. Linear circuit **D.** Non-linear circuit

Q.56 In a parallel R-L circuit the if I_R is the current through the resistor and I_L is the current through the inductor then:

A. I_R lags I_L by 90°

B. I_L lags I_R by 90°
C. I_R and I_L are in phase
D. I_R lags I_L by 270°

Q.57 Calculate the impedance of a circuit when the resistance is 3 ohms and the inductive reactance of the circuit is 4 ohms.

A. 49 ohms **B.** 1 ohm **C.** 7 ohms **D.** 5 ohms

Q.58 On what factors does the resistance of a conductor depend?

A. All the options
B. Thickness of conductor
C. Nature of material of the conductor
D. Length of conductor

Q.59 An a.c. sinusoidal voltage source is connected across a series circuit consisting of a resistor and capacitor. The rms value of the voltage across the resistor and capacitor are 100 V and 200 V respectively. The rms value of the voltage of the source is

A. 300 V **B.** 100 $\sqrt{5}$ V
C. 100 $\sqrt{3}$ V **D.** 100 V

Q.60 In a series RC circuit, the current ____ the voltage by an angle ____ degrees.

A. lags, of 45
B. lags, of 0
C. leads, between 0 and 90
D. leads, of 90

Q.61 The coil having a resistance of 5 ohm and inductance of 38.22 mH is connected to 220 V, 50 Hz supply. Calculate the current (in A) flowing in the circuit.

A. 15.45 **B.** 17.92 **C.** 16.92 **D.** 14.45

Q.62 The impedance of the circuit is (4 + j3) ohms. The power factor of the circuit is

A. 0.6 lead **B.** 0.8 lead **C.** 0.6 lag **D.** 0.8 lag

Q.63 Two coils having equal resistances but different inductances are connected in series. The time constant of the series combination is the

A. sum of time constant of the individual coils
B. average of time constants of the individual coils
C. geometric mean of time constants of the individual coils
D. product of the time constant of the individual coils

Q.64 An RLC circuit in series resonance at the frequency of f Hz. If the value of all the components doubled, the new frequency will be

A. f/4 **B.** f/2 **C.** 2f **D.** f

Q.65 Like a series resonant RLC circuit, a parallel resonant circuit also

A. has a power factor of unity
B. offers minimum impedance
C. draws maximum current
D. magnifies current

Q.66 An LC circuit resonant at 1000 kHz has a Q of 100. The band width between half power points equals:

A. 10 kHz between 995 kHz and 1005 kHz
B. 10 kHz between 1000 kHz and 1010 kHz
C. 5 kHz between 995 kHz and 1000 kHz
D. 200 kHz between 900 kHz and 1100 kHz

Q.67 For an RL circuit, R = 3.14 Ω and L = 1 H connected across 220 V, 50 Hz (resonant frequency) supply, the quality factor is
A. 1   B. 100   C. 50.001   D. 314.16

Q.68 What is the value of the total impedance (in ohms) of a tank circuit working at resonant frequency having a capacitance of 0.01 mF and an inductance of 0.01 mH?
A. 0   B. 10   C. 100   D. ∞

Q.69 An RLC series resonant circuit has a Q of 15 and a source voltage of 50 V. The voltage across the capacitor at resonance is _______
A. 750 V   B. 50 V   C. 15 V   D. 375 V

Q.70 A series RLC circuit has Q of 100 and an impendence of $(100 \pm j0)\Omega$ at its resonant angular frequency of 10^7 rad/s. The value of R and L respectively –
A. 100 Ω, 10^{-3}H   B. 10 Ω, 10^2 H
C. 1000 Ω, 10 H   D. 100 Ω, 100 H

Q.71 A balanced star connected a load of (8 + j6) Ω per phase is connected to a balanced 3-phase 400 V supply. Find the power factor
A. 0.8 lead   B. 0.8 lag   C. 1   D. 0.6 lag

Q.72 Determine the total power consumed by a three-phase delta connected system supplied by a line voltage of 230 V when the value of phase current is 15 A and the current lags the voltage by 60 degree
A. 5.18 kW   B. 2.98 kW   C. 8.96 kW   D. 7.32 kW

Q.73 Three equal impedances (10 + j10) Ω are connected in delta across a three-phase balanced supply, the angle between the line current IR and line voltage VRY is given by
A. 45°   B. 75°   C. 15°   D. 0°

Q.74 Which of the following is true about an ideal voltage source?
A. Zero resistance   B. Small emf
C. Large emf   D. Infinite resistance

Q.75 What is the value of line voltage (in kV) of a 3-phase star connected system having a phase voltage of 3.3 kV?
A. 2.1   B. 3.3   C. 5.7   D. 6.8

Q.76 A DC voltage source is connected across a series RC circuit. Under steady state conditions, the applied DC voltage drops entirely across the
A. R only
B. C only
C. R and C combination
D. None of these

Q.77 A step voltage E is applied to a series R-L circuit. The rate of change of current is maximum at t =
A. Zero   B. Infinite   C. L/R   D. R/L

Q.78 In series RL circuit, the voltage across the resistance is 40 V and voltage across the inductance is 40 V. Then the total voltage across the series circuit is
A. 40 V   B. 56.56 V   C. 80 V   D. 5.656 V

Q.79 Magnetic circuit with the cross-sectional area of 25 cm^2 is to be operated at 50 Hz from 150 V$_{rms}$ supply. The number of turns required to active a peak magnetic flux density of 2 T in the core flux is
A. 175   B. 200   C. 250   D. 135

Q.80 Determine the value of current (in A) in a coil, if it has 60 numbers of turns and produces a mmf of 30 Amp-turns.
A. 0.8   B. 1.4   C. 1.2   D. 0.5

Q.81 A coil is wound uniformly with 300 turns over a steel ring of relative permeability 900, having a mean circumference of 40 mm and cross-sectional area of 50 mm2. If a current of 25 A is passed through the coil, find reluctance of the ring
A. 0.707×10^6 AT/Wb   B. 1.707×10^6 AT/Wb
C. 3.876×10^6 AT/Wb   D. 0.765×10^{-6} AT/Wb

Q.82 A coil is wound uniformly with 300 turns over a steel ring of relative permeability 900, having a mean circumference of 40 mm and cross-sectional area of 50 mm^2. If a current of 25 A is passed through the coil, find MMF
A. 7000 AT   B. 7500 AT   C. 6500 AT   D. 6000 AT

Q.83 A long straight wire carries a current I = 10 A, the magnetic field at a distance of 1.59 m is
A. 0.1 Am^{-1} B. 1 Am^{-1}
C. 10 Am^{-1} D. 100 Am^{-1}

Q.84 A metallic ring has a mean length of 20 cm. it is wound with a 1000 turns of wire. If the current through the wire is 1 A then H is____
A. 5000 AT/m   B. 1000 AT/m
C. 2000 AT/m   D. 500 AT/m

Q.85 A magnetic flux of 6 Wb-turn sets up in the coil, when a current of 3 A flows through it. What is the inductance (in H) of the coil?
A. 1   B. 2   C. 3   D. 4

Q.86 A solenoid has a diameter of 6 cm and a length of 60 cm and it comprises of 7000 turns. Calculate the energy stored (in J) in the solenoid, if 10 A current flows through it.
A. 11   B. 14   C. 17   D. 20

Q.87 A circular loop has its radius increasing at a rate of 1 m/s. The loop placed perpendicular to a constant magnetic field of 0.8 wb/m^2. When the radius of the loop is 2 m, the emf induced in the will be
A. 3.2π V   B. 4π V   C. 2π V   D. Zero

Q.88 Which one of the following meters exhibits creeping phenomena?
A. Ammeter   B. Voltmeter
C. Watt meter   D. Energy meter

Q.89 A dynamometer wattmeter can be used for
A. Both D.C. and A.C. if scales are calibrated

B. D.C. only

C. A.C. only

D. Both AC and DC without any calibration of scale

Q.90 The power factor of a single-phase load can be calculated if the instruments available are

A. one voltmeter and one ammeter

B. one voltmeter, one ammeter and one wattmeter

C. one voltmeter, one ammeter and one energy meter

D. any of the above

Q.91 Eddy current damping cannot be used for dynamometer type instruments because

A. The presence of a permanent magnet required for such purpose would affect the deflection and hence the reading of the instrument

B. Eddy current will pass through the iron and thereby causing loss

C. The size of the instrument will increase

D. All of the above

Q.92 The potential coil of wattmeter is designed for

A. Very high inductance

B. Minimum inductance

C. Very low inductance

D. 1 to 10 H

Q.93 In two wattmeter method of power measurement, one of the wattmeters will show negative reading when the load power factor angle is strictly:

A. Less Than 30°　　**B.** Less than 60°

C. Greater than 30°　　**D.** Greater than 60°

Q.94 A power factor meter has _______ control spring.

A. One　　**B.** Two　　**C.** Four　　**D.** No

Q.95 The current coil of a wattmeter is connected to the CT of R-phase. The potential coil is connected across Y and B phases. The wattmeter measures

A. Active power in R phase

B. Active power of Y phase

C. Reactive power of R phase

D. Power proportional to 3 phase power if the load is balanced

Q.96 Which of the following is a disadvantage of renewable energy?

A. High pollution

B. Available only in few places

C. High running cost

D. Unreliable supply

Q.97 A Solar cell is an electrical device that converts the energy of light directly into electricity by the _________

A. Photovoltaic effect　　**B.** Chemical effect

C. Atmospheric effect　　**D.** Physical effect

Q.98 In hydroelectric power, what is necessary for the production of power throughout the year?

A. Dams filled with water

B. High amount of air

C. High intense sunlight

D. Nuclear power

Q.99 The main composition of biogas is _____________

A. Methane　　　　**B.** Carbon dioxide

C. Nitrogen　　　　**D.** Hydrogen

Q.100 Which Ministry is mainly responsible for research and development in renewable energy sources such as wind power, small hydro, biogas and solar power?

A. Human Resource Development

B. Agriculture and Farmers Welfare

C. Ministry of New and Renewable Energy

D. Health and Family Welfare

Q.101 Which among the following have a large amount of installed grid interactive renewable power capacity in India?

A. Wind power　　　　**B.** Solar power

C. Biomass power　　　**D.** Small Hydro power

Q.102 The world's first 100% solar powered airport located at __________

A. Cochin, Kerala

B. Bengaluru, Karnataka

C. Chennai, Tamil Nadu

D. Mumbai, Maharashtra

Q.103 Which of the following is not under the Ministry of New and Renewable Energy?

A. Wind energy　　　　**B.** Solar energy

C. Tidal energy　　　　**D.** Large hydro

Q.104 Where is the largest Wind Farm located in India?

A. Jaisalmer Wind Park, Rajasthan

B. Muppandal Wind Farm, Tamil Nadu

C. Vaspet Wind Farm, Maharashtra

D. Chakala Wind Farm, Maharashtra

Q.105 Which Indian enterprise has the Motto "ENERGY FOREVER"?

A. Indian Renewable Energy Development Agency

B. Indian Non-Renewable Energy Development

C. Indian Agricultural Development

D. Indian Biotechnology Development

Q.106 What is meaning of a Carbon Positive Area?

A. Area with carbon emissions more than carbon sequestration

B. Area with carbon emissions balanced with carbon sequestration

C. Area with carbon emissions are zero

D. Area with more renewable energy generation than needed to sustain the area

Q.107 Which of the following are parts of government's urban development strategy for the next 20 years?

1) Reducing water use by 50 per cent

2) Reducing electricity use by 40 per cent

3) Generating half of power from renewable sources

A. 2, 3
B. 1, 2
C. 1, 3
D. All of the above

Q.108 The first Pilot-cum- demonstration project of Small Wind Solar Hybrid System of 25 KW capacity will be installed at

A. Tamil Nadu
B. Gujarat
C. Rajasthan
D. Maharashtra

Q.109 The theme of Ministry of New & Renewable Energy in the republic day parade will be

A. Mega Watt To Giga Watt – Sustainable Power
B. Mega Watt To Giga Watt – Land of Thousand Suns
C. Mega Watt - Thousand Suns in India
D. Mega Watt To Giga Watt – Making The Sun Brighter, Even At Night

Q.110 Which energy accounts for largest share in the renewable energy basket of India?

A. Wind **B.** Nuclear **C.** Hydel **D.** Solar

Q.111 Which of the following statements is/are correct about renewable energy sector in India?

1. The renewable energy sector is governed by the Electricity Act, 2003.
2. National Renewable Energy Fund (NREF) has a corpus of over Rs.17,000 crore.

A. Only 1 **B.** Only 2 **C.** Both **D.** None

Q.112 With some initial change at t = 0+, a capacitor will act as __________.

A. Open circuit
B. Short circuit
C. A current source
D. A voltage source

Q.113 Which of the following statement/s is/are correct?

1) Biomass is a renewable energy resource derived from plants and animal waste.
2) However, burning of biomass increases atmospheric carbon dioxide.

A. Only 1
B. Only 2
C. Both 1 and 2
D. None of the above

Q.114 Which of the following can be used as a biofuel?

1) Bagasse
2) Jatropha
3) Pongamia

A. Only 2
B. Only 2 and 3
C. Only 3
D. All of the above

Q.115 Which of the following is not a renewable source of energy?

A. Nuclear Energy
B. Energy from Waste
C. Hydropower
D. Biomass

Q.116 The Ministry of New and Renewable Energy, Government of India is organizing the first Renewable Energy Global Investors Meet & Expo. What is the name of event?

A. RE-Invest 2015
B. RE-Invent 2015
C. RE-Innovation 2015
D. Re-Imagination 2015

Q.117 Which of the following statements are correct?

1. The National Clean Energy Fund (NCEF) is a fund created in 2010-11.
2.It is a clean energy cess on coal produced or imported in India has been introduced. It is Rs.50 per tonne of coal.
3. The fund is a non lapsable fund under Public Accounts.
4. It Utilized for funding research and innovative projects in clean energy technologies of public sector or private sector entities, upto the extent of 40% of the total project cost.

A. 1,3,4 **B.** 2,3 **C.** 2,3,4 **D.** All

Q.118 Which state in India ranks first in renewable energy capacity?

A. Rajsthan
B. Kerela
C. Gujarat
D. Tamil Nadu

Q.119 Which of the following statements are correct?

1. The renewable energy sector is governed by the Electricity Act, 2003 which will be replaced by National Renewable Energy Act.
2. Under the National Renewable Energy Act, the central government would set up 'National Renewable Energy Fund' and also push states to set up their own 'State Green Funds'.

A. Only 1 **B.** Only 2 **C.** Both **D.** None

Q.120 Determine the capacity (in-vehicle per hour, rounded up to nearest integer) of the rotary roadway for the following data: Width of weaving section = 12 m, proportion of weaving traffic = 0.3, length of weaving section = 24 m, entry radius of rotary = 20 m, exit radius of rotary = 27 m, entry width = 3 m and exit width = 5 m

A. 2688 **B.** 2800 **C.** 3024 **D.** 3360

// Smart Answer Sheet //

Correct Indicates percentage of students who answered questions correctly.

Skipped Indicates percentage of students who skipped questions.

Q.	Ans.	Correct / Skipped	Q.	Ans.	Correct / Skipped	Q.	Ans.	Correct / Skipped	Q.	Ans.	Correct / Skipped	Q.	Ans.	Correct / Skipped
1	A	21.7 % / 31.13 %	17	A	32.83 % / 38.11 %	33	C	23.58 % / 36.42 %	49	C	10.75 % / 42.27 %	65	A	12.45 % / 45.47 %
2	C	31.51 % / 31.89 %	18	A	33.21 % / 42.26 %	34	C	32.26 % / 29.25 %	50	A	20.57 % / 44.52 %	66	A	8.49 % / 47.55 %
3	A	27.55 % / 37.92 %	19	B	23.96 % / 44.15 %	35	C	36.98 % / 42.27 %	51	D	26.04 % / 41.51 %	67	B	11.89 % / 47.36 %
4	C	23.21 % / 38.11 %	20	A	27.92 % / 13.21 %	36	C	33.77 % / 39.44 %	52	C	18.49 % / 38.68 %	68	D	12.26 % / 35.1 %
5	B	16.04 % / 44.34 %	21	A	33.21 % / 35.85 %	37	B	14.91 % / 42.45 %	53	C	14.34 % / 46.98 %	69	A	9.81 % / 46.79 %
6	A	12.64 % / 45.47 %	22	B	33.02 % / 33.4 %	38	D	29.62 % / 41.51 %	54	C	33.4 % / 36.79 %	70	A	13.4 % / 38.11 %
7	B	17.92 % / 38.87 %	23	B	25.85 % / 44.34 %	39	D	21.89 % / 40.94 %	55	C	24.34 % / 43.58 %	71	B	16.79 % / 43.96 %
8	A	16.6 % / 43.02 %	24	A	24.53 % / 26.04 %	40	A	26.23 % / 43.39 %	56	B	18.87 % / 41.88 %	72	A	7.74 % / 43.77 %
9	B	21.13 % / 42.45 %	25	C	14.91 % / 44.52 %	41	A	21.7 % / 38.3 %	57	D	22.08 % / 40.56 %	73	B	5.85 % / 42.83 %
10	D	14.15 % / 45.1 %	26	C	9.25 % / 46.6 %	42	C	32.26 % / 31.7 %	58	A	5.66 % / 44.91 %	74	A	12.64 % / 33.59 %
11	A	32.08 % / 41.32 %	27	B	23.96 % / 41.51 %	43	A	17.17 % / 42.26 %	59	B	13.58 % / 46.42 %	75	C	15.28 % / 44.91 %
12	C	32.64 % / 39.44 %	28	D	24.53 % / 32.83 %	44	D	32.64 % / 36.42 %	60	C	26.98 % / 21.32 %	76	B	13.02 % / 40.94 %
13	C	24.53 % / 42.83 %	29	A	11.89 % / 43.96 %	45	A	13.4 % / 43.39 %	61	C	11.13 % / 40.0 %	77	A	11.13 % / 41.7 %
14	A	19.62 % / 34.34 %	30	B	16.79 % / 36.61 %	46	C	14.15 % / 42.83 %	62	D	14.72 % / 34.9 %	78	B	14.15 % / 45.85 %
15	D	23.4 % / 43.96 %	31	C	13.77 % / 42.65 %	47	D	29.43 % / 39.44 %	63	B	7.17 % / 46.23 %	79	D	1.89 % / 48.3 %
16	B	19.06 % / 41.32 %	32	C	12.45 % / 44.91 %	48	C	10.75 % / 42.27 %	64	B	23.77 % / 27.93 %	80	D	20.19 % / 45.85 %

Q.	Ans.	Correct		Q.	Ans.	Correct		Q.	Ans.	Correct		Q.	Ans.	Correct		Q.	Ans.	Correct
		Skipped				Skipped				Skipped				Skipped				Skipped
81	A	3.96 %		89	A	15.28 %		97	A	38.3 %		105	A	27.36 %		113	A	14.15 %
		49.06 %				43.21 %				42.27 %				44.9 %				36.6 %
82	B	15.66 %		90	B	16.04 %		98	A	36.6 %		106	D	8.68 %		114	D	22.08 %
		39.06 %				43.77 %				42.83 %				40.94 %				43.58 %
83	B	5.47 %		91	A	6.04 %		99	A	41.89 %		107	C	9.43 %		115	A	37.55 %
		48.87 %				42.83 %				40.75 %				42.27 %				41.88 %
84	A	13.77 %		92	B	6.98 %		100	C	42.64 %		108	A	12.08 %		116	A	8.68 %
		40.38 %				38.49 %				38.68 %				45.47 %				46.23 %
85	B	18.49 %		93	D	9.43 %		101	A	11.89 %		109	D	13.21 %		117	D	11.89 %
		46.42 %				39.44 %				36.6 %				43.02 %				43.96 %
86	B	8.3 %		94	D	10.75 %		102	A	27.17 %		110	C	11.89 %		118	D	14.91 %
		41.51 %				45.48 %				41.89 %				43.58 %				41.51 %
87	A	5.09 %		95	C	7.92 %		103	D	32.26 %		111	C	18.11 %		119	C	19.81 %
		48.87 %				44.16 %				41.51 %				44.91 %				43.77 %
88	D	25.28 %		96	D	25.66 %		104	A	19.25 %		112	D	12.45 %		120	A	4.34 %
		40.0 %				39.06 %				39.81 %				29.06 %				38.87 %

Performance Analysis

Avg. Score (%)	15.83%
Toppers Score (%)	99.17%
Your Score	

//Hints and Solutions//

1. Mulching is one of the simplest and most beneficial practices you can use in the garden. Mulch is simply a protective layer of a material that is spread on top of the soil. Mulches can either be organic, such as grass clippings, straw, bark chips, and similar materials or inorganic such as stones, brick chips, and plastic. Both organic and inorganic mulches have numerous benefits.

Hence, the correct option (a).

2. In earth science, erosion is the action of surface processes (such as water flow or wind) that removes soil, rock, or dissolved material from one location on the Earth's crust, and then transport it away to another location. The particulate breakdown of rock or soil into clasticsediment is referred to as physical or mechanical erosion; this contrasts with chemical erosion, where soil or rock material is removed from an area by its dissolving into a solvent (typically water), followed by the flow away of that solution.

Hence, the correct option (c).

3. In Microsoft word font color allows us to change the color of selected text.

Hence, the correct option (a).

4. The name Arthropod means jointed legs. These animals are meteorically segmented, coelomate and triploblastic.

It is the largest phylum of Animal kingdom. Some of their feature are:

1. These animals are multicellular triploblastic, bilaterally symmetrical animals. Some of the anterior segments show cephalization forming a distinct cephalic region.

2. Body is segmented. Segments are limited. Each segment bears a pair of appendages. They are jointed.

3. The body is covered by exoskeleton. It is made by chitin. The exoskeleton project inside. The projections are useful for muscle attachment.

4. The exoskeleton is cast off periodically and new one is secreted. It is called ecdysis.

Hence, the correct option (c).

5. Brahmadeya (given to Brahmin) was tax free land gift either in form of single plot or whole villages donated to Brahmans in the early medieval India. It was initially practiced by the ruling dynasties and was soon followed up by the chiefs, merchants, feudatories, etc.

Hence, the correct option (b).

6. Prithvirāja III (reign. c. 1168–1192 CE), popularly known as Prithviraj Chauhan or Rai Pithora in the folk legends, was an Indian king from the Chahamana (Chauhan) dynasty. He ruled Sapadalaksha, the traditional Chahamana territory, in present-day north-western India.

He also repulsed the early invasions by Muhammad of Ghor, a ruler of the Muslim Ghurid dynasty. However, in 1192 CE, the Ghurids decisively defeated Prithviraj at the Second battle of Tarain. His defeat at Tarain is seen as a landmark event in the Islamic conquest of India.

Hence, the correct option (a).

7. Sir Frederick Grant Banting (November 14, 1891 – February 21, 1941) was a Canadian medical scientist, physician, painter, and Nobel laureate noted as the co-discoverer of insulin and its therapeutic potential.

In 1923 Banting and John James Rickard Macleod received the Nobel Prize in Medicine.

Hence, the correct option (b).

8. In 2016, oracle lost its high profile legal battles with HP and Google.

Hence, the correct option (a).

9. The total sale of English newspapers in all the localities together=40000

The total sale of English newspapers in all the localities together=31500

Required difference = 40,000 – 31,500 = 8500

Hence, the correct option is (B).

10. Required $\% = \left(\dfrac{7500}{7500+9000+9500+7500+6500}\right) \times 100$

$= \left(\dfrac{7500}{40000}\right) \times 100$

$= \dfrac{7500}{400}\%$

$= 18.75\%$

$\simeq 19\%$

Hence, the correct option is (D).

11. Required ratio = 5500 : 9500

= 55 : 95

= 11 : 19

Hence, the correct option is (A).

12. Required $\% = \left(\dfrac{16,500}{23,500}\right) \times 100$

$= \dfrac{16500}{235}\% = 70.21\% \simeq 70\%$

Hence, the correct option is (C).

13. Reqd. average expenditure,

$= \dfrac{(200+250+210+100+140)}{5}$

= Rs. 180 lakhs.

Hence, the correct option (c).

14. Read. difference,

=Rs. [(190+170)-(210+140)] lakh

= Rs. [360-350] =10 lakh
= Rs. 1000000.

Hence, the correct option (a).

15. Reqd. Ratio,
= 210:140
= 3:2

Hence, the correct option (d).

16. Total expenditure of 3 companies in 2005,
= (80+140+200)
= Rs. 420 lakh Total expenditure of 3 companies in 2006,
= (100+190+250)
= Rs. 540 lakh
Total expenditure of 3 companies in 2007,
= Rs. 580 lakh
Total expenditure of 3 companies in 2008,
= Rs. 470 lakh
Total expenditure of 3 companies in 2009,
= Rs. 530 lakh
The reqd. answer is 2006.

Hence, the correct option (b).

17. Let the Cost Price(C.P.) of good to a wholesaler be Rs. 100x

Cost Price(C.P.) of good for retailer = 105% of 100x = Rs. 105x

Cost Price(C.P.) of good for customer = 110% of 105x =Rs. 115.5x

115.5x = Rs. 2,000

$\therefore$ x = 17.316

$\therefore$ Cost Price(C.P.) of good to a wholesaler = Rs. 100x = Rs. 1,731.6

Hence, the correct option (a).

18. 518=13×39+11

$\therefore$ 11 must be the required number to be subtracted from 518.

Hence, the correct option (a).

19. $\tan 45° + \dfrac{1}{3}\cosec 60°$

$= 1 + \dfrac{1}{3} \times \dfrac{2}{\sqrt{3}}$

$= \dfrac{3\sqrt{3}+2}{3\sqrt{3}} \times \dfrac{\sqrt{3}}{\sqrt{3}}$

$= \dfrac{9+2\sqrt{3}}{9}$

Hence, the correct option (b).

20. Given ;

$\cot\theta = \dfrac{21}{20}, \tan\theta = \dfrac{1}{\cot\theta} = \dfrac{20}{21}$

$\therefore sec\theta = \sqrt{1+\tan^2\theta} = \sqrt{1+\left(\dfrac{20}{21}\right)^2}$

$= \dfrac{29}{21}$

Hence, the correct option (a).

21. Romance and Fiction genres have the lowest percentage of likes of the film, which is 3 and 5% respectively.

Hence, the correct option is (A).

22. Number of people who liked historical movies

$= \dfrac{6}{100} \times 1200 = 72$

Hence, the correct option (b).

23. Number of people who liked drama movies more than romance movies = $\left[\left(\dfrac{11}{100}\right) - \left(\dfrac{3}{100}\right)\right] 1200 = 96$

Hence, the correct option (b).

24. Number of people to whom survey questionnaire was mailed

$= \dfrac{1200}{24} \times 100 = 5000$

Hence, the correct option (a).

25.

1. A joint India-New Development Bank workshop was held in New Delhi.

2. The workshop was organized to enhance the NDB's engagement with the India's private and public sector.

3. The NDB is the first Multilateral Development Bank established by developing countries and emerging economies: Brazil, Russia, India, China and South Africa.

4. President of NDB: K V Kamath; Headquarters: Shanghai, China.

Hence, the correct option (c).

26.

1. In Meghalaya, a four-day international symposium on buckwheat is being organised by North Eastern Hills University, Shillong from 3-6 September 2019.

2. The theme for it is diversifying food systems for health and nutritional security.

3. The flour of buckwheat can be used either as food or as medicine.

4. Buckwheat is used to improve blood flow by strengthening veins and small blood vessels.

Hence, the correct option (c).

27.

1. Steve Smith dethroned India captain Virat Kohli to reclaim the top spot in ICC Test rankings.

2. Kohli was dismissed for a first-ball duck in the second innings of the final Test against the West Indies, which saw him slip to the No.2 spot.

3. Steve Smith (904) and Virat Kohli (903) are separated by a single rating point in the latest Test rankings.

Hence, the correct option (b).

28.

1. CBI Director Rishi Kumar Shukla inaugurated the 1st National Conference on Cyber Crime Investigation and Cyber Forensics in New Delhi on 4 September 2019.

2. The two-day conference covers one of the mandates of CBI which is to investigate crimes with inter-state and international ramifications.

3. The conference is aimed at creating a platform to discuss challenges related to cybercrime.

Hence, the correct option (d).

29.

1. ECL Finance Limited, a subsidiary of Edelweiss Financial Services Limited and State Bank of India (SBI) have signed a co-origination agreement.

2. The aim of the agreement is to increase access to credit for micro, small and medium enterprises.

3. It plans to provide business loans, machinery loans and SME asset-backed loans ranging from Rs 3 lakh to Rs 50 lakh at a blended rate of interest.

Hence, the correct option (a).

30.

1. England cricket greats Geoffrey Boycott and Andrew Strauss have been given knighthoods by Theresa May in her resignation honours list.

2. Both received the honour for their services to sport after outstanding careers for England.

3. Geoffrey played 108 tests between 1964-1982 for England and scored 8,114 Test runs.

4. Andrew played 100 tests for England from 2004-12, scoring more than 7,000 runs.

Hence, the correct option (b).

31. Nobel Laureate from Bangladesh Professor Muhammad Yunus was conferred the 'Lamp of Peace of Saint Francis ' award by the Vatican for his contribution towards establishing peace and harmony.

The award is a recognition for distinguished work by an individual for promoting peace and dialogue among people.

The award was first given to the Polish trade union leader Lech Walesa in 1981.

Hence, the correct option (c).

32.

1. UN Secretary-General Antonio Guterres appointed Lieutenant General (retired) Abhijit Guha as the Chair of the Redeployment Coordination Committee (RCC) and head of the UNMHA.

2. He is tasked with leading the UN oversight of a ceasefire agreement in Hodeidah.

3. He will succeed Lieutenant General Michael Lollesgaard, who served as RCC Chair and head of UNMHA.

4. UNMHA stands for UNITED NATIONS MISSION TO SUPPORT THE HUDAYDAH AGREEMENT.

Hence, the correct option (c).

33. It is an interrogative sentence. The tense of the sentence changes into 'past' because the reporting verb in direct voice (said) is in past tense.

Hence, the correct option (c).

34. The usage of 'upon' is wrong. Replace it by 'while'. The correct sentence is:

The lady was knocked down by a speeding car while crossing the road.

Hence, the correct option (c).

35. valiant

possessing or showing courage or determination.

"she made a valiant effort to hold her anger in check"

stout

(of a person) rather fat or of heavy build.

"stout middle-aged men"

foolhardy

recklessly bold or rash.

"it would be foolhardy to go into the scheme without support"

Hence, the correct option (c).

36. Drink and Drinking means the same thing but we need a gerund here. Therefore option 3 is correct for above sentence.

drinking- the habit of consuming alcohol.

"she is drinking again"

Hence, the correct option (c).

37. stupor -a state of near-unconsciousness or insensibility.

"a drunken stupor"

sensibility -the quality of being able to appreciate and respond to complex emotional or aesthetic influences; sensitivity.

"the study of literature leads to a growth of intelligence and sensibility"

slumber -sleep.

"Sleeping Beauty slumbered in her forest castle"

liveliness- the quality of being outgoing, energetic, and enthusiastic.

"he radiated liveliness and good humour"

consciousness- the state of being aware of and responsive to one's surroundings.

"she failed to regain consciousness and died two days later"

Hence, the correct option (b).

38. The sentence "Rahul went out without (saying) good bye." is a correct sentence and no improvement needed.

Hence, the correct option (d).

39. The sentence "Grandfather led a peaceful life after his retirement from the army" is a correct sentence and there is no error.

Hence, the correct option (d).

40. bereave- gerund or present participle: bereaving

be deprived of a close relation or friend through their death.

"she had recently been bereaved"

Hence, the correct option (a).

41. Advantage of synchronous sequential circuit over asynchronous ones is faster operation.

Asynchronous sequential logic is not synchronized by a clock signal; the outputs of the circuit change directly in response to changes in inputs. The advantage of asynchronous logic is that it can be faster than synchronous logic, because the circuit doesn't have to wait for a clock signal to process inputs.

Hence, the correct option (c).

42. The synchronous motor operates at a constant speed which is equivalent to synchronous speed. Hence we use these motors at specific applications where the load is to be driven at constant speed.

Hence, the correct option (c).

43.

1. Synchronous motor is not a self-starting motor.
2. We use a pony motor to start the synchronous motor.
3. We need to bring the rotor of the synchronous motor to synchronous speed before we switch on the motor.
4. For that reason, we directly couple a small induction motor (pony motor) with the synchronous motor.
5. The number of poles of the induction motor should be less than the synchronous motor else it will never be able to achieve the synchronous speed of the synchronous motor.
6. This is because an induction motor always has a speed less than the synchronous speed and for it to become equal to the synchronous speed of the synchronous motor, its own speed must be increased.
7. After the rotor of the synchronous motor is brought to the synchronous speed, we switch on the DC supply to the rotor.
8. After that, we simply de-couple the induction motor from the synchronous motor shaft.

Hence, the correct option (a).

44. The advantages of synchronous motor:

1. It runs at a constant speed (at synchronous speed)
2. It can run over a wide range of power factors both lagging and leading
3. Its torque is less sensitive to change in supply frequency
4. Synchronous motors can be constructed with wider air gaps than induction motors which makes these motors mechanically more stable
5. Electro-magnetic power varies linearly with the voltage
6. usually, operate with higher efficiencies especially in low speed and unity power factor applications compared to induction motors

The disadvantages of synchronous motor:

1. It requires dc excitation which must be supplied from an external source.
2. It is inherently not self-starting and needs some arrangement for its starting and synchronizing.
3. These motors cannot be used for variable speed applications.
4. It cannot be started on load; Its starting torque is zero.
5. When loading on the synchronous motor increases beyond its capability, the synchronism between rotor and stator rotating magnetic field is lost and motor comes to halt.
6. Collector rings and brushes are required resulting in an increase in maintenance.
7. Synchronous motors cannot be useful for applications requiring frequent starting or high starting torques required.

Hence, the correct option (d).

45. The reciprocal of resistance is known as conductance. It is denoted by the letter C.

We know that,

Resistance (R): The resistance offered to the flow of current is known as resistance. SI unit of resistance is the ohm (Ω).

Mathematically resistance can be written as:

$$R = \frac{\rho l}{A}$$

Where R = resistance, l = length, A = area of cross-section and ρ = resistivity

Hence, the correct option is (A).

46. Rotors of an electrical machine are classified as:

1. Salient pole rotors
2. Non-salient pole rotors

In salient pole type, rotor consist of large number of projected poles (salient poles) mounted on a magnetic wheel. Construction of a salient pole rotor is as shown in the figure. The projected poles are made up from laminations of steel. The rotor winding is provided on these poles and it is supported by pole shoes.

Non-salient pole rotors are cylindrical in shape having parallel slots on it to place rotor windings. It is made up of solid steel. The construction of non-salient pole rotor (cylindrical rotor) is as shown in figure.

As salient pole synchronous machines are more stable than the cylindrical rotor machines, most of synchronous motors are of salient pole type machines.

Hence, the correct option (c).

47. The power factor of a synchronous motor depends on excitation. If we change excitation it can be made to operate at lagging, leading and unity power factor.

Hence, the correct option (d).

48. Q is directly proportional to V. The constant of proportionality, in this case, is C.

So, Q=CV, where C is capacitance.

Hence, the correct option (C).

49. Variation in dc excitation of a synchronous motor causes variation in both power factor and armature current. These both can be represented by inverted v curve.

Hence, the correct option (c).

50. According to maximum power transfer theorem, in AC circuits the load impedance should be the complex conjugate of the internal impedance of the active network

$$Z_L = Z_{th}^*$$

Hence, the correct option (a).

51. The superposition theorem can be applied to solve networks when the network contains two or more than two sources of anyone, or both types.

The superposition theorem for electrical circuits states that for a linear system the response (voltage or current) in any branch of a bilateral linear circuit having more than one independent source equals the algebraic sum of the responses caused by each independent source acting alone, where all the other independent sources are replaced by their internal impedances. This theorem is essentially based on linearity.

Hence, the correct option (d).

52. Tellegen theorem can be applied to any network- linear or non-linear, active or passive, time-variant or time-invariant.

Important:

According to Tellegen's theorem, the summation of instantaneous powers for the n number of branches in an electrical network is zero.

Let n number of branches in an electrical network have I_1, I_2, I_3, ... In respective instantaneous currents through them.

These branches have instantaneous voltages across them are V_1, V_2, V_3, ... V_n respectively.

According to Tellegen's theorem, $\sum_{k=1}^{n} V_k I_k = 0$

It is applicable to both linear and non-linear circuits

Hence, the correct option (c).

53. Concept:

According to maximum power transfer theorem,

In DC circuits, $R_L = R_S$

In AC circuits, $Z_L = Z_S^*$

Calculation:

For pure resistive load R_L to extract the maximum power

$$R_L = \sqrt{R_S^2 + X_S^2} = \sqrt{6^2 + 8^2} = 10\Omega$$

Hence, the correct option (c).

54. A solar cell takes solar energy directly from the sunlight and converts it into electrical energy.

Hence, the correct option (C).

55. Reciprocity theorem states that in any branch of a network, the current (I) due to a single source of voltage (V) elsewhere in the network is equal to the current through the branch in which the source was originally placed when the source is placed in the branch in which the current (I) was originally obtained.

It is applicable for only single source networks.

Hence, the correct option (c).

56. Current through the resistor:

$$I_R = \frac{V}{R}$$

Current through the Inductor:

$$I_L = \frac{V}{j\omega L} = \frac{V}{\omega L} \angle -90°$$

Hence I_L LAGS I_R by 90°

Hence, the correct option (c).

57. Concept:

In series RL circuit, impedance is given by

$$Z = \sqrt{R^2 + X_L^2}$$

Where, R is resistance and X_L is inductive reactance

Calculation:

Given that,

Resistance (R) = 3 ohms

Inductive reactance (X_L) = 4 ohms

Impedance $Z = \sqrt{3^2 + 4^2} = 5\Omega$

Hence, the correct option (d).

58. The resistance of a conductor depends on all the given options.

We know that,

The property of any conductor that opposes the flow of electric current through it is called resistance. It is denoted by R and the SI unit is the ohm (Ω).

The resistance is given by:

$$R = \rho L/A$$

Where ρ is resistivity, L is the length, and A is the area of the cross-section.

According to the above formula of the resistance:

- The resistance of a conductor is directly proportional to its length. So option D is correct.
- It is inversely proportional to the area of the conductor. Thickness decides the area. So option B is correct.
- Resistivity, a characteristic property of the conductor also determines the resistance. It depends on the nature of the material of the conductor. So option C is correct.

Hence, the correct option is (A).

59. Given that, V_R = 100 V, V_C = 200 V

We know that, $V_s= \sqrt{V_R^2 + V_c^2} = \sqrt{100^2 + 200^2} = 100\sqrt{5}V$

Hence, the correct option (b).

60.

1. In pure capacitive circuit, the current leads the voltage by 90°.
2. In series RC circuit, the current leads the voltage by an angle in between 0 to 90°.
3. In pure inductive circuit, the current lags the voltage by 90°.
4. In series RL circuit, the current lags the voltage by an angle in between 0 to 90°.

Hence, the correct option (c).

61. Resistance (R) = 5 Ω

Inductance (L) = 38.22 mH

Inductive reactance (X) = 2πfL = 2π × 50 × 38.22 × 10⁻³ = 12 Ω

Impedance Z= $\sqrt{R^2 + X^2} = \sqrt{5^2 + 12^2} = 13\Omega$

Current (I) = $\dfrac{V}{Z} = \dfrac{220}{13}$ = 16.92 A

Hence, the correct option (c).

62. Z = R + jX = 4 + j3

It represents lagging load.

|Z| = 5 ohms

Power factor = $\cos\phi = \dfrac{R}{Z} = \dfrac{4}{5} = 0.8\ lag$

Hence, the correct option (d).

63. Suppose the coils have resistance R and inductances L_1 and L_2.

Total inductance = L_1 + L_2

Total resistance = 2R

Then the time constant of series connection will be (L_1 + L_2)/2R.

The individual time constants were L_1/R and L_2/R.

Thus the time constant of series combination is the average of the individual time constants.

Hence, the correct option (b).

64. The frequency of a series RLC circuit at resonance is,

$$f= \dfrac{1}{2\pi\sqrt{LC}}$$

If the value of all the components doubled, the new frequency will be

$$f_{new}= \dfrac{1}{2\pi\sqrt{2L\times 2C}} = \dfrac{1}{4\pi\sqrt{LC}} = \dfrac{f}{2}$$

Hence, the correct option (b).

65.

Series	Parallel resonance
Inductive reactance is equal to capacitive reactance and hence the impedance will be pure resistive.	Inductive reactance is equal to capacitive reactance and hence the impedance will be pure resistive.
Offers minimum impedance	Offers maximum impedance
Draws maximum current	Draws minimum current
Power factor is unity	**Power factor unity**
Magnifies voltage	Magnifies current

Hence, the correct option (a).

66. We know that

Band width = resonant frequency/Quality factor = $\dfrac{1000}{100}$ = 10 kHz

Half power point = $\omega_1 = \omega_0 + \dfrac{\Delta\omega}{2}$ = 1000 + $\dfrac{10}{2}$ = 1005 kHz

Half power point = $\omega_2 = \omega_0 + \dfrac{\Delta\omega}{2}$ = 1000 - $\dfrac{10}{2}$ = 995 kHz

Hence, the correct option (a).

67. R = 3.14 Ω and L = 1 H

Quality factor Q= $\dfrac{\omega L}{R} = \dfrac{2\pi\times 50\times 1}{3.14} = 100$

Hence, the correct option (b).

68. Impedance of tank circuit is,

$$Z= \dfrac{(j\omega L)\left(\frac{1}{j\omega C}\right)}{j\omega L} = \dfrac{j\omega L}{1-\omega^2 LC}$$

Resonant frequency of tank circuit, $\dfrac{1}{\sqrt{LC}}$

At resonant frequency, impedance is infinity.

Hence, the correct option (d).

69. Quality factor Q$= \dfrac{\omega L}{R} = \dfrac{V_L}{V}$

At resonance, VL = VC

$Q= \dfrac{V_C}{V}$

$\Rightarrow 15= \dfrac{Vc}{50}$

$V_C = 15 \times 50 = 750V$

Hence, the correct option (a).

70. $\omega = 10^7$ rad/s

Q = 100

R = 100 Ω

$Q= \dfrac{1}{R}\sqrt{\dfrac{L}{C}}$

$\Rightarrow 100 - \dfrac{1}{100}\sqrt{\dfrac{L}{C}}$

$= \sqrt{\dfrac{L}{C}} = 10^4$ ----(1)

for resonance condition,

$X_L = X_C$

$\Rightarrow \omega L = \dfrac{1}{\omega C}$

$\Rightarrow \omega^2 = \dfrac{1}{LC}$

$\Rightarrow \dfrac{1}{LC} = 10^{-14}$ ----(2)

By (1) and (2)

$\Rightarrow$ L = 10^{-3} H

Hence, the correct option (a).

71. Load in each phase = (8 + j6) Ω

It is an inductive load.

R = 8 Ω and X = 6 Ω

Impedance Z$= \sqrt{R^2 + X^2} = \sqrt{8^2 + 6^2} = 10\Omega$

Power factor = cos φ $= \dfrac{R}{Z} = \dfrac{8}{10} = 0.8$ lag

Hence, the correct option (b).

72. Given that, line voltage (VL) = 230 V

Phase current (I_{ph}) = 15 A

For delta connection, $I_L = \sqrt{3}I_{ph} = 15\sqrt{3}A$

Phase difference (φ) = 60°

Total power P$= \sqrt{3}V_{L}I_{L}\cos\varphi = \sqrt{3}\times 230\times 15\times$ $\sqrt{3}\times\cos 60 = 5.175$kW

Hence, the correct option (a).

73. Impedance = (10 + j10) Ω

In a delta connected balanced supply, the angle between the line current IR and line voltage VRY is given by

φ = (30 + θ)

Where θ is the impedance angle.

$\theta = \tan^{-1}\dfrac{X}{R} = 45°$

φ = 30 + 45 = 75°

Hence, the correct option (b).

74. The internal resistance of an ideal voltage source is zero; it is able to supply or absorb any amount of current. When connected to a load resistance, the current through the source approaches infinity as the load resistance approaches zero (a short circuit). Thus, an ideal voltage source can supply unlimited power.

Hence, the correct option is (A).

75.

Connection	Relation between voltages	Relation between currents
Star (Y)	$V_L = \sqrt{3}V_{ph}$	$I_L = I_{ph}$
Delta	$V_L = V_{ph}$	$I_L = \sqrt{3}I_{ph}$

$V_L = \sqrt{3}V_{ph} = \sqrt{3} \times 3.3 = 5.71kV$

Hence, the correct option (c).

76. Under steady state, the capacitor acts as an open circuit. Hence the current flowing in the circuit will be zero. The total DC voltage drops across the capacitor only

Hence, the correct option (b).

77. When a step voltage E is applied to a series R-L circuit, the rate if the change of current will get maximum at t = 0 and it is equal to

$\left(\dfrac{di}{dt}\right)_{t=0^+} = \dfrac{v}{L}$

Hence, the correct option (a).

78. Voltage across resistor (V_R) = 40 V

Voltage across (V_L) = 40 V

$V= \sqrt{V_R^2 + V_L^2} = \sqrt{40^2 + 40^2} = 56.56V$

Hence, the correct option (b).

79. Given that, cross sectional area (A) = 25 cm^2 = 25 × 10-4 m^2

Frequency (f) = 50 Hz

Magnetic flux density (B) = 2 T

Emf (E) = 150 V

We know that,

E = 4.44 fNBA

$\Rightarrow$ 150 = 4.44 × 50 × N × 2 × 25 × 10^{-4}

$\Rightarrow$ N = 135 turns

Hence, the correct option (d).

80. Given that, number of turns (N) = 60

MMF = 30 Amp-turns

MMF = NI

$\Rightarrow$ 30 = 60 × I $\Rightarrow$ I = 0.5 A

Hence, the correct option (d).

81. We know that

Reluctance of the ring = $\dfrac{1}{\mu_0 \mu_r A}$

$= \dfrac{40 \times 10^{-3}}{4\pi \times 10^{-7} \times 900 \times 40 \times 10 - 50 \times 10^{-6}}$ = 0.707 × 10^6 AT/Wb.

Hence, the correct option (a).

82. We know that

MMF = NI

Here, MMF = Magnetomotive force, N = Number of turns, I = Current

MMF = 300 × 25 = 7500 AT.

Hence, the correct option (b).

83. We know that

Magnetic field H = $\dfrac{I}{2}\pi r$

Here I = current, r = radius of wire

H= $\dfrac{I}{2\pi r} = \dfrac{10}{2\pi 1.59}$ =1Am^{-1}

Hence, the correct option (b).

84. Given:

Mean length = 20 cm, Turn N = 1000, Current = 1 A

We know that

$$H = \frac{NI}{l} = \frac{1000 \times 1}{0.2} = 5000 AT/m$$

Hence, the correct option (a).

85. Given that, magnetic flux (φ) = 6 Wb-turn

Current (I) = 3 A

We know that, φ = LI

$\Rightarrow$ 6 = L × 3 $\Rightarrow$ L = 2 H

Hence, the correct option (b).

86. Given that, length (l) = 60 cm

Number of turns (N) = 7000

Current (I) = 10 A

Diameter (d) = 6 cm

The inductance of a solenoid is given by,

$$L= \frac{\mu_0 N^2 A}{l} \; H = \frac{\mu_0 N^2 \pi d^2}{4l} = \frac{4\pi \times 10^{-7} \times 7000^2 \times \pi \times (6 \times 10 - 2)^2}{4 \times 60 \times 10^{-2}} = 0.29$$

Energy stored E= $\dfrac{1}{2}LI^2 = \dfrac{1}{2} \times 0.29 \times 10^2 = 14.5J$

Hence, the correct option (b).

87. Given that,

Rate of radius (dr/dt) = 1 m/s

Magnetic field (B) = 0.8 wb/m^2

Radius of the loop (r) = 2 m

Emf induced E=2πrB $\dfrac{dr}{dt}$

= 2π × 2 × 0.8 × 1 = 3.2π V

Hence, the correct option (a).

88. Creeping is the phenomenon in which the energy meter still shows some minimal energy consumption when there is no load attached to the meter. Overcompensation for friction is the main reason for creeping.

Hence, the correct option (d).

89.

1. Electrodynamics instruments are capable of serving as transfer instruments.
2. The transfer instrument is first calibrated on D.C.; This calibration is then transferred to the A.C. instrument on alternating current.
3. Dynamometer wattmeter can be used for both D.C. and A.C.
4. Electrodynamometer types of instruments are used as A.C. voltmeters and ammeters both in the range of power frequencies and lower part of the audio power frequency range.
5. They are used as wattmeters, voltmeters and with some modification as power factor meters and frequency meters.

Hence, the correct option (a).

90. We know that, Power factor cosφ= $\dfrac{P}{VI}$

To calculate power factor, we need the values of power (P), voltage (V) and current (I). So, we need one voltmeter, one ammeter and one wattmeter.

Hence, the correct option (b).

91.

1. Eddy current damping cannot be used in electrodynamometer type instruments as the operating field is very weak on account the fact that the coils are air cored.

2. Any introduction of permanent magnet required for eddy current damping would distort the operating magnetic field of the instrument.

3. The distortion of magnetic field affects the deflection and hence the reading of the instrument.

4. Air friction damping is employed for these instruments and is provided by a pair of aluminium vanes, attached to the spindle at the bottom.

Hence, the correct option (a).

92.

1. In an ideal dynamometer type wattmeter, the current in pressure coil in phase with the applied voltage.

2. But in practically the pressure coil of wattmeter has an inductance and current in it will lag the applied voltage.

3. If there is no inductance the current in pressure coil will be in phase with the applied voltage.

4. In the absence of inductance in pressure coil of wattmeter, it will read correctly in all power factors and frequency.

5. The wattmeter will read high when the load power factor is lagging, as in that case the effect of pressure coil inductance is to reduce the phase angle between load current and pressure coil current.

6. The wattmeter will read low when the load power factor is leading as in that case the effect of pressure coil inductance is to increase the phase angle between load current and pressure coil current.

Hence, the correct option (b).

93.

1. If one of the wattmeter shows -ve value then this indicates that the load is a reactive.

2. Element i.e. an inductor or a capacitor which consumes the reactive power.

3. When p.f. angle = 60°, only single wattmeter measures entire 3-phase power.

4. When p.f. angle = 60°, only one wattmeter shows zero deflection.

5. When p.f. angle > 60°, one of the wattmeter shown -ve deflection.

6. When p.f. angle < 60°, one of the wattmeter shown +ve deflection.

7. When one of the wattmeter shows -ve deflection, the range of p.f. is from 0 to 0.5.

8. When two wattmeter show +ve deflection, then range of the p.f. is from 0 to 1.

Hence, the correct option (d).

94.

1. Power factor meter consists of a fixed coil which acts as the current coil.

2. This coil split up into two parts and carries the current of the circuit under test.

3. Therefore, the magnetic field produced by this coil is proportional to the main current.

4. Two identical pressure coils A and B are pivoted on a spindle as shown constitute the moving system.

5. Pressure coil A is non-inductive resistance R connected in series with it, and coil B has a highly inductive choke coil L connected in series with it.

6. These two coils are connected across the voltage of the circuit.

7. These two pressure coils have the same dimensions and the same number of turns.

8. There is no requirement of the controlling system because at equilibrium there exist two opposite forces which balance the movement of the pointer without any requirement of controlling force.

9. As there is no need for controlling torque, it doesn't have any control springs.

Hence, the correct option (d).

95. Wattmeter reading = V_{PC} I_{CC} cos ($V_{PC} {}^{I_{CC}}$)

A current coil of wattmeter is connected to the CT of R-phase. So, wattmeter takes the current flowing through the R phase.

Pressure coil is connected across the Y phase and B phase. So, wattmeter takes the voltage V_{YB}

Now, the wattmeter reading is,

W = V_{YB} I_R cos ($V_{YB} {}^{I_R}$)

Let the load angle is φ, the angle between V_{YB} and I_R is (90 − φ)

⇒ W = V_{YB} I_R sin φ = reactive power of the R phase.

Hence, the correct option (c).

96. Explanation: Renewable energy often relies on the weather for its sources of power. Hydro generators need rain to fill dams and thereby provide electricity. Wind turbines need wind to turn the blades. Solar collectors need clear skies and sunshine.

Hence, the correct option (d).

97. The photovoltaic effect was first discovered in 1839 by Edmond Becquerel. The hotovoltaic effect is a process that generates voltage or electric current in a photovoltaic cell when it is exposed to sunlight.

Hence, the correct option (a).

98. Dams are used for power generation. The reservoir water is stored at a higher level than the turbines, which are housed in a power station. The dam feed water directly to the turbines in the power station.

Hence, the correct option (a).

99. Biogas is one of the types of bio fuel that is produced from the decomposition of organic waste. Biogas is known as the environmentally-friendly energy source since it is converting organic waste into energy. The composition of biogas is as follows: – Methane 50-75%, Carbon dioxide 25-50%, Nitrogen 0-10%, Hydrogen 0-1%.

Hence, the correct option (a).

100. Ministry of New and Renewable Energy is a ministry of the Government of India. The ministry is working to develop renewable energy for supplementing the energy requirements of India. It is headquartered in Lodhi Road, New Delhi.

Hence, the correct option (c).

101. Wind power having capacity 29000 MW holds 56.8%, Solar power having capacity 9500 MW holds 18.5%, Biomass power having capacity 8200 MW holds 16%, Small Hydro power having capacity 4400 MW holds 8.5%.

Hence, the correct option (a).

102. Cochin International airport, the fourth-largest airport in India in terms of international traffic, now runs entirely on solar power. Cochin International Airport became the world's first fully solar powered airport on 18 August 2015.

Hence, the correct option (a).

103. According to a recent survey large hydro installed capacity was 44.41 GW. The large hydro is administered separately by the Ministry of Power and not included in Ministry of New and Renewable Energy.

Hence, the correct option (d).

104. The 1,600MW Jaisalmer wind park is India's biggest wind farm. Developed by Suzlon Energy, the project features a group of wind farms located in the Jaisalmer district of Rajasthan, India.

Hence, the correct option (A).

105. Indian Renewable Energy Development Agency established in 1987 as Non-Banking Financial Institution. It is engaged in promoting, developing and extending financial assistance for setting up projects which are relating to new and renewable sources of energy.

Hence, the correct option (a).

106.

1. The terms 'carbon zero', 'carbon neutral', 'zero energy' or 'zero emission' apply to buildings that use renewable energy sources on site to generate energy for their operation, so that over a year the net amount of energy generated on site equals the net amount of energy required by the building.

2. Carbon positive moves beyond carbon zero by making additional 'positive' or 'net export' contributions by producing more energy on site than the building requires and feeding it back to the grid.

3. Carbon positive projects can make significant contributions by helping to address the carbon intensity and damaging impacts of past building

practices and lifestyles, and by offsetting situations where carbon zero homes are not possible.

4. Also in such areas carbon sequestration is more than carbon emissions and not just zero emissions.

Hence, the correct option (d).

107.

1. The outcomes of new urban agenda based on sustainable urban planning would include reducing water and electricity use by 50 per cent from that of normal use, enabling over 60 per cent of urban travel by public transport, generating half of power from renewable sources, and promoting walking and cycling for last mile connectivity.

2. Promoting natural drainage patterns, reducing waste generation of all kind and promoting greenery are some of the government agenda for sustainable urban development.

3. Housing and Urban Poverty Alleviation Minister released the India Habitat III-National Report on World Habitat Day today, ahead of the UN Habitat III Conference in Quito, Ecuador later this month where a global new urban agenda for the next 20 years is going to be adopted.

4. India's strategy for urban development intends to give a big push to use growing urbanisation for rapid economic development while at the same time committing itself to address issues of sustainable development and climate change.

Hence, the correct option (c).

108.

1. Ministry of New and Renewable Energy is implementing a programme to promote the installation of Small Wind Energy and Hybrid Systems (SWES) with the objective to provide electricity in un-electrified areas or areas with intermittent electric supply.

2. The first- such Pilot-cum- demonstration project of 25 KW capacity will be installed at the wind turbine test station of National Institute of Wind Energy at Kayathar, Tootikudi District, Tamil Nadu.

3. The success of programme would lead towards launching of National Programme on Grid connected small wind and solar hybrid system in future.

4. The SWES projects have been highly successful in USA and European countries.

5. Under the programme, MNRE provides Central Financial Assistance (CFA) to community users for installation of such systems. The total installed capacity as on 31st March 2016 is 2.69 MW.

Hence, the correct option (a).

109. Ministry of New & Renewable Energy will be showcasing its various activities and initiatives for the first time in Republic Day Parade. The Theme of display is "Mega Watt To Giga Watt – Making The Sun Brighter, Even At Night". The tableau highlights its ambitious project of renewable energy capacity target of 175 GW to be achieved by the year 2022. All systems on the tableau are being run by the energy produced through the solar panels and energy stored in a device called Eco grid. The new and renewable energy sources have been accepted universally as the foremost choice for being clean, non-polluting and inexhaustible sources of energy. Being environment-friendly, they preserve nature, promote greenery, health, happiness and prosperity for the mankind. India has announced a very ambitious renewable energy capacity target of 175 GW by 2022. We already have an impressing cumulative existing installed capacity of approximately 38 GW of solar, wind, small hydro and bio-energy. The vision 2022 of achieving the installed capacity of 175 GW, aims to transform India through rapid strides in the renewable energy sector, job creation and skill development. To meet these targets, the Ministry of New and Renewable Energy is spearheading research and technology development in new areas such as ocean, tidal energy, hydrogen, etc.

Hence, the correct option (d).

110.

1. Wind currently accounts for 8.63%, Nuclear for 2.13%, Hydel for 15.19%, and solar for 1.38%.

2. Coal currently accounts for 54 percent of installed generation capacity and some 69 percent in actual production.

Hence, the correct option (c).

111.

1. Electricity Act, 2003 for governing renewable energy sector will be replaced by proposed Renewable Energy Act.

2. The act will also establish National Renewable Energy Fund (NREF) with corpus of over Rs.17,000 crore.

3. The NREF would be used for supporting all the objectives of the Act.

4. It mentions funding for R&D, resource assessment, demonstrations and pilot projects, low cost financing, investments for skills development, supporting RE technology manufacturing, infrastructure development, promoting all forms of decentralised renewable energy.

5. The Ministry of New and Renewable Energy "may offer a starting corpus" to such State Green Fund(s) from the National Renewable Energy Fund.

Hence, the correct option (c).

112. At t=0+, the capacitor starts charging to a particular voltage and acts as a voltage source.

Hence, the correct option (D).

113. Burning of biomass does not increase atmospheric carbon dioxide because to begin with biomass was formed by atmospheric carbon dioxide and the same amount of carbon dioxide is released on burning.

Hence, the correct option (a).

114. Indian sugar mills are rapidly turning to bagasse, the leftover of cane after it is crushed and its juice extracted, to generate electricity. Jatropha and Pongamia seeds are used to extract oil which can be used to mix in diesel.

Hence, the correct option (d).

115. Nuclear energy is non renewable as the source i.e. Uranium is non - renewable. Rest of them are renewable sources of energy.

Hence, the correct option (a).

116. This is in line with the government's initiative to create a category of investors ready to put in at least $1 billion in five years into renewables.

Hence, the correct option (a).

117. All statements are correct, the statements are-

1. The National Clean Energy Fund (NCEF) is a fund created in 2010-11.

2. It is a clean energy cess on coal produced or imported in India has been introduced. It is Rs.50 per tonne of coal.

3. The fund is a non lapsable fund under Public Accounts.

4. It Utilized for funding research and innovative projects in clean energy technologies of public sector or private sector entities, upto the extent of 40% of the total project cost.

Hence, the correct option (d).

118. Tamil Nadu was the number one state in renewable energy capacity in India. It was also the number one in installed wind power capacity in the country and number ten in global installed capacity of wind power.

Hence, the correct option (d).

119. Through a separate law, MNRE would get freedom to execute projects and not depend on other ministries and departments for necessary clearances. The Bill would be placed in Parliament next year.

Hence, the correct option (c).

120. For calculating the capacity of rotary or turnabout:

$$Q_r = \frac{280w\left[1+\frac{e}{w}\right]\left[1+\frac{p}{3}\right]}{1+\frac{W}{L}}$$

Where,

W = width of the weaving section

L = length of weaving section

P = Proportion of crossing (weaving) traffic

e = average of entry and exit width

Calculation:

$$Q_r(\text{veh/hour}) = \frac{280\times12\times\left(1+\frac{4}{12}\right)\times\left(1-\frac{0.3}{3}\right)}{1+\frac{12}{24}}$$

Q_r = 2688 veh/hour

Hence, the correct option (a).

Mock Test 02

Part - I

Q.1 Brownish film formed on iron when left in open is called?

A. Dust   **B.** Shovel   **C.** Spade   **D.** Rust

Q.2 Classes comprising animals like fishes, amphibians, reptiles, birds along with mammals constitute the category called?

A. Species   **B.** Genus
C. Kingdom   **D.** Phylum

Q.3 Which of the statements given below are correct?

1. The author of the novel 'Air' is Geoff Ryman.

2. The author of the novel 'Ulysses' is James Joyce.

3. The author of the novel 'The Great Gatsby' is F. Scott Fitzgerald.

A. 1 and 2   **B.** 2 and 3
C. 1 and 3   **D.** 1, 2 and 3

Q.4 For an object, the state of rest is considered to be the state of _____ speed

A. increasing   **B.** decreasing
C. invers   **D.** zero

Q.5 Which nation will host the Summer Olympics in the year 2020?

A. China   **B.** South Korea
C. Canada   **D.** Japan

Q.6 "Public health and sanitation; hospitals and dispensaries" is listed in the _______ list given in the Seventh Schedule in the Constitution of India.

A. Union   **B.** State
C. Global   **D.** Concurrent

Q.7 _______ elects the President and the Vice President and removes judges of Supreme Court and High Court.

A. Ministry of Defence
B. Lok Sabha
C. Prime Minister's Office
D. Securities and Exchange Board of India

Q.8 Which of the following is India's highest award in cinema given annually by the Government of India for lifetime contribution to Indian cinema?

A. Ashok Chakra
B. Dada Saheb Phalke Awards
C. Arjuna Award
D. Padma Shri

Q.9 Direction: Answer the following question from the data mentioned in caselet.

Three banks A, B, and C started their smart application services together in the month of March 2020. 25% customers of Bank A, 35% of Bank C, and 20% customers of Bank B registered themselves for the applications. The number of customers in Bank C is 1.5 times that Bank A and the number of customers in Bank A is 50,000 more than Bank B. The number of customers in bank A is 300,000. It should also be noted that Bank B has 10% of its registered customers as common with bank C. Ratio of common registrations between bank B with bank C to Bank A with bank B is 1 : 3. Bank A and C have 20,000 common registrations. From the total customers of all three banks, 2% have registered on smart application with all three banks. It should be noted that the data of common registrations are only between the two banks mentioned hence the third bank is excluded.

What is the ratio between the number of registered customers with only Bank A to Bank B?

A. 1 : 3   **B.** 2 : 5   **C.** 3 : 5   **D.** 4 : 3

Q.10 Direction: Answer the following question from the data mentioned in caselet.

A contractor builds an arcade with 25 apartments and 15 shops. Also, his site consists of 16 houses wherein he has partnered with fellow contractors wherein the profits are distributed in $2:1$ ratio. His share in the house site is more than his partner. $\frac{4}{5}$th of the shops and apartments were sold at 10% profit (each) but the rest cumulated up to 2% loss of what was projected. An apartment's C. P. is 20% less than the house C. P. and shop C. P. is 25% less than the house C. P. The C. P. of the house was $Rs. 60$ lakhs and 75% of houses got sold at 10% profit whereas the rest incurred 12% loss. Calculate cumulative loss from the percentage mentioned in the caselet.

A. $Rs. 7.5$ lakhs   **B.** $Rs. 5.3$ lakhs
C. $Rs. 6.0$ lakhs   **D.** $Rs. 6.5$ lakhs

Q.11 Direction: Answer the following question by selecting the most appropriate option.

Ram loses the cost of 6 pens of selling of 144 pens. What is the percentage of loss?

A. 14   **B.** 5   **C.** 8   **D.** 4

Q.12 Directions: Study the table and answer the questions:

The table given here

Year	English		Maths		Science		Social Science	
	High	Ave.	High	Ave.	High	Ave.	High	Ave.
2007	80	70	94	60	89	70	65	55
2008	82	65	85	62	65	64	66	58
2009	71	56	92	68	97	68	68	48
201	75	52	91	64	92	75	77	58

<table>
<tr><td>0</td><td></td><td></td><td></td><td></td><td></td><td></td><td></td></tr>
</table>

<table>
<tr><td>0</td><td></td><td></td><td></td><td></td><td></td><td></td><td></td></tr>
</table>

What is the overall average of marks in the four subjects in the year 2009?

A. 63   **B.** 64   **C.** 65   **D.** 60

Q.13 Directions: Study the table and answer the questions:

The table given here

Year	English		Maths		Science		Social Science	
	High	Ave.	High	Ave.	High	Ave.	High	Ave.
2007	80	70	94	60	89	70	65	55
2008	82	65	85	62	65	64	66	58
2009	71	56	92	68	97	68	68	48
2010	75	52	91	64	92	75	77	58

Supposing that there were 40 students in science in the year 2009. How much total of marks did they receive combined together?

A. 2800   **B.** 2720   **C.** 2560   **D.** 3000

Q.14 Directions: Study the table and answer the questions:

The table given here

Year	English		Maths		Science		Social Science	
	High	Ave.	High	Ave.	High	Ave.	High	Ave.
2007	80	70	94	60	89	70	65	55
2008	82	65	85	62	65	64	66	58
2009	71	56	92	68	97	68	68	48
2010	75	52	91	64	92	75	77	58

In which year, the difference between the highest and the average marks in Maths was maximum?

A. 2009   **B.** 2010   **C.** 2007   **D.** 2008

Q.15 Directions: Study the table and answer the questions:

The table given here

Year	English		Maths		Science		Social Science	
	High	Ave.	High	Ave.	High	Ave.	High	Ave.
2007	80	70	94	60	89	70	65	55
2008	82	65	85	62	65	64	66	58
2009	71	56	92	68	97	68	68	48
2010	75	52	91	64	92	75	77	58

In which year, the difference between the highest and the average marks in Social Science was least?

A. 2009   **B.** 2010   **C.** 2007   **D.** 2008

Q.16 Directions: Study the following table and answer the question.

Number of Students from various school Playing Various Games: (one student play one game only)					
Games			Schools		
	A	B	C	D	E
Cricket	150	200	250	230	200
Football	250	125	175	100	250
Basketball	200	195	245	200	225
Badmintan	100	130	60	40	65
Tennis	120	180	150	130	165

The difference between the total number of students playing Basketball from the all schools and the total number of students playing Cricket from all the schools is:

A. 27   **B.** 35   **C.** 28   **D.** 26

Q.17 ΔDEF is right angled at E. If ∠F = 45°, then what is the value of sinF x tanF?

A. $\sqrt{2}$ **B.** $1/\sqrt{3}$ **C.** $1/\sqrt{2}$ **D.** $2/\sqrt{3}$

Q.18 If $\frac{2}{3}\left[\frac{6x}{5} - \frac{1}{4}\right] + \frac{1}{3} = \frac{9x}{5}$, then what is the value of x?

A. 1/6   **B.** -1/6   **C.** 1/5   **D.** -1/5

Q.19 What is the reflection of the point (-4, 3) in the line x = -2?

A. (-4 , -7)   **B.** (4 , 3)   **C.** (0 , 3)   **D.** (-4 , 7)

Q.20 When a number is increased by 69, it becomes 103% of itself. What is the number?

A. 1,300   **B.** 3,300   **C.** 2,300   **D.** 4,300

Q.21 The ratio of present ages of P and Q is 7:9. Before 10 years the ratio of their ages was 5:7. What is Q's present age (in years)?

A. 35   **B.** 45   **C.** 25   **D.** 55

Q.22 What is the sum of the first 13 terms of an arithmetic progression if the 5th term is 1 and the 8th term is -17?

A. -140   **B.** 61   **C.** -143   **D.** 166

Q.23 If $a^3 + b^3 = 341$ and $ab = 30$, then what is the value of a + b?

A. 1   **B.** 9   **C.** 7   **D.** 11

Q.24 What is the slope of the line parallel to the line passing through the points (3 , -4) and (-2, 5)?

A. $\frac{9}{5}$ **B.** $\frac{-5}{9}$ **C.** $\frac{-9}{5}$ **D.** $\frac{5}{9}$

Q.25 In which of the following states was 'Mukhyamantri Dal Poshit Yojana' launched in September 2019?

A. Uttarakhand   **B.** Punjab

C. Assam   **D.** Andhra Pradesh

Q.26 India has become a part of the Global Antimicrobial Resistance Research and Development Hub in September 2019. In which year was the hub launched?

A. 2015　　**B.** 2016　　**C.** 2017　　**D.** 2018

Q.27 Where was the first-ever public information portal, Jan Soochna Portal-2019, launched in September 2019?

A. Rajasthan　　　　　　**B.** Bihar
C. Haryana　　　　　　**D.** Uttar Pradesh

Q.28 In September 2019, the central government has set up a task force to draw up plans for building infrastructure worth Rs _______ lakh crore over the next five years.

A. 25　　**B.** 50　　**C.** 75　　**D.** 100

Q.29 Who has been appointed as the Chancellor of the Haryana sports university at Rai in Sonepat district in September 2019?

A. Sunil Gavaskar　　　　**B.** Kapil Dev
C. Anil Kumble　　　　　**D.** Ravi Shastri

Q.30 In September 2019, Former Union Minister Bandaru Dattatreya took oath as the 27th Governor of _______.

A. Bihar　　　　　　　**B.** Uttar Pradesh
C. Himachal Pradesh　　**D.** Rajasthan

Q.31 What is the name of India's second Scorpene-class attack submarine which is to be commissioned into the Navy in Mumbai in September 2019.

A. INS Kalvari　　　　　**B.** INS Karanj
C. INS Khanderi　　　　**D.** INS Vela

Q.32 Where did the Union Minister of Commerce & Industry and Railways, Piyush Goyal and Minister of State for Commerce & Industry, Hardeep Singh Puri launch Steel Import Monitoring System (SIMS) in September 2019?

A. Pune　　　　　　　**B.** New Delhi
C. Raipur　　　　　　**D.** Ranchi

Q.33 In the following question, out of the four alternatives, select the word opposite in meaning to the word given.

Summon

A. Dismiss　　**B.** Draft　　**C.** Invite　　**D.** Mobilize

Ques (34-38): In the following passage, some of the words have been left out. Read the passage carefully and select the Answer for the given blank out of the four alternatives.

The promise of nuclear power has so _______ (1) outweighed all of these concerns, and India has reason to be proud of its technology and determination to look for non-fossil _______(2) in its energy planning. However, _______(3) rapid progress in technology in other _______(4) energy sources such as wind and solar power, the collapse of oil prices and the expansion in gas projects as a viable and clean alternative, that promise _______.(5)

nuclear power has so _______(6) outweighed all of these concerns.

Q.34 What will come in place of 1st.

A. far　　**B.** less　　**C.** near　　**D.** closely

Q.35 look for non-fossil _______ in its energy planning.

A. compulsions　　　　**B.** obligations
C. alternatives　　　　**D.** constraints

Q.36 However, _______ rapid progress in technology

A. to　　**B.** from　　**C.** with　　**D.** for

Q.37 Other _______ energy sources such as wind and solar power.

A. brief　　　　　　**B.** renew able
C. untenable　　　　**D.** temporary

Q.38 Projects as a viable and clean alternative, that promise _______.

A. to dim　　　　　**B.** dimming
C. was dim　　　　**D.** has dimmed

Q.39 In the following question, the sentence given with blank to be filled in with an appropriate word. Select the correct alternative out of the four and indicate it by selecting the appropriate option.

At night, the winding roads can make driving up the mountain a _______ journey.

A. carefree　　　　**B.** beastly
C. obnoxious　　　　**D.** treacherous

Q.40 The question below consists of a set of labelled sentences. Out of the four options given, select the most logical order of the sentences to form a coherent paragraph.

I've taken out my

X-and stay poised and vigilant

Y-ear buds so I can

Z-listen for announcements

A. ZXY　　**B.** YZX　　**C.** XZY　　**D.** YXZ

Part - II

Q.41 An incandescent lamp is rated at 100 W, 230 V. What will be its resistance when measured with the help of multimeters?

A. 529 Ω　　**B.** 5 Ω　　**C.** Zero　　**D.** infinite

Q.42 What is one Henry equal to?

A. Joule/Ampere^2　　　**B.** Ohm-Second
C. Weber/Ampere　　　　**D.** All the above

Q.43 What is the total charge of capacitor when 300 V is applied across a series combination of 5 μF and 10 μF?

A. 100 μC　　　　　**B.** 1000 μC
C. 10 μC　　　　　**D.** None of these

Q.44 What is the current when 4 Coulombs pass through a point for 5 seconds?

A. 0.8 A　　　　　**B.** 20 A
C. 1.2 A　　　　　**D.** None of these

Q.45 A series circuit has 100 resistors, each having a resistance of 1 Ω and 1 A current is flowing through this circuit. What will be the current in the circuit when these 100 resistors are connected in parallel?

A. 100 A   **B.** 1000 A
C. 10000 A   **D.** None of these

Q.46 Which one of the following is NOT an active element?
A. Current source
B. Resistance
C. Voltage dependent current source
D. Voltage source

Q.47 Direction: What will come in place of question mark (?) in the following questions?

368 ÷ 23 × 9 -104 = ? - 43

A. 83   **B.** 73   **C.** 59   **D.** 84

Q.48 What is the unit of measure for electrical pressure or electromotive force?
A. Amps   **B.** Ohms   **C.** Volts   **D.** Watts

Q.49 A point where two or more branches connect is called as _________.

A. branch   **B.** node   **C.** terminal   **D.** circuit

Q.50 The resistance of a wire of length L metres is R ohms. What happens to the resistance if the wire is stretched to 2L?
A. Remains the same
B. Increases by 2 times
C. Increases by 4 times
D. Decreases by 2 times

Q.51 A, B and C enter into business and invest in the ratio of $\frac{5}{2} : \frac{1}{3} : \frac{4}{5}$. After four months, A increases his capital by 66.66%. If the profit share of C is 9000 at the end of the year then find the total profit at the end of the year-
A. Rs. 75652   **B.** Rs. 75285
C. Rs. 75875   **D.** Rs. 74123

Q.52 When parallel resistors are of three different values, which has the greatest power loss?
A. The smallest resistance
B. The largest resistance
C. They have the same power loss
D. Voltage and resistance values are needed

Q.53 The current in an inductor changes from 0 to 200 mA in 4 ms and induces a voltage of 100 mV. The value of inductor is
A. 2 mH   **B.** 2 mH   **C.** 8 mH   **D.** 4 mH

Q.54 Find the current through a 5-H inductor if the voltage across it is

$$V(t) = \begin{cases} 30t^2 & t > 0 \\ 0 & t < 0 \end{cases}$$

Also, find the energy stored within 0 < t < 4 sec
A. 29.78 kJ   **B.** 72.78 kJ
C. 40.96 kJ   **D.** None of these

Q.55 The resistance of copper wire 2000 m long is 21 Ω. If its diameter is 0.44 mm, its specific resistance is around
A. 1.2×10^{-9} Ω -m   **B.** 1.4×10^{-9} Ω -m
C. 1.6×10^{-9} Ω -m   **D.** 1.8×10^{-9} Ω -m

Q.56 Kirchhoff's current law (KCL) is applicable to networks that are ____
A. unilateral or bilateral
B. active or passive
C. linear or non-linear
D. all the above

Q.57 Three equal resistances of 3 ohms each are connected in delta. The star equivalent value of resistance in ohms is
A. 2   **B.** 1   **C.** 2/3   **D.** 2/6

Q.58 Which type of winding is generally preferred for generating large currents on DC generators?
A. Progressive wave winding
B. Lap winding
C. Retrogressive wave winding
D. Current depends on design

Q.59 Brushes are provided in DC machine for:
A. smooth rotation
B. preventing sparking
C. providing a path for flow of current
D. reducing the losses

Q.60 Which of the following statement about D.C. generators is false?
A. Interpole winding in a D.C. machine helps in commutation
B. In a D. C. generator interpoles winding is connected in series with the armature winding
C. Back pitch and front pitch are both odd and approximately equal to the pole pitch
D. Equalizing bus bars are used with parallel running of D.C. shunt generators

Q.61 In a DC machine, on no-load the magnetic neutral axis
A. Moves from the geometrical neutral axis in the direction of rotation
B. Moves from geometrical neutral axis in the opposite direction of rotation
C. Coincides with the geometrical neutral axis
D. None of the above

Q.62 Match List-I (types of DC machines) with List-II (applications) and select the correct answer using the given options.

List-I	List-II
A. Series Generator	1. Arc welding
B. Shunt Generator	2. Supply of distant loads
C. Cumulative Compounded	3. Booster
D. Differentially Compounded	4. battery Charging

A. A-1, B-4, C-3, D-2   **B.** A-3, B-4, C-2, D-1
C. A-3, B-4, C-1, D-2   **D.** A-4, B-3, C-2, D-1

Q.63 The essential condition for parallel operation of two dc generators is they have the same
A. kW rating   **B.** Terminal voltage
C. Operating speed   **D.** All of these

Q.64 A 4 pole, 1200 rpm DC lap wound generator has 1520 conductors. If the flux per poles is 0.01 weber the emf of generator is

A. 608 volts

B. 304 volts

C. 152 volts

D. 76 volts

Q.65 Field winding of a DC series motor is usually provided with thick wire.

A. to provide large flux

B. to reduce the use of insulating materials

C. as it carries large load current

D. in order to reduce eddy current

Q.66 200 V DC motor draws an armature current of 25 A. Its armature resistance is 0.8 ohm. The induced emf in the motor will be:

A. 240 V

B. 220 V

C. 180 V

D. 200 V

Q.67 An electrical appliance has a yoke, stator winding, rotor, commutator, carbon brush. The appliance could be a

A. DC motor

B. AC induction motor

C. AC generator

D. Both 2 and 3

Q.68 Armature reaction in DC motor results:

A. decrease in speed

B. increase in speed

C. short circuit

D. open circuit

Q.69 Which of the following motor has the poorest speed regulation?

A. Shunt motor

B. Series motor

C. Differential compound motor

D. Cumulative compound motor

Q.70 At the time of starting the motor consumes current ______ than normal

A. Same

B. High

C. Low

D. None of these

Q.71 When the direction of power flow reverses, a differentially compounded motor becomes

A. Differentially compounded generator

B. A shunt generator

C. Cumulatively compounded generator

D. A series generator

Q.72 The current drawn by a 120 V DC motor of armature resistance 0.5 Ω and back emf 110 V is ______ ampere.

A. 20

B. 240

C. 220

D. 5

Q.73 Insulation used in commutator is:

A. Wood

B. PVC

C. Mica

D. Glass

Q.74 Which of the following does not change in transformer?

A. Current

B. Voltage

C. Frequency

D. All of the above

Q.75 Transformer operates on the principle of ________ between two coils

A. binding

B. magnetic field

C. mutual inductance

D. duality

Q.76 Due to magnetostriction, which of the following problem occurs in the transformer?

A. Oil leakage

B. Humming sound

C. Speed destruction

D. No problem occurs

Q.77 The eddy current loss in the transformer occurs in the

A. primary winding

B. core

C. secondary winding

D. None of these

Q.78 he maximum flux density in the core of 250/3000 volts, 50-Hz single-phase transformer is 1.2 Wb/m^2. If the emf per turn is 8 volt, determine secondary turns.

A. 3000

B. 320

C. 375

D. 230

Q.79 At light load, the efficiency of the transformer is low. It is because

A. copper loss is small

B. copper loss is high

C. secondary output is low

D. fixed loss is high with respect to output

Q.80 Transformers are connected in parallel for supplying:

A. Load in excess of the rating of an existing transformer

B. Load less than the rating of an existing transformer

C. Load equal to the rating of an existing transformer

D. Load less or equal to the rating of an existing transformer

Q.81 A transformer is working at full load with maximum efficiency. Its iron loss is 1000 W. What will be its copper loss at half full load?

A. 1000 W

B. 250 W

C. 500 W

D. 2000 W

Q.82 Oil in a transformer is used for

A. insulation

B. insulation and cooling

C. lubrication

D. insulation, cooling and lubrication

Q.83 The purpose of an open-circuit test is

A. to determine full-load copper loss

B. to determine magnetising resistance

C. to determine the equivalent resistance

D. to determine the equivalent reactance

Q.84 The power delivered by a source of internal resistance 'r' to a load resistance R is maximum when:

A. R= r

B. R> r

C. R <r

D. R >> r

Q.85 **Direction**: What will come in place of question mark(?) in the given number series?

4, 5, 12, 39, ?, 805

A. 156

B. 178

C. 280

D. 160

Q.86 The parallel axis theorem can be applied to

A. Any two parallel axes

B. Any two parallel axes of which one must lie within the body

C. Any two parallel axes of which one must pass through the centre of mass of the body

D. Any two parallel axes lying in the plane of the body

Q.87 A body takes 5 minutes for cooling from 50°C to 40°C. Its temperature comes down to 33.33°C in the next 5 minutes. The temperature of the surroundings is-

A. 15°C   **B.** 20°C   **C.** 25°C   **D.** 10°C

Q.88 According to Millman's Theorem, if there are n voltage sources with n internal resistances respectively, are in parallel, then these sources are replaced by?

A. single current source I' in series with R'

B. single voltage source V' in series with R'

C. single current source I' in parallel to R'

D. single voltage source V' in parallel to R'

Q.89 The synchronous motor is:

A. Not a self-starting machine and does not run at synchronous speed

B. A self-starting machine and does not run at synchronous speed

C. Not a self-starting machine and runs at synchronous speed

D. A self-starting machine and runs at synchronous speed

Q.90 Which of the following is not a combinational circuit

A. Encoders   **B.** Decoders

C. Registers   **D.** Multiplexers

Q.91 A pony motor is basically a

A. small induction motor

B. D.C. series motor

C. D.C. shunt motor

D. double winding A.C./D.C. motor

Q.92 Which of the following metals is used as connecting wires that connect solar cells in a solar panel?

A. copper   **B.** Iron

C. Aluminium   **D.** silver

Q.93 A quarter horse power motor runs at a speed of 600 rpm. Assuming 40% efficiency, the work done by the motor in one rotation will be

A. 7.46 J   **B.** 7400 J   **C.** 74.6 J   **D.** 746 J

Q.94 The magnitude of the e.m.f. across the secondary of a transformer does not depend on :

A. the number of the turns in the primary

B. the number of the turns in the secondary

C. the magnitude of the e.m.f applied across the primary

D. the resistance of the primary and the secondary

Q.95 Which of the following energy has the greatest potential among all the sources of renewable energy?

A. Solar energy

B. Wind Energy

C. Thermal energy

D. Hydro-electrical energy

Q.96 What is a compound microscope?

A. A microscope that has one lens

B. A microscope that has two sets of lenses: an ocular lens and an eyepiece

C. A microscope whose lenses are concave

D. A microscope whose lenses are convex

Q.97 The velocity of light is maximum in _____.

A. Diamond   **B.** Vacuum

C. Water   **D.** Glass

Q.98 Which is most common source of energy from which electricity is produced?

A. Hydroelectricity   **B.** Wind energy

C. Coal   **D.** Solar energy

Q.99 Oil is estimated to last for _______ more.

A. 100 years   **B.** 500 years

C. A decade   **D.** 800 years

Q.100 Complete the following reaction.

$H_2O + CO_2 \rightarrow$ _____

A. $CH_2O + O_2$ **B.** $CO_2 + O_2$

C. $H + CO_2 + O_2$ **D.** $CH_2O + H_2O + O_2$

Q.101 In what form is solar energy is radiated from the sun?

A. Ultraviolet Radiation

B. Infrared radiation

C. Electromagnetic waves

D. Transverse waves

Q.102 What does MHD stands for in the energy field?

A. Magneto Hydro Dynamic

B. Metal Hydrogen Detox

C. Micro Hybrid Drive

D. Metering Head Differential

Q.103 Solar radiation which reaches the surface without scattering or absorbed is called __________

A. Beam Radiation   **B.** Infrared radiation

C. Ultraviolet radiation   **D.** Diffuse radiation

Q.104 The scattered solar radiation is called _________

A. Direct Radiation   **B.** Beam Radiation

C. Diffuse radiation   **D.** Infrared Radiation

Q.105 Solar radiation received at any point of earth is called __________

A. Insolation   **B.** Beam Radiation

C. Diffuse Radiation   **D.** Infrared rays

Q.106 Insolation is less _________

A. when the sun is low

B. when the sun right above head

C. at night

D. at sun rise

Q.107 HHW stands for _________

A. High and Low water

B. High Level Waste

C. Heated Low Level water

D. High and Low Waste

Q.108 What is unit of nuclear radiation?

A. Reaumur   **B.** Roentgen

| C. Rankine | D. Pascal | A. 350,000 | B. 3500 | C. 350 | D. 35,000 |

Q.109 Which type of fuel is removed from the reactor core after reaching end of core life service?

A. Burnt Fuel　　　　B. Spent fuel
C. Engine oil　　　　D. Radioactive fuel

Q.110 How much solar energy reaches the Earth's surface at any given moment?

A. 173 terawatts　　　　B. 1.73 terawatts
C. 17,300 terawatts　　　　D. 173,000 terawatts

Q.111 Of all new generating capacity added to the U.S. electrical grid in 2015, what percentage was solar?

A. 5.5%　　B. 13.6%　　C. 29.4%　　D. 17.2%

Q.112 Which U.S. state generates the most utility-scale solar power?

A. California　　　　B. Arizona
C. Texas　　　　D. Florida

Q.113 What does the word photovoltaic mean?

A. Sun-powered　　　　B. Light-cells
C. Light-electricity　　　　D. Solar-energy

Q.114 Who discovered the photovoltaic effect?

A.　American physicist Enrico Fermi
B.　Italian physicist Alessandro Volta
C.　German physicist Heinrich Rudolf Hertz
D.　French physicist Edmond Becquerel

Q.115 Photovoltaic cells are used in

(i) static charge generator

(ii) printers

(iii) solar panels

(iv) xerox

A. (i), (ii)　　　　B. (i), (iii)
C. (i),(ii), (iii)　　　　D. None

Q.116 Roughly how much did the cost of PV solar panels decrease between 2008 and 2015?

A. 40%　　B. 80%　　C. 20%　　D. 60%

Q.117 Which of these is NOT considered a "soft cost" of solar power?

A. Connection fees　　　　B. Labor
C. Permits　　　　D. Solar panels

Q.118 What form of energy do concentrating solar power technologies use to generate electricity?

A. Static　　　　B. Chemical
C. Thermal　　　　D. Magnetic

Q.119 Which of the following is NOT a technology used in concentrating solar power?

A. Power tower　　　　B. Linear fresnel
C. Cathode ray tube　　　　D. Parabolic trough

Q.120 About how many mirrors are used at Ivanpah Solar Electric Generating System, the largest concentrating solar power facility in the U.S.?

// Smart Answer Sheet //

Correct — Indicates percentage of students who answered questions correctly.

Skipped — Indicates percentage of students who skipped questions.

Q.	Ans.	Correct / Skipped	Q.	Ans.	Correct / Skipped	Q.	Ans.	Correct / Skipped	Q.	Ans.	Correct / Skipped	Q.	Ans.	Correct / Skipped
1	D	50.0 % / 30.3 %	17	C	33.33 % / 48.49 %	33	A	34.85 % / 42.42 %	49	B	60.61 % / 36.36 %	65	C	28.79 % / 36.36 %
2	D	13.64 % / 37.88 %	18	A	31.82 % / 46.97 %	34	A	37.88 % / 40.91 %	50	C	22.73 % / 39.39 %	66	C	30.3 % / 42.43 %
3	D	12.12 % / 57.58 %	19	C	19.7 % / 57.57 %	35	C	43.94 % / 45.45 %	51	C	24.24 % / 45.46 %	67	A	40.91 % / 36.36 %
4	D	53.03 % / 39.39 %	20	C	42.42 % / 27.28 %	36	C	37.88 % / 43.94 %	52	A	42.42 % / 36.37 %	68	B	18.18 % / 39.4 %
5	D	46.97 % / 40.91 %	21	B	40.91 % / 48.48 %	37	B	42.42 % / 42.43 %	53	A	16.67 % / 43.94 %	69	B	19.7 % / 48.48 %
6	B	12.12 % / 45.46 %	22	C	25.76 % / 48.48 %	38	D	19.7 % / 45.45 %	54	C	13.64 % / 53.03 %	70	B	63.64 % / 34.84 %
7	B	51.52 % / 40.9 %	23	D	27.27 % / 51.52 %	39	D	25.76 % / 50.0 %	55	C	27.27 % / 46.97 %	71	C	19.7 % / 45.45 %
8	B	56.06 % / 40.91 %	24	C	25.76 % / 50.0 %	40	B	46.97 % / 43.94 %	56	D	51.52 % / 34.84 %	72	A	36.36 % / 43.94 %
9	B	15.15 % / 57.58 %	25	A	24.24 % / 46.97 %	41	A	54.55 % / 36.36 %	57	B	42.42 % / 36.37 %	73	C	53.03 % / 36.36 %
10	A	9.09 % / 60.61 %	26	D	10.61 % / 54.54 %	42	D	34.85 % / 36.36 %	58	B	22.73 % / 43.94 %	74	C	63.64 % / 31.81 %
11	D	13.64 % / 54.54 %	27	A	15.15 % / 51.52 %	43	B	36.36 % / 42.43 %	59	C	46.97 % / 37.88 %	75	C	57.58 % / 36.36 %
12	D	43.94 % / 42.42 %	28	D	13.64 % / 45.45 %	44	A	54.55 % / 34.84 %	60	D	4.55 % / 43.93 %	76	B	60.61 % / 34.84 %
13	B	39.39 % / 50.0 %	29	B	30.3 % / 43.94 %	45	C	18.18 % / 43.94 %	61	C	30.3 % / 45.46 %	77	B	59.09 % / 34.85 %
14	C	48.48 % / 40.91 %	30	C	33.33 % / 43.94 %	46	B	51.52 % / 36.36 %	62	B	19.7 % / 40.91 %	78	C	19.7 % / 56.06 %
15	D	31.82 % / 46.97 %	31	C	25.76 % / 45.45 %	47	A	31.82 % / 40.91 %	63	B	24.24 % / 36.37 %	79	D	36.36 % / 34.85 %
16	B	48.48 % / 42.43 %	32	B	22.73 % / 43.94 %	48	C	59.09 % / 34.85 %	64	B	22.73 % / 45.45 %	80	A	40.91 % / 39.39 %

Q.	Ans.	Correct / Skipped
81	B	19.7 % / 37.88 %
82	B	45.45 % / 33.34 %
83	B	24.24 % / 37.88 %
84	A	48.48 % / 34.85 %
85	D	36.36 % / 40.91 %
86	C	46.97 % / 42.42 %
87	B	25.76 % / 48.48 %
88	B	34.85 % / 40.91 %

Q.	Ans.	Correct / Skipped
89	C	40.91 % / 34.85 %
90	C	46.97 % / 40.91 %
91	A	39.39 % / 40.91 %
92	D	37.88 % / 34.85 %
93	A	33.33 % / 46.97 %
94	D	34.85 % / 36.36 %
95	A	36.36 % / 34.85 %
96	B	25.76 % / 46.97 %

Q.	Ans.	Correct / Skipped
97	C	13.64 % / 51.51 %
98	C	51.52 % / 37.87 %
99	A	45.45 % / 37.88 %
100	A	46.97 % / 37.88 %
101	C	36.36 % / 34.85 %
102	A	30.3 % / 43.94 %
103	A	46.97 % / 33.33 %
104	C	51.52 % / 36.36 %

Q.	Ans.	Correct / Skipped
105	A	30.3 % / 34.85 %
106	A	15.15 % / 39.4 %
107	B	30.3 % / 46.97 %
108	B	48.48 % / 34.85 %
109	B	10.61 % / 40.91 %
110	D	12.12 % / 48.49 %
111	C	16.67 % / 53.03 %
112	A	24.24 % / 39.4 %

Q.	Ans.	Correct / Skipped
113	C	36.36 % / 36.37 %
114	D	27.27 % / 43.94 %
115	B	56.06 % / 37.88 %
116	B	16.67 % / 45.45 %
117	D	30.3 % / 39.4 %
118	C	45.45 % / 34.85 %
119	C	45.45 % / 42.43 %
120	A	24.24 % / 43.94 %

Performance Analysis	
Avg. Score (%)	30.0%
Toppers Score (%)	95.83%
Your Score	

//Hints and Solutions//

1. Rust is an iron oxide, usually red oxide formed by the redox reaction of iron and oxygen in the presence of water or air moisture. Several forms of rust are distinguishable both visually and by spectroscopy, and form under different circumstances. Rust consists of hydrated iron(III) oxides $Fe_2O_3 \cdot nH_2O$ and iron(III) oxide-hydroxide (FeO(OH), Fe(OH)$_3$).

Given sufficient time, oxygen, and water, any iron mass will eventually convert entirely to rust and disintegrate. Surface rust is flaky and friable, and it provides no protection to the underlying iron, unlike the formation of patina on copper surfaces. Rusting is the common term for corrosion of iron and its alloys, such as steel. Many other metals undergo similar corrosion, but the resulting oxides are not commonly called rust.

Hence, the correct option (d).

2. A phylum (plural: phyla) is the third highest rank used in the biological taxonomy of all organisms. The second rank is kingdom. And the highest is domain. However, since genome analysis, groups of phyla have been put together based on evolutionary relationships. These are informal, not part of the standard classification.

Botanists usually use the word division instead of phylum.

Hence, the correct option (d).

3. All the statements are correct, the statements are-

1. The author of the novel 'Air' is Geoff Ryman.

2. The author of the novel 'Ulysses' is James Joyce.

3. The author of the novel 'The Great Gatsby' is F. Scott Fitzgerald.

Hence, the correct option (d).

4. For an object, the state of rest is considered to be the state of zero speed.

The state of rest is considered as state of no speed or of 0 speed. Reason - when velocity (speed) is 0 then it means their is not change in position, and no change in position means that object is at rest.

Hence, the correct option (d).

5. Summer Olympics 2020 are planned to be held from 24 July to 9 August 2020 in Tokyo. The city was announced as the host at the 125th IOC Session in Buenos Aires on 7 September 2013.

Hence, the correct option (d).

6. The State List or List-II is a list of 61 items (Initially there were 66 items in the list) in Schedule Seven to the Constitution of India. The legislative section is divided into three lists: Union List, State List and Concurrent List.

Hence, the correct option (b).

7. The Lok Sabha (House of the People) is the Lower house of India's bicameral Parliament, with the Upper house being the Rajya Sabha. Members of the Lok Sabha are elected by adult universal suffrage and a first-past-the-post system to represent their respective constituencies, and they hold their seats for five years or until the body is dissolved by the President on the advice of the council of ministers. The house meets in the Lok Sabha Chambers of the Sansad Bhavan in New Delhi.

The maximum strength of the House allotted by the Constitution of India is 552. Currently the house has 545 seats which is made up by election of up to 543 elected members and at a maximum, 2 nominated members of the Anglo-Indian Community by the President of India. A total of 131 seats (24.03%) are reserved for representatives of Scheduled Castes (84) and Scheduled Tribes (47). The quorum for the House is 10% of the total membership.

Hence, the correct option (b).

8. The Dadasaheb Phalke Award is India's highest award in cinema. It is presented annually at the National Film Awards ceremony by the Directorate of Film Festivals, an organisation set up by the Ministry of Information and Broadcasting. The award comprises a Swarna Kamal (Golden Lotus) medallion, a shawl, and a cash prize of ₹1,000,000 (US$16,000).

First presented in 1969, the award was introduced by the Government of India to commemorate Dadasaheb Phalke's contribution to Indian cinema. Phalke (1870–1944), who is popularly known as and often regarded as "the father of Indian cinema", was an Indian film-maker who directed India's first full-length feature film, Raja Harishchandra (1913).

The first recipient of the award was actress Devika Rani, who was honoured at the 17th National Film Awards.

Hence, the correct option (b).

9. Given:

Number of customers with bank $A = 300{,}000$

Number of customers with bank $C = 300{,}000 \times 1.5 = 450{,}000$

Number of customers with bank $B = 250{,}000$ (i.e. 300,000 50,000)

Bank A and C common registrations $= 20{,}000$

Formula used: Ratio of A to $B = A : B$

Number of registered customers for only Bank A = Total number of registered customers for bank A - Common registered customers with B - Common registered customers with Bank C - All common registered customers

Number of registered customers with bank $A = 0.25 \times 300{,}000 = 75{,}000$

Number of registered customers with bank $C = 0.35 \times 450{,}000 = 157{,}500$

Number of registered customers with Bank B $= 0.20 \times 250{,}000 = 50{,}000$

Number of common registrations between bank B an C but not with $A = 10\%$ of customers Bank B's registered customers $= 5,000$ (i.e. 10% of 50,000)

Ratio of common registrations between bank B with bank C to Bank A with bank $B = 1:3$

Common registration between Bank A and Bank B but not $C = 3 \times 5000 = 15000$

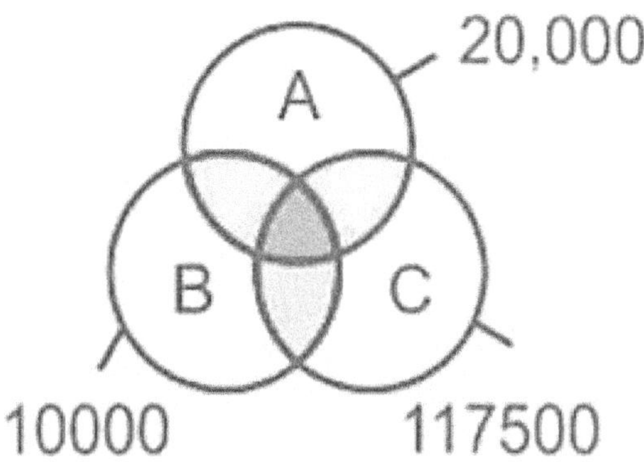

Bank A, B and C has 2% of common registration from total customers $= 0.02 \times 1,000,000 = 20,000$

Values in the Venn diagram includes only A, only B, and only C.

Number of registered customers with only Bank $A = 75,000$ $20,000 - 15,000 - 20,000 = 20,000$

Required Ratio $=$ Registered customers with only bank A : Registered customers with Bank $B = 20,000 : 50,000 = 2:5$

Hence, the correct option is (B).

10. Given:

C.P. of house $= Rs.\ 60$ lakhs

C.P. of apartment $= \dfrac{4}{5}$ times C.P. of house

C.P. of shop $= \dfrac{3}{4}$ times C.P of house

Site $= 25$ shops $+15$ apartments $+16$ houses (Partnered with fellow contractor)

$\dfrac{4}{5}$ of shops and apartment sold at profit $= 20$ apartments $+12$ shops were sold at profit rest at loss

Cumulative loss $= 2\%$

Profit on each apartment and shop $= 10\%$

C.P. of apartment $= \left(\dfrac{4}{5} \times 60\right) = 48$ lakhs

C.P. of shop $= \left(\dfrac{3}{4} \times 60\right) = 45$ lakhs

Total cost price of 5 apartments and 3 shops $= (5 \times 48) + (3 \times 45) = 240 + 135 = 375$ lakhs

Now, Cumulative loss of $2\% = $ C.P. $\times \left(\dfrac{\text{Loss }\%}{100}\right) = 375 \times \left(\dfrac{2}{100}\right) = 7.5$ lakhs

Hence, the correct option is (A).

11. Let the selling price of each pen $= x$

Total selling price $= 144x$

Loss $= 6x$

Total cost price $= 144x + 6x = 150x$

Percentage loss $= \left(\dfrac{6x}{150x}\right) \times 100 = \left(\dfrac{6}{150}\right) \times 100 = 4\%$

Hence, the correct option is (D).

12. Average in four subjects,

$= \dfrac{(56+68+68+48)}{4} = \dfrac{240}{4} = 60 = 60.$

Hence, the correct option (d).

13. Total marks$= (40 \times 68) = 2720.$

Hence, the correct option (b).

14. Difference in 2007 is 34 which is maximum.

Hence, the correct option (c).

15. Difference in 28 is minimum in 2008 i.e. 8.

Hence, the correct option (d).

16. Required difference,

$= (200+195+245+200+225)-(150+200+250+230+200)$

$= 1065-1030$

$=35$

Hence, the correct option (b).

17.

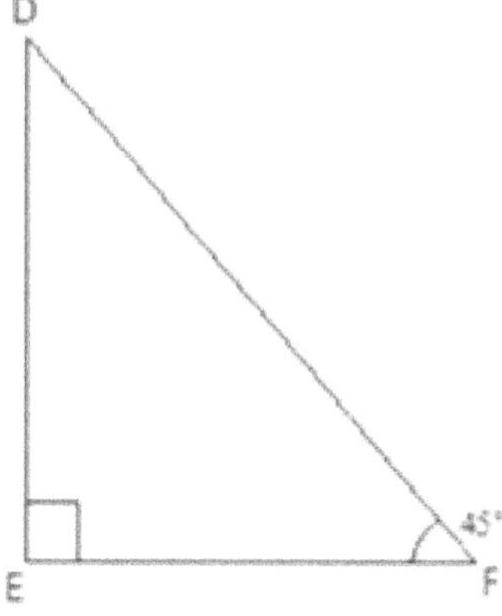

Given :-

∠E=90°;∠F=45°,

So,sinF×tanF=sin45°×tan45°

$$\frac{1}{\sqrt{2}} \times 1 = \frac{1}{\sqrt{2}}$$

Hence, the correct option (c).

18. $\frac{2}{3}\left[\frac{6x}{5} - \frac{1}{4}\right] + \frac{1}{3} = \frac{9x}{5}$

$$\frac{48x - 10 + 20}{60} = \frac{9x}{5}$$

$$48x + 10 = 108x$$

$$60x = 10$$

$$\therefore x = \frac{1}{6}$$

Hence, the correct option (a).

19. Reflection of the point [-4,3] in the line x = -2

=[x−2a,y]

=[(−4)−2(−2),3]

=[0,3]

Hence, the correct option (c).

20. Let the number be N

So,

$$N + 69 = \frac{103 \times N}{100}$$

100N+6,900=103N

∴   N = 2,300

Hence, the correct option (c).

21. Let the present ages of P and Q be 7x and 9x respectively.

According to the question

$$\frac{7x - 10}{9x - 10} = \frac{5}{7}$$

49x−70=45x−50

4x=20

∴x=5

∴Q's present age=9x=45yrs

Hence, the correct option (b).

22. Let the first term and common difference of an arithmetic progression be 'a' and 'd' respectively.

5th term $=> a + 4d = 1$..........(i)

8th term $=> a + 7d = -17$.......(ii)

Now, by (ii) - (i) we get

$$3d = -18$$

$$\therefore d = -6$$...............(iii)

From (iii) and (i) we get;

$$\therefore a = 25$$

∴ Sum of first 13 terms $= \frac{n}{2}[2a + (n - 1)d]$

$$= \frac{13}{2}[2 \times 25 + 12 \times (-6)]$$

$$= -143$$

Hence, the correct option (c).

23. $a^3 + b^3 = 341, ab = 30$
$[a^3 + b^3] = [a + b][a^2 + b^2 - ab]$
$341 = [a + b][(a + b)^2 - 3ab]$
$341 = [a + b][(a + b)^2 - 90]$
$11 \times 31 = [a + b][(a + b)^2 - 90]$
$\therefore a + b = 11$

Hence, the correct option (d).

24. Slope of line parallel to the line passing through two given points =

$$\frac{y_2 - y_1}{x_2 - x_1} = \frac{5 - (-4)}{-2 - 3} = \frac{-9}{5}$$

Hence, the correct option (c).

25.

1. 'Mukhyamantri Dal Poshit Yojana' was launched in Uttarakhand on 13 September 2019.

2. Under the scheme, two kilogrammes of pulses per month would be made available to 23.32 lakh ration card holders.

3. Under the Dal Poshit Yojana, chick pea is being made available at a rate of Rs 44 per kg this month. The current market rate of this pulse is Rs 65 to 70 per kg.

Hence, the correct option (a).

26. India has become a part of the Global Antimicrobial Resistance Research and Development Hub on 12 September 2019.

The hub is aimed at helping countries decide the allocation of resources for research and development (R&D) on antimicrobial resistance (AMR) by identifying gaps and overlaps.

The hub was launched during the 71st session of the World Health Assembly in 2018.

Hence, the correct option (d).

27. The first-ever public information portal - Jan Soochna Portal-2019 - was launched in Rajasthan on 13 September 2019.

The portal will provide information about government authorities and departments suo motu to the public in the true spirit of the Right To Information Act.

The State government has collaborated with the civil society groups to develop the portal.

Hence, the correct option (a).

28. The central government has set up a task force to draw up plans for building infrastructure worth Rs 100 lakh crore over the next five years.

The task force under the chairmanship of Secretary (DEA) has been constituted to draw up a 'national infrastructure pipeline' from 2019-20 to 2024-25.

The national infrastructure pipeline project would include greenfield and brownfield projects.

Hence, the correct option (d).

29. The government of Haryana appointed Kapil Dev as Chancellor of the Haryana sports university at Rai in Sonepat district.

Kapil Dev was also known as Haryana Hurricane.

The sports university at Rai would be the third varsity set up by a state government in the country after the Swarnim Gujarat Sports University at Gandhinagar and Tamil Nadu Physical education and sports university at Chennai.

Hence, the correct option (b).

30. Former Union Minister Bandaru Dattatreya took oath as the 27th Governor of Himachal Pradesh on 11 September 2019.

The Chief Justice of Himachal Pradesh High Court, Justice Sanjay Karol administered him oath of Office and Secrecy at Rajbhavan in Shimla.

Duttatreya has replaced Kalraj Mishra who is now the Governor of Rajasthan.

He has served as a Member of Parliament for five terms.

Hence, the correct option (c).

31. India's second Scorpene-class attack submarine INS Khanderi will be commissioned into the Navy by Defence Minister Rajnath Singh in Mumbai on September 28, 2019.

The conventional diesel-electric submarine has been manufactured by Mazagon Dock Shipbuilders Ltd in Mumbai.

The first Scorpene-class submarine INS Kalvari had been commissioned into the Indian Navy in December 2017.

Hence, the correct option (c).

32. Union Minister of Commerce & Industry and Railways, Piyush Goyal and Minister of State for Commerce & Industry, Hardeep Singh Puri launched Steel Import Monitoring System (SIMS) in New Delhi.

The system has been developed in consultation with Ministry of Steel on the pattern of US Steel Import Monitoring and Analysis (SIMA) system.

It will provide advance information about steel imports.

Hence, the correct option (b).

33. summon- order (someone) to be present.

"a waiter was summoned"

dismiss -order or allow to leave; send away.

"she dismissed the taxi at the corner of the road"

draft- a preliminary version of a piece of writing.

"the first draft of the party's manifesto"

mobilize - (of a country or its government) prepare and organize (troops) for active service.

"the government mobilized regular forces, reservists, and militia"

Hence, the correct option (a).

34. "so far" is the correct option as per the context of the passage

so far- (of a trend that seems likely to continue) up to this time.

"diplomatic activity so far has failed"

Hence, the correct option (a).

35. alternative- one of two or more available possibilities.

"audio cassettes are an interesting alternative to reading"

constraint- a limitation or restriction.

"time constraints make it impossible to do everything"

obligation- an act or course of action to which a person is morally or legally bound; a duty or commitment.

"I have an obligation to look after her"

compulsion- the action or state of forcing or being forced to do something; constraint.

"the payment was made under compulsion"

Hence, the correct option (c).

36. Out of all the given options 'with' conveys the correct meaning when placed in given blank.

Hence, the correct option (c).

37. Wind and solar power are renewable sources of energy. Therefore option 2 is right.

renewable- (of a natural resource or source of energy) not depleted when used.

"a shift away from fossil fuels to renewable energy"

untenable- (especially of a position or view) not able to be maintained or defended against attack or objection.

"this argument is clearly untenable"

temporary- lasting for only a limited period of time; not permanent.

"a temporary job"

brief- of short duration; not lasting for long.

"the president made a brief working visit to Moscow"

Hence, the correct option (b).

38. As per the context of the passage, the last sentence should be in present perfect. Therefore option 4 is right.

dim- make or become less intense.

"the difficulty in sleeping couldn't dim her happiness"

Hence, the correct option (d).

39. treacherous- guilty of or involving betrayal or deception.

"a treacherous Gestapo agent"

obnoxious- extremely unpleasant.

"obnoxious odours"

beastly- very unpleasant.

"this beastly war"

carefree- free from anxiety or responsibility.

"we were young and carefree"

Hence, the correct option (d).

40. 'YZX' is the most logical flow of given sentences.

Hence, the correct option (b).

41. We know that

$$P = \frac{v^2}{R}$$

Here P = Power, V = Voltage, R = Resistance

Calculation:

$$R = \frac{230^2}{100} = 529 \, \Omega$$

Hence, the correct option (a).

42. Inductance is the property of an electrical conductor which induces an electromotive force because of change in the electric current in the conductor. Its SI unit is Henry.

One henry = Joule/Ampere^2 = Ohm-Second = Weber/Ampere

Hence, the correct option (d).

43. When two capacitors C_1 and C_2 are connected in series then total capacitance $=$
$$\frac{C_1 \times C_2}{C_1 + C_2}$$
$$C_{eq} = \frac{5 \times 10}{15} = \frac{50}{15} = 3.33 \mu F$$
Total charge $= Q = CV = 3.33 \times 300 = 1000 \mu C$
Hence, the correct option (b).

44. We know that
$$i = \frac{Q}{t}$$
Here, $i =$ current, $Q =$ Charge, $t =$ Time
$$i = \frac{Q}{t} = \frac{4}{5} = 0.8A$$
Hence, the correct option (a).

45. We know that,

In parallel circuit sum of the currents through each path is equal to the total current that flows from the source.

Total resistor in the circuit = 100

The value of each resistor = 1 Ω

The current in each resistor when connected in series = 1 A

Source voltage = 1 × 100 = 100 V

The current in the circuit when these 100 resistors are connected in parallel = 100 × 100 = 10000 A.

Hence, the correct option (c).

46. An active element is the one which can act as a source of power. On this basis, the current source, Voltage-dependent current source, and the Voltage source is the active element. Resistance, inductance, and capacitance do not have the power of their own.

Hence, the correct option (b).

47. $\left(\frac{368}{23} \times 9\right) - 104 = ? - 43$

$\Rightarrow 144 - 104 = ? - 43$

$\Rightarrow\ = 40 + 43 = 83$

Hence, the correct option is (A).

48.

Electrical Quantity	Unit
Electrical pressure	**Volts**
Resistance	Ohms
Current	Amps
Power	Watts

Hence, the correct option (c).

49. In an electrical network, connecting point of two or more branches at a common point is called Node.

A junction is a point where at least three circuit paths meet.

A branch is a path connecting two junctions.

The closed path made by the combination of several branches of the network is called loop.

Hence, the correct option (b).

50. $R = \frac{\rho L}{A}$
R is resistance
L is length
A is area
Calculation:
Let the length of the wire is L_1
And the area of the wire is A_1
For volume remains to be same
$$L_1 A_1 = L_2 A_2$$
$$\Rightarrow L_1 A_1 = (mL_1)A_2$$
$$\Rightarrow A_1 = m A_2$$
We know that,
$$R = \frac{\rho L}{A}$$
$$\frac{R_1}{R_2} = \frac{\rho L_1}{A_1} \times \frac{A_2}{\rho L_2}$$
$$\Rightarrow R_2 = m^2 R_1 = m^2 R$$
Here $m = 2$

$$\Rightarrow r_2 = 4r$$

Hence, the correct option (c).

51. Ratio of initial investment,

$$A:B:C = \frac{5}{2}:\frac{7}{3}:\frac{4}{5} = 75:70:24$$

Let the initial investment of A, B and C be $75x$, $70x$ and $24x$ respectively.

Ratio of the share of profit:

$$\left(75x \times 4 + 75x \times \frac{5}{3} \times 8\right):(70x \times 12):(24x \times 12)$$

$$(300x + 1000x):840x:288x = 325:210:72$$

Let total profit be Rs. P.

C's profit share $= \frac{72P}{607} = 9000$

$$P = 9000 \times \frac{607}{72} = \text{RS. } 75875.$$

Hence, the correct option is (C).

52. We know that, power P$= \dfrac{V^2}{R}$

In the parallel connection, the voltage across all the branches is same.

As the voltage is same, power is inversely proportional the resistance.

The resistor with lesser resistance causes greater power loss.

Hence, the correct option (a)

53. Voltage across inductor is given as

$$V_L = L \cdot \frac{di}{dt}$$

$$100 \times 10^{-3} = L\left(\frac{200}{4}\right)$$

$$\Rightarrow L = 2mH$$

Hence, the correct option (a).

54. $i = \frac{1}{L}\int_{t_o}^{t} V(t)dt + i(t_o)$ and $L = 5H$

$$i = \frac{1}{5}\int_0^t 30\, t^2 dt + 0 = 6 \times \frac{t^3}{3} = 2t^3 A$$

Power $P = Vi = 60t^5$ and the energy stored is then

$$W = \int P dt = \int_0^5 60\, t^5 dt = 40.96 kJ$$

Hence, the correct option (c).

55. We know that the resistance of the conductor,

is directly proportional to the length of the conductor (R $\propto$ L)

inversely proportional to its cross-sectional area of the conductor

Depends on the material with which it is made

$$R = \frac{\rho l}{A}$$

$$\rho = R \times \frac{A}{l} = \frac{21 \times 3.14 \times 0.00022^2}{2000} = 1.595 \times 10^{-9}\Omega - m$$

Hence, the correct option (c).

56. Kirchhoff's current law (KCL) is applicable to networks that are:

1. Unilateral or bilateral
2. Active or passive
3. Linear or non-linear
4. Lumped network

<u>Important:</u>

Kirchhoff's law is applicable to both AC and DC circuits. It is not applicable for time-varying magnetic fields.

Kirchhoff's Current Law (KCL)- It states that the amount of current flowing into a node or junction is equal to the sum of the currents flowing out of it.

Kirchhoff's Voltage Law (KVL)- It states that the sum of the voltages or electrical potential differences in a closed network is zero.

Hence, the correct option (d).

57. Given that impedance of delta connection is, Z = 3 Ω

So, impedance of star connection is $Z_{eq} = \dfrac{Z}{3} = 1\Omega$

Hence, the correct option (b).

58. In case of lap winding, number of parallel paths (A) are equal to number of parallel paths. As number of parallel paths are more compared to wave winding it is used preferred for large current and low voltage applications.

Hence, the correct option (b).

59.

1. Brushes are provided in a DC machine to carry current. These are placed on the rotating part which is known as an armature.

2. In DC generator, the emf produced in armature conductors is passed through the brushes to output terminals mounted on the generator yoke. From these terminals, the electrical power is connected to the bus bar for further distribution.

3. In DC motor, the electrical power is passed to external mounted terminals and then to armature through brushes placed on the armature. Thus enabling torque being created due to the interaction between two magnetic fields.

Hence, the correct option (c).

60.

1. For stable parallel operation of series generators, over and level compound generators, equalizer bus bars are used.

2. It is connected to the armature ends of the series coils of the generators.

3. No need of equalizing bars in case of shunt generators.

Hence, the correct option (d).

61. In DC machines, two kinds of magnetic fluxes are present (armature flux and main field flux). The effect of armature flux on the main field flux is called an armature reaction.

EMF is induced in the armature conductors when they cut the magnetic field lines. There is an axis along which armature conductors move parallel to the flux lines hence, they do not cut the flux lines while on that plane. This axis is called the MNA (Magnetic Neutral Axis).

GNA (Geometrical Neutral Axis) is perpendicular to the stator field axis.

When a machine is running on no-load, no current is flowing in the armature conductors and only the field winding is energized. In this case, magnetic flux lines of the field poles are uniform and symmetrical to the polar axis. The magnetic neutral axis coincides with the geometric neutral axis.

Hence, the correct option (c).

62. Applications of shunt generator:

1. Used for general lighting.
2. Used to charge battery because they can be made to give constant output voltage.
3. Used for giving the excitation to the alternators.
4. Used for small power supply (such as a portable generator).

Applications of series generator:

1. Used for supplying field excitation current in DC locomotives for regenerative breaking.
2. Used as boosters to compensate the voltage drop in the feeder in various types of distribution systems such as railway service.
3. Used in series arc lightening.

Applications of compound generator:

1. Cumulative compound generators (over compounded) are generally used for lighting, power supply purpose and for heavy power services because of their constant voltage property; These are also used for driving a motor.
2. The flat compounded generators are generally used for small distance operation, such as power supply for hotels, offices, homes and lodges.
3. The differential compound wound generators are used for arc welding where huge voltage drop and constant current is required because of their large demagnetization armature reaction.

Hence, the correct option (b).

63. Essential and desirable conditions of parallel operation of DC generators are:

1. Same drooping voltage characteristics.
2. Same voltage rating.
3. Same percentage voltage regulation.
4. Same percentage speed regulation of the prime movers.

Hence, the correct option (b).

64. $E = \dfrac{\phi NZP}{60A}$

Given that $\phi = 0.01$ weber

$N = 1200 rpm, Z = 1520$

For lap winding, $A = P = 4$

$E = \dfrac{0.01 \times 1520 \times 1200 \times 4}{60 \times 4} = 304V$

Hence, the correct option (b).

65.

1. In the series motor, field winding is in series with the armature.
2. The same load current is passes through the filed winding.
3. It consists of thicker wire and fewer turns as it carries large load current.

Hence, the correct option (c).

66. In a DC generator, generated emf is given by

Eg = Vt + IaRa

In a DC motor, back emf is given by

Eb = V – IaRa

Where, Ia is armature current

Ra is armature resistance

Calculation:

Armature current (Ia) = 25 A

Armature resistance (Ra) = 0.8 ohm

Voltage (V) = 200 V

Eb = V – IaRa = 200 – 25(0.8) = 180 V

Hence, the correct option (c).

67.

1. DC motor has a yoke, stator winding, rotor, commutator, carbon brush.
2. Carbon brushes are provided in a DC machine to carry current. These are placed on the rotating part which is known as an armature.
3. Yoke is used to provide mechanical protection to the machine and flux path completion to enable poles produce working flux.
4. The commutator in a dc machine acts as bot mechanical inverter and rectifier. In dc motor it acts as inverter and in dc generator is acts as rectifier.

Hence, the correct option (a).

68. Concept:

Armature reaction in DC motor:

1. There are two windings in a dc motor, armature winding (on the rotor) and field winding (on stator); When we excite the field winding, it produces a flux which links with the armature.

2. This causes an emf and hence a current in the armature.

3. This current in armature produces another flux which lags the main flux.

4. This effect of armature flux on main field flux is referred to as armature reaction.

5. It has two effects on the machine, demagnetizing effect which reduces the strength of the main flux and cross magnetizing effect which distorts the main flux line along the conductor.

Application:

In DC motor, speed is $N \propto \dfrac{E_b}{\varphi}$

Because of armature reaction, flux reduces. As speed is inversely proportional to flux, speed will get an increase with the reduction in flux.

Hence, the correct option (b).

69. The speed regulation of a DC motor is defined as the change in speed from no load to full load. It is expressed as a fraction or a percentage of the full load speed.

Percentage speed regulation =

$\dfrac{N_{nl} - N_{fl}}{N_{fl}} \times 100$

No load speed of a DC series motor is very high. So, it has poorest speed regulation.

Hence, the correct option (b).

70.

1. While starting a motor, it draws heavy current (5 to 7 times of rated current) which damages the motor.

2. At the time of starting of motor, starter provides extra resistance.

3. This extra resistance is added so that a safe value of the motor is maintained and to limit the starting current until the motor has attained its stable speed.

4. Starter supplies lower initial voltage for proper starting of the motor.

5. It also provides protection to the induction motor against overloading loading and low voltage situations.

6. The protection against single phasing is also provided by the starter.

Hence, the correct option (b).

71.

1. The direction of rotation of a DC compound motor may be conveniently reversed by reversing the connection of both series and shunt field winding or may be reversing the armature connection but not both at the same time.

2. When the direction of power flow reverses, a differentially compounded motor becomes a cumulatively compounded generator.

3. When the direction of power flow reverses, a cumulatively compounded motor becomes a differentially compounded generator.

Hence, the correct option (c).

72. Back emf in a DC motor is given by,

Eb = V - IaRa

Where Eb is back emf

V = applied voltage

Ia = armature current

Ra = armature resistance

Calculation:

Given that, voltage (V) = 120 V

Armature resistance (Ra) = 0.5 Ω

Back emf (Eb) = 110 V

Eb = V - IaRa

$\Rightarrow$ 110 = 120 - Ia(0.5)

$\Rightarrow$ Ia = 20 A

Hence, the correct option (a).

73.

1. Mica sheets are used for the insulating leaves between commutator segments.

2. Insulation on a motor prevents interconnection of windings and the winding to earth.

3. Mica is a good electrical insulator at the same time as being a good thermal conductor.

4. Micanite is used for slot linings of H.V. machines and for making bushes.

Hence, the correct option (c).

74. Let $i = i_0 \sin(\omega t)$ be the input alternating current to the primary coil with a frequency ω then the voltage induced in the secondary coil of transformer is given as

$V_{in} = -M \dfrac{di}{dt}$

where M is the mutual inductance setting the value of i,

$V_{in} = -M \dfrac{d}{dt}(i_0 \sin(\omega t)) = -M i_0 \omega \cos(\omega t) = -M i_0 \omega \sin(\omega t + \pi/2)$

It is clear that the frequency of output/induced voltage Vin is ω which is same as that of the input current.

Hence, in a transformer the frequency remains unchanged (constant) as flux changes.

Hence, the correct option (c).

75. A Transformer is a device used to transfer electrical energy from one circuit to another circuit based on the principle of mutual inductance without any direct connection. Since induction is the property of AC circuits only, therefore, a transformer can work on AC only.

Hence, the correct option (c).

76. Magnetostriction:

1. Any magnetic material contains magnetic dipole and each dipole produces some flux.

2. At no magnetic field is applied, the magnetic dipoles are irregularly distributed, and their corresponding fluxes are nullified.

3. When the magnetic field is applied, during magnetization all the dipoles align themselves as a string, these magnetic dipoles produce flux in the forward direction.

4. Due to this alignment of dipoles, there is a slight change in physical dimension which is called magnetostriction.

Effect on the transformer:

Magnetostriction causes transformer noise. The contraction and expansion of the iron core (laminations) due to the magnetic effect of alternation current flowing through the transformer coils. This produces an audible hum.

Hence, the correct option (b).

77.

1. The changing flux induces voltages in the material according to Faraday's laws of electromagnetic induction.

2. Since the material is conducting, these induced voltages circulate currents within the body of the material.

3. These induced currents do no useful work and are known as eddy currents.

4. Eddy current loss in the transformer is basically I^2R loss present in the core due to the production of eddy current in the core.

5. Eddy current losses are directly proportional to the conductivity of core.

Important Point:

Eddy current loss in the transformer is given by,

$$P_e = K_e B_m^2 t^2 f^2 V \quad \text{watts}$$

Where,

K - coefficient of eddy current. Its value depends upon the nature of magnetic material

Bm - Maximum value of flux density in Wb/m^2

t - Thickness of lamination in meters

f - Frequency of reversal of the magnetic field in Hz

V - Volume of magnetic material in m^3

Thus, we can say that eddy current loss depends on frequency, flux density, and thickness of the core.

Hence, the correct option (b).

78. Emf in a transformer is given by

E = 4.44fφN

E/N=4.44fφEN

Where N = no of turns

Given E/N=8

Now in secondary side E = 3000 volt

4.44fφN=3000

8 × N = 3000

N = 375 turns

Hence, the correct option (c).

79.

1. Transformer efficiency is defined as the ratio of its output power to input power.

2. At light load, hysteresis losses (magnetization and demagnetization of the core of the transformer) and eddy current losses are high compared to output power; Hence, the efficiency is low at this condition.

3. When the load on the transformer is further increased, its efficiency increases.

4. At heavy loads, copper losses are high compared to the output power; Hence the efficiency is low at this condition.

5. Efficiency is maximum at both copper losses are equal to iron losses.

Hence, the correct option (d).

80.

1. The transformer is said to be in parallel operation when their primary windings are connected to a common voltage supply, and the secondary windings are connected to a common load.

2. The parallel operation of a transformer has some advantages likes it increases the efficiency of the system, makes the system more flexible and reliable. But it increases the short-circuit current of the transformers.

Parallel operation of a transformer is necessary because of the following reasons are given below.

1. It is impractical and uneconomical to have a single large transformer for heavy and large loads; Transformers are connected in parallel for supplies load in excess of the rating of an existing transformer.

2. In substations, the total load required may be supplied by an appropriate number of the transformer of standard size; As a result, this reduces the spare capacity of the substation.

3. If there will be any breakdown of a transformer in a system of transformers connected in parallel, there will be no interruption of power supply.

Hence, the correct option (a).

81. In a transformer maximum efficiency occurs when copper loss is equal to constant loss

If Pcu = full load copper loss

Pi = constant loss or core loss

i.e. Pi = x²Pcu

Calculation:

Given that maximum load occurs at full load i.e. x = 1

Hence, Pcu = Pi = 1000 watt

Now copper loss at half load i.e. x = 0.5

Copper loss at half load = (0.5)² × 1000 = 250 watt

Hence, the correct option (b).

82. The type of oil used in the transformer is mineral oil. Transformer oil is stable at high temperatures and has excellent electrical insulating properties. It is used for cooling purpose and to provide the required insulation between the two windings of the transform.

Hence, the correct option (b).

83. These two transformer tests are performed to find the parameters of equivalent circuit of transformer and losses of the transformer. Open circuit test and short circuit test on transformer are very economical and convenient because they are performed without actually loading of the transformer.

Hence, the correct option (b).

84. Effective resistance of circuit= $R + r$

Current in circuit $= I = \dfrac{V}{R+r}$

Power delivered to R is $P = I^2 R = \dfrac{V^2 R}{(R+r)^2}$

Differentiating with respect to R :

$\dfrac{dP}{dR} = V^2 \dfrac{(R+r)^2 - 2R(R+r)}{(R+r)^4}$

$\Rightarrow \dfrac{dP}{dR} = V^2 \dfrac{(R+r)(r-R)}{(R+r)^4} = 0$ for maximum

$\Rightarrow r - R = 0$

$\Rightarrow r = R$

Hence, the correct option (a).

85. The pattern of the series is:

4 × 1 + 1 = 5

5 × 2 + 2 = 12

12 × 3 + 3 = 39

39 × 4 + 4 = 160

160 × 5 + 5 = 805

Hence, the correct option (D).

86. As parallel theorem states that the moment of inertia of a planar body about an axis parallel to an axis passing through the center of mass is equal to the sum of the moment of inertia of body about an axis passing through center of mass and product of mass & square of the distance between two axes.

$$I_z = I_{cm} + MR_d^2$$

Hence, the correct option (c).

87. In first case $\dfrac{50-40}{5} = K \left[\dfrac{50+40}{2} - \theta_0\right]$

In second case $\dfrac{40-33.33}{5} = K \left[\dfrac{40+33.33}{2} - \theta_0\right]$

By solving $\theta_0 = 20°C$

Hence, the correct option (b).

88. Milliman's Theorem states that if there are voltage sources V₁, V₂ ----------- Vₙ with internal resistances R₁, R₂, ... Rₙ, respectively, are in parallel, then these sources are replaced by single voltage source V' in series with R'.

This theorem is nothing but a combination of Thevenin's Theorem and Norton's Theorem. It is very useful theorem to find out voltage across the load and current through the load. This theorem is also called as parallel generator theorem.

Hence, the correct option (b).

89.

1. The synchronous motor is a constant speed motor and it always runs as at synchronous speed.

2. Due to the magnetic locking between stator and rotor poles synchronous motor is not self-starting and there is no starting device to accelerate the rotor to near synchronous speed.

3. It can be made self-starting by providing damper windings on rotor poles or by using pony motors.

Hence, the correct option (c).

90. Registers is not a combinational circuit.

A combinational logic circuit performs an operation assigned logically by a Boolean expression or truth table.

Examples of common combinational logic circuits include: half adders, full adders, multiplexers, demultiplexers, encoders and decoders.

A processor register (CPU register) is one of a small set of data holding places that are part of the computer processor. A register may hold an instruction, a storage address, or any kind of data (such as a bit sequence or individual characters).

Hence, the correct option (c).

91.

1. Synchronous motor is not a self-starting motor.

2. We use a pony motor to start the synchronous motor.

3. We need to bring the rotor of the synchronous motor to synchronous speed before we switch on the motor.

4. For that reason, we directly couple a small induction motor (pony motor) with the synchronous motor.

5. The number of poles of the induction motor should be less than the synchronous motor else it will never be able to achieve the synchronous speed of the synchronous motor.

6. This is because an induction motor always has a speed less than the synchronous speed and for it to become equal to the synchronous speed of the synchronous motor, its own speed must be increased.

7. After the rotor of the synchronous motor is brought to the synchronous speed, we switch on the DC supply to the rotor.

8. After that, we simply de-couple the induction motor from the synchronous motor shaft.

Hence, the correct option (a).

92. Silver is the metal which is used for connecting wires that connect solar cells in a solar panel, due to its large conductivity.

Hence, the correct option (d).

93. $P = \frac{1}{4}hp = \frac{746}{4}W = 186.5W$

$e = 40\%$

Poner used $= 40\%$ of $186.5W$

$P = \frac{40}{100} \times 186.5$

$P = 74.6W$

Angular velocity , $w = 600rpm = 10$ rps.

$w = \frac{(600)2\pi}{60}rad/s$

$w = 2\pi rad/s$

Torque $= \dfrac{\text{Power}}{\omega} = \dfrac{74.6}{20\pi}$

$W = \frac{74.6}{20\pi} \times 2\pi = 7.46J$

Hence, the correct option (a).

94. The magnitude of emf across the secondary of a transformer depends on the number of turns in the primary and secondary coils, and also on the emf applied across the primary coils. It does not depend on the resistance of the primary and the secondary coils.

Hence, the correct option (d).

95. Solar energy has the greatest potential of all the sources of renewable energy which comes to the earth from sun. This energy keeps the temperature of the earth above that in colder space, causes wind currents in the ocean and the atmosphere, causes water cycle and generates photosynthesis in plants.

Hence, the correct option (a).

96. A compound microscope has two lenses that bend light so that a specimen is magnified and projected. Having two lenses is very important because this is where the microscope gets its name. To compound something means to add to it - like compound interest, or a chemical compound, which is a sum of multiple parts.

Hence, the correct option is (B).

97. The speed of light is a universal physical constant. Its value in a vacuum is exactly 299792458 meters per second.

Hence, the correct option is (C).

98. Coal is the most common source of energy that is being used since industrialization. Modern steam boilers can burn coal in any of its form as a primary fuel. Different ranks of coal available are peat, lignite, bituminous and anthracite.

Hence, the correct option (c).

99. Almost 40% of energy needs is met by oil alone. With present consumption and a resource of 250,000 million tonnes of oil, it is estimated to be last for only 100 years, unless more oil is discovered. Major chunk of oil comes from petroleum.

Hence, the correct option (a).

100. $H_2O + CO_2 \rightarrow CH_2O + O_2$

∵under solar energy CH_2O is stable at low temperature but breaks at higher temperature releasing heat equal to 469 Kj/mole.

Hence, the correct option (a).

101. Solar energy is radiated from the sun in the form of electromagnetic waves of shorter wavelength of 0.2 to 0.4 micrometers. Out of all the solar energy radiations reaching the earth's atmosphere, 8% is ultraviolet radiation, 40% is visible range light and 46% is by infrared radiation.

Hence, the correct option (c).

102. Magneto hydro dynamic is a generator which is used for direct conversion of thermal energy into electrical energy. They work on faraday principle. When an electric conductor moves across a magnetic field, electric current is produced.

Hence, the correct option (a).

103. Solar radiation that has not been absorbed or scattered and reaches the ground from the sun is called direct radiation or beam radiation. It is the radiation which produces a shadow when interrupted by an opaque object.

Hence, the correct option (a).

104. Diffuse radiation received from the sun after its direction has been changed by reflection and scattering by the atmosphere. Since the solar radiation is scattered in all direction in the atmosphere, diffuse radiation comes to the earth from all parts of the sky.

Hence, the correct option (c).

105. Insolation is the total solar radiation received at any point on any point on the earth's surface. In other words insolation is the sum of the direct and diffuse radiation. More specifically insolation is defined as the total solar radiation energy received on a horizontal surface of unit area on the ground in unit time.

Hence, the correct option (a).

106. The insolation at a given point or location on the earth's surface depends among other factors, on the altitude of the sun in the sky. As a result of absorption and scattering, the insolation is less when the sun is low in the sky than when it is higher.

Hence, the correct option (a).

107. These are generated in reprocessing of spent fuel. They contain all fission products and contain of the transuranium elements not separated during reprocessing. Such wastes are to be disposed of carefully.

Hence, the correct option (b).

108. Units of nuclear radiation is Roentgen- amount of radiation which will on passing through pure air under standard condition produce 1 electrostatic unit of ions/cm^3 of air -> 86.9 ergs of energy absorbed/gm of air.

Hence, the correct option (b).

109. Spent fuel is the unprocessed fuel that is removed from the reactor core after reaching end of core life service. It is removed and then stored for 3 to 4 months under water in the plant site to give time for the most intense radioactive isotopes to decay.

Hence, the correct option (b).

110. Solar energy is the most abundant energy source on the planet. Enough sunlight hits the Earth's surface in 1 1/2 hours to power the entire world's electricity consumption for a year.

Hence, the correct option (d).

111. While solar accounts for less than 2% of U.S. electrical generating capacity overall, it is one of the fastest-growing energy markets in the country. With solar power continuing to get more affordable and new installations happening every day, the solar industry is booming. For the first time, more solar generating capacity was added in 2015 than natural gas in the U.S.

Hence, the correct option (c).

112. In 2014, California became the first state to generate more than 5 percent of its annual utility-scale electricity from solar power, according to the Energy Information Administration. With several large solar plants phased into operation in 2014, California's utility-scale (1 megawatt or larger) facilities generated a record 9.9 million megawatthours (MWh) of electricity in 2014, an increase of 6.1 million MWh from 2013 and more than three times the output of the next-highest state, Arizona. In total, nearly 1,900 MW of new utility-scale solar capacity was added, bringing the state's utility-scale capacity for all solar technologies to 5,400 MW by the end of 2014.

Hence, the correct option (a).

113. Photovoltaics (PV) is the conversion of light into electricity using semiconducting materials that exhibit the photovoltaic effect, a phenomenon studied in physics, photochemistry, and electrochemistry.

Hence, the correct option (c).

114. Edmond Becquerel was the first person to realize that sunlight could produce an electric current in a solid material in 1839, but it took more than a century for scientists to fully understand this process and develop a practical solar cell.

Hence, the correct option (d).

115. Photovoltaic cells are used in Solar panels, Static charge generator.

when light falls on them, it produces electricity.

Hence, the correct option (b).

116. The trend that the developing economies invest more in renewable energy capacity than the developed ones continued for the fourth year. Out of the USD 140 billion (EUR 122 billion) investments in solar energy, 54% or USD 75 billion (EUR 65 billion) were invested in developing economies.

Between 2008 and 2014, PV module prices have decreased rapidly by more than 80 %, then 2015 saw a short levelling out due to industry consolidation and increasing markets, mainly in China and Japan [Blo 2013, 2016]. However, since the beginning of 2016 module prices have again seen a sharp decrease in prices, which put all solar companies along the value chain under enormous pressure.

Hence, the correct option (b).

117. Today, soft costs that is, all the costs and fees aside from the solar hardware itself account for more than half of the price of installing a solar energy system. By taking steps to help reduce soft costs, the Department of Energy is working to make affordable solar power a reality for those who want it.

Hence, the correct option (d).

118. Concentrating solar power technologies use mirrors to reflect and concentrate sunlight onto receivers that collect solar energy and convert it to heat. This thermal energy can then be used to produce electricity via a steam turbine or heat engine that drives a generator.

Hence, the correct option (c).

119. Parabolic trough, linear fresnel and power tower are all types of concentrating solar power systems. They may look very different, but they operate on the same principle, focusing the sun's rays on a central receiver.

The cathode-ray tube (CRT) is a vacuum tube that contains one or more electron guns and a phosphorescent screen, and is used to display images. It modulates, accelerates, and deflects electron beam(s) onto the screen to create the images.

Hence, the correct option (c).

120. Spanning 3,500 acres of Southern California desert, Ivanpah's 173,500 "heliostats" (each made up of two mirrors) focus the sun's rays on three 459-foot-tall, heat-collecting "power towers." Water circulated through these towers turns to steam, driving turbines that can generate up to 377 megawatts of electricity enough to power 140,000 homes in California.

Hence, the correct option (a).

Part - I

Q.1 Goods which are consumed together are called?
A. Inferior goods
B. Normal goods
C. Complementary goods
D. Substitute goods

Q.2 Dhamek Stupa was built by?
A. Akbar **B.** Humayun
C. Ashoka **D.** Nar asimha

Q.3 The substances which have very low ignition temperature and can easily catch fire with a flame are called ___________ substances.
A. hazardous **B.** perilous
C. incombustible **D.** inflammable

Q.4 The predominant stage of the life cycle of a moss is the gametophyte which consists of two stages. The first stage is the __________ stage.
A. Agar **B.** Leafy
C. Chlorella **D.** protonema

Q.5 The marginal product curve is inverse ___ shaped.
A. X **B.** W **C.** V **D.** U

Q.6 __________ scheme has been introduced by the Central Government to provide equal primary education to all budding children across India.
A. Gram Uday Se Bharat Uday Abhiyan
B. Pradhan Mantri Ujjwala Yojana
C. Pradhan Mantri Su rakshit Matritva Yojana
D. Vidyanjali Yojana

Q.7 Which of the following is a major river in Bangladesh which is also the main distributary of the Ganges?
A. Gandak **B.** Kosi **C.** Gomati **D.** Padma

Q.8 The laws which govern the motion of planets are called ________________.
A. Newton's Laws **B.** Kepler's Laws
C. Avogadro' s Laws **D.** De Morgan's Laws

Ques (9-12):Directions: Study the chart and answer the questions: The pie chart given here represents the domestic expenditure of a family in percent. Study the chart and answer the following questions if the total monthly income of the family is Rs. 33,650

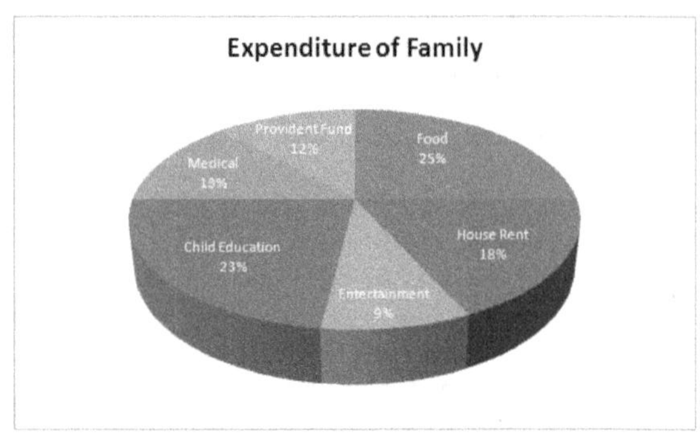

Q.9 The house rent per month is:
A. Rs. 6000 **B.** Rs. 6152 **C.** Rs. 6057 **D.** Rs. 6048

Q.10 The annual savings in the form of provident fund would be:
A. Rs. 48456 **B.** Rs. 48540
C. Rs. 44856 **D.** Rs. 45480

Q.11 After providential fund deductions and payment of house rent, the total monthly income of the family remains:
A. Rs. 23545 **B.** Rs. 24435
C. Rs. 23555 **D.** Rs. 25355

Q.12 The total amount per month, the family spends on food and entertainment combined together, is:
A. Rs. 11432 **B.** Rs. 11441
C. Rs. 12315 **D.** Rs. 12443

Q.13 Directions : The proportion of male student and proportion of vegetarian in a school are given below. The school has a total of 800 students, 80% of whom are in the Secondary Section and rest equally divided between Class 11 and 12.

	Male (M)	Vegetarian (V)
Class 12	0.60	
Class 11	0.55	0.50
Secondary Section		0.55
Total	0.475	0.53

What is the percentage of vegetarian students in class 12?
A. 40 **B.** 45 **C.** 50 **D.** 55

Q.14 Directions : The proportion of male student and proportion of vegetarian in a school are given below. The school has a total of 800 students, 80% of whom are in the Secondary Section and rest equally divided between Class 11 and 12.

	Male (M)	Vegetarian (V)
Class 12	0.60	
Class 11	0.55	0.50
Secondary Section		0.55
Total	0.475	0.53

In class 12, twenty 25% of the vegetarian are male. What is the difference between number of female vegetarian and male non-vegetarian?

A. 10   **B.** 12   **C.** 14   **D.** 16

Q.15 Directions : The proportion of male student and proportion of vegetarian in a school are given below. The school has a total of 800 students, 80% of whom are in the Secondary Section and rest equally divided between Class 11 and 12.

	Male (M)	Vegetarian (V)
Class 12	0.60	
Class 11	0.55	0.50
Secondary Section		0.55
Total	0.475	0.53

What is the percentage of male students in Secondary Section?

A. 40   **B.** 45   **C.** 50   **D.** 55

Q.16 Directions : Study the table and answer the questions:

The table given here

Year								
	English		Maths		Science		Social Science	
	High.	Ave.	High.	Ave.	High.	Ave.	High.	Ave.
2007	80	70	94	60	89	70	65	55
2008	82	65	85	62	95	64	66	58
2009	71	56	92	68	97	68	68	48
2010	75	52	91	64	92	75	77	58

What is the overall average of marks in the four subjects in the year 2009?

A. 63   **B.** 64   **C.** 65   **D.** 60

Q.17 Point A divides segment BC in the ratio 5:1. Co-ordinates of B are (6 ,-4) and C are (0,8). What are the co-ordinates of point A?

A. (1 , 6)   **B.** (1 , -6)   **C.** (-1 , -6)   **D.** (1 , 6)

Q.18 What is the area (in sq cm) of a regular hexagon of side 9 cm?

A. $50\sqrt{3}$ **B.** $300\sqrt{3}$ **C.** $243\sqrt{3}/2$ **D.** $200\sqrt{3}$

Q.19 If 1 shirt is offered free on purchase of 4 shirts, what is the effective discount (in %) on each shirt?

A. 25   **B.** 20   **C.** 16   **D.** 24

Q.20 Sum of a fraction and thrice its reciprocal is $\frac{31}{6}$. What is the fraction?

A. $\frac{2}{9}$ **B.** $\frac{9}{4}$ **C.** $\frac{9}{2}$ **D.** $\frac{4}{9}$

Q.21 A sum fetched a total simple interest of Rs. 5,400 at the rate of 12.5 % yearly in 4 years. What is the sum (in Rs.)?

A. 11,800   **B.** 12,800   **C.** 9,800   **D.** 10,800

Q.22 A and B together do a job in 12 days and A could do the job in 20 days if he worked alone. How many days would B take to do the job if he worked alone?

A. 30 days   **B.** 25 days   **C.** 24 days   **D.** 15 days

Q.23 The average marks of 40 students in an examination was 34. It was later found that the marks of one student had been wrongly entered as 62 instead of 26. What is the correct average?

A. 33.1   **B.** 33.3   **C.** 33.5   **D.** 33.7

Q.24 ΔXYZ is similar to ΔPQR. If ratio of Perimeter of ΔXYZ and Perimeter of ΔPQR is 4:9 and if PQ = 27 cm, then what is the length of XY (in cm)?

A. 9   **B.** 12   **C.** 16   **D.** 15

Q.25 Where did a maiden trilateral exercise, involving Republic of Singapore Navy (RSN), Royal Thailand Navy (RTN) and Indian Navy (IN) commence in September 2019?

A. Chennai   **B.** Kochi

C. Port Blair   **D.** Mumbai

Q.26 Where did Union Minister of Science & Technology, Dr. Harsh Vardhan inaugurate the National Centre for Clean Coal Research and Development in September 2019?

A. IIT Bombay   **B.** IIT Delhi

C. IIT Kanpur   **D.** IISc-Bengaluru

Q.27 In September, 2019, India's Sumit Nagal jumped 15 places to achieve a career-high ranking of _______ in the latest ATP rankings.

A. 172   **B.** 165   **C.** 159   **D.** 143

Q.28 Who was conferred the Dr Kalam Smriti International Excellence Award 2019 in September 2019?

A. Sheikh Hasina   **B.** Narendra Modi

C. Sajeeb Wazed   **D.** Amit Shah

Q.29 With which of the following did the Directorate General of Training sign an agreement in September 2019 to carry out a nationwide Train-the-Trainer programme in basic artificial intelligence?

A. Microsoft   **B.** IBM

C. Accenture   **D.** Oacle

Q.30 What is the rank of the Indian football team in the FIFA rankings released in September 2019?

A. 102   **B.** 104   **C.** 106   **D.** 108

Q.31 To which country will Prime Minister Narendra Modi embark on a seven-day visit in September 2019?

A. USA   **B.** Poland

C. Germany   **D.** Russia

Q.32 Who will be the chief of Indian Air force from 30 September 2019?

A. Karambir Singh

B. Rakesh Kumar Singh Bhadauria

C. Anil Khosla

D. Shirish Baban Deo

Q.33 The question below consists of a set of labelled sentences. Out of the four options given, select the most logical order of the sentences to form a coherent paragraph.

I've taken out my

X-and stay poised and vigilant

Y-ear buds so I can

Z-listen for announcements

A. ZXY   **B.** YZX   **C.** XZY   **D.** YXZ

Q.34 The question below consists of a set of labelled sentences. Out of the four options given, select the most logical order of the sentences to form a coherent paragraph.

In the Northeast, the sun
X-sets by four in the evening
Y-morning and in winter it
Z-rises as early as four in the

A. XYZ   **B.** YZX   **C.** ZYX   **D.** ZXY

Q.35 In the following question, out of the four alternatives, select the alternative which is the best substitute of the words/sentence.

A person or thing that is likely to cause harm

A. Menace   **B.** Cordial   **C.** Festal   **D.** Blithe

Q.36 In the following question, out of the four alternatives, select the word similar in meaning to the word given.

Subtle

A. Harsh   **B.** Open
C. Ignorant   **D.** Understated

Q.37 In the following question, four words are given out of which one word is correctly spelt. Select the correctly spelt word.

A. deligence   **B.** diligence
C. delegence   **D.** dilegence

Q.38 In the following question, out of the four alternatives, select the alternative which best expresses the meaning of the idiom/phrase.

At the drop of a hat

A. Without any hesitation; instantly.
B. Show outward respect to someone you hate.
C. Forcibly let go of something which is very personal to you.
D. A mistake which is of not much consequence.

Q.39 In the following question, out of the four alternatives, select the word opposite in meaning to the word given.

Sullen

A. Glum   **B.** Silent
C. Crabby   **D.** Agreeable

Q.40 In the following question, the sentence given with blank to be filled in with an appropriate word. Select the correct alternative out of the four and indicate it by selecting the appropriate option.

Since my father was an __________ from India, he brought his Indian culture and traditions to the United States with him.

A. emigrant   **B.** immigrant
C. native   **D.** citizen

Part - II

Q.41 Three equal resistors are conntected as shown in figure. Find the eqcivalent resistance between poits A and B ?

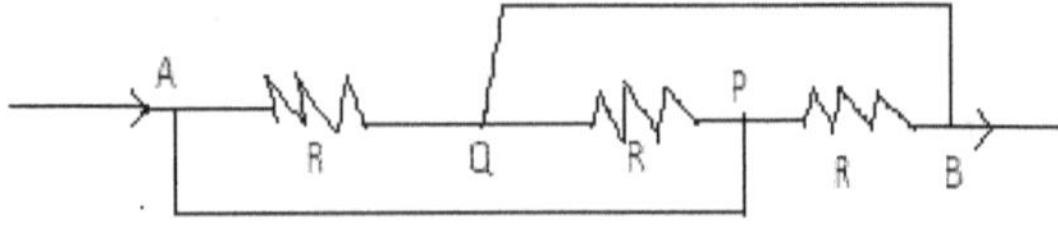

A. 3R   **B.** $\frac{R}{3}$ **C.** $\frac{R}{2}$ **D.** $\frac{2R}{3}$

Q.42 The short circuit KVA is maximum when fault occurs
A. Near the generator
B. At the end of transmission line
C. In the middle of transmission line
D. None of these

Q.43 Electrical appliances are not connected in series because-
A. Series circuit is complicated
B. Power loss is more
C. Appliances have different current ratings
D. None of the above

Q.44 Which of the following motors is preferred for tape recorder.
A. Hystersis motor
B. Shaded-pole motor
C. Two value capacitor motor
D. Universal motor

Q.45 It is known that the potential difference across 6 Ω resistor in figure is 48V. The entering current I is

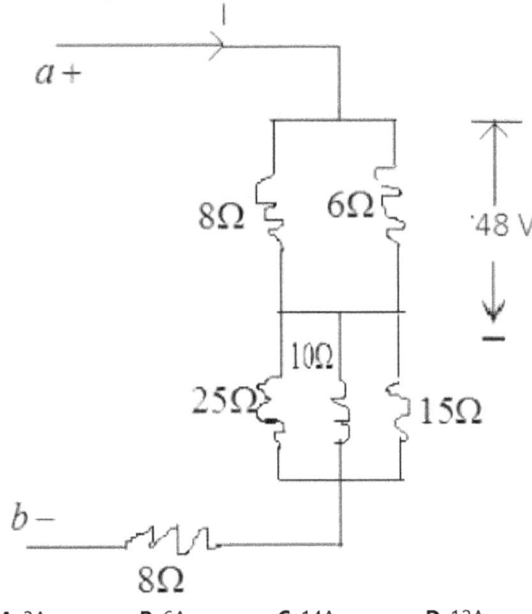

A. 3A   **B.** 6A   **C.** 14A   **D.** 12A

Q.46 Give the number of electrons passing through a wire per minute. The current flowing through it is 500mA.
A. 1.875×10^{20} **B.** 6.875×10^{20}
C. 1.875×10^{-20} **D.** 6.875×10^{-20}

Q.47 Find the Norton equivalent current source at terminal (a, b) in figure.

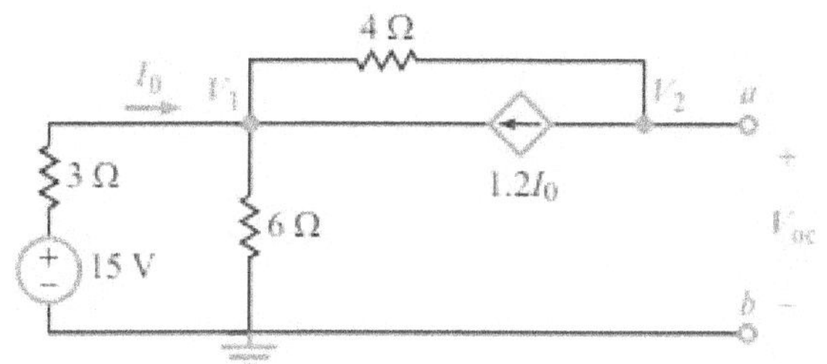

A. In=4MA,Rn=5Ω
B. I_n=1A, R_n=3.5Ω
C. I_n=2.5A, R_n=6Ω
D. I_n=0.217A, R_n=9.2Ω

Q.48 When the relative permeability of a material is slightly less than 1 , it is called a-
A. Diamagnetic Material
B. Paramagnetic Material
C. Ferro Magnetic Material
D. None of the above

Q.49 In figure

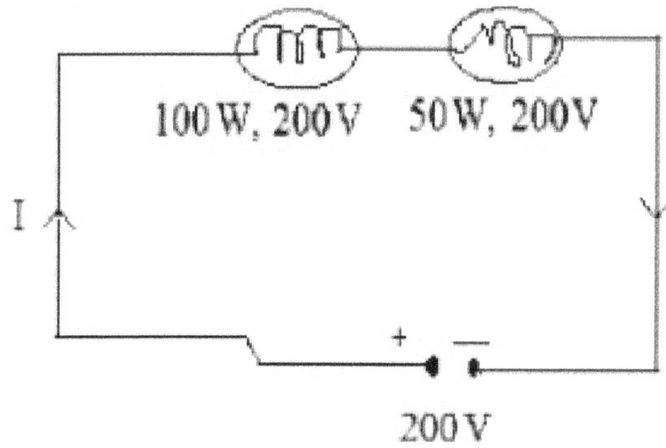

100 watts = lamp A
50 watts = lamp B
A. The lamp A will be brighter than lamp B
B. The lamp B will be brighter than lamp A
C. The two lamp will be equally bright
D. None of the above

Q.50 Dielectric is introduced between the plates of a capacitor kept at a constant potential difference. The capacitance of the capacitor-
A. Increases
B. Decreases
C. Remains the same
D. None of the above

Q.51 2cm long coil has 10 turns and curries a current of 750 MA. The magnetizing force of the coil is
A. 225 AT/M
B. 675 AT/M
C. 450 AT/M
D. 375 AT/M

Q.52 The ohm's law for magnetic circuit is
A. Reluctance = $\frac{flux}{mmf}$
B. mmf = $\frac{Reluctance}{flux}$
C. mmf = $\frac{flux}{Reluctance}$
D. mmf = flux × reluctance

Q.53 The curie temperature of iron is-
A. 200 ° C
B. 430 ° C
C. 770 ° C
D. 550 ° C

Q.54 The coupling between two magnetically coupled coils is said to be ideal if the cofficeint of coupling is-
A. Zero
B. 0.1
C. 2
D. 1

Q.55 The form factor of a ....wave is-
A. Sinusoidal
B. Square
C. Triangular
D. Saw tooth

Q.56 The reactance of 1F capacitance when connected to a D.C. circuit is-
A. Zero
B. Infinite
C. 1Ω
D. 0.5Ω

Q.57 A series RLC circuit is resonant at 150 KHz and has a D of 50. What is the bandwidth-
A. 3KHz
B. 4 KHz
C. 6 KHz
D. 8 KHz

Q.58 The purpose of choke in a fluorescent tube is-
A. To increase the current
B. To decrease the current
C. To decrease the voltage momentarily
D. To increase the voltage momentarily

Q.59 If current through the operating coil of a moving iron instrument is doubled, the operating force becomes-
A. Two times
B. Four times
C. One half time
D. Three time

Q.60 In a dynomo meter wattmeter, the moving coil is the-
A. Current coil
B. Potential coil
C. Current coil
D. None of the above

Q.61 For the measurement of high direct voltage (Says 10KV) one would use..........volt meter-
A. PMMC
B. Electro static
C. Not wire
D. Moving Iron

Q.62 The rated voltage of a 3 phase power system is given as-
A. RMS phase voltage
B. Peak phase voltage
C. RMS line to line voltage
D. Peak line to line voltage

Q.63 In a single phase energy meter, braking torque is provided by-
A. Permanent magnet
B. Air friction
C. Fluid friction
D. None of the above

Q.64 The yoke of a DC. Machine is made of-
A. Silicon steel
B. Soft iron
C. Aluminium
D. Cost steel

Q.65 What is the correct sequence of the following type of ammeter and voltmeter with increasing accuracy
(a) Moving Iron
(b) PMMC
(c) Induction Instrument
A. c, a, b
B. a, c, b
C. b, a, c
D. a, b, c

Q.66 Electric traction in comparison to other traction systems has the advanges of____.
A. higher acceleration and breaking retardation
B. cleanest system and so ideally suitable for the underground and tube railways.
C. better speed control
D. All of these

Q.67 Armature reaction in a D.C. motor is increased.
A. When the armature current increase
B. When the armature current decrease
C. When the field current increase
D. By interpoles

Q.68 ....motor is most suitable for push and pull action
A. Shunt
B. Series
C. Differentialy compounded
D. Cumulatively compound

Q.69 The resistance of the field regulator of a DC shunt motor is of order of
A. 0.1 Ω B. 1 Ω C. 10 Ω D. 100 Ω

Q.70 In a DC motor, unidirectional torque is produced with the help of-
A. Brushes   B. Commutator
C. End Plates   D. Both (A) and (B)

Q.71 Which materials are used for Superheater tubes?
A. Nickel chromium
B. Alnico
C. Chromium-Molybdenum
D. Magnox

Q.72 A D.C. generator has 6 poles. A brush shift of actual means a brush shift-
A. 6 ° electrical   B. 18 ° electrical
C. 30 ° electrical   D. 2 ° electrical

Q.73 If the load on an over compounded D.C. generator is reduced the terminal voltage.
A. Increases   B. Remains the same
C. Decreases   D. None of these

Q.74 The path of the magnetic flux in a transformer has-
A. High reluctance   B. Low resistance
C. High conductivity   D. Low reluctance

Q.75 As compared to an Amplifier a transformer can not-
A. Increase the output voltage
B. Increase the output current
C. Increase the output power
D. None of these

Q.76 The full load copper-loss in a transformer is 400W. At half load, the copper-loss will be
A. 100 W   B. 200 W
C. 150 W   D. None of these

Q.77 In any transformer, the voltage per turn in primary and secondary remains-
A. Always same
B. Always in ratio of K
C. Always different
D. Some time same

Q.78 What is the phase difference between the low and the high voltage of a YZ5 power transformer-
A. 0 °   B. 75 °   C. 5 °   D. 150 °

Q.79 Transformer oil is used as-
A. Insulant only
B. Coolant only
C. Both insulant and coolant
D. Ihert medium

Q.80 At full load, the current induced in the rotor conductor of a 3 phase squirrel cafe induction motor is-
A. More than rated current
B. Les than rated current
C. nearly equal to rated current
D. None of these

Q.81 What is the unit for inductive reactance?
A. Henry   B. Ohm   C. Farad   D. Volts

Q.82 A three phase, 50 Hz induction motor has a full load speed of 1440 rpm. Rotor frequency is?
A. 2 Hz   B. 50 Hz   C. 52 Hz   D. 58 Hz

Q.83 Which of the following lubricants is the shaft of the motor lubricated-
A. Graphite   B. Grease
C. Silicon oil   D. Mineral oil

Q.84 A change of 5% in supply voltage to a 3 phase induction motor will produce the appropriate change in the torque of-
A. 5%   B. 7.5   C. 10%   D. 25%

Q.85 The simplest way to eliminate the harmonic induction torques is-
A. Integral slot winding
B. Skewing
C. Chording
D. None of these

Q.86 In an induction motor, skew of the rotor BQR reduces-
A. Noise   B. Vibration
C. Synchronous cusps   D. All of the these

Q.87 A multimeter has different shunts, which increase the-
A. Current Range   B. Voltage Range
C. Resistance Range   D. Impedance Range

Q.88 The megger voltage for testing 250 V installation should be-
A. 100 V   B. 500 V   C. 300 V   D. 100 V

Q.89 In two wattmeter method of measuring 3 phase power, power factor is 0.5 , then one of the wattmeter will read-

A. $\frac{W}{2}$ **B.** Zero   **C.** $\sqrt{2}W$ **D.** $\frac{W}{\sqrt{3}}$

Q.90 Inductance is measured in terms of capacitance and resistance by-
A. Schering bridge
B. De- Sauty Bridge
C. Maxwell -wein bridge
D. Wein bridge

Q.91 Which of the following is electro mechanical device ?
A. D.C. motor   **B.** LVDT
C. Induction relay   **D.** None of these

Q.92 Two impedances 5+j5 and 5-j5 ohms are connected in parallel. The combined impedance is-
A. (10+j0)   **B.** (2.5−j2.5)
C. (5+j0)   **D.** (j10)

Q.93 A capacitor used on 230 V AC Supply should have a peak voltage rating of-
A. 325 V   **B.** 230 V   **C.** 115 V   **D.** $\frac{230}{\sqrt{2}}V$

Q.94 If I be the current, C the capacitance and V the potential differences, then $\frac{I}{CV}$ will have the unit of-
A. Power   **B.** Reactive Power
C. Time   **D.** Frequency

Q.95 Which of the resistances is represented by the curve shown in figure.

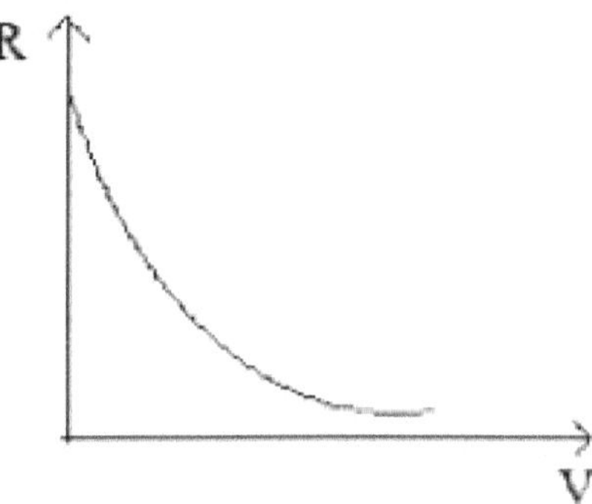

A. Potentio meter
B. Layer resistance
C. Hot conductor (NTC)
D. Cold Conductor (PTC)

Q.96 The period of a sine wave is $\frac{1}{60}$ seconds. Its frequency is:
A. 30 Hz   **B.** 60 Hz   **C.** 120 Hz   **D.** 15 Hz

Q.97 The maximum power in the shown load is

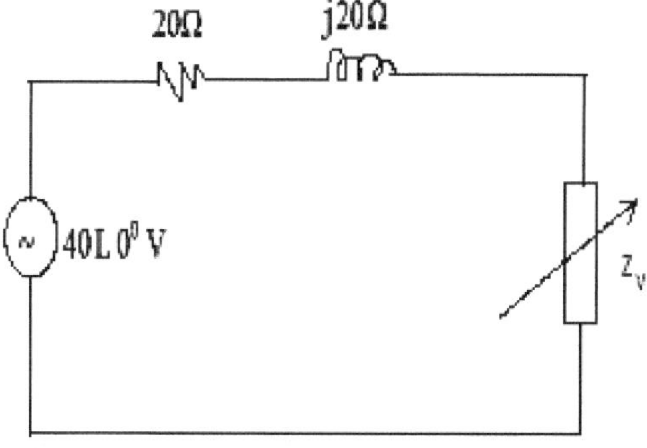

A. 25W   **B.** 20W   **C.** 62.5W   **D.** 110W

Q.98 In an RLC series circuit, the impedance at resonance is
A. Maximum   **B.** Minimum
C. Infinity   **D.** Zero

Q.99 In the circuit shown, the value of currents I_1, I_2 and I_3 are.

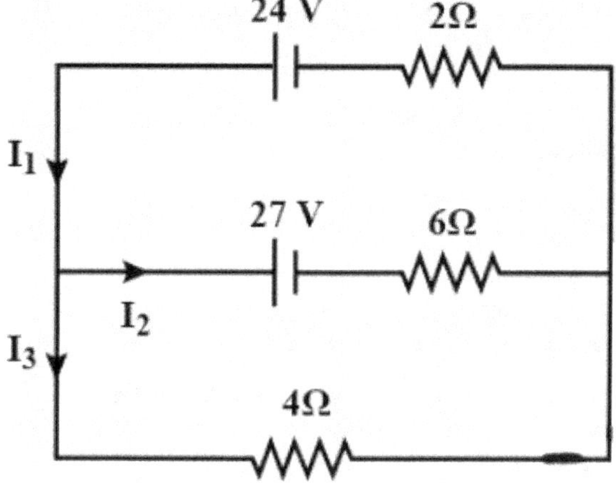

A. 3A, $\frac{-3}{2}A$, $\frac{9}{2}A$ **B.** $\frac{9}{2}A$, 3A, $\frac{-3}{2}A$
C. 5A, 4A, -3A   **D.** 7A, $\frac{5}{4}A$, $\frac{9}{2}A$

Q.100 The ripple factor in case of a full wave rectifier-
A. 1.12   **B.** 1.21   **C.** 0.48   **D.** 0.50

Q.101 The acceptor type of impurity is impurity is-
A. Phosporus   **B.** Boron
C. Freon   **D.** None of these

Q.102 Secondary emission occurs in-
A. Diode   **B.** Triode   **C.** Tetrode   **D.** Pentode

Q.103 As compared to CE amplifier, the frequency response of an emitter follower is-
A. Worse   **B.** Better
C. Similar   **D.** None of these

Q.104 Which of the following transistors can be used in enhancement mode ?
A. UJT   **B.** JFET
C. MOSFET   **D.** NPN Transistor

Q.105 In a steam power plant water is used for cooling purposes in-

A. Condenser
B. Turbine only
C. Boiler tubes
D. Boiler tubes and turbine both

Q.106 Induced draft fans are bacted at :-
A. The top
B. The bottom
C. In the middle part
D. Can be anywhere, in the cooling tower

Q.107 The fissile material is-
A. 232
B. Thorium
C. Plutonium
D. None of these

Q.108 In a power plant, a reserve generating capacity which is not in service but is in operation is known as-
A. Hot Reserve
B. Cold Reserve
C. Firm Power
D. Spinning Reserve

Q.109 Running cost of a power plant is based on the cost of-
A. Energy or fuel
B. Consumable items
C. Maintenance and operation
D. All of these

Q.110 Stringing chart represents a graph of-
A. Tension - Temperature
B. Sag - Temperature
C. Load - Temperature
D. option a and b both are correct

Q.111 The most important cause of power loss in the transmission line is the-
A. Resistance
B. Reactance
C. Capacitance
D. None of these

Q.112 If the P.F of load decreases, the line losses
A. Increases
B. Decreases
C. Remain constant
D. None of these

Q.113 The line constants of a transmission line are-
A. Uniformly distributed
B. Lumped
C. Non- uniformly distributed
D. None of these

Q.114 The skin effect does not depend on-
A. A natural of material
B. Size of wire
C. Supply frequency
D. Ambient temperature

Q.115 By using guard ring, string efficiency is-
A. Increased
B. Decreased
C. Constant
D. Independent of shunt capacitance

Q.116 The material generally used for armour of high voltage cable is-
A. Aluminium
B. Steel
C. Brass
D. Copper

Q.117 The life of under ground cable is taken as-
A. 10 years
B. 20 years
C. 25 years
D. 40 years

Q.118 The minimum clearance between the ground and a 220 KV line is about-
A. 5.5 m
B. 10.5 m
C. 7.0 m
D. 4.3 m

Q.119 In an interconnected grid system, the diversity factor of the whale system
A. Decreases
B. Increases
C. Remains same
D. None of these

Q.120 The economic size of conductor is determined by-
A. Current carrying capacity
B. Transmission voltage
C. Kelvin's law
D. None of these

// Smart Answer Sheet //

Correct Indicates percentage of students who answered questions correctly.

Skipped Indicates percentage of students who skipped questions.

Q.	Ans.	Correct / Skipped	Q.	Ans.	Correct / Skipped	Q.	Ans.	Correct / Skipped	Q.	Ans.	Correct / Skipped	Q.	Ans.	Correct / Skipped
1	C	24.59 % / 16.39 %	17	D	21.31 % / 54.1 %	33	B	45.9 % / 45.9 %	49	B	26.23 % / 45.9 %	65	C	19.67 % / 54.1 %
2	C	27.87 % / 52.46 %	18	C	16.39 % / 59.02 %	34	C	45.9 % / 45.9 %	50	A	29.51 % / 49.18 %	66	D	36.07 % / 47.54 %
3	D	49.18 % / 40.98 %	19	B	29.51 % / 45.9 %	35	A	22.95 % / 52.46 %	51	D	29.51 % / 49.18 %	67	A	34.43 % / 47.54 %
4	D	8.2 % / 59.01 %	20	C	29.51 % / 42.62 %	36	D	14.75 % / 49.18 %	52	D	32.79 % / 44.26 %	68	D	8.2 % / 44.26 %
5	D	19.67 % / 54.1 %	21	D	32.79 % / 52.46 %	37	B	22.95 % / 45.9 %	53	D	6.56 % / 57.37 %	69	D	14.75 % / 54.1 %
6	D	27.87 % / 54.1 %	22	A	40.98 % / 47.54 %	38	A	22.95 % / 54.1 %	54	D	45.9 % / 44.26 %	70	D	31.15 % / 44.26 %
7	D	32.79 % / 45.9 %	23	A	37.7 % / 52.46 %	39	D	6.56 % / 59.01 %	55	B	14.75 % / 50.82 %	71	C	9.84 % / 49.18 %
8	B	37.7 % / 47.55 %	24	B	32.79 % / 47.54 %	40	A	9.84 % / 47.54 %	56	B	36.07 % / 44.26 %	72	B	9.84 % / 52.46 %
9	C	37.7 % / 54.1 %	25	C	16.39 % / 54.1 %	41	B	29.51 % / 42.62 %	57	A	32.79 % / 54.1 %	73	C	9.84 % / 47.54 %
10	A	34.43 % / 57.37 %	26	D	16.39 % / 54.1 %	42	A	42.62 % / 40.99 %	58	D	32.79 % / 49.18 %	74	D	34.43 % / 40.98 %
11	C	0 % / 100 %	27	C	6.56 % / 60.65 %	43	C	37.7 % / 49.19 %	59	B	27.87 % / 47.54 %	75	C	39.34 % / 49.18 %
12	B	36.07 % / 52.45 %	28	A	22.95 % / 50.82 %	44	A	16.39 % / 47.54 %	60	B	31.15 % / 37.7 %	76	A	11.48 % / 42.62 %
13	A	11.48 % / 59.01 %	29	B	13.11 % / 54.1 %	45	C	24.59 % / 52.46 %	61	B	22.95 % / 44.26 %	77	A	24.59 % / 42.62 %
14	D	4.92 % / 60.65 %	30	B	16.39 % / 50.82 %	46	A	6.56 % / 47.54 %	62	C	31.15 % / 42.62 %	78	D	8.2 % / 57.37 %
15	B	9.84 % / 59.01 %	31	A	27.87 % / 49.18 %	47	D	9.84 % / 55.73 %	63	A	27.87 % / 50.82 %	79	C	50.82 % / 45.9 %
16	D	37.7 % / 49.19 %	32	B	36.07 % / 45.9 %	48	A	27.07 % / 50.82 %	64	D	19.67 % / 39.35 %	80	C	27.87 % / 50.82 %

Q.	Ans.	Correct / Skipped		Q.	Ans.	Correct / Skipped		Q.	Ans.	Correct / Skipped		Q.	Ans.	Correct / Skipped		Q.	Ans.	Correct / Skipped
81	B	8.2 % / 49.18 %		89	B	21.31 % / 50.82 %		97	B	11.48 % / 52.45 %		105	A	37.7 % / 49.19 %		113	A	32.79 % / 47.54 %
82	A	6.56 % / 45.9 %		90	C	6.56 % / 50.82 %		98	B	29.51 % / 47.54 %		106	A	16.39 % / 47.54 %		114	D	24.59 % / 49.18 %
83	B	36.07 % / 47.54 %		91	B	14.75 % / 45.91 %		99	A	6.56 % / 57.37 %		107	C	16.39 % / 50.82 %		115	A	31.15 % / 50.82 %
84	C	19.67 % / 49.18 %		92	C	21.31 % / 45.9 %		100	C	14.75 % / 45.91 %		108	A	16.39 % / 50.82 %		116	B	37.7 % / 49.19 %
85	C	11.48 % / 52.45 %		93	A	32.79 % / 44.26 %		101	B	34.43 % / 47.54 %		109	D	47.54 % / 47.54 %		117	C	9.84 % / 47.54 %
86	D	36.07 % / 47.54 %		94	D	24.59 % / 50.82 %		102	C	4.92 % / 57.38 %		110	D	9.84 % / 54.09 %		118	C	8.2 % / 52.46 %
87	A	31.15 % / 49.18 %		95	A	16.39 % / 54.1 %		103	B	21.31 % / 54.1 %		111	B	13.11 % / 47.55 %		119	B	21.31 % / 52.46 %
88	B	26.23 % / 49.18 %		96	B	3.28 % / 42.62 %		104	C	27.87 % / 54.1 %		112	A	37.7 % / 39.35 %		120	C	16.39 % / 40.99 %

Performance Analysis

Avg. Score (%)	21.67%
Toppers Score (%)	91.67%
Your Score	

//Hints and Solutions//

1. A complementary good is a good whose use is related to the use of an associated or paired good. Two goods (A and B) are complementary if using more of good A requires the use of more of good B. For example, the demand for one good (printers) generates demand for the other (ink cartridges).

Hence the correct answer is option (c).

2. Ashoka was an Indian emperor of the Maurya Dynasty, who ruled almost all of the Indian subcontinent from c. 268 to 232 BCE. He was the grandson of the founder of the Maurya Dynasty, Chandragupta Maurya,

There are lovely elaborate carvings halfway on the monument on some sides. Dhamek Stupa is said to have been built in the year 500 CE while the construction was ordered by Emperor Ashoka in the 3rd Century BC. There's a small museum right after the entrance which has a few basic details of the monument.

Hence the correct answer is option (c).

3. The substances which catch fir easily are called inflammable substances such as oil, kerosene etc.

Hence the correct answer is option (d).

4. The life cycle of most mosses begins with the release of spores from a capsule, which opens when a small, lid like structure, called the operculum, degenerates. A single spore germinates to form a branched, filamentous protonema, from which a leafy gametophyte develops.

Hence the correct answer is option (d).

5. MARGINAL PRODUCT CURVE:

According to the law of variable proportions, the marginal product of an input initially rises and then after a certain level of employment, it starts falling. The MP curve in the input-output plane, therefore, looks like an inverse 'U'-shaped curve. Let us now see what the AP curve looks like.

Hence the correct answer is option (d).

6. A unique scheme named the Vidyanjali Yojana has been launched by the Ministry of Education in India which aims to fill up the Govt. schools with volunteer teachers willing to provide their service. With this unique scheme, one can fulfil the dream of becoming a teacher and teaching in a govt. school without having a teaching degree or becoming a certified teacher. There is an acute shortage of school teachers in govt. schools, mostly in rural areas all across the nation. Vidyanjali Yojana aims to fulfill this gap.

Hence the correct answer is option (d).

7. The Padma is a major river in Bangladesh. It is the main distributary of the Ganges, flowing generally southeast for 120 kilometres (75 mi) to its confluence with the Meghna River near the Bay of Bengal. The city of Rajshahi is situated on the banks of the river.

Hence the correct answer is option (d).

8. In astronomy, Kepler's laws of planetary motion are three scientific laws describing the motion of planets around the Sun.

- The orbit of a planet is an ellipse with the Sun at one of the two foci.
- A line segment joining a planet and the Sun sweeps out equal areas during equal intervals of time.
- The square of the orbital period of a planet is proportional to the cube of the semi-major axis of its orbit.

Hence the correct answer is option (b).

9. House rent per month= 18% of Rs. 33650; = Rs.

$\frac{18}{100} \times 36650$ = Rs. 6057

Hence the correct answer is option (c).

10. Annual provident fund saving= 12% of (Rs. 33650 $\times$ 12)

$= \frac{12}{100} \times 36650 \times 12$

= Rs. 48456.

Hence the correct answer is option (a).

11. Remaining income= [100-12-18]% of Rs. 33650,

$= Rs. \frac{70}{100} \times 36650$

= Rs. 23555.

Hence, the correct answer is option (C).

12. Spent on food and entertainment,

= 34% of Rs. 33650

$= Rs. \frac{34}{100} \times 36650$

=Rs. 11441.

Hence the correct answer is option (b).

13. Total Students = 800.

No. of students in secondary = 80% of 800 = 640.

Rest Students = 800 - 640 = 160.

Rest students are divided equally into class 12 and 11. So,

No. of students in class 12 = $\frac{160}{2}$ = 80.

Now, total vegetarian = 53%

No. of Total vegetarian = 53% of 800 = 424.

55% of secondary students are vegetarian.

No. of vegetarian in secondary = 55% of 640 = 352.

No. vegetarian in 11 = 50% of 80 = 40

Thus, no. of vegetarian in 12,

= 424- 352 - 40 = 32.

Thus,

In class 12 total vegetarian = 32.

So, % of vegetarian = $\dfrac{32}{80} \times 100$ = 40%.

Hence the correct answer is option (a).

14. male vegetarian= 32-8 =24; Difference= 24-8=16.

Hence the correct answer is option (d).

15. % of male students in secondary section,

$= \dfrac{288}{800} \times 100$ = 45%

Hence the correct answer is option (b).

16. Average in four subjects,

$= \dfrac{56+68+68+48}{4} = \dfrac{240}{4} = 60.$

Hence the correct answer is option (d).

17. Let the co-ordinates of point A be [x, y]

So,

$x = \dfrac{6\times1+0\times5}{5+1} = 1$

$y = \dfrac{-4\times1+8\times5}{5+1} = 6$

Hence the correct answer is option (d).

18. Side of a hexagon = a = 9 cm

$\therefore$Area of hexagon = $6 \times \dfrac{\sqrt{3}}{4}a^2 = 6 \times \dfrac{\sqrt{3}}{4} \times 81$

$=243\ \dfrac{\sqrt{3}}{2}$ sqcm.

Hence the correct answer is option (c).

19. Effective discount % = $\dfrac{1}{5} \times 100$ = 20%

Hence the correct answer is option (b).

20. Let the fraction be 'x'

According to the question,

$x + \dfrac{3}{x} = \dfrac{31}{6}$

$6x^2 - 31x + 18 = 0$

$6x^2 - 4x - 27x + 18 = 0$

$(2x - 9)(3x - 2) = 0$

$\therefore x = \dfrac{9}{2}, \dfrac{2}{3}$

Required answer = $\dfrac{9}{2}$

Hence the correct answer is option (c).

21. Let the sum be Rs. P

Simple Interest(SI) = $\dfrac{P \times R \times T}{100}$

$5400 = \dfrac{P \times 12.5 \times T}{100}$

$\therefore P = Rs.\ 10800$

Hence the correct answer is option (d).

22. Let the total work be 60 units

We know that,

Work = Efficiency × Time

From (i) and (ii) We get;

3 +B = 5

$\therefore$B = 2 units/day

$\therefore$Time taken by B alone to complete the work = $\dfrac{60}{2}$

=30 days.

Hence the correct answer is option (a).

23. Correct average = $Old\ Average - \dfrac{Error}{No.\ of\ student} =$

34-0.9 = 33.1 $= 34 - \dfrac{(62-26)}{40}$

Hence the correct answer is option (a).

24. Since ΔXYZ ~ ΔPQR

$\dfrac{Perimeter\ of\ XYZ}{Perimeter\ of\ PQR} = \dfrac{XY}{PQ}$

$\dfrac{4}{9} = \dfrac{XY}{27}$

$\therefore XY = 12\ cm$

Hence the correct answer is option (b).

25. A maiden trilateral exercise, involving Republic of Singapore Navy (RSN), Royal Thailand Navy (RTN) and Indian Navy (IN) commenced at **Port Blair** on 16 September 2019.

The five-day-long exercise is aimed at bolstering the maritime inter-relationships amongst Singapore, Thailand and India.

This would also strengthen the mutual confidence amongst three navies in terms of interoperability.

Hence the correct answer is option (c).

26. Union Minister of Science & Technology, Dr. Harsh Vardhan inaugurated the National Centre for Clean Coal Research and Development at Indian Institute of Science (IISc)-Bengaluru.

Dr. Harsh Vardhan also dedicated an Interdisciplinary Centre for Energy Research(ICER) to the Nation which is India's first of its kind center equipped with state-of-art facilities.

Hence the correct answer is option (d).

27. India's Sumit Nagal jumped 15 places to achieve a career-high ranking of 159 in the latest ATP rankings released on 16 September 2019.

He ended runners up in the Banja Luka ATP Challenger following a first round appearance at the US Open in August 2019.

Meanwhile, Prajnesh Gunneswaran continued his run in the top-100. He rose three places to be world no. 82.

Hence the correct answer is option (c).

28. PM Sheikh Hasina of Bangladesh was conferred the Dr Kalam Smriti International Excellence Award 2019 in Dhaka on 16 September 2019.

The award has been instituted in the memory of former Indian President Dr. A.P.J. Abdul Kalam.

The award citation lauded Prime Minister Hasina for her vision of a peaceful and prosperous South Asia, free of tension, conflicts and terrorism.

Hence the correct answer is option (a).

29. The Directorate General of Training signed an agreement with IBM to carry out a nationwide Train-the-Trainer programme in basic artificial intelligence.

As part of the programme, ITI trainers will be trained on basic AI skills towards using technology in their day-to-day training activities.

This programme aims at enabling the trainers with the basic approach, workflow and application of AI.

Hence the correct answer is option (b).

30. The Indian football team slipped a place to 104th position in the latest FIFA rankings released.

Indian Football Team in recent times is playing under the leadership of new coach Igor Stimac.

Belgium managed to hold on to the top position, while France has surpassed Brazil to reach the second spot.

Hence the correct answer is option (b).

31. Prime Minister Narendra Modi will embark on a seven-day visit to the United States on 21 September 2019.

During his visit, he will be in Houston and New York and address the United Nations General Assembly on 27 September 2019.

He will also be honoured with Bill and Melinda Gates Foundation's Global Goalkeeper's Award for his leadership in field of sanitation through Swachh Bharat Abhiyan.

Hence the correct answer is option (a).

32. Air Marshal Rakesh Kumar Singh Bhadauria will be the next chief of Indian Air force.

Air Marshal Bhadauria, will take charge from the incumbent Chief Air Chief Marshal BS Dhanoa on 30 September 2019.

The Cost Negotiation Committee (CNC) for the Rafale deal was headed by Mr. Bhadauria.

Hence the correct answer is option (b).

33. 'YZX' is the most logical flow of given sentences.

"I've taken out my ear buds so I can listen for announcements and stay poised and vigilant."

Hence the correct answer is option (b).

34. 'ZYX' is the correct sequence of given sentences.

"In the Northeast, the sun rises as early as four in the morning and in winter it sets by four in the evening."

Hence the correct answer is option (c).

35. Menace - a person or thing that is likely to cause harm; a threat or danger.

eg:- a new initiative aimed at beating the menace of drugs.

Hence the correct answer is option (a).

36. understated - presented or expressed in a subtle and effective way.

eg:- understated elegance.

Hence the correct answer is option (d).

37. diligence - careful and persistent work or effort.

eg:- few party members challenge his diligence as an MP.

Hence the correct answer is option (b).

38. at the drop of a hat - without hesitation or good reason.

eg:- he used to be very bashful, blushing at the drop of a hat.

Hence the correct answer is option (a).

39. agreeable - quite enjoyable and pleasurable; pleasant.

eg:- a cheerful and agreeable companion.

Hence the correct answer is option (d).

40. emigrant - a person who leaves their own country in order to settle permanently in another.

eg:- she was a Polish emigrant who came to Scotland during the Second World War.

Hence the correct answer is option (a).

41. Now point S& Q are at same potential . Similarly point P &T are at same potential.

Joining resistance between S & P, P&Q and Q&T we find thst they all are in parallel.

Equivalent resistance across AB

$$\frac{1}{R_{eq}} = \frac{1}{R} + \frac{1}{R} + \frac{1}{R}$$
$$= \frac{3}{R}$$
$$R_{eq} = \frac{R}{3}$$

Hence the correct answer is option (b).

42. The short circuit KVA is maximum when fault occurs near the generator.

Hence the correct answer is option (a).

43. It is because of the entire electrical network of the city, which is parallel. In serial circuits, if only one element is disconnected, the entire circuit is disconnected. would you like your fridge to shut down as soon as you turn your computer off? Would you like your microwave oven to shut down when you turn your hair drier off? NO!!!

And then there is the problem with current and voltage. In a serial circuit, the current passing all elements is equal, but each have different voltages. Current is not dangerous, but high or low voltage is dangerous for all electrical elements.

So, a network of power plugs must be used, that connecting and disconnecting an element does not shut the whole city's network down, and it does not affect the voltage of other elements.

Also, this network should work in a way that all voltages for all elements be the same (usually about 220 volts) but the current can be different according to the element, no problems there. While the air conditioner uses 10 amperes of current, a laptop computer only uses about 1 ampere. but the voltage for both is 220 V, regardless of how many electrical appliances are connected to the network.

So, a parallel network satisfies both above problems, and is ideal.

Hence the correct answer is option (c).

44. Hysteresis motor is particularly useful for high-quality record players and tape-recorders because it develops hysteresis torque which is extremely steady both in amplitude and phase.

Hence the correct answer is option (a).

45. Since, 6 and 8 ohms resistors are in parallel so, volatge acroos both of them will be same i.e., 48 volts,

Total current entering is equals to the sum of current through 6ohms and 8 ohms

Current through 6 ohms is $\dfrac{48}{6}$=8 Amps

Current through 8 ohms is $\dfrac{48}{8}$=6 Amps

Total entering current is 6+8 = 14 Amps.

Hence the correct answer is option (c).

46. Number of electrons, $n = \dfrac{It}{e}$

$$= \dfrac{\left(500 \times 10^{-3} \times 60\right)}{\left(1.6 \times 10^{-19}\right)}$$

$$= 1.875 \times 10^{20}$$

Hence, the correct option is (A).

47. $\dfrac{V_1-15}{3} + \dfrac{V_1}{6} + \dfrac{V_1-V_2}{4} - 1.2I_0 = 0$

$\dfrac{V_2-V_1}{4} + 1.2I_0 = 0$

Additionally,

$I_0 = \dfrac{15-V_1}{3}$

Solution yields:

$V_1 = 10V, \quad V_2 = 2V$

$V_{Th} = V_{oc} = V_2 = 2V$

To find R_{Th}, we will calculate I_{sc}

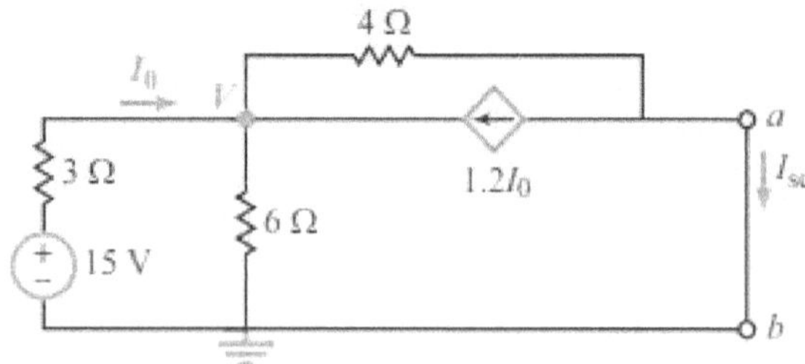

$\dfrac{V-15}{3} + \dfrac{V}{4} + \dfrac{V}{6} - 1.2I_0 = 0$

$I_0 = \dfrac{15-V}{3}$

Hence,

$V = 9.57V$

$I_{sc} = \dfrac{V}{4} - 1.2I_0 = \dfrac{9.57}{4} - 1.2\left(\dfrac{15-9.57}{3}\right) = 0.217A$

$R_{Th} = \dfrac{V_{oc}}{I_{sc}} = \dfrac{2}{0.217} = 9.2\Omega$

Hence the correct answer is option (d).

48. A diamagnetic material has a constant relative permeability slightly less than 1. When a diamagnetic material, such as bismuth, is placed in a magnetic field, the external field is partly expelled, and the magnetic flux density within it is slightly reduced.

Hence the correct answer is option (a).

49. That lamp will glow brighter whose resistance will be greater.

For 100 watts bulb, R= $\dfrac{200 \times 200}{100}$ = 400 ohms

For 50 watts bulb, R= $\dfrac{200 \times 200}{50}$ = 800 ohms

So 50 watts bulbs will glow brighter.

Hence the correct answer is option (b).

50. The electric field between the plates of parallel plate capacitor is directly proportional to capacitance C of the capacitor. The strength of the electric field is reduced due to the presence of dielectric. If the total charge on the plates is kept constant, then the potential difference is reduced across the capacitor plates. In this way, dielectric increases the capacitance of the capacitor.

Hence the correct answer is option (a).

51. For a coil of wire Magnetizing force (H)

$= \dfrac{NI}{I} = \dfrac{10 \times 750 \times 10^{-3}}{2 \times 10^{-2}}$

= 375 AT/m

Hence the correct answer is option (d).

52. mmf = flux × reluctance where;

f is the magneto motive force (MMF) across a magnetic element, φis the magnetic flux through the magnetic element, and Rm is the magnetic reluctance of that element. (It will be shown later that this relationship is due to the empirical relationship between the H-field and the magnetic field B, B=μH, where μ is the permeability of the material). Like Ohm's law, Hopkin son's law can be interpreted either as an empirical equation that works for some materials, or it may serve as a definition of reluctance.

Hence the correct answer is option (d).

53. Curie point, also called Curie Temperature, temperature at which certain magnetic materials undergo a sharp change in their magnetic properties. In the case of rocks and minerals, permanent magnetism appears below the Curie point—about 550° C (1,060° F) for the common magnetic mineral magnetite.

Hence the correct answer is option (d).

54. An ideal transformer is a useful approximation of very tightly coupled transformer (k≈1) in which both the primary and secondary inductive reactance are extremely large compared to the load impedance.

Hence the correct answer is option (d).

55. The ratio of the root mean square value to the average value of an alternating quantity (current or voltage) is called Form Factor. The average of all the instantaneous values of current and voltage over one complete cycle is known as the average value of the alternating quantities. Mathematically, it is expressed as

$$\text{Form Factor} = \frac{I_{rms}}{I_{av}} \text{ or } \frac{E_{rms}}{E_{av}}$$

Hence the correct answer is option (b).

56. Impedance is just the sum of the DC component, resistance, and the AC component, called reactance. If a circuit has only DC applied to it, then the inductive reactance is zero (short circuit) and the capacitive reactance is infinite (open circuit). The equations you derive for AC analysis will, in principle, work for DC analysis if you recognize that the AC frequency is zero. This will mean replacing inductors with shorts and capacitors with opens. This transition can sometimes be handled by just setting the frequency parameter to a small non-zero value. Or you may have to rework your equations. The concept of impedance in AC circuits really converts to one of resistance in DC circuits.

Hence the correct answer is option (b).

57. $BW = \dfrac{fc}{Q}$

Where fc = resonant frequency

Q = quality factor

$\dfrac{150}{50} = 3KHz$

Hence the correct answer is option (a).

58. It is required to limit the current in the tube while in operation the design also provides necessary resistance for the filament to glow for starting the lamp.

Hence the correct answer is option (d).

59. If current through the operating coil of a moving iron instrument is doubled, the operating force becomes Four times.

Hence the correct answer is option (b).

60. The dynamometer is connected as a wattmeter. This is one of the advantages of this type of-meter. If the coils are connected so that a value of current proportional to the load voltage flows in one, and a value of current proportional to the load current.

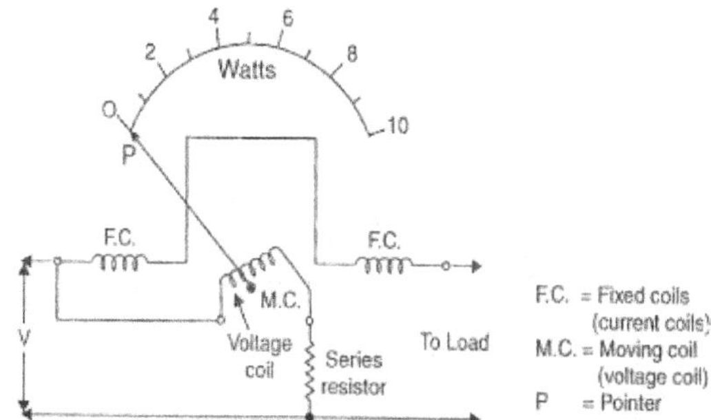

Connection of dynamometer for measuring power.

Hence the correct answer is option (b).

61. In a plasma application (Helium or Argon Plasma), we would like to measure the current. The voltage is around 10kV AC and modulated with a function generator.

Hence the correct answer is option (b).

62. The rated voltage of a 3 phase power system is given as rms line to line voltage.

Hence the correct answer is option (c).

63. Single phase induction type energy meter is also popularly known as watt-hour meter. This name is given to it. This article is only focused about its constructional features and its working. Induction type energy meter essentially consists of following components:

1. Driving system
2. Moving system
3. Braking system and
4. Registering system

Hence the correct answer is option (a).

64. To provide low reluctance path, it must be made up of some magnetic material. It is prepared by using cast iron because it is cheapest. For large machines rolled steel, cast steel, silicon steel is used which provides high permeability i.e. low reluctance and gives good mechanical strength.

Hence the correct answer is option (d).

65. Bridges and potentiometers; PMMC, moving iron, dynamometer and induction type instruments; measurement of voltage, current, power, energy and power factor; instrument transformers; digital voltmeters and multi meters; phase, time and frequency measurement; Q-meters; oscilloscopes; potentiometric recorders; error analysis.

Hence the correct answer is option (c).

66. The above given are all advantages of electric traction.

Electric traction has many advantages as compared to other non-electrical systems of traction including steam traction.

Electric traction is used in: Electric trains, Trolley buses, Tram cars, Diesel-electric vehicles etc.

Hence the correct answer is option (d).

67. In the armature, an electromotive force is created by the relative motion of the armature and the field. When the machine is used as a motor, this EMF opposes the armature current, and the armature converts electrical power to mechanical power in the form of torque, and transfers it via the shaft. When the machine is used as a generator, the armature EMF drives the armature current, and the shaft's movement is converted to electrical power. In an induction generator, these distinctions are blurred, since the generated power is drawn from the stator, which would normally be considered the field.

A growler is used to check the armature for shorts, opens and grounds.

Hence the correct answer is option (a).

68. A cumulative compound motor has a fairly constant speed and good starting torque. Such motors are used where series characteristics are required and the load is likely to be removed totally. These motors are used in driving machines which are subject to the sudden application of heavy loads; they are used in rolling mills, punching and shearing machines, mine-hoists etc.

Hence the correct answer is option (d).

69. In DC shunt motors, Field Resistance is kept high so as to flow minimum amount of current through it and thus maximum amount of current through armature for the rated voltage supply and current.

The resistance of the field regulator of a DC shunt motor is of order of 100 Ω

Hence the correct answer is option (d).

70. In a DC motor, unidirectional torque is produced with the help of - **brushes and commutator**.

Hence the correct answer is option (d).

71. The superheater is made of coils of tubes forming parallel tube circuits connected between heaters. The superheater tubes are made of high-temperature strengths special alloy steels such as chromium-molybdenum. The coils are heated by the heat of combustion gas during their passage from the furnace to the chimney.

Hence, the correct option is (C).

72. Rotating field machines are used for the high power generating plant in most of the world's national electricity grid systems. The field excitation power needed for these huge machines can be as much as 2.5% of the output power (25 KW in a 1.0 MW generator) though this reduces as the efficiency improves with size so that a 500 MW generator needs 2.5 MW (0.5%) of excitation power. If the field voltage is 1000 Volts, the required field current will be 2500 Amps. Providing such excitation through slip rings is an engineering challenge which has been overcome by generating the necessary power within the machine itself by means of a pilot, three phase, stationary field generator on the same shaft. The AC current generated in the pilot generator windings is rectified and fed directly to the rotor windings to supply the excitation for the main machine.

Hence the correct answer is option (b).

73. Applied voltage is defined as the voltage that is delivered across the load. This voltage should be the same as terminal voltage; however, various circuit faults and losses may reduce the terminal voltage.

Hence the correct answer is option (c).

74. The magnetic path length (MPL) is analogous to the length of a conductor for electrical current - increasing the MPL will increase its reluctance (magnetic 'resistance'). For a given magneto-motive force (MMF) in ampere-turns the flux produced will depend upon the value of reluctance in ampere-turns per Weber and so an increase in reluctance will produce a decrease in flux. (See Hopkinson's Law) Permeability is analogous to 'conductivity' and depends upon the material as well as the path length and cross-sectional area. Increasing reluctance will decrease permeability.

Hence the correct answer is option (d).

75. As compared to an Amplifier a transformer can not Increase the output power.

Hence the correct answer is option (c).

76. for full load, copper loss $= I^2 \times R = 400$

For half load, $I = \dfrac{I}{2}$

therefore, half load copper loss $= \left(\dfrac{I}{2}\right)^2 \times R$

$= \left(\dfrac{1}{4}\right) \times (I)^2 \times R$

$= \dfrac{1}{4} \times 400$

$= 100$

Hence the correct answer is option (a).

77. If the primary has the same number of turns as the secondary the outgoing voltage will be the same as what comes in .

Hence the correct answer is option (a).

78. When the primary and secondary windings are connected differently, the secondary voltage waveforms will differ from the corresponding primary voltage waveforms by 30 electrical degrees. This is called a 30 degree phase shift.

Here, YZ5 indicates that primary winding is in Star and Secondary winding is in Z connection and the phase difference between them is 5 $\times$30= 150 degrees.

Hence the correct answer is option (d).

79. Transformer oil or insulating oil is an oil that is stable at high temperatures and has excellent electrical insulating properties. It is used in oil-filled transformers, some types of high-voltage capacitors, fluorescent lamp ballasts, and some types of high-voltage switches and circuit breakers.

Hence the correct answer is option (c).

80. According to Faraday's law an emf induced in any circuit is due to the rate of change of magnetic flux linkage through the circuit. As the rotor winding in an induction motor are either closed through an external resistance or directly shorted by end ring, and cut the stator rotating magnetic field, an emf is induced in the rotor copper bar and due to this emf a current flows through the rotor conductor. Here the relative speed between the rotating flux and static rotor conductor is the cause of current generation; hence as per Lenz's law the rotor will rotate in the same direction to reduce the cause i.e. the relative velocity.

Hence the correct answer is option (c).

81. Inductive reactance is nothing but the impedance. Impedance is the AC equivalent of resistance, hence the unit for inductive reactance is ohm.

82. $s = 0.04,$

rotor frequency $= s \times f = 0.04 \times 50 = 2Hz.$
Hence, the correct option is (A).

83. The motor-stopped and motor-running test conditions were repeated with a new low-noise polyurea grease from another major U.S. lubricants supplier to determine if its formulation provided any performance advantages over the previous test grease.

Hence the correct answer is option (b).

84. A change of 5% in supply voltage to a 3 phase induction motor will produce the appropriate change in the torque of the stable operating region of the motor is increased instead of simply running at its base rated speed the motor can be run typically from 5% of the synchronous speed up to the base speed the torque generated by the motor can be kept constant throughout this region.

Hence the correct answer is option (C).

85. Crawling and cogging are related to space harmonics. The above question is about time harmonics. The speed of an IM with respect to n^{th} harmonic is Ns where Ns is the synchronous speed of the motor with respect to fundamental voltage harmonic Moreover 3rd harmonic is destroyed in 3 phase windings of IM. 5th harmonic is negative sequence harmonic .hence it rotates at -5Ns with respect to the rotor speed. 7th is a positive sequence harmonic and rotates at 7Ns ,11th negative and so on. For negative sequence harmonics ,slip is >1 where as for positive sequence harmonics s<1 In this way the rotor gets the tendency to reverse its direction of rotation back and forth .Also additional losses are attached with these harmonics which all together result in a pulsating nature of torque under non sinusoidal voltage supply(combination of harmonics).

Hence the correct answer is option (c).

86. In Squirrel cage rotor, slots in lamination or rotor core is not made parallel to the rotor shaft. A slight angle is maintained due to some advantages. This is called the rotor Skew.

Rotor of an Induction Motor skewed due to following reason:-

- With the bar skewed, the amount of the bar cutting the field line grows continuously and the next bar starts cutting the field lines as the first finishes. Due to this, we get Uniform Torque.

- To run quietly by reducing the magnetic hum , reduce rotor locking tendency. Rotor locking tendency occurs when rotor teeth remain directly under stator teeth thus they might be magnetically attracted.

- Primarily to prevent the cogging phenomenon. It is a phenomenon in which, if the rotor conductors are straight, there are chances of magnetic locking or strong coupling between rotor & stator.

- Increase effective Magnetic Coupling between Stator and Rotor Fluxes.

Hence the correct answer is option (d).

87. A meter shunt is a useful means of extending the current range of an ammeter. As current divides between two resistors in parallel it is possible to increase the range of a DC microammeter or milliammeter by paralleling an additional resistance with the inherent DC resistance of the meter itself. This is called a meter shunt.

Hence the correct answer is option (a).

88. Take a look at many of the latest insulation testers and multifunction installation testers (MFTs) and you'll see that they offer a choice of DC insulation test voltages. Almost all offer testing at 250 V, 500 V and 1,000 V but increasingly an option for testing at 100 V is also available.

Hence the correct answer is option (b).

89.

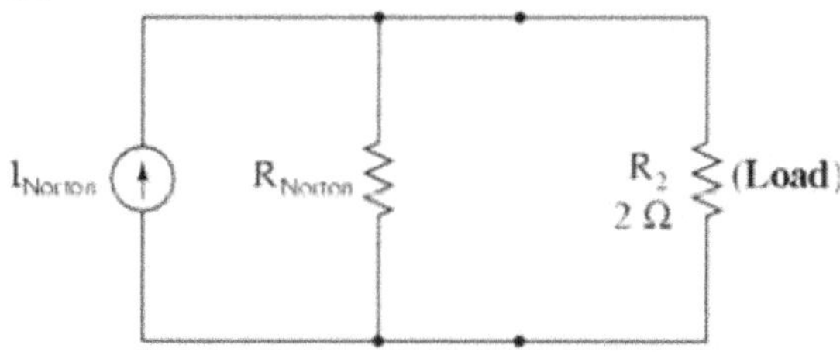

The resultant sum of all the readings of wattmeter will give the.

total power of the circuit. Mathematically we can,

$P = P_1 + P_2 + P_3 = V_1 I_1 + V_2 I_2 + V_3 I_3 = 0$

Hence the correct answer is option (b).

90. Maxwell's inductance Bridge circuit measures an inductance by comparison with a variable standard self-inductance.The connections and the phasor diagrams for balance conditions are shown in the Maxwell's Inductance Bridge figure.

Hence, the correct answer is option (C).

91. LVDT is an acronym for Linear Variable Differential Transformer. It is a common type of electromechanical transducer that can convert the rectilinear motion of an object to which it is coupled mechanically into a corresponding electrical signal.

Hence the correct answer is option (b).

92. Two impedances 5+j5 and 5-j5 ohms are connected in parallel. The combined impedance is (5+j0).

Hence the correct answer is option (c).

93. First, there is the voltage rating. The voltage rating on a capacitor is of course a maximum DC (i.e. a peak) rating. For $50/60Hz$ mains we're talking about a sinusoidal voltage waveform with an RMS value of for instance $230V$, so the DC peak value of such a supply $V_{rms}.2 - \sqrt{V_{rms}}.2$ is or about 1.4 times this quoted value. If you're already dealing with a DC system, there is no math involved. The peak rating of your cap should be more than the peak DC voltage you expect over the device.For longevity and nonlinear effects at high stresses, it is recommended to keep ample margin on these ratings, especially on the voltage rating. For $230VAC$ applications, even though typical you wouldn't expect more than about $325V$ peak over your lines, choose at least a $400V$ or better even a $450V$ capacitor. And yes, even when the manufacturer specifies survivability of the part at higher voltages. Survivability does not mean proper operation. It just means that it doesn't blow up and cause a mess.

Hence the correct answer is option (a).

94. $\dfrac{I}{CV} = \dfrac{1}{RC}$ which is reciprocal of the time constant in steady state analysis of the network which in turn gives frequency.

Hence the correct answer is option (d).

95. A potentiometer is defined as a 3 terminal variable resistor in which the resistance is manually varied to control the flow of electric current. A potentiometer acts as an adjustable voltage divider.

PTC stands for "Positive Temperature Coefficient". PTC thermistors are resistors with a positive temperature coefficient, which means that the resistance increases with increasing temperature.

With NTC thermistors, resistance decreases as temperature rises. An NTC is commonly used as a temperature sensor, or in parallel with a circuit as an inrush current limiter.

Hence the correct answer is option (a).

96. $Frequency = \dfrac{1}{Period}$

$f = \dfrac{1}{60} = 60$ Hz

Hence, the correct option is (B).

97. Then by using the following Ohm's Law equations:

$I = \dfrac{V_S}{R_S+R_L}$ and $P = I^2 R_L$

Hence the correct answer is option (b).

98. In series RLC circuit current, I $= \dfrac{V}{Z}$ but at resonance current I $= \dfrac{V}{R}$, therefore the current at resonant frequency is maximum as at resonance in impedance of circuit is resistance only and is minimum.

Hence the correct answer is option (b).

99. Applying Kirchoff's voltage law, In loop. I $= -27 - 6I_2 - 2I_1 + 24 = 0$

$\Rightarrow 6I_2 + 2I_1 = -3 \quad ...(1)$

In loop- II $-27 - 6I_2 + 4I_3 = 0$

$6I_2 - 4I_3 = -27 \quad ...(2)$

Junction 'p

$I_1 = I_2 + I_3 \quad ...(3)$

Solving equation (1),(2) and (3) we get, $I_1 = 3A, I_2 = \dfrac{-3}{2}A, I_3 = \dfrac{9}{2}A$

Hence the correct answer is option (a).

100. Ripple factor may be defined as the ratio of the root mean square (rms) value of the ripple voltage to the absolute value of the DC component of the output voltage, usually expressed as a percentage. It is expressed as peak to peak value.

Now for the full wave rectifier,

RMS value$= \dfrac{Vm}{1.414}$

Avg. Value$= 2 \times \dfrac{Vm}{3.14}$

Ripple factor $= \dfrac{rms}{avg} = 0.48$

Hence the correct answer is option (c).

101. The impurity atom can be made available as free electron or negative charge carrier even if a very small amount of energy is applied.

Hence the correct answer is option (b).

102. Secondary electron emission is the emission of free electrons from the metal surface, which occurs when the high-speed electrons or primary electrons hit the free electrons or secondary electrons in the metal.

Hence the correct answer is option (c).

103. In electronics, a common-emitter amplifier is one of three basic single-stage bipolar-junction-transistor (BJT) amplifier topologies, typically used as the voltage amplifier. In this circuit the base terminal of the transistor serves as the input, the collector is the output, and the emitter is common to both (for example, it may be tied to ground reference or a power supply rail), hence its name. The analogous FET circuit is the common-source amplifier, and the analogous tube circuit is the common-cathode amplifier.

Hence the correct answer is option (b).

104. In field effect transistors (FETs), depletion mode and enhancement mode are two major transistor types, corresponding to whether the transistor is in an ON state or an OFF state at zero gate–source voltage. Enhancement-mode MOSFETs are the common switching elements in most MOS.

Hence the correct answer is option (c).

105. Thermoelectric power plants boil water to create steam, which then spins turbines to generate electricity. The heat used to

boil water can come from burning of a fuel, from nuclear reactions, or directly from the sun or geothermal heat sources underground. Once steam has passed through a turbine, it must be cooled back into water before it can be reused to produce more electricity. Colder water cools the steam more effectively and allows more efficient electricity generation.

Hence the correct answer is option (a).

106. Our Induced Draft Fans are fabricated in compliance with predefined standards, so as to go hand in hand with material conveying machines, air pollution machines, etc. These I.D. Fans are made of high-grade components, using the best manufacturing practices. They are rolled off in different flow rates and pressure, as per the requirement. And, we can make them available in varied specifications. We are standing tall.

Hence the correct answer is option (a).

107. In nuclear engineering, fissile material is material capable of sustaining a nuclear fission chain reaction. By definition, fissile material can sustain a chain reaction with neutrons of any energy. The predominant neutron energy may be typified by either slow neutrons (i.e., a thermal system) or fast neutrons.

Hence the correct answer is option (c).

108. Cold Reserve It is that reserve generating capacity which is not in operation but can be made available for service.

Hence the correct answer is option (a).

109. All plants in India has their different electricity generation cost depends on their location, age, maintenance practices, operation efficiency etc.

It would range between 2.5 - 6.5 Rs/kWh currently in India.

Hence the correct answer is option (d).

110. Stringing chart is basically a graph between Sag, Tension with Temperature. As we want low Tension and minimum sag in our conductor but that is not possible as sag is inversely proportional to tension. It is because low sag means a tight wire and high tension whereas a low tension means a loose wire and increased sag. Therefore, we make compromise between two but if the case of temperature is considered and we draw graph then that graph is called Stringing chart.

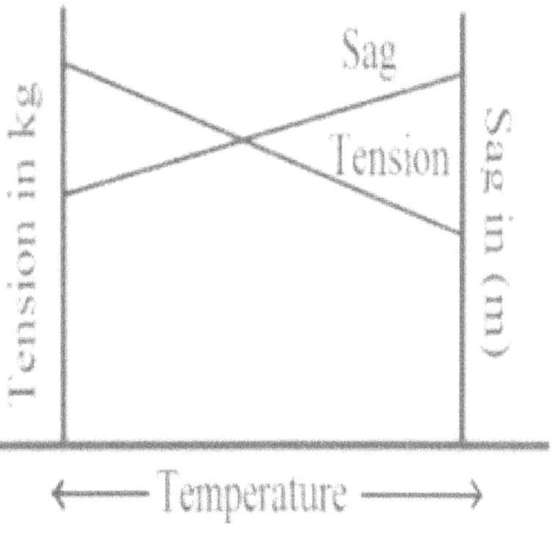

As Temperature increases then sag will increase but sag is inversely proportional to Tension so Tension will decrease.

Hence, the correct answer is option (D).

111. Technical losses are normally 22.5%, and directly depend on the network characteristics and the mode of operation.

Hence the correct answer is option (b).

112. Taking that the pf of the load is improved (say from 0.7 lag to 0.85 lag) for the same real power P, then the magnitude of the line current will decrease, decreasing the line losses. So transmission efficiency will improve.

Hence the correct answer is option (a).

113. The line constant of the transmission line is uniformly distributed all over the line and it is not lumped at any point of the transmission line.

The values of the line constant is always given as- per unit length of the line such as Henry/meters, Micro Farad/meters or Reactance/meters.

It is not that somewhere the values are high and somewhere low.

Hence the correct answer is option (a).

114. Impedance of round wire[edit] The internal impedance of round wire is given by:

The internal impedance is complex and may be interpreted as a resistance in series with an inductance. The inductance accounts for energy stored in the magnetic field inside the wire. It has a maximum value of H/m at zero frequency and goes to zero as the frequency increases. The zero frequency internal inductance is independent of the radius of the round wire.

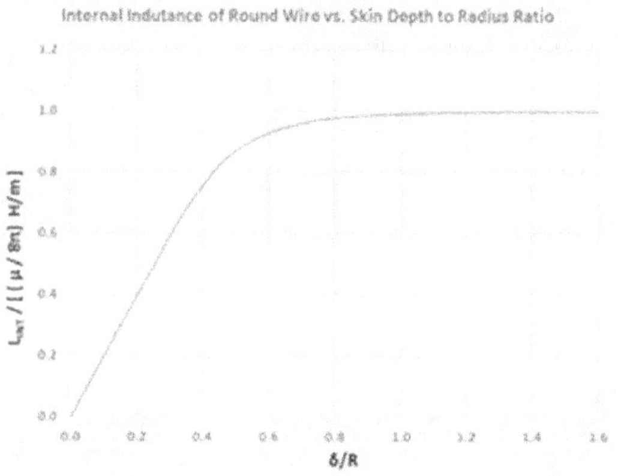

The internal inductance of round wire vs. the ratio of skin depth to radius. The inductance asymptotically approaches $(\mu / 8\pi)$ H/m for large skin depth. The internal inductance is associated with the magnetic field inside the wire. As skin depth becomes small, the inductance goes linearly to zero.

Hence the correct answer is option (d).

115. By using a guard ring. The potential across each unit in a string can be equalised by using a guard ring which is a metal ring electrically connected to the conductor and surrounding the bottom insulator. The guard ring introduces capacitance between metal fittings and the line conductor. The guard ring is contoured in such a way that shunt capacitance currents i_1, i_2 etc. are equal to metal fitting line capacitance currents i_1, i_2 etc. The result is that same charging current I flows through each unit of string. Consequently, there will be uniform potential distribution across the units.

Hence the correct answer is option (a).

116. Typically, the armor is made of one or two layers of wires, round or flat in shape, made of steel with low to medium carbon content (for example ranging from less than 0.015% to up to 2%). Steel is generally used due to its low cost, availability of supply and good mechanical properties. Other materials used for the cable armour can be galvanized (e.g. zinc-coated) steel, copper, brass, bronze. Galvanized steel is preferably used when the armor wires are exposed to the environment without any polymeric sheath or yarn layer, to ensure better resistance to corrosion.

Hence the correct answer is option (b).

117. Permissible Min ground Clearance of Electrical Line:

KV	Ground Clearance	Over National Highway
66 KV	6.1 Meter	8.0 Meter
132 KV	6.1 Meter	8.6 Meter
220 KV	7.0 Meter	9.8 Meter
400KV	8.8 Meter	10.8 Meter

The life of under ground cable is taken as - **25 years**

Hence the correct answer is option (c).

118. Minimum ground clearance of 33KV uninsulated electrical conductor is 5.2 meter and 0.3 meter for every 33KV above 33KV.

So, for first 33 kV, 5.2 meters and for next (220-33)= 187kv, $\frac{187}{33}$=5.66 for which 5.66 ✕0.3mt= 1.7 mt

In total 5.2+1.7= 6.9 meters for 220 kV

Hence the correct answer is option (c).

119. Increases diversity factor:

- The load curves of different interconnected stations are generally different.

- The result is that the maximum demand on the system is much reduced as compared to the sum of individual maximum demands of different stations.

- In other words, the diversity factor of the system is improved, so increasing the effective capacity of the system.

Hence the correct answer is option (b).

120. Kelvin's law for finding economic size of a conductor Let, area of cross-section of conductor = a annual interest and depreciation on capital cost of the conductor = C1 annual

running charges $= C_2$ Now, annual interest and depreciation cost is directly proportional to the area of conductor.

i.e., $C_1 = K_1 a$ And, annual running charges are inversely proportional to the area of conductor. $C_2 = \dfrac{K_2}{a}$

Where, K_1 and K_2 are constants. Now, Total annual cost $=$

$$C = C_1 + C_2 \quad C = \frac{K_1 a + K_2 a}{a}$$

For C to be minimum, the differentiation of C w.r.t a must be zero. i.e. $\dfrac{dC}{da} = 0$. Therefore, $\dfrac{dC}{da} = \dfrac{d}{da}\left[K_2 a + \dfrac{K_2}{a}\right] = 0$

$$\therefore K_2 - \frac{K_2}{a^2} = 0$$

$$\therefore K_1 = \frac{K_2}{a^2}$$

$$\therefore K_1 a = \frac{K_2}{a}$$

$$\therefore C_1 = C_2$$

"The Kelvin's law states that the most economical size of a conductor is that for which annual interest and depreciation on the capital cost of the conductor is equal to the annual cost of energy loss." From the above derivation, the economical cross-sectional area of a conductor can be calculated as, $\mathbf{a} = \sqrt{\dfrac{K_2}{K_1}}$

Hence the correct answer is option (c).

Mock Test 04

Part - I

Q.1 In January 2020, a team of astronomers of which country have discovered a mysterious ring of hydrogen gas, of diameter of about 380,000 light-years, around a distant galaxy?

A. China   B. India   C. Japan   D. Australia
E. USA

Q.2 In January 2020, who took charge as the executive director of SEBI?

A. P.V. Bharathi   B. G Babita Rayudu
C. Rajkiran Rai G.   D. Roli Singh
E. Nikeeta Diwan

Q.3 In January 2020, who has been appointed as the new chancellor of Queen's University, Belfast (QUB)?

A. Elizabeth Warren   B. Hillary Clinto
C. Bernie Sanders   D. Tulsi Gabbard
E. Kamala Harris

Q.4 In January 2020, in which state did Prime Minister Narendra Modi electronically release 12,000 crore rupees under Pradhan Mantri Samaan Yojana to six crore farmers?

A. Tamil Nadu   B. Maharashtra
C. Karnataka   D. Kerala
E. Gujarat

Q.5 Which of the following is hosting the 5th Asia Pacific Drosophila Research Conference (APDRC5) and Indian Drosophila Research Conference in January 2020?

A. Indian Institute of Science Education and Research, Kolkata
B. Bose Institute, Kolkata
C. Indian Institute of Science Education and Research, Pune
D. Raman Research Institute, Bengaluru
E. Indian Institute of Science, Bengaluru

Q.6 Which of the following won the Best motion picture — Drama at the 77th annual Golden Globes Awards, held in January 2020 in Beverly Hills, California?

A. 1917   B. War Horse
C. Joker   D. American Beauty
E. Judy

Q.7 By how much per cent did the Gujarat government hike the dearness allowance (DA) for over nine lakh state government employees and pensioners, in January 2020?

A. 2   B. 3   C. 4   D. 5
E. 6

Q.8 By January 2020, how many massive black holes were found as per the study published in the Astrophysical Journal?

A. 3   B. 7   C. 11   D. 13
E. 19

Q.9 'Dakshin Ganga' name is given to:

A. Indus   B. Ganga
C. Yamuna   D. Godavari

Q.10 What is the average salinity of the water present in the oceans?

A. 65 per thousand   B. 35 per thousand
C. 10 per thousand   D. 80 per thousand

Q.11 The Gandhara Art was mainly patronized by:

A. Satvahanas   B. Guptas
C. Mauryans   D. Sakas and Kushans

Q.12 What was the name of the person who first discovered the ruins of 'Mohenjo-daro'?

A. R. D. Banerji   B. Daya ram Sahni
C. Marshall   D. John Clay

Q.13 Which of the following city have the remains of the Vijayanagara dynasty?

A. Hampi   B. Baroda
C. Golconda   D. Bijapur

Q.14 Which of the following is not a significant event of Indian National Movement in 1919?

A. Montague Chelmsford Reforms
B. Rowlett Act
C. Jallianwala Bagh Massacre
D. Khilafat Movement

Q.15 'The Story of My Experiments with Truth' is written by a famous leader of India. This book was also included in the '100 Best Spiritual Books of the 20th Century'. Who is the author of this book?

A. A. P. J. Abdul Kalam
B. Maulana Abul Kalam Azad
C. Mahatma Gandhi
D. Jawaharlal Nehru

Q.16 The name of the first Kushana ruler to issue gold coins in India was:

A. Kujala Kadphises   B. Vima Kadphises
C. Vasishka   D. Huvishka

Q.17 Direction : In the following questions out of the four alternatives, choose the one which is best express the meaning of the given word.
PESTER

A. Carefree   B. Bother   C. Relaxed   D. Gratify

Q.18 Direction : In the following questions out of the four alternatives, choose the one which is best express the meaning of the given word.
HIATUS

A. Pause   B. Continue
C. Run   D. Contempt

Q.19 Direction : In the following questions, four alternatives are given for the meaning of the given Idiom/Phrase. Choose the alternative which best express the meaning of the Idiom/Phrase.
To get cold feet

A. To be afraid **B.** To run for life
C. To fall sick **D.** To be discourteous

Q.20 Direction : In the following questions, four alternatives are given for the meaning of the given Idiom/Phrase. Choose the alternative which best express the meaning of the Idiom/Phrase.
Hush money

A. Easy money
B. Black money
C. Money kept in the safe
D. Bribe paid to keep someone silent

Q.21 Direction : In the following questions, out of the given alternatives, choose the one which can be substituted for the given words/sentence.
The custom of having many wives.

A. Matrimony **B.** Celibacy
C. Polyandry **D.** Polygamy

Q.22 Direction : In the following questions, out of the given alternatives, choose the one which can be substituted for the given words/sentence.
A name adopted by an author in his writings.

A. Title **B.** Nomenclature
C. Surname **D.** Pseudonym

Q.23 Direction : In the following questions, some of the sentences have errors and some have none. Find out which part of the sentence has an error. The number of that part is your answer. If there is no error, the answer would be (D).
Parliament and state assemblies (A)/ are places which (B)/ reflection the true character of the country. (C)/ No error. (D)

A. A **B.** B **C.** C **D.** D

Q.24 Direction : In the following questions, some of the sentences have errors and some have none. Find out which part of the sentence has an error. The number of that part is your answer. If there is no error, the answer would be (D).
The crisis they are facing (A)/ is the most critical (B)/ natural disaster what ever happened in Thai history (C) / No error. (D)

A. A **B.** B **C.** C **D.** D

Q.25 If x+y=25 and $x^2y^3+x^3y^2$=25 ,what is the value of xy?
A. 5 **B.** 10 **C.** 25 **D.** ±1

Q.26 If $5^{k+3} = 3125$, what is the value of k?
A. 2 **B.** 3 **C.** 4 **D.** 5

Q.27 What is the value of $x =$
$$\sqrt{6 + \sqrt{6 + \sqrt{6} + \cdots \ldots + \infty}}$$
A. 3 **B.** -2 **C.** 1 **D.** 4

Q.28 Veer can complete a work in 20 days, the same work Ram complete in 18 day. If they worked together for 5 day then what fraction of work is left after 5 days?
A. $\frac{19}{36}$ **B.** $\frac{17}{36}$ **C.** $\frac{5}{18}$ **D.** $\frac{5}{20}$

Q.29 The sum of Rs 9000 becomes Rs 10800 in 10 years at Simple Interest. Find the rate per annum?
A. 2% **B.** 3% **C.** 2.5% **D.** 1.67%

Q.30 Ramesh borrowed Rs. 15000 as a loan for two years with compound interest 20% compounded annually. After 1 year, he pays Rs. 12000. What is the principal amount for next year?
A. Rs. 6000 **B.** Rs. 7500
C. Rs. 1500 **D.** Rs. 18000

Q.31 A Metro train of 120 m length is running on a bridge at the rate of 40 km/hr. The train crosses the bridge in 20 second. What is the length of the bridge?
A. 102.22 m **B.** 60 m
C. 52.2 m **D.** 150 m

Q.32 In the food Bazaar, the profit is 300% of the cost. Due to the demand the cost of food products increases by 25% but the selling price remains same what percentage of the selling price will be the profit?
A. 68% **B.** 68.75% **C.** 60% **D.** 69.75%

Ques (33-35):Direction :The following is a multiple bar chart showing man's and women's average daily earnings in certain industries. Study the chart and answer the questions given below.

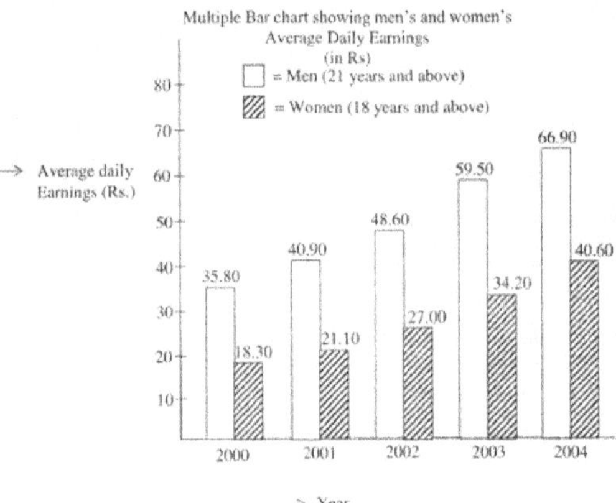

Q.33 In which year is the percentage increase in the average daily earnings of men over the preceding year, the maximum ?
A. 2001 **B.** 2002 **C.** 2003 **D.** 2004

Q.34 The difference between the average daily earnings of men and women over successive years :
A. Increase **B.** Decrease
C. Remains the same **D.** None of these

Q.35 In which year is the ratio of man's average daily earnings to women's average daily earnings is the highest ?
A. 2000 **B.** 2001
C. 2003 **D.** All of the above

Ques (36-40):Directions : Study the chart and answer the questions:

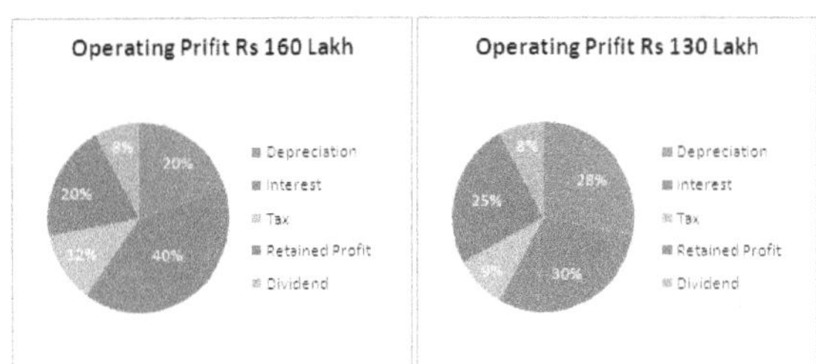

Q.36 The operating Profit in 1991-92 increased over in 1990-91 by

A. 23% **B.** 22% **C.** 25% **D.** 24%

Q.37 The interest burden in 1991-92 was higher than that in 1990-91 by

A. 50% **B.** Rs. 25 lakh
C. 90% **D.** Rs 41 lakh

Q.38 If on an average, 20% rate of interest was charged on borrowed funds, then the total borrowed funds used by this company is the given 2 yr amounted to

A. Rs 221 lakh **B.** Rs 195 lakh
C. Rs 368 lakh **D.** Rs 515 lakh

Q.39 The retained profit in 1991-92, as compared to that in 1990-91 was:

A. Higher by2.5 % **B.** higher by 1.5
C. lower by 2.5 % **D.** lower by 1.5%

Q.40 The equity base of those companies remained unchanged. Then, the total dividend earnings by the share holders in 1991-92 is

A. Rs 104 lakh **B.** Rs. 9 lakh
C. Rs. 12.8 lakh **D.** Rs 15.6 lakh

Part - II

Q.41 The effective resistance between points P and Q of the electrical circuit shown in the figure is

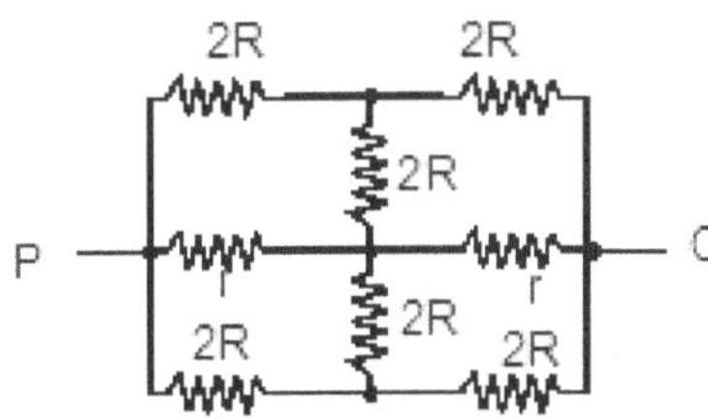

A. $\frac{2Rr}{R+r}$ **B.** $\frac{8R(R+r)}{3R+r}$ **C.** $2r + 4R$ **D.** $\frac{5R}{2} + 2r$

Q.42 Find the resultant resistance when 3 resistance of 2 ohm each are connected as shown in the figure below.

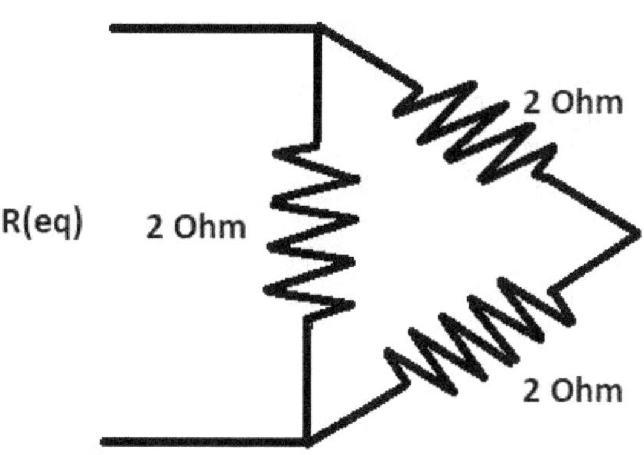

A. 4 ohm **B.** 1.33 ohm
C. 6 ohm **D.** 1.5 ohm

Q.43 The D.C armature resistance of a delta connected alternator measured across its two terminates is 1Ω. The per phase DC resistance is________.

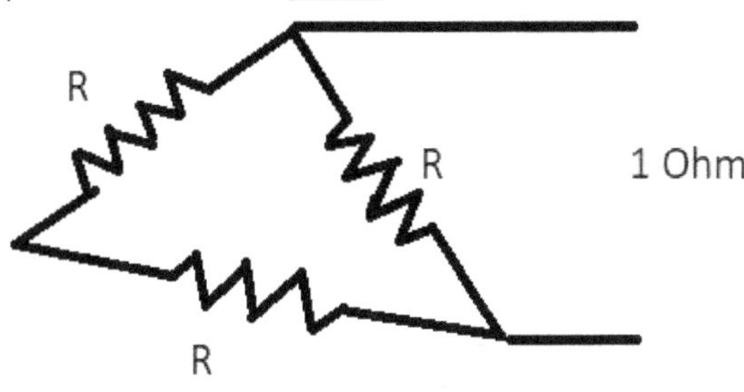

A. 3 Ohm **B.** 1.5 Ohm
C. 0.33 Ohm **D.** 4 Ohm

Q.44 What will be the current through the circuit when 2 resistance of 5 ohm and 50 ohm each are connected as shown in the figure below?

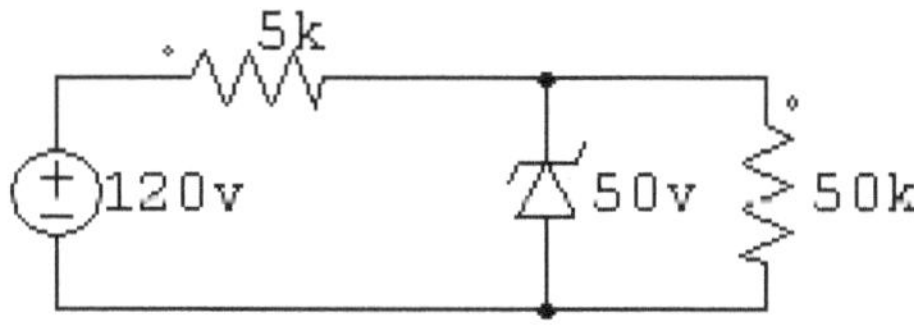

A. 28 A **B.** 56 mA
C. 14 mA **D.** None of these

Q.45 The voltage drop is main consideration for design of______.

A. Feeder **B.** Distribution
C. Service mains **D.** None of these

Q.46 A crystal diode is________ device.

A. Linear **B.** An amplifier
C. Non-linear **D.** None of these

Q.47 The voltage regulation of DC generator is zero this implies that generator is________.

A. Differentially compounded
B. Shunt wound
C. Flat compounded
D. Series wound

Q.48 The wattmeter measures_______ power.
A. Instantaneous
B. Reactive
C. Average
D. Apparent

Q.49 Which instruments are used for high voltage and high current measurement?
A. CT
B. PT
C. Instrument transformer
D. Wattmeter

Q.50 High speed alternators are driven by___________.
A. Diesel engine
B. Hydraulic turbines
C. Steam turbines
D. None of these

Q.51 Three phase wound rotor motors are also called_______ motors.
A. Synchronous
B. Slip ring
C. Series
D. Commutator

Q.52 A four speed squirrel cage induction motor uses_______ stator winding.
A. Four
B. Three
C. One
D. Two

Q.53 The average value of $\sin\theta$ over complete cycle is_______.
A. 0
B. 1
C. -1
D. $\frac{1}{2}$

Q.54 The inductive reactance of a circuit is_______ .
A. Directly proportional to Frequency
B. Inversely proportional to Frequency
C. Independent of Frequency
D. None of the above

Q.55 An AND gate_______.
A. Implements logic addition
B. High output when all inputs low
C. Is equivalent to a series switching circuit
D. Is equivalent to a parallel switching circuit

Q.56 An XOR gate produces output only when two inputs are_________.
A. High
B. Low
C. Different
D. Equal

Q.57 A crystal diode is used as______.
A. An amplifier
B. An rectifier
C. An oscillator
D. A voltage regulator

Q.58 Transistor turn off time is______.
A. Sum of storage and fall time
B. Maximum value of storage time
C. Maximum value of fall time
D. Sum of rise and fall time

Q.59 A non-uniform moving electric charge will produce _______.
A. Electric field only
B. Both electric and magnetic fields
C. Magnetic field
D. None of these

Q.60 For the process of electrolysis, we require______.
A. DC supply
B. AC supply
C. Varying voltage
D. both DC and AC supply

Q.61 A magnetic field is produced by_______.
A. Current carrying conductor
B. Moving charge
C. Changing electric field
D. All of the above

Q.62 The superposition theorem applies to_______.
A. current or voltage calculation
B. power calculation
C. current and power calculation
D. voltage and power calculation

Q.63 If in a transistor $I_E=10.5mA$,$I_C=10mA$,then the value of is______.
A. 20
B. 200
C. 100
D. 150

Q.64 A transistor is ....operated device.
A. Current
B. Voltage
C. Both voltage and current
D. None of the above

Q.65 Zener diode are used primarily as......
A. Amplifiers
B. Voltage regulators
C. Rectifiers
D. Oscillators

Q.66 Which type of charge carrier has the greatest mobility in semiconductor?
A. Positive ions
B. Negative ions
C. Free electrons
D. Holes

Q.67 Which single phase motor has the lowest speed?
A. Universal
B. Shaded pole
C. Hysteresis
D. Repulsion

Q.68 Which of the following motors are AC synchronous type motors?
A. Universal motor
B. Reluctance motor
C. Hysteresis motor
D. Both B and C

Q.69 The rotor of hysteresis motor is made of magnetic material having area of hysteresis loop____.
A. Very small
B. Medium
C. Very large
D. Any of above

Q.70 A reluctance motor runs at_________.
A. Synchronous speed
B. Slightly less than synchronous speed
C. Half the synchronous speed
D. Above synchronous speed

Q.71 The single phase shaded pole motor has_________.
A. Squirrel cage rotor
B. Wound rotor
C. High p.f
D. High stating torque

Q.72 In regenerative cycle, bled steam is________.
A. Discharged to atmosphere
B. Condensed in steam condenser
C. Used to beat feed water for boiler
D. Is mixed with steam supplied to turbine.

Q.73 Permissible pH value of water for the boiler is________.
A. 1
B. 7
C. Slightly more than 7
D. 10

Q.74 Efficiency of thermal power plant improve with________.
A. Increased quantity of coal burnt
B. Larger quantity of water used
C. Lower load in the plant
D. Use of high steam pressure

Q.75 Hysteresis loss least depends on________.
A. Volume of material
B. Frequency
C. Stein mertz coefficient of material
D. Ambient temperature

Q.76 If area of hysteresis loop of a material is large, the hysteresis loss in the material will be________.
A. Zero
B. Small
C. Large
D. None of these

Q.77 Permanent magnets are normally mode of________.
A. Al-Ni-Co alloys
B. Aluminum
C. Cast iron
D. Wrought iron

Q.78 Dynamic equalization circuit is used for________.
A. Equal division of voltage across each thyrister in series.
B. Equal division of current across each thyrister in parallel.
C. Equal division of voltage across each thyrister in parallel.
D. Equal division of current across each thyrister in series.

Q.79 IGBT combines advantages of________.
A. BJTs and SITs
B. BJTs and MOSFETs
C. SITs and MOSFETs
D. None of these

Q.80 Leakage current flows through the thyrister in________.
A. Forward blocking mode.
B. Reverse blocking mode.
C. Both forward and reverse blocking mode.
D. Forward conduction mode.

Q.81 The arc voltage in a CB________.
A. Is in phase with arc current
B. Lags are current by 90 °
C. Leads arc current by 90 °
D. Lags arc current by 180 °

Q.82 Reactors are used at various locations in power system to________.

A. Increase short-circuit current
B. Avoid short-circuit current
C. Limit short –circuit current
D. None of these

Q.83 In AC system, the skin effect________.
A. Reduces effective area of conductor
B. Increase resistance of conductor
C. Causes greater power loss
D. All of the above

Q.84 Which among the following are suitable discrete time system?
1. $y(n) = x(4n)$
2. $y(n) = x(-n)$
3. $y(n) = ax(n) + 8$
4. $y(n) = -\cos x(n)$

A. 1 and 3
B. 2 and 4
C. 1, 3 and 4
D. 1, 2, 3 and 4

Q.85 As compared to capacitor-short induction motors or split phase motor, a permanent split capacitor motor has lower________.
A. Efficiency
B. Cost
C. Noise
D. Power-factor

Q.86 In a split phase motor________.
A. The starting winding is connected through a centrifugal switch.
B. The running winding is connected through a centrifugal switch.
C. Both starting and running windings are connected through a centrifugal switch.
D. Centrifugal switch is used to control supply voltage.

Q.87 If the capacitor of a single phase motor is short circuited________.
A. The motor will not start.
B. The motor will run.
C. The motor will run in reverse direction
D. The motor will run in same direction at reduced rpm.

Q.88 An overexcited synchronous motor behave as ______.
A. An inductor
B. A capacitor
C. A resister
D. None of these

Q.89 Unsymmetrical faults______.
A. Introduce unbalance in the system.
B. Indicated abnormal condition in the system.
C. Are more frequent than symmetrical faults.
D. All of above

Q.90 The knowledge of diversity factor helps in determining______.
A. Average load
B. Units generated
C. Plants capacity
D. None of these

Q.91 The load factor (LF), maximum demand (MD), average load (AG) are related as______.

A. LF = AL/MD   **B.** LF = AL x MD
C. LF = MD/AL   **D.** LF = MD

Q.92 When the number of poles is equal to zero then how many branches of root locus tends towards infinity?
A. 1
B. 2
C. 0
D. Equal to number of poles

Q.93 Root locus is used to calculate____.
A. Marginal Stability
B. Absolute Stability
C. Conditional stability
D. Relative stability

Q.94 An alternating voltage or current is a_________.
A. Scalar quantity   **B.** Vector quantity
C. Phasor   **D.** None of the above

Q.95 The forward voltage drop across a silicon diode is about_______.
A. 2.5V   **B.** 3V   **C.** 0.7V   **D.** 10V

Q.96 The torque speed characteristics of a repulsion motor resembles which one of the following d.c motor characteristics?
A. Separately executed
B. Shunt
C. Series
D. Cumulatively compounded

Q.97 Overall efficiency of gas turbine is_______.
A. Equal to runtime cycle efficiency
B. Equal to carrot cycle efficiency
C. More than otto or diesel cycle efficiency
D. Less than diesel cycle efficiency

Q.98 Zinc Oxide is
A. Acidic   **B.** Basic
C. Neutral   **D.** Amphoteric

Q.99 The positive and negative sequence impedance of transmission lines are_______.
A. Equal   **B.** Zero   **C.** Different   **D.** Infinite

Q.100 Steam engine used in Locomotive is __________.
A. Single acting, condensing type.
B. Single acting, non-conducting type.
C. Double acting, non-conducting type
D. Double acting, condensing type

Q.101 Which of the following is a non-renewable resource?
A. Coal   **B.** Forests   **C.** Water   **D.** Wildlife

Q.102 Which among the following is not a renewable source of energy?
A. Solar energy   **B.** Biomass energy
C. Hydro-power   **D.** Geothermal energy

Q.103 If electrical conductivity increases with the increase of temperature of a substance, then it is a:

A. Conductor   **B.** Semiconductor
C. Insulator   **D.** Carborator

Q.104 Which of the following is a disadvantage of most of the renewable energy sources?
A. Highly polluting
B. High waste disposal cost
C. Unreliable supply
D. High running cost

Q.105 Photovoltaic energy is the conversion of sunlight into:
A. Chemical energy   **B.** Biogas
C. Electricity   **D.** Geothermal energy

Q.106 Horizontal axis and vertical axis are the types of:
A. Nuclear reactor   **B.** Wind mills
C. Biogas reactor   **D.** Solar cell

Q.107 Which among the following is not an adverse environmental impact of tidal power generation?
A. Interference with spawing and migration of fish
B. Pollution and health hazard in the estuary due to blockage of flow of polluted water into the sea
C. Navigational hazard
D. All of the above

Q.108 Steam reforming is currently the least expensive method of producing:
A. Coal   **B.** Biogas
C. Hydrogen   **D.** Natural gas

Q.109 A fuel cell, in order to produce electricity, burns:
A. Helium   **B.** Nitrogen
C. Hydrogen   **D.** None of the above

Q.110 Fuel cells are:
A. Carbon cell   **B.** Hydrogen battery
C. Nuclear cell   **D.** Chromium cell

Q.111 Both power and manure is provided by:
A. Nuclear plants   **B.** Thermal plants
C. Biogas plants   **D.** Hydroelectric plant

Q.112 The outermost layer of the earth is:
A. Magma   **B.** Mantle
C. Crust   **D.** Solid iron core

Q.113 Common energy source in Indian villages is:
A. Electricity
B. Coal
C. Sun
D. Wood and animal dung

Q.114 The one thing that is common to all fossil fuels is that they:
A. Were originally formed in marine environment
B. Contain carbon
C. Have undergone the same set of geological processes during their formation
D. Represent the remains of one living organisms

Q.115 The process that converts solid coal into liquid hydrocarbon fuel is called:

A. Liquefaction
B. Carbonation
C. Catalytic conversion
D. Cracking

Q.116 Lignite, bituminous and anthracite are different ranks of:

A. Nuclear fuel
B. Coal
C. Natural gas
D. Biogas

Q.117 Cruid oil is:

A. Colourless
B. Odourless
C. Smelly yellow to black liquid
D. Odourless yellow to black liquid

Q.118 BTU is measurement of:

A. Volume
B. Area
C. Heat content
D. Temperature

Q.119 The first controlled fission of an atom was carried out in Germany in:

A. 1920   B. 1928   C. 1925   D. 1938

Q.120 Boiling water reactor and pressurised water reactors are:

A. Nuclear reactor
B. Solar reactor
C. OTEC
D. Biogas reactor

// Smart Answer Sheet //

Correct — Indicates percentage of students who answered questions correctly.

Skipped — Indicates percentage of students who skipped questions.

Q.	Ans.	Correct / Skipped	Q.	Ans.	Correct / Skipped	Q.	Ans.	Correct / Skipped	Q.	Ans.	Correct / Skipped	Q.	Ans.	Correct / Skipped
1	B	21.62 % / 32.43 %	17	B	16.22 % / 48.64 %	33	C	40.54 % / 40.54 %	49	C	45.95 % / 40.54 %	65	B	40.54 % / 40.54 %
2	B	24.32 % / 45.95 %	18	A	27.03 % / 48.65 %	34	A	45.95 % / 37.83 %	50	C	32.43 % / 43.25 %	66	C	35.14 % / 43.24 %
3	B	21.62 % / 48.65 %	19	A	43.24 % / 43.25 %	35	D	5.41 % / 40.54 %	51	B	32.43 % / 48.65 %	67	B	24.32 % / 43.25 %
4	C	18.92 % / 40.54 %	20	D	32.43 % / 24.33 %	36	A	24.32 % / 48.65 %	52	D	8.11 % / 40.54 %	68	D	54.05 % / 37.84 %
5	C	18.92 % / 51.35 %	21	D	40.54 % / 40.54 %	37	B	43.24 % / 48.65 %	53	A	40.54 % / 40.54 %	69	C	27.03 % / 43.24 %
6	A	27.03 % / 48.65 %	22	D	43.24 % / 40.54 %	38	D	2.7 % / 51.35 %	54	A	48.65 % / 35.13 %	70	A	37.84 % / 40.54 %
7	D	18.92 % / 43.24 %	23	C	51.35 % / 40.54 %	39	D	10.81 % / 48.65 %	55	C	32.43 % / 45.95 %	71	A	10.81 % / 45.95 %
8	C	10.81 % / 51.35 %	24	C	37.84 % / 32.43 %	40	C	16.22 % / 48.64 %	56	C	27.03 % / 43.24 %	72	C	27.03 % / 43.24 %
9	D	45.95 % / 40.54 %	25	D	43.24 % / 43.25 %	41	A	10.81 % / 45.95 %	57	B	24.32 % / 43.25 %	73	C	43.24 % / 40.54 %
10	B	24.32 % / 48.65 %	26	A	48.65 % / 40.54 %	42	B	54.05 % / 37.84 %	58	A	24.32 % / 48.65 %	74	D	54.05 % / 32.44 %
11	D	24.32 % / 51.36 %	27	A	40.54 % / 45.95 %	43	B	24.32 % / 43.25 %	59	B	35.14 % / 43.24 %	75	D	27.03 % / 40.54 %
12	A	21.62 % / 43.24 %	28	B	43.24 % / 40.54 %	44	C	21.62 % / 43.24 %	60	A	54.05 % / 32.44 %	76	C	37.84 % / 40.54 %
13	A	29.73 % / 48.65 %	29	A	48.65 % / 43.24 %	45	C	16.22 % / 40.54 %	61	D	56.76 % / 35.13 %	77	A	43.24 % / 37.84 %
14	D	18.92 % / 40.54 %	30	A	48.65 % / 40.54 %	46	C	32.43 % / 48.65 %	62	A	56.76 % / 35.13 %	78	A	18.92 % / 48.65 %
15	C	29.73 % / 40.54 %	31	A	43.24 % / 40.54 %	47	C	27.03 % / 45.94 %	63	A	18.92 % / 48.65 %	79	B	35.14 % / 45.94 %
16	B	18.92 % / 45.94 %	32	B	32.43 % / 45.95 %	48	C	18.92 % / 40.54 %	64	A	32.43 % / 32.43 %	80	C	21.62 % / 43.24 %

Q.	Ans.	Correct / Skipped	Q.	Ans.	Correct / Skipped	Q.	Ans.	Correct / Skipped	Q.	Ans.	Correct / Skipped	Q.	Ans.	Correct / Skipped
81	A	18.92 % / 43.24 %	89	D	35.14 % / 43.24 %	97	D	13.51 % / 45.95 %	105	C	32.43 % / 40.54 %	113	D	45.95 % / 40.54 %
82	C	43.24 % / 35.14 %	90	C	24.32 % / 43.25 %	98	D	16.22 % / 48.64 %	106	B	43.24 % / 40.54 %	114	B	48.65 % / 37.84 %
83	D	51.35 % / 40.54 %	91	A	32.43 % / 45.95 %	99	A	37.84 % / 43.24 %	107	D	16.22 % / 40.54 %	115	A	43.24 % / 43.25 %
84	D	18.92 % / 45.94 %	92	C	21.62 % / 43.24 %	100	C	16.22 % / 45.94 %	108	C	21.62 % / 43.24 %	116	B	54.05 % / 40.54 %
85	C	10.81 % / 45.95 %	93	D	21.62 % / 43.24 %	101	A	54.05 % / 40.54 %	109	C	51.35 % / 40.54 %	117	C	51.35 % / 40.54 %
86	A	35.14 % / 37.83 %	94	C	24.32 % / 43.25 %	102	B	24.32 % / 40.54 %	110	B	43.24 % / 40.54 %	118	C	48.65 % / 32.43 %
87	A	43.24 % / 40.54 %	95	C	48.65 % / 43.24 %	103	B	37.84 % / 40.54 %	111	C	43.24 % / 37.84 %	119	D	21.62 % / 48.65 %
88	B	43.24 % / 40.54 %	96	C	16.22 % / 48.64 %	104	C	54.05 % / 40.54 %	112	C	37.84 % / 43.24 %	120	A	37.84 % / 43.24 %

Performance Analysis

Avg. Score (%)	26.67%
Toppers Score (%)	90.83%
Your Score	

//Hints and Solutions//

1.

- A team of astronomers at the National Centre for Radio Astrophysics (NCRA) in Pune, India have discovered a mysterious ring of hydrogen gas around a distant galaxy.
- Giant Meter wave Radio Telescope (GMRT) was used to discover it.
- The ring is much bigger than the galaxy it surrounds and has a diameter of about 380,000 light-years (about 4 times that of our Milky Way).

Hence the correct answer is option (b).

2.

- G Babita Rayudu took charge as the executive director of SEBI.
- Rayudu will handle the legal affairs department, enforcement department, and special enforcement cell.
- The Securities and Exchange Board of India is the Regulator for the Securities market in India owned by the Government of India.
- It was founded on 2 April 1992.

Hence the correct answer is option (b).

3.

- Hillary Clinton is appointed as the new chancellor of Queen's University, Belfast (QUB).
- The former US secretary of state is the university's 11th chancellor and the first woman to take up the post.
- She took her role immediately and will serve for a period of five years, succeeding Dr Tom Moran - who died last year.

Hence the correct answer is option (b).

4.

- In Karnataka, Prime Minister Narendra Modi electronically released 12,000 crore rupees under Pradhan Mantri Samaan Yojana to six crore farmers in Tumakuru.
- Under the Scheme, income support of Rs.6000 per year is provided to all farmer families.
- The fishermen of Tamil Nadu and Karnataka were also given deep sea fishing boats and transponders that will help them to navigate in the deep sea.

Hence the correct answer is option (c).

5.

- Indian Institute of Science Education and Research Pune is hosting the 5th Asia Pacific Drosophila Research Conference (APDRC5) and Indian Drosophila Research Conference.
- It is being held from 6-10 January 2020.

- Asia Pacific Drosophila Research Conference happens every two years, and this is the first time it is coming to India.

Hence the correct answer is option (c).

6.

- The 77th annual Golden Globes Awards were held on 5 Jan 2020 in Beverly Hills, California.
- Best motion picture — Drama was won by '1917'.
- Best performance by an actress in a motion picture — Drama was won by Renee Zellweger for "Judy".
- Best performance by an actor in a motion picture — Drama was won by Joaquin Phoenix for "Joker".
- Best Director was won by Sam Mendes for '1917'.

Hence the correct answer is option (a).

7.

- The Gujarat government has hiked the dearness allowance (DA) by five per cent for over nine lakh state government employees and pensioners.
- With this, the DA would be 17 per cent, on par with Central government employees.
- The hike will come into effect retrospectively from July 1, 2019.
- It will benefit 5.11 lakh employees and 4.5 lakh pensioners.

Hence the correct answer is option (d).

8.

- Astronomers have discovered some smallest galaxies known to host massive black holes.
- The study published in the Astrophysical Journal found 13 massive black holes, about 4,00,000 times as heavy as the Sun, in dwarf galaxies which are 100 times smaller than our Milky Way.
- These galaxies are situated so far away that light from the Earth would take less than a billion years to reach them.

Hence the correct answer is option (c).

9. The Godavari is India's second longest river after Ganga. Its length is 1,465 kilometers. The river is also known as Dakshin Ganga. Its another name is Vriddha Ganga. The Godavari River rises from Trimbakeshwar in the Nashik district of Maharashtra. Godavari flows from north to south in Dharmapuri, hence the river is locally called 'Dakshina Vahini'. Its famous tributaries are Pranahita, Indravati, Manjira, Purna etc. After crossing Rajahmundry, the river divides itself into two main streams, Gautami Godavari on the east and Vashishta Godavari on the west.

Hence the correct answer is option (d).

10. The salinity of the ocean water is calculated in part of per thousand. It is the weight of salt present in 1000 grams of the sea water. The average salinity of the water present in the oceans is 35 per thousand.

Hence the correct answer is option (b).

11. Gandhara was the northwestern region of the Indian subcontinent. The Sakas and Kushans were the chief patrons of the Gandhara Art.

Hence the correct answer is option (d).

12. R. D. Banerji first excavated the sites of 'Mohenjo-daro' while the sites of Harappa were first discovered by Daya Ram Sahni.

Hence the correct answer is option (a).

13. Hampi is located in the northern areas of Karnataka. It was the main city of Vijayanagar dynasty in its earlier days.

Hence the correct answer is option (a).

14. Khilafat movement was started in 1920 against the British Policy towards Turkey. Other events are the significant events of Indian national movement happened in 1919.

Hence the correct answer is option (d).

15. The Story of My Experiments with Truth is the autobiography of Mohandas K. Gandhi, covering his life from early childhood through to 1921. It was written in weekly installments and published in his journal Navjivan from 1925 to 1929.

Hence the correct answer is option (c).

16. Vima Kadphises is known for issuing a large number of gold coins, silk routes, and trade routes.

Hence the correct answer is option (b).

17. 'Pester' means to 'annoy', or 'harass'. Therefore, the synonym for 'pester' is 'bother.'

Gratify refers to giving (someone) pleasure or satisfaction.

Hence the correct answer is option (b).

18. Hiatus refers to a pause or break in continuity in a sequence or activity.

Thus the synonym for the word 'hiatus' is 'pause'.

Contempt: the feeling that a person or a thing is worthless or beneath consideration.

Hence the correct answer is option (a).

19. 'To get cold feet' is an idiom which means to become frightened to do something.

Example: Do you still want to do this parachute jump or are you getting cold feet?

Hence the correct answer is option (a).

20. 'Hush money' is the money paid so that someone will keep information secret.

Example : Bob gave his younger sister hush money so that she wouldn't tell Jane that he had gone to the movies with Sue.

Hence the correct answer is option (d).

21. The custom of having many wives is usually termed as 'polygamy'.

Hence the correct answer is option (d).

22. A name adopted by an author in his writings is 'pseudonym' which means 'a false name'.

Hence the correct answer is option (d).

23. "Reflection" should be replaced by "reflect". "Reflection" is a noun but a verb is required here.

Hence the correct answer is option (c).

24. "What" should be replaced by "that" because "that" would come as a relative pronoun coming from natural disaster. 'That' is used to introduce an explanatory dependent clause and indicates a specific quality of the object in question while 'What' indicates the object in question itself.

Hence the correct answer is option (c).

25. $x^2y^2(x+y)=25$

$x^2y^3+x^3y^2=25$

$(xy)^2=1$

$xy=\pm 1$

Hence the correct answer is option (d).

26. $5^{k+3} = 3125$
$5^{k+3} = 5^5$
$k + 3 = 5$
$k = 2$

Hence the correct answer is option (a).

27. $x = \sqrt{6 + \sqrt{6 + \sqrt{6} + \cdots + \infty}}$
$x = \sqrt{6 + x}$
$x^2 - x - 6 = 0$
$(x - 3)(x + 2) = 0$
$x = 3, -2 (-2 \text{ is rejected })$

Hence the correct answer is option (a).

28. Veer's 1 day's work $= \dfrac{1}{20}$ Ram's 1 day's work $= \dfrac{1}{18}$

Together their 1 day's work $= \dfrac{1}{20} + \dfrac{1}{18}$

Together their 5 day's work $\left(\dfrac{1}{20} + \dfrac{1}{18}\right) \times 5 = \dfrac{19}{36}$ Therefore,

Left work $= 1 - \dfrac{19}{36} = \dfrac{17}{36}$

Hence the correct answer is option (b).

29. Sum $=$ Rs 9000

Time $= 10$ years $SI = 10800 - 9000 = 1800$

Now, calculate the rate of interest:

$SI = \dfrac{P \times R \times T}{100}$

$1800 = \dfrac{9000 \times R \times 10}{100}$

$$R = \frac{1800 \times 100}{9000 \times 10}$$
$$R = 2\%$$

Hence the correct answer is option (a).

30. Given, $P =$ Rs. $15000, r = 20\% \& n = 1$ year

We know that, $A = P\left(1 + \frac{r}{100}\right)^n$

$$A = 15000\left(1 + \frac{20}{100}\right)^1$$
$$A = 15000 \times \left(\frac{6}{5}\right)$$
$$A = \frac{15000 \times 6}{5}$$
$$A = 18000$$

since he pay Rs. 12000 at the end of the first year. Therefore, Principle amount for next year is $= (18000 - 12000) = 6000$ Hence, the required amount is Rs. 6000.

Hence the correct answer is option (a).

31. Speed of Metro $= 40 \times \frac{5}{18} = \frac{100}{9} m/\sec$

Let, the length of bridge be $\overline{x}m$. Therefore. $\frac{120+x}{20} = \frac{100}{9}$

$$9(120 + x) = 2000$$
$$9x = 2000 - 1080$$
$$9x = 920$$
$$x = 102.22$$

Hence the correct answer is option (a).

32. Let The cost price be Rs 100

Then Profit = Rs 300 and Selling price = Rs 400.

New cost price = 125% of 100 = Rs 125

New Selling price = Rs 400 .

Profit = (400 - 125) = Rs 275

Percentage Profit $\frac{275}{400} \times 100 = 68.75\%$

Hence the correct answer is option (b).

33. % increase in 2004,

$$= \frac{66.90 - 59.50}{59.50} \times 100] = 12.43\%$$

% increase in 2003,

$$= \frac{59.50 - 48.60}{48.60} \times 100 = 22.24\%$$

% increase in 2002,

$$= \frac{48.60 - 40.90}{40.90} \times 100 = 18.82\%$$

% increase in 2001,

$$= \frac{40.90 - 35.80}{35.80} \times 100] = 14.25$$

Thus, maximum increase in daily earning of men over preceding year is in 2003.

Hence the correct answer is option (c).

34. Difference between earning of man and women in 2000,

= 35.8 -18.3 = 17.5

Difference between earning of man and women in 2012,

= 40.90 - 21.10 = 19.8

Difference between earning of man and women in 2002,

= 48.60 - 27.0 = 21.6

Difference between earning of man and women in 2003,

= 59.50 -34.20 = 25.3

Difference between earning of man and women in 2004,

= 66.90 - 40.60 = 26.3

pattern show, its increasing.

Hence the correct answer is option (a).

35. Required ratio in 2000,

$$= \frac{35.80}{18.30} = 1.9$$

Required ration in 2001,

$$= \frac{40.9}{21.1} = 1.93$$

Required ration in 2002,

$$= \frac{48.60}{27.0} = 1.8$$

Required ration in 2003,

$$= \frac{59.5}{34.20} = 1.73$$

Required ration in 2004,

$$= \frac{66.90}{40.60} = 1.64$$

It is highest in 2001.

Hence the correct answer is option (d).

36. Required % increase$= \frac{160 - 130}{130} = 23\%$.

Hence the correct answer is option (a).

37. Interest in 1990-91= 30% of 130= 39 lakh

Interest in 1991-92= 40% of 160= 64 lakh

Hence, difference= Rs. 25 lakh.

Hence the correct answer is option (b).

38. Total interest= (39+64)= Rs 103 lakh

Given that,

this interest is calculated on 20% of borrowed fund.

Hence, borrowed funds$= \frac{103}{20} \times 100$

= Rs 515 lakh.

Hence the correct answer is option (d).

39. Retained profit in 1990-91= 25% of 130= Rs 32.5 lakh

Retained profit in 1991-92= 20% of 160= Rs 32 lakh;

Decrease= $\dfrac{32.5-32}{32.5} \times 100$ = 1.5%.

Hence the correct answer is option (d).

40. Total dividend earned by share holder in 1991-92,

= 8 of 160= Rs 12.8 lakh.

Hence the correct answer is option (c).

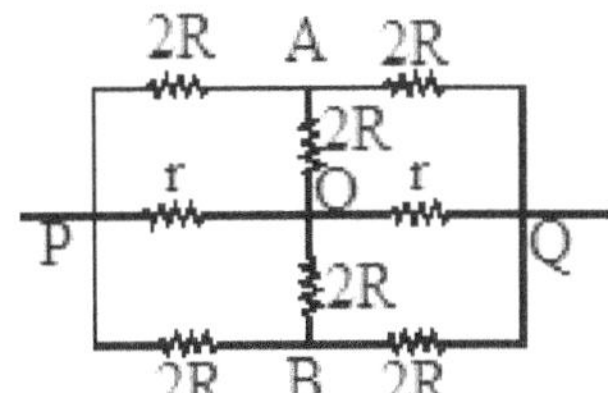

41.

The circuit is symmetrical about axis POQ. Therefore the equivalent circuit is drawn

$$\therefore \frac{1}{R_{PQ}} = \frac{1}{4R} + \frac{1}{4R} + \frac{1}{2r} = \frac{1}{2R} + \frac{1}{2r} = \frac{R+r}{2Rr}$$

$$\Rightarrow R_{PQ} = \frac{2Rr}{R+r}$$

Hence the correct answer is option (a).

42. 2 ohm resistance is connected in parallel with 2 resistances of 2 ohm each.

the resultant resistance = $\dfrac{1}{\frac{1}{2}+\frac{1}{4}}$

$= \dfrac{1}{\frac{3}{4}} = \dfrac{4}{3} = 1.333$ohm

Hence the correct answer is option (b).

43. $\Rightarrow 2R \times \dfrac{R}{2R+R} = 1\Omega$

$\Rightarrow R = \dfrac{3}{2} = 1.5\Omega$

Hence the correct answer is option (b).

44. Voltage across the circuit = 120 - 50 = 70 V

$I = \dfrac{V}{R} = \dfrac{70}{5000} = 14$ mA

[Note: 50 K resistor will be short circuited in the reverse bias because the zener diode will be on]

Hence the correct answer is option (c).

45. The voltage drop is the main consideration for design of service mains. For feeder the main consideration be its current carrying capacity and voltage drop can be compensated using voltage regulating equipments. Even in distribution, voltage drop is not a significant factor and minor voltage +6 V of voltage fluctuation is permissible.

Hence the correct answer is option (c).

46. The V-I characteristics of crystal diode is **non-linear**.

Hence the correct answer is option (c).

47. Zero voltage regulation of DC generator means that full load terminal voltage is equal to the no load terminal voltage. This characteristics is exhibited by flat compound generator.

Hence the correct answer is option (c).

48. This measuring instrument indicates directly the average power dissipated by the load. Only one wattmeter is used in case of single phase power measurement while two wattmeters are needed to measure the three phase power.

Hence the correct answer is option (c).

49. Current transformer is used for high current measurement purpose.

Potential transformer is used for high voltage measurement purpose.

Instrument transformer is used for high voltage and high current measurement purpose.

Hence the correct answer is option (c).

50. An alternator with small diameter and large length of rotor bar is used for high speed Application. This type of rotor is driven by stream turbine.

The alternator with large diameter and small length of rotor is used for low speed application. This type of rotor is driven by hydraulic or diesel engine.

Hence the correct answer is option (c).

51. In three phase wound rotor motors, each one of the three phase is connected to the slip ring, which provides there additional resistance to the rotor. That is why three phase wound rotor motors are also called slip ring motors.

Hence the correct answer is option (b).

52. Four speed squirrel cage motor are equipped with two separate stator winding, each of which provide two speeds. This can be done by pole changing of stator side for speed control of motor.

This is not possible in slipring rotor type motor. Only in squirrel cage motor possible.

Hence the correct answer is option (d).

53. Alternating current can be represented by $I = I_0\sin(2\pi t/T)$ $I_{avg} = \int_0^T I_0 \sin(2\pi t/T)dt = 0$

Hence the correct answer is option (a).

54. AS $X = 2\pi f L$

where X: inductive reactance

f = frequency

L = inductance

it is directly proportional to reactance and frequency.

for capacitive reactance

$$X = \frac{1}{2\pi f c}$$

c=capacitance

it is inverse proportional to each other.

Hence the correct answer is option (a).

55. An AND gate is equivalent to a series switching circuit.

AND gate out is one(high) only when all the input are one(high).

other its output is zero.

It is similar to series connected switching circuit.if one of the switch is open then output is zero.

Note: OR gate is used for logical addition.

for OR gate switch is connected in parallel.

Hence the correct answer is option (c).

56. An XOR gate produces output only when two inputs are different.

XOR gate produces the result irrespective of the magnitude of the input. So, low or high input does not make any difference.

Hence the correct answer is option (c).

57. A crystal diode act as a switch, when forward biased as a closed switch and open switch in reverse biased.

BJT-amplifier

zenor diode-voltage regulator.

op-amp & bjt-oscillator.

Hence the correct answer is option (b).

58. Device turn off time= storage time + fall time.

Circuit turn off time is always greater than device turn off time.

Because gate circuit require some time recovery purpose.

For proper circuit operation. Otherwise it turn on any time. This is causes maloperation of circuit.

Circuit turn off time =device turn off time+gate recovery time.

Hence the correct answer is option (a).

59. A non uniform moving electric charge will produce both electric and magnetic fields. Both are dependent on each other.

Uniform moving charge produce only magnetic field.

Charge is at rest produces only electric field.

Above 2 condition both are independent on each other.

Hence the correct answer is option (b).

60. Electrolysis is possible only if DC potential difference is applied to the electrode .It is because we are to attract ions of only one kind on each electrode.

Hence the correct answer is option (a).

61. All options are correct.

- In static field the charge is moving with uniform velocity it produces magnetic field.
- In time variable field, both field are depend on each other.
- change in electric field density with time produces magnetic field.
- If current flow though in conductor, it always produces magnetic field around the conductor.

Hence the correct answer is option (d).

62. As superposition principal is applicable for linear, active, bilateral network.

Current & voltage are linear to each other.

but power = $I^2 \times R$

Power is direct propositional to square of current, which is non linear.

There for it is applicable only for current & voltage calculation.

Hence the correct answer is option (a).

63. If transistor is operating in active mode, then use this formula for active region emitter junction is forward bias & collector junction is reverse bias.

IE=IC+IB

$$\beta = \frac{IC}{IB}$$

10.5=10+IB

IB=0.5mA

$$\beta = 20$$

Hence the correct answer is option (a).

64. Input to the transistor is bias current & collector to ground voltage.

Change in base current is main responsible for change in output of circuit voltage and current.

There for BJT is current control device.

Note-FET is voltage control device.

Hence the correct answer is option (a).

65. When voltage applied across the diode is forward bias then zener diode act as normal diode, maintain output voltage constant. But during voltage across diode is reverse bias then diode act as zener diode operates in reverse blocking mode for maintaining output voltage constant.There for zener diode is called as voltage regulator.

Hence the correct answer is option (b).

66. The electron mobility is often greater than hole mobility because quite often, the electron effective mass is smaller than hole effective mass. The relaxation times are often of the same order of magnitude for electrons and holes and therefore, they do not make too much difference.

Hence the correct answer is option (c).

67. Shaded pole motor has the lowest speed due to shaded pole present.

Note-shaded pole motor has very poor power factor.

Hysteresis motor run at synchronous speed.

Universal motor is dc series motor.

Hence the correct answer is option (b).

68. Reluctance motor and Hysteresis motor are AC synchronous motors.

If field winding is unexcited then synchronous motor act as reluctance motor.

Hysteresis motor is excited by A.C. supply on stator side, both the winding present on stator and motor is rotating always at synchronous speed.

Universal motor is excited both AC & DC supply.

Hence the correct answer is option (d).

69. The rotor of hysteresis motor is made of magnetic material having area of hysteresis loop very large.

Rotor of hysteresis motor is made of harden steel with high retentivity.

High retentivity is responsible for large hysteresis loop on B-H curve.

Hence the correct answer is option (c).

70. A reluctance motor runs at synchronous speed.

Synchronous motor is act as a reluctance motor ,if field winding excitation is zero.

It run same as synchronous motor.

It receive both active power and reactive power for motoring operation.

Hence the correct answer is option (a).

71. The single phase shaded pole motor has squirrel cage rotor.

Rotor winding of shaded pole motor is permanently short circuit. There for it is similar to squirrel cage motor.

Shaded pole motor has low power factor & low starting torque.

Hence the correct answer is option (a).

72. In regenerative cycle, bled steam is used to beat feed water for boiler.

As in gas-turbine plants, the thermal efficiency of a steam power plant is raised by means of heat regeneration. In actual steam power cycles regeneration is effected with the aid of surface-type or direct-contact regenerative feed-water heaters, either of which is supplied with steam from intermediate turbine stages (the regenerative take off). The steam condenses in the regenerative feed-water heaters Heating steam condensate is also delivered to the boiler or mixes with the main flow of feed water.

Hence the correct answer is option (c).

73. Permissible pH value of water for the boiler is slightly more than 7.

Natural water is usually between 6.5 and 7.5 pH. A common recommendation is to maintain boiler water at 8.5 pH. Acidic water is corrosive. Alkalinic water is more prone to scaling. Alkalinity is a measure of the bicarbonate, (HCO_3) carbonate (CO_3) and hydroxyl (OH) ions in the water.

Hence the correct answer is option (c).

74. Efficiency of thermal power plant improve with use of high steam pressure.

Steam power plants use pressurized, superheated steam generators to boost the temperature and pressure of the steam to improve efficiency. After the steam exits the turbine and is condensed back to water, it is passed through a series of heat exchangers to extract the last drop of residual heat energy.

Hence the correct answer is option (d).

75. Hysteresis loss least depends on ambient temperature.

Hysteresis loss is mainly depends upon volume of material, frequency, flux density and hysteresis coefficient.

Hence the correct answer is option (d).

76. If area of hysteresis loop of a material is large, the hysteresis loss in the material will be Large.

Hysteresis loss is directly proportional to the area under the curve on B-H axis.

Hence the correct answer is option (c).

77. Permanent magnets are normally mode of Al-Ni-Co alloys.

Usually ferromagnetic or ferromagnetic materials are used for making permanent magnets these materials includes iron, nickel, cobalt and some rare earth metals. These materials were exposed to strong magnetic fields until it retains its magnetic field.

Hence the correct answer is option (a).

78. Dynamic equalization circuit is used for equal division of current through each thyristor in series. Dynamic equalizing circuit is nothing but snubber circuit which is used to equalize the voltage division under transient condition.

Hence the correct answer is option (a).

79. The Insulated Gate Bipolar Transistor also called an IGBT for short, is something of a cross between a conventional Bipolar Junction Transistor, (BJT) and a Field Effect Transistor, (MOSFET) making it ideal as a semiconductor switching device.

Hence the correct answer is option (b).

80. In forward blocking mode junction J_2 and in reverse blocking mode junction J_1 and J_3 acts as capacitor hence, leakage current present in both direction.

Hence the correct answer is option (c).

81. The arc voltage in a CB **is in phase with arc current**.

Since arc path is purely resistive.

The arc voltage in a CB is in phase with arc current.

Hence the correct answer is option (a).

82. Reactors are used at various locations in power system to limit short-circuit current.

Reactors are also used to protect the circuit breakers of different ratings. They are used to limit the short circuit currents according to the capacity of circuit breakers. Therefore while doing changes in the system, we don't have to replace the circuit breakers, instead we can add reactors and utilize the same circuit breaker, due to which, time and money, both can be saved.

Hence the correct answer is option (c).

83. All of the options are correct.

Skin effect is the tendency of an alternating electric current (AC) to become distributed within a conductor such that the current density is largest near the surface of the conductor, and decreases with greater depths in the conductor.

Hence the correct answer is option (d).

84. All are suitable discrete time system.

Above options are related to properties of discrete time system. Option 1 – Scaling operation on signal is performed.

Option (b) is reverse operation.

Option (c) signal is multiplied by constant plus dc component.

Option (d) Cosine operation, even cosine is continuous function but cosine of the discrete signal is a discrete signal system.

Hence the correct answer is option (d).

85. As compared to capacitor-short induction motors or split phase motor, a permanent split capacitor motor has lower noise.

In Split phase IM main and auxiliary winding are connected in parallel during starting condition. When motor reaches to 70% to 80% of the speed starting winding is automatically disconnected

Capacitor start IM has good starting condition but poor running char. Efficiency and Power factor is less as compared to split phase IM.

Hence the correct answer is option (c).

86. In a split phase motor the starting winding is connected through a centrifugal switch.

When the motor is started, the centrifugal switch is in the closed position allowing current to flow through both the run winding and the start winding. Because the motor has two distinct windings (a stronger magnetic field is created) which causes the motor to begin rotation and accelerate towards operating speed.

Once the motor reaches about 70% to 80% of its rated-speed, the centrifugal switch opens and disconnects the starting winding. From this point on to operating speed, the single-phase motor can maintain enough magnetic field strength to operate using only the run winding.

Hence the correct answer is option (a).

87. If the capacitor of a single phase motor is short circuited the motor will not start.

Hence the correct answer is option (a).

88. Overexcited synchronous motor delivers reactive factor to 3-phase lines, behave like source of reactive power. Thus we can call it synchronous capacitor.

An overexcited synchronous motor operate at leading power factor, under-excited synchronous motor operate at lagging power factor and normal excited synchronous motor operate at unity power factor.

Hence the correct answer is option (b).

89. All options are correct.

- Fault is an abnormal condition in the electrical system due to this leads to damage or abnormal operation of the electrical appliances.
- Basically faults are classified into Open and Short circuit faults.
- Short circuit faults are further classified into Symmetrical and unsymmetrical faults.
- Line to ground (unsymmetrical) Fault is the most severe in power system (Up to 70%).

Hence the correct answer is option (d).

90. The knowledge of diversity factor helps in determining plants capacity.

Diversity factor is the ratio of the sum of the individual maximum demands of the various subdivisions of a system (or part of a system) to the maximum demand of the whole system (or part of the system) under consideration. Diversity is usually more than one.

Diversity factor is a measure of the probability that a particular piece of equipment will turn on coincidentally to another piece of equipment.

Hence the correct answer is option (c).

91. According to definition of load factor:

Load factor = Average load/Max demand

Load factor is the ratio of the average load to the maximum demand during a given period. Normally, if load factor and diversity factor is higher then energy per unit is less.

Hence the correct answer is option (a).

92. number of branches of root locus tends towards infinity is equal to

$=P-Z$

P=number of poles of open loop system

Z=number of zero of open loop system.

in given problem P=Z then branches toward infinity is zero.

Hence the correct answer is option (c).

93. Root locus is used to calculate Relative Stability.

Hence the correct answer is option (d).

94. AC current is certainly not a scalar quantity.

The quantity represented by value and displacement is termed as Phasor whereas the one represented by value and direction is termed as the vector quantity.

Because it act like rotating vector so it is Phasor quantity and not vector.

Hence the correct answer is option (c).

95. As the forward voltage drop across a silicon diode is almost constant at about 0.7V, while the current through it varies by relatively large amounts, a forward-biased signal diode can make a simple voltage regulating circuit.

Hence the correct answer is option (c).

96. The torque speed characteristics of a repulsion motor resembles in series of DC motor characteristics.

Starting torque of repulsion motor is very high at low speed, when speed goes on increasing the torque goes on decreasing.

Speed torque characteristics of both motor are similar.

NOTE-series motor is used for under loaded condition not for starting purpose.

Hence the correct answer is option (c).

97. Overall efficiency of gas turbine is less than diesel cycle efficiency.

The overall efficiency of gas turbine is low, because a greater part of power developed by the turbine (about 65%) is used in driving the compressor.

Hence the correct answer is option (d).

98. Metals which form an amphoteric oxide are zinc, tin, lead, aluminium and beryllium. e.g., zinc
Amphoteric oxides react with acids as well as bases. Thus ZnO will react with HCl as well as with $NaOH$.
$$ZnO + 2HCl \rightarrow ZnCl_2 + H_2O$$
$$ZnO + 2NaOH \rightarrow Na_2ZnO_2 + H_2O$$

Hence the correct answer is option (d).

99. In static and balanced power system components like transformer and lines, the sequence impedance offered by the system are the same for positive and negative sequence currents. In other words, the positive sequence impedance and negative sequence impedance are same for transformers and power lines.

Hence the correct answer is option (a).

100. Steam engine used in Locomotive is double acting, non-conducting type.

Hence the correct answer is option (c).

101. The most common examples of non-renewable resources are fossil fuels, such as coal, oil and natural gas. Although these resources form naturally within the earth, they take billions of years to do so. Other non-renewable resources include metals, minerals and stone.

Hence the correct answer is option (a).

102. Among the following biomass is a non renewable source of energy.

Hence the correct answer is option (b).

103. If electrical conductivity increases with the increase of temperature of a substance then that substance is a semiconductor. - The electrical conductivity of a substance is dependent on the electrical resistance of that substance.

Hence the correct answer is option (b).

104. Energy- abundant, versatile, reliable, portable, and affordable, fossil fuels provide over 80 percent of the worlds energy because they are superior to the current alternatives, Disadvantage of most of the renewable energy sources is its unreliable supply.

Hence the correct answer is option (c).

105. Photovoltaic energy is the conversion of sunlight into electricity. A photovoltaic cell, commonly called a solar cell or PV, is the technology used to convert solar energy directly into electrical power.

Hence, the correct option is (C).

106. Wind turbines have two main design categories: horizontal and vertical axis. The horizontal-axis turbine typically has a three-blade vertical propeller that catches the wind face-on. The vertical turbine has a set of blades that spins around a vertical axis.

Hence the correct answer is option (b).

107.

1. Interference with spawning and migration of fish
2. Pollution and health hazard in the estuary due to blockage of flow of polluted water into the sea
3. Navigational hazard

Hence the correct answer is option (d).

108. Steam reforming of natural gas is currently the least expensive method of producing hydrogen and is used for about half of the world's production of hydrogen.

Hence the correct answer is option (c).

109. A fuel cell, in order to produce electricity, Hydrogen burns.

Hence the correct answer is option (c).

110. Fuel cells work like batteries, but they do not run down or need recharging. They produce electricity and heat as long as fuel is supplied. A fuel cell consists of two electrodes—a negative electrode (or anode) and a positive electrode (or cathode)—sandwiched around an electrolyte.

Hence the correct answer is option (b).

111. As the biogas plant is based on the gas produced by a huge amount of cow dung and feces of other firm animals, after utilization of the produced gas power is produced, and the remaining feces material is used as manure, fertilizers in agricultural grounds.

Hence the correct answer is option (c).

112. The outermost layer, called the crust, is solid, too. Together, these solid parts are called the lithosphere. Earth's crust is made up of hard rocks.

Hence the correct answer is option (c).

113. Common energy source in Indian villages is wood and animal dung which is burnt to form biogas.

Hence the correct answer is option (d).

114. The one thing that is common to all fossil fuels is that they **contain carbon**.

Hence the correct answer is option (b).

115. The process that converts solid coal into liquid hydrocarbon fuel is called Liquefaction.

Hence the correct answer is option (a).

116. Lignite, bituminous and anthracite are different ranks of coal. Coal is classified on the basis of its rank. The rank of coal denotes its degree of maturity.

Hence the correct answer is option (b).

117. Petroleum—or crude oil—is a fossil fuel that is found in large quantities beneath the Earth's surface and is often used as a fuel or raw material in the chemical industry. It is a smelly, yellow-to-black liquid and is usually found in underground areas called reservoirs.

Hence the correct answer is option (c).

118. BTU measures the amount of heat required to raise or lower the temperature of one pound of water one degree Fahrenheit. When it comes to heat pumps or furnaces, the BTU number refers to the heat output of a unit. With air conditioners, the BTU number refers to the amount of energy used to remove heat from the air.

Hence the correct answer is option (c).

119. Nuclear fission of heavy elements was discovered on December 17, 1938 by German Otto Hahn and his assistant Fritz Strassmann, and explained theoretically in January 1939 by Lise Meitner and her nephew Otto Robert Frisch.

Hence the correct answer is option (d).

120. A boiling water reactor (BWR) is a type of light water nuclear reactor used for the generation of electrical power. The main difference between a BWR and PWR is that in a BWR, the reactor core heats water, which turns to steam and then drives a steam turbine. In a PWR, the reactor core heats water, which does not boil.

Hence the correct answer is option (a).

Mock Test 05

Part - I

Q.1 If two numbers are given, each number multiplied by sum of both numbers,. Then the multiplication is 247 and 114 respectively. Find the sum of these two numbers.

A. 19   **B.** 20   **C.** 21   **D.** 23

Q.2 How many numbers between 6 and 1300 are completely divisible by 6 or 9 or by both?

A. 293   **B.** 297   **C.** 289   **D.** 288

Q.3 The sum of n terms of an A.P is $3n^2 + 5n$ then 164 is which digit?

A. 24th   **B.** 27th   **C.** 26th   **D.** 25th

Q.4 Solve the following equation :

$$\frac{1\frac{1}{4} \div 1\frac{1}{2}}{\frac{1}{15} + 1 - \frac{9}{10}}$$

A. $\frac{2}{5}$ **B.** 5   **C.** 6   **D.** 3

Q.5 If p : q = 7 :9 and q : r = 15 :7 then p : r is-

A. 3 : 5   **B.** 5 : 3   **C.** 7 : 15   **D.** 7 : 21

Q.6 If $\frac{x}{a} = \frac{y}{b} = \frac{z}{c}$ then $\frac{x}{y} : \frac{y}{z} : \frac{z}{x}$ will be:

A. 1:2:3   **B.** $a^2c : ab^2 : bc^2$

C. $ab : bc : ca$ **D.** $a : b : c$

Q.7 Ankit, Bhusan and Chetan enter into a partnership in the ratio $\frac{7}{2} : \frac{4}{3} : \frac{6}{5}$.After 4 months, Ankit increases his share 50%. If the total profit at the end of one year be Rs. 10,800, then Chetan's share in the profit is:

A. Rs. 1200   **B.** Rs. 1800   **C.** Rs. 1600   **D.** Rs. 2000

Q.8 Δ ABC is an isosceles triangle with AB=AC, A circle through B touching AC at the middle point intersects AB at P. Then AP: AB is :

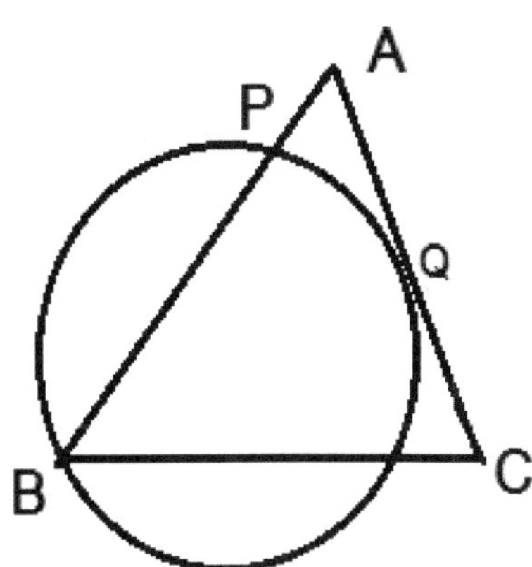

A. 4:1   **B.** 2:3   **C.** 3:5   **D.** 1:4

Q.9 Direction : In the following questions, some of the sentences have errors and some have none. Find out which part of the sentence has an error. The number of that part is your answer. If there is no error, the answer would be (D).
I am waiting/(A) for my friend/(B) since this morning./(C) No error. (D)

A. A   **B.** B   **C.** C   **D.** D

Q.10 In the following question, select the missing number from the given series.
9, 18, 72, 576, ?

A. 8116   **B.** 8216   **C.** 9016   **D.** 9216

Q.11 Which one set of letters when sequentially placed at gap in the given letter series shall complete it.
_nmmn_mmnn_mnnm_

A. nnmm   **B.** nmnm   **C.** mnnm   **D.** nmmn

Q.12 Direction : In the following questions a part of sentence is bold. Below are given alternatives to the part of sentence given in bold, which may improve the sentence. Choose the alternative which makes the sentence grammatically and contextually correct. In case the sentence is correct as it is, choose 'No Improvement' as your option.

We need honest workers, not people of redoubtable integrity.

A. doubting   **B.** doubtful

C. doubtless   **D.** No improvement

Q.13 Direction : In the following question, a sentence is given with a blank to be filled in with appropriate word(s). Some alternatives are suggested for each question. Choose the correct alternative from the given alternatives.

The deceased left ______ children.

A. behind   **B.** for   **C.** with   **D.** by

Q.14 Direction : In the following question, a sentence is given with a blank to be filled in with appropriate word(s). Some alternatives are suggested for each question. Choose the correct alternative from the given alternatives.

The statue ______ a global symbol of freedom.

A. stands against   **B.** stands to

C. stands for   **D.** stands as

Q.15 Direction : In the following questions, a sentence has been given in Active Voice/ Passive Voice. Out of the four alternatives suggested, select the one which best expresses the same sentence in Passive/Active Voice.

Has anybody answered your question.

A. Your question has been answered ?

B. Anybody has answered your question

C. Has your question been answered ?

D. Have you answered your question ?

Q.16 Direction : In the following questions , a sentence has been given in Direct/Indirect . Out of the four alternatives suggested, select the one which best expresses the same sentence in Indirect/ Direct .

The teacher said, "Students, which of you would volunteer to convene the Annual Day celebration this year.?"

A. The teacher asked the student whether they would volunteer to convene the Annual Day celebration that year.

B. The teacher said to the students to volunteer to convene the Annual Day celebration this year.

C. The teacher said to the students that they would have volunteered to convene the Annual Day celebration that year.

D. The teacher asked the students which of them would volunteer to convene the Annual Day celebration that year.

Q.17 Who is turning entrepreneur with the launch of a male grooming and hygiene products line '23 Yards'?

A. Anil Kumble **B.** Ravi Shastri

C. Rahul Dravid **D.** Yuvraj Singh

Q.18 Which state will become the first state to cap the prices of masks?

A. Karnataka **B.** Maharashtra

C. Haryana **D.** Bihar

Q.19 When is the 'International Day of Commemoration and Dignity of the Victims of the Crime of Genocide and of the Prevention of this Crime' observed?

A. 7 December **B.** 8 December

C. 9 December **D.** 10 December

Q.20 IRCTC will restart the first set of which of the following private Tejas Express trains from October 2020?

A. Lucknow-New Delhi

B. Ahmedabad-Mumbai

C. New Delhi-Mumbai

D. Both 1 and 2

Q.21 Which of the following is launching pressurized metered-dose inhaler for patients suffering from Chronic Obstructive Pulmonary Disease (COPD) in India?

A. Cipla **B.** Zydus Cadila

C. Sun Pharma **D.** Lupin Limited

Q.22 Which of the following has announced an end to its five-year-old joint venture partnership with German luxury brand Montblanc?

A. Fastrack **B.** Titan Co. Ltd

C. Fossil Group **D.** Cromā

Q.23 In order to boost its economic ties with Bangladesh, which country will open its Foreign Commercial Service Office in Dhaka?

A. US **B.** Germany

C. France **D.** Sweden

Q.24 The Union Cabinet has given its approval for signing a Memorandum of Cooperation (MoC) in the field of cybersecurity between India and which of the following countries?

A. Japan **B.** Sweden **C.** Norway **D.** Australia

Q.25 When is the International Workers' Day?

A. 15th April **B.** 12th December

C. 1st May **D.** 1st August

Q.26 The first death anniversary day of Sri Rajiv Gandhi was observed as the

A. National Integration Day

B. Peace and Love Day

C. Secularism Day

D. Anti-Terrorism Day

Q.27 Water vapor is:

A. A gas **B.** A cloud droplet

C. A rain drop **D.** A snowflake

Q.28 What is the cause of the Exxon Valdez?

A. Oil Tanker which sank in 1989 along the coast of Alaska and marine life seriously affected.

B. a plane which crashed and caused death of human life.

C. a ship which wrecked on the coast of India.

D. None of these

Q.29 Article 359 of the Constitution authorizes the president of India to suspend the right to move any court for the enforcement of Fundamental Rights during :

A. A National Emergency

B. A failure of constitutional machinery in States.

C. A financial emergency.

D. None of Above.

Q.30 The correct chronological order of the formation of Haryana, Sikkim, Arunanchala Pradesh and Nagaland as full states of Indian Union is :

A. Haryana-Sikkim-Arunaachal Pardesh- Nagaland

B. Nagaland –Arunaachal Pradesh- Haryana-Sikkim

C. Nagaland –Haryana-Arunaachal Pardesh

D. Nagaland –Haryana-Sikkim-Arunaachal Pradesh

Q.31 The Kolkata East-West Metro Corridor project will have how many stations between Salt Lake Sector-V and Howrah Maidan?

A. 8 **B.** 10 **C.** 12 **D.** 14

Q.32 Which was the 1st non Test playing country to beat India in an international match?

A. Canada **B.** Sri Lanka

C. Zimbabwe **D.** East Africa

Ques (33-36):Directions : The cumulative bar chart below gives us the production of four Products A, B, C and D for four years. It is known that the total production increases @20% over its value in the previous year. the difference between C's production in 2003 and A's production in 2001 is 2640 units.

Production of A, B, C and D.

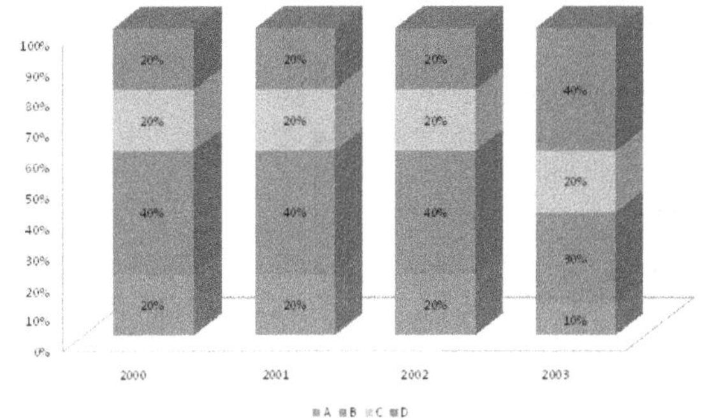

Q.33 If the price of B is Rs. 125 per unit, what is the sales revenue in the same year due to sale of B (in Rupees Lakhs)?

A. 15   **B.** 12.5   **C.** 20   **D.** 25

Q.34 Assuming no pile up of inventory at the beginning or the end of the year, what is the ratio of the number of units of C produced in these four years?

A. 120 : 175 : 260 : 228
B. 125 : 135 : 240 : 224
C. 125 : 165 : 270 : 216
D. 175 : 150 : 180 : 216

Q.35 If the price of four products is in ratio of 3 : 5 : 7 : 8, what is the ratio of the ratio of the revenue generated by these products in 2002?

A. 6 : 15 : 21 : 16   **B.** 4 : 10 : 14 : 9
C. 9 : 16 : 24 : 20   **D.** 3 : 10 : : 7 : 8

Q.36 If due to extra set up time required, the production in 2001 drops by 12.5% over that in 2000, what should be the growth rate of production in 2002 to maintain the compounded annual growth rate (CAGR) of 20% (Approx)?

A. 56%   **B.** 48%   **C.** 52%   **D.** 65%

Ques (37-40):Direction: Study the pie chart and answer the following question based on it.

The following pie chart gives the language-based composition of the people of India.

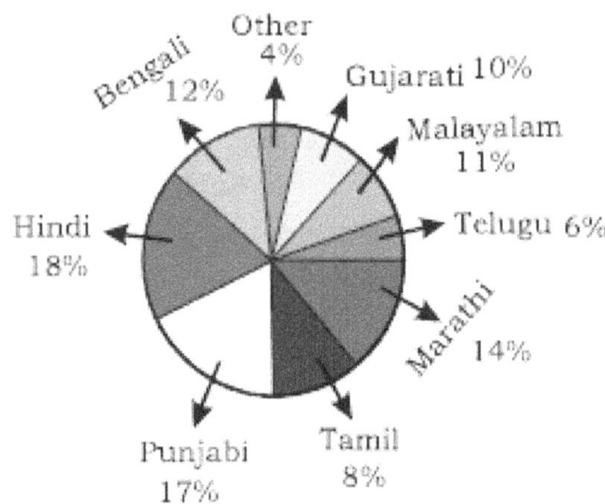

Q.37 What is the percentage of Telugu speaking people to Hindi speaking people?

A. $66\frac{1}{3}$%   **B.** $33\frac{2}{3}$%   **C.** $30\frac{2}{3}$%   **D.** $33\frac{1}{3}$%

Q.38 What is the central angle for Gujarati speaking people?
A. 72°   **B.** 36°   **C.** 30°   **D.** 45°

Q.39 What is the population of Bengali speaking in thousands nearly?
A. 900   **B.** 500
C. 600   **D.** Data is inadequate

Q.40 Which two sections of people forms majority in India?
A. Hindi + Telugu
B. Hindi + Marathi
C. Malayalam + Punjabi
D. Punjabi + Hindi

Part - II

Q.41 An incandescent lamp is rated at 100 W, 230 V. What will be its resistance when measured with the help of a multimeters?

A. 529 Ω   **B.** 5 Ω   **C.** Zero   **D.** infinite

Q.42 For the circuit shown in figure the total impedance is

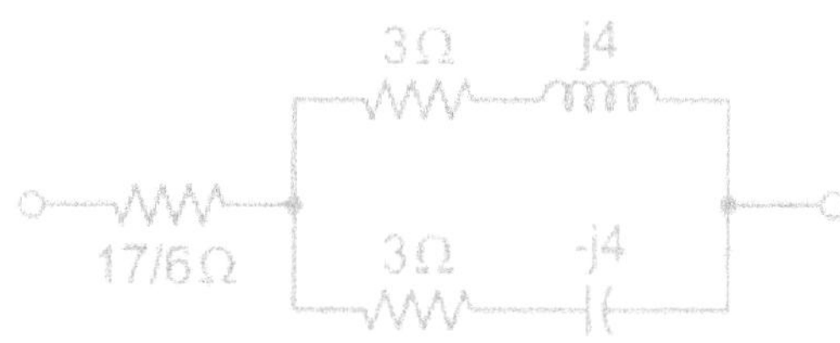

A. (7 + j0)   **B.** (5 + j0)   **C.** (0 + j8)   **D.** (7 + j10)

Q.43 Two coils have inductances of 4 mH and 9 mH and a coefficient of coupling of 0.5. If the two coils are connected in series aiding, the total inductance will be:
A. 19 mH   **B.** 16 mH   **C.** 7 mH   **D.** 10 mH

Q.44 The input characteristics of a CB transistor resembles____
A. Forward biased diode
B. Illuminated photo diode
C. LED
D. Zener diode

Q.45 Which of the following is true with regenerative braking?
A. It uses an energy recovery mechanism which slows down a vehicle by converting its kinetic energy into another form.
B. It uses an energy recovery mechanism which transforms the braking energy into kinetic energy of the vehicle.
C. It uses an energy recovery mechanism which reduces the speed of a vehicle by converting the electrical energy into kinetic energy.
D. It regenerates the brake fluids for use at a future period.

Q.46 The deflection sensitivity of the CRO is 10 m/V. What is the value of deflection factor (in V/m)?
A. 10   **B.** 0.1   **C.** 1   **D.** 0.01

Q.47 Which of the following currents can induce the maximum induced voltage in a coil?

A. 1 A, DC
C. 1 A, 1 Hz
B. 1 A, 100 Hz
D. 20 A, DC

Q.48 Which among these is a demerit of underground service mains?

A. Ugly appearance
B. Frequent fault occurrence
C. Costly
D. All of these

Q.49 In 4 wire electric circuit, the black conductor is used for

A. Phase
C. Earth wire
B. Neutral
D. Armour

Q.50 In a series RC circuit, the current ___ the voltage by an angle ___ degrees.

A. lags, of 45
B. lags, of 0
C. leads, between 0 and 90
D. leads, of 90

Q.51 Most of the fractional horsepower motors have either

A. hard and annealed bearings
B. ball or roller bearings
C. soft and porous bearings
D. plain or sleeve bearings

Q.52 In a three-phase induction motor:

A. The developed torque is approximately directly proportional to slip in normal running range and inversely proportional to it in the low-speed range.
B. The developed torque is approximately directly proportional to slip in normal running range as well as in the low-speed range.
C. The developed torque is approximately inversely proportional to slip in normal running range as well as in the low-speed range.
D. The developed torque is approximately inversely proportional to slip in normal running range and directly proportional to it in the low-speed range.

Q.53 A shunt resistor is connected across the contacts of a circuit breaker in order to:

A. Damp out the restriking transients
B. Bypass the arc current
C. Limit the short circuit current
D. Reduce the damage to contacts due to arcing

Q.54 Find the maximum power is delivered to the load

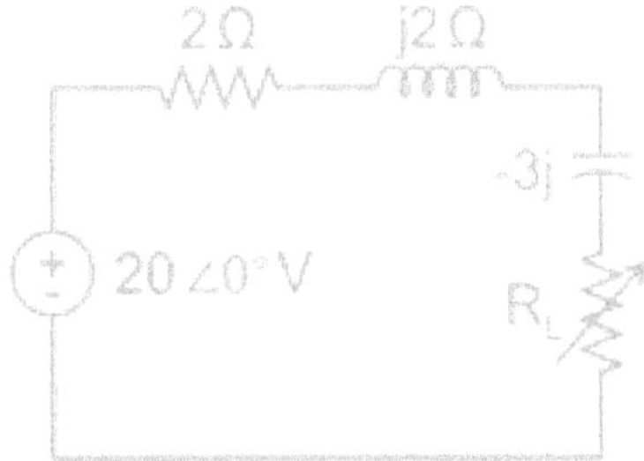

A. 34.82 W **B.** 88.74 W **C.** 44.72 W **D.** 50.72 W

Q.55 The traction motor used in composite system employed in India is

A. AC single phase motor
B. DC series motor
C. DC shunt motor
D. three-phase induction motor

Q.56 An ideal rectifier should have –

A. Efficiency = 100%; Vac = 0; Transformer Utilization Factor = 1 and Total harmonic distortion = 0
B. Efficiency = 90%; Vac = 0.1; Transformer Utilization Factor = 0.9 and Total harmonic distortion = 0
C. Efficiency = 90%; Vac = 0.1; Transformer Utilization Factor = 0.9 and Total harmonic distortion = 5%
D. Efficiency = 100%; Vac = 0.2; Transformer Utilization Factor = 0.8 and Total harmonic distortion = 5%

Q.57 The split-phase induction motor has

A. Low starting current and high starting torque
B. Moderate starting current and moderate starting torque
C. Low starting current and moderate starting torque
D. Moderate starting current and low starting torque

Q.58 What will be the produced mmf (in Amp-turns) in a magnetic circuit, if it has 100 number of turns and carrying a current of 0.2 A?

A. 20 **B.** 40 **C.** 500 **D.** 200

Q.59 The electric drives possess the following drawback

A. Requires hazardous fuel requirement
B. Not adoptable to various environments
C. Not available with various rating
D. Requires a continuous power supply

Q.60 Windage losses are caused by

A. Air friction
B. Bearing friction
C. Non-uniform airflow
D. Window in a transformer

Q.61 Which of the following statements correctly defines "Utilization factor" or "Co-efficient of Utilization"?

A. Lumens received on the working plane/Lumens emitted by the lamp
B. Lumens received on the working plane/Lux of the lamp
C. Lux of the lamp/Lumens received on the working plane
D. Lux of the lamp/Foot-candle on the working plane

Q.62 In the following circuit find the value of V_{TH} and R_{TH}

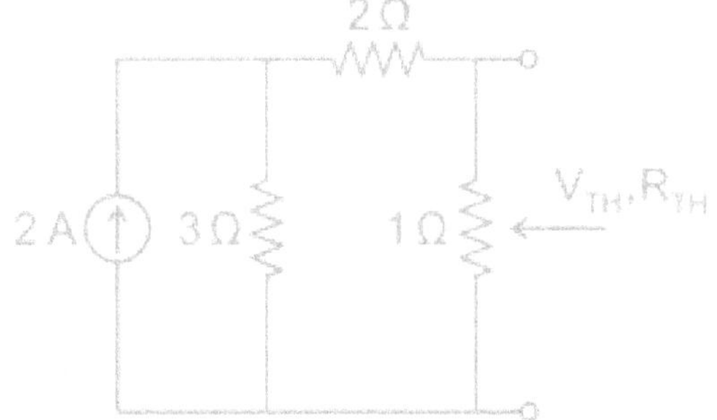

A. 1 V, $\frac{5}{3}$ Ω

B. 2 V, $\frac{5}{6}$ Ω

C. 1 V, $\frac{7}{6}$ Ω

D. 1 V, $\frac{5}{6}$ Ω

Q.63 _______ is the torque developed by the motor when full voltage is applied to its stator winding.

A. Starting torque

B. Running torque

C. Pull-in torque

D. Pull-out torque

Q.64 For a transformer:

A. iron loss can be found by short-circuit test and copper loss by open-circuit test

B. iron loss can be found by open-circuit test and copper loss by short-circuit test

C. open-circuit test results can enable us to determine voltage regulation

D. short-circuit test results can enable us to determine efficiency

Q.65 A battery had a short-circuit current of 30 A and an open circuit voltage of 24 V. If the battery is connected to an electric bulb of resistance 2 Ω the power dissipated by the bulb is:

A. 80 W **B.** 1800 W **C.** 112.5 W **D.** 228 W

Q.66 As there is no _______ on conductors, therefore an entire cross-section of conductor is usefully utilized in DC transmission.

A. skin effect

B. resistance

C. corona loss

D. capture effect

Q.67 Two coils of inductances 4 H and 6 H are connected in parallel. If their mutual inductance is 3H, calculate the equivalent inductance of the combination mutual inductance opposes the self-inductance.

A. 0.9375 H

B. 1.9375 H

C. 0.5643 H

D. 1.6753 H

Q.68 Equalizer bus is necessary for the parallel operation of the:

A. Series generator only

B. series and over compound generators

C. series and under compound generators

D. Over compounded generator only

Q.69 What does the fourth colour band on a resistor mean?

A. The value of the resistor in ohms

B. The power rating in watts

C. The resistance material

D. The resistance tolerance in percent

Q.70 Common Mode Rejection ratio for a differential amplifier is the ratio of:

A. $\dfrac{Differential\ gain}{Common\ mode\ gain}$

B. $\dfrac{Differential\ gain}{Integrated\ gain}$

C. $\dfrac{Integrated\ gain}{Differential\ gain}$

D. $\dfrac{Common\ mode\ gain}{Differential\ gain}$

Q.71 By reducing the thickness of laminations, the Eddy current losses in a transformer _______.

A. is reduced

B. remains the same

C. is increased

D. keeps fluctuating

Q.72 In an open device, current through it is

A. Zero and voltage is unknown

B. Known and voltage is zero

C. Zero and voltage is also zero

D. Unknown and voltage is also unknown

Q.73 The critical temperature above which ferromagnetic materials lose their magnetic property is known as

A. Curie point

B. Hysteresis

C. Transition temperature

D. Recrystallization temperature

Q.74 If a DC series motor is operated on AC supply, it will

A. spark excessively

B. have poor efficiency

C. have a poor power factor

D. all of the above

Q.75 A 100 µH coil has a Q value of 200 at 2 MHz. The effective resistance of the coil is_______.

A. 2π Ω **B.** 4π Ω **C.** 6π Ω **D.** π Ω

Q.76 A 3-phase synchronous generator connected to infinite bus is operating at full load at lagging power factor. Suddenly, the prime mover fails, the machine will

A. Continue to operate as generator without delivering any power

B. Continue to operate as generator with increased armature current

C. Operate as motor at leading power factor

D. Operate as motor at lagging power factor

Q.77 The impedance of an ideal parallel LC circuit at resonance is

A. Infinite

B. Zero

C. 1K ohms

D. None of the above

Q.78 A table fan draws 350 mA from a 230 V AC supply at 0.75 power factor. Find the real power taken by the fan.

A. 75.785 watt

B. 34.657 watt

C. 55.453 watt

D. 60.375 watt

Q.79 200 V DC motor draws an armature current of 25 A. Its armature resistance is 0.8 ohm. The induced emf in the motor will be:

A. 240 V **B.** 220 V **C.** 180 V **D.** 200 V

Q.80 The trip coil of a circuit breaker is energized by:

A. DC voltage

B. AC voltage

C. Any voltage (AC or DC)

D. No supply is required

Q.81 If a phase sequence indicator rotates clockwise for a phase sequence of RYB, then what happens when the phase sequence is changed to BRY.

A. It will not rotate.

B. It will rotate anticlockwise only.

C. It will rotate clockwise or anticlockwise.

D. It will rotate clockwise only.

Q.82 In a series R-L-C circuit, R = 200, X_L = 350 and X_C = 150. The phase angle of the circuit is _______ degrees.

A. 0   **B.** 90   **C.** 45   **D.** 60

Q.83 The difference between an emf and potential difference is

A. Both are same

B. emf is generated and potential difference is across two points

C. emf is the voltage measured in open circuit and there is a potential difference when the load is connected.

D. potential difference is higher than emf.

Q.84 The diode in which impurities are heavily doped is

A. Varactor diode   **B.** PIN diode

C. Tunnel diode   **D.** Zener diode

Q.85 Which among these is a part of distribution system?

A. Feeders   **B.** Distributors

C. Service mains   **D.** All of these

Q.86 What will be the flux density (in T) of a material in free space, if the field strength of the material is 2×10^5 A-m^{-1} and the magnetic susceptibility of the material is 0.44×10^{-3}?

A. 0.25   **B.** 0.5   **C.** 0.75   **D.** 1

Q.87 It is required to measure the true open circuit e.m.f. of a battery. The best device is

A. D.C. voltmeter

B. Ammeter and a known resistance

C. D.C. potentiometer

D. None of the above

Q.88 Which device protects the high voltage surges on the power system?

A. Circuit breaker   **B.** Isolator

C. Insulator   **D.** Lightning arrester

Q.89 The current capacity of the battery depends upon

A. The kind of electrode metals used

B. The size of the electrodes

C. Volume of the electrolyte contained

D. All the above

Q.90 Which of the following statement is true about RMS voltage?

A. RMS voltage of a sinusoidal waveform is inversely proportional to the peak voltage

B. Most multi-meters measure RMS value assuming a non-sinusoidal waveform

C. The RMS value of a sinusoidal waveform gives double the heating effect than a DC current of the same value

D. The ratio of the RMS value of voltage to the maximum value of voltage is the same as the ratio of the RMS value of current to the maximum value of current

Q.91 A voltage divider is always a _______

A. series-parallel circuit

B. series circuit

C. parallel circuit

D. bridge circuit

Q.92 Consider a situation where a particular laboratory has several resisters of 100 Ω only. Which of the following combinations is the best for replacing a 150 Ω resistor in a circuit using the resistors available in the laboratory?

A. Three in series

B. Two in parallel and one in series

C. Two in parallel and two in series

D. Three in parallel

Q.93 If α = 0.995, I_E = 10 mA and I_{CO} = 0.5 μA, then I_{CEO} will be

A. 100 μA   **B.** 25 μA   **C.** 10.1 μA   **D.** 10.5 μA

Q.94 The hot resistance of a bulb's filament is higher than its cold resistance because the temperature coefficient of the filament is:

A. Zero

B. Negative

C. Positive

D. About 2 Ω per degree C

Q.95 A milliammeter of resistance 100 Ω is connected in series with a circuit. Its power consumption is 0.1 mW. Supposing it is replaced with a milliammeter of 200 Ω resistance, the power consumed will be:

A. 0.2 mW   **B.** 0.05 mW

C. 0.1 mW   **D.** 1 mW

Q.96 The power drawn from the source in the circuit of the figure is:

A. Zero   **B.** 160 watts

C. 240 watts   **D.** 250 watts

Q.97 A transformer on no load has an induced emf of 230V (rms), draws a current of 2A (rms) and having angle between them is 60°, then the value of core loss is _______.

A. 150 W   **B.** 100 W   **C.** 230 W   **D.** 200 W

Q.98 The drift current in semiconductors depends upon:

A. Mobility of charge carriers

B. Type of circuit

C. Current source

D. None of these

Q.99 Potier triangle is required to calculate voltage regulation in which of the following method?

A. Synchronous impedance method

B. Ampere-turn method

C. MMF method

D. ZPF method

Q.100 In order to separate iron losses of a transformer into its components, we keep

A. Ratio $\frac{V}{f}$ constant

B. V (i.e. voltage constant)

C. Frequency (f) constant

D. None of these

Q.101 Energy can neither be created nor destroyed but still everybody discuss about the energy crisis because

A. Energy transform into different form continuously.

B. Usable form of energy is dissipated to the surroundings in less usable forms.

C. Energy is consumed and cannot be used again.

D. All of these

Q.102 An ideal source of energy should have

A. higher calorific value

B. easy transportability

C. easy accessibility

D. All of these

Q.103 Fossil fuels are

A. non-renewable source of energy

B. renewable source of energy

C. both (a) and (b)

D. Neither (a) nor (b)

Q.104 Dead organisms are transformed into petroleum and natural gas in

A. presence of air   **B.** absence of air

C. presence of sunlight   **D.** none of the above

Q.105 Which of the following problem is associated with a burning of coal?

A. Carbon-dioxide emission

B. acid rain

C. ash with toxic metal supurity

D. all of these.

Q.106 Select the important factor for the site selection of a thermal power plant.

A. Distance from the populated area

B. Availability of fuel

C. Availability' of water

D. Cost of plant

Q.107 Which of these is a 'working fluid' in the liquid phase?

A. Water   **B.** Steam   **C.** Mercury   **D.** Oxygen

Q.108 Biogas is a better fuel than animal dung cake because

A. biogas has lower calorific value.

B. animal dung cake has high calorific value

C. biogas bums smoke and leaves no residue

D. biogas is used as a fuel for cooking only wheareas dung cake can be used for cooking, illuminant the lanterns.

Q.109 Which of the following organism produces biogas from cow drug sherry in the biogas plant?

A. aerobic bectria   **B.** anaerobic bectria

C. protozoa   **D.** fungi

Q.110 Wind is caused due to

A. uneven heating of earth's surface

B. rotation of earth

C. local conditions

D. All of these

Q.111 What are the disadvantage of solar energy

A. A large surface area is required collect the solar.

B. Daily average of solar energy varies from 4 to 7 kwh/m^2.

C. Highly hazardous toxic material is used in the manufacturing of solar device.

D. All of the above are disadvantages.

Q.112 The temperature inside the solar cooker ranges from

A. 500-100°C   **B.** 100-140°C

C. 150-200°C   **D.** 70-80°C

Q.113 The use of reflector in the solar cooker is to

A. Decrease efficiency

B. create green house effect

C. increase efficiency

D. none of these

Q.114 Solar cells are made of

A. germanium   **B.** silicon

C. silver   **D.** aluminium

Q.115 The material used for interconnection the solar cells in the solar panel is

A. silicon   **B.** silver

C. aluminium   **D.** copper

Q.116 A solar panel is made by combining in an arrangement

A. solar concentrator   **B.** solar cookers

C. solar cells   **D.** solar chimney

Q.117 Tidal energy is a farm of energy obtained from the

A. motion of surface water in ponds

B. ocean in the form of tidal waves

C. tides occurs in the river water

D. motion of the wave in sea

Q.118 Tidal energy is harnessed by constructing a dam across

A. narrow opening to the sea

B. wide opening to the sea

C. the river in hilly trains

D. the river in plane areas

Q.119 Wave energy is caused due to

A. strong winds blowing across the sea

B. kinetic energy possessed by huge waves near the sea shore

C. potential energy possessed by the stored water

D. both (a) and (b)

Q.120 The working fluid in ocean thermal power plant is

A. Volatile liquid like ammonia

B. petrol

C. charcoal

D. liquified petroleum gas

// Smart Answer Sheet //

Correct   Indicates percentage of students who answered questions correctly.

Skipped   Indicates percentage of students who skipped questions.

Q.	Ans.	Correct / Skipped	Q.	Ans.	Correct / Skipped	Q.	Ans.	Correct / Skipped	Q.	Ans.	Correct / Skipped	Q.	Ans.	Correct / Skipped
1	A	36.11 % / 30.56 %	17	B	19.44 % / 55.56 %	33	A	5.56 % / 61.11 %	49	B	36.11 % / 47.22 %	65	C	8.33 % / 50.0 %
2	D	11.11 % / 50.0 %	18	B	16.67 % / 58.33 %	34	D	5.56 % / 47.22 %	50	C	36.11 % / 47.22 %	66	A	33.33 % / 47.23 %
3	B	13.89 % / 61.11 %	19	C	11.11 % / 61.11 %	35	D	11.11 % / 61.11 %	51	D	11.11 % / 55.56 %	67	A	5.56 % / 58.33 %
4	B	38.89 % / 52.78 %	20	D	19.44 % / 58.34 %	36	D	2.78 % / 61.11 %	52	A	19.44 % / 55.56 %	68	B	27.78 % / 50.0 %
5	B	44.44 % / 55.56 %	21	B	27.78 % / 52.78 %	37	D	16.67 % / 63.89 %	53	A	19.44 % / 47.23 %	69	D	33.33 % / 52.78 %
6	B	30.56 % / 58.33 %	22	B	16.67 % / 55.55 %	38	B	11.11 % / 66.67 %	54	C	13.89 % / 52.78 %	70	A	25.0 % / 50.0 %
7	B	16.67 % / 58.33 %	23	A	11.11 % / 63.89 %	39	D	5.56 % / 66.66 %	55	B	25.0 % / 50.0 %	71	A	30.56 % / 47.22 %
8	D	22.22 % / 63.89 %	24	A	19.44 % / 55.56 %	40	D	13.89 % / 66.67 %	56	A	30.56 % / 52.77 %	72	A	47.22 % / 47.22 %
9	A	8.33 % / 55.56 %	25	C	36.11 % / 55.56 %	41	A	47.22 % / 47.22 %	57	C	11.11 % / 47.22 %	73	A	38.89 % / 47.22 %
10	D	25.0 % / 55.56 %	26	D	27.78 % / 55.55 %	42	A	27.78 % / 47.22 %	58	A	44.44 % / 47.23 %	74	D	47.22 % / 47.22 %
11	A	25.0 % / 55.56 %	27	A	36.11 % / 55.56 %	43	A	19.44 % / 50.0 %	59	C	16.67 % / 50.0 %	75	A	30.56 % / 50.0 %
12	B	19.44 % / 55.56 %	28	A	25.0 % / 58.33 %	44	B	8.33 % / 55.56 %	60	A	27.78 % / 47.22 %	76	D	13.89 % / 55.55 %
13	A	30.56 % / 55.55 %	29	A	27.78 % / 58.33 %	45	A	30.56 % / 47.22 %	61	A	27.78 % / 50.0 %	77	A	22.22 % / 47.22 %
14	D	30.56 % / 50.0 %	30	D	16.67 % / 52.77 %	46	B	27.78 % / 50.0 %	62	D	13.89 % / 50.0 %	78	D	38.89 % / 47.22 %
15	C	30.56 % / 55.55 %	31	C	13.89 % / 61.11 %	47	B	30.56 % / 50.0 %	63	A	27.78 % / 47.22 %	79	C	41.67 % / 47.22 %
16	D	33.33 % / 58.34 %	32	B	19.44 % / 52.78 %	48	C	30.56 % / 47.22 %	64	B	41.67 % / 47.22 %	80	C	19.44 % / 47.23 %

Q.	Ans.	Correct		Q.	Ans.	Correct		Q.	Ans.	Correct		Q.	Ans.	Correct		Q.	Ans.	Correct
		Skipped				Skipped				Skipped				Skipped				Skipped
81	D	22.22 %		89	B	13.89 %		97	C	36.11 %		105	D	47.22 %		113	C	47.22 %
		47.22 %				47.22 %				50.0 %				47.22 %				47.22 %
82	C	27.78 %		90	D	41.67 %		98	A	50.0 %		106	C	27.78 %		114	B	44.44 %
		50.0 %				47.22 %				47.22 %				47.22 %				47.23 %
83	C	16.67 %		91	B	38.89 %		99	D	19.44 %		107	A	27.78 %		115	B	33.33 %
		47.22 %				47.22 %				52.78 %				47.22 %				47.23 %
84	C	19.44 %		92	B	41.67 %		100	A	30.56 %		108	C	38.89 %		116	C	50.0 %
		50.0 %				47.22 %				52.77 %				47.22 %				47.22 %
85	D	50.0 %		93	A	16.67 %		101	D	33.33 %		109	B	38.89 %		117	B	41.67 %
		47.22 %				55.55 %				47.23 %				47.22 %				47.22 %
86	A	8.33 %		94	C	33.33 %		102	D	50.0 %		110	D	38.89 %		118	A	22.22 %
		55.56 %				47.23 %				47.22 %				47.22 %				47.22 %
87	C	30.56 %		95	A	22.22 %		103	A	44.44 %		111	D	33.33 %		119	D	38.89 %
		47.22 %				50.0 %				47.23 %				47.23 %				44.44 %
88	D	36.11 %		96	B	13.89 %		104	B	33.33 %		112	B	27.78 %		120	A	30.56 %
		47.22 %				47.22 %				47.23 %				47.22 %				47.22 %

Performance Analysis

Avg. Score (%)	25.0%
Toppers Score (%)	90.83%
Your Score	

//Hints and Solutions//

1. $x(x + y) = 247$
$y(x + y) = 114$
$\Rightarrow x^2 + y^2 + 2xy = 361$
$(x + y)^2 = 361$
$\therefore x + y = 19$
Hence, the correct option is (a).

2. We need to find the number from 7 to 1299

The numbers which are divided by the $6 = \dfrac{1299}{6} = $ integral part 216

Number which is divisible by $9 = $ integral part of $\dfrac{1299}{9} = 144$

Number which are divisible by $18 = $ Integral part $\dfrac{1299}{18} = $ integral part, 72

The number which is divided by 6 or 9 or both
$= 216 + 144 - 72 = 288$
Hence, the correct option is (d).

3. $s(n) = 3n^2 + 5n$
$\Rightarrow$ First term $= S(1) = 8$
$\Rightarrow$ Sum of first two term
$= S(2) = 3(2)^2 + 5(2) = 22$
$\Rightarrow$ Second term $= 22 - 8 = 14$
So, $a = 8$ and $d = 6$
$T_n = 164$
$8 + (n - 1)6 = 164$
$n = 27$
Hence, the correct option is (b).

4. $\dfrac{1\frac{1}{4} \div 1\frac{1}{2}}{\frac{1}{15} + 1 - \frac{9}{10}}$

$\Rightarrow \dfrac{\frac{5}{4} \div \frac{3}{2}}{\frac{2 + 30 - 27}{30}}$

$\Rightarrow \dfrac{\frac{5}{6}}{\frac{5}{30}}$

$\Rightarrow \dfrac{\frac{5}{6}}{\frac{1}{6}} = 5$

Hence, the correct option is (b).

5. $p : q = 7 : 9$
$q : r = 15 : 7$
$\dfrac{p}{q} = \dfrac{7}{9} \dots \dots (i)$
$\dfrac{q}{r} = \dfrac{15}{7} \dots \dots (ii)$
Now multiplying equation (i) and (ii)
$\dfrac{p}{q} \times \dfrac{q}{r} = \dfrac{7}{9} \times \dfrac{15}{7} \Rightarrow \dfrac{p}{r} = \dfrac{5}{3}$
Hence, the correct option is (b).

6. $\dfrac{x}{a} = \dfrac{y}{b} \Rightarrow \dfrac{x}{y} = \dfrac{a}{b}$
$\dfrac{y}{b} = \dfrac{z}{c} \Rightarrow \dfrac{y}{z} = \dfrac{b}{c}$
and $\dfrac{z}{c} = \dfrac{x}{a} \Rightarrow \dfrac{z}{x} = \dfrac{c}{a}$
$\dfrac{a}{b} : \dfrac{b}{c} : \dfrac{c}{a} = a^2c : ab^2 : bc^2$
Hence, the correct option is (b).

7. Ratio of initial investments $= \dfrac{7}{2} : \dfrac{4}{3} : \dfrac{6}{5} = 105 : 40 : 36$

Let the initial investments be $105x, 40x$ and $36x$.
Ankit: Bhusan : Chetan
$= \left(105x \times 4 + \frac{150}{100} \times 105x \times 8\right) : (40x \times 12) : (36x \times 12)$
$= 35 : 10 : 9$

Hence, Chetan's share in the profit $= Rs. \left(\dfrac{9}{54} \times 10800\right) = Rs. 1800$
Hence, the correct option is (b).

8. Let, $AB = AC = 2x$
$\Rightarrow AQ = QC = x$
Let, $AP = a$
$\Rightarrow AP \times AB = AQ^2$
$\Rightarrow a \times 2x = x^2$
$\Rightarrow a = \dfrac{x}{2}$
$\Rightarrow AP : AB$
$\Rightarrow \dfrac{x}{2} : 2x$
$\Rightarrow 1 : 4$
Hence, the correct option is (d).

9. The correct sentence is "I have been waiting for my friend since morning."
replace 'I am waiting' with 'I have been waiting' because the given sentence is in present perfect continuous tense thus the structure is:
Subject + has/have + been + present participle (verb + ing) + time reference.
Hence, the correct option is (a).

10. From the given series-
$9 \times 2 = 18$
$18 \times 4 = 72$
$72 \times 8 = 576$
$576 \times 16 = 9216$
Hence, the correct option is (d).

11. The series is nnmm/nnmn/nnmm/nnmm. Thus, the pattern 'nnmm' is repeated.
Hence, the correct option is (a).

12. We need honest workers, not people of doubtful integrity.
Redoubtable (adj.) (Of a person): causing fear and respect
Doubtful : Uncertain, undecided and contingent, often use to admitting of doubt.
Hence, the correct option is (b).

13. The word 'behind' will fill in the blank. The sentence means that the deceased (the person who recently died), left behind him two young children.
Hence, the correct option is (a).

14. The phrase 'stands as' will fill in the blank because it means to signify.Hence, the correct option is (d).

15. The sentence is an interrogative sentence and started with has. The passive voice will also start with has.
Rule : Has + subject + been + V_3 + Optional Agents.
Passive: Has your question been answered ?
Hence, the correct option is (c).

16. Rules for such interrogative sentences changed to indirect speech :
(a) Reporting verb is changed into ask or enquire of.
(b) If or whether is used as a linking word.
(c) The auxiliary verb in the reported speech is used after the subject.
(d) If the sentence begins with who, which, what, how, when, where, why etc., these are not changed and if or whether is not used.
Hence, the correct option is (d).

17.

1. Former cricketer and Indian cricket team coach Ravi Shastri is turning entrepreneur with the launch of a male grooming and hygiene products line '23 Yards'.

2. He has partnered with personal care manufacturer Ador Multi products Ltd, which will help create grooming products.

3. These will include beard oils, body wash, aftershave, deodorant and hand sanitizer for a target group of 25 to 40 years
Hence, the correct option is (b).

18.

1. In Maharashtra, the committee appointed to control the price of masks and sanitizers, has submitted a report to the State Government.

2. After the approval of the government, it will be mandatory to sell masks at the revised rate.

3. With this, Maharashtra will become the first state to cap the prices of masks.

4. The prices of sanitizers are also being capped as well.
Hence, the correct option is (b).

19.

1. The United Nations General Assembly established 9 December as the International Day of Commemoration and Dignity of the Victims of the Crime of Genocide and of the Prevention of this Crime.

2. On this day in 1948, the Convention on the Prevention and Punishment of the Crime of Genocide was adopted.

3. The purpose of the day is to raise awareness of the Genocide Convention.
Hence, the correct option is (c).

20.

1. IRCTC will restart the first set of private Tejas Express, Lucknow-New Delhi and Ahmedabad-Mumbai trains from 17th of October 2020.

2. The operation of these two Tejas Trains was suspended from 19th of March 2020 due to spread of COVID-19 pandemic.

3. Every alternate seat will be kept vacant following the social distancing norms for the initial period.
Hence, the correct option is (d).

21.

1. Drug firm Zydus Cadila is launching pressurized metered-dose inhaler for patients suffering from Chronic Obstructive Pulmonary Disease (COPD) in India.

2. Forglyn pMDI is India's first pressurized Metered Dose Inhaler.

3. Forglyn pMDI is priced at ₹495 per pack and has been developed in-house using Zydus' innovations in formulation technology.
Hence, the correct option is (b).

22.

1. Titan Co. Ltd has announced an end to its five-year-old joint venture partnership with German luxury brand Montblanc.

2. Titan's decision to exit the joint venture agreement was driven by the company's consolidation strategy to focus on its primary business and proprietary brands such as Tanishq Jewellery and Titan watches.
Hence, the correct option is (b).

23.

1. In order to boost its economic ties with Bangladesh, the US will open its Foreign Commercial Service Office in Dhaka.

2. Bangladesh and the US agreed to implement reforms to improve the investment climate for US-sourced Foreign Direct Investment (FDI) in Bangladesh.

3. The US agreed to ask the American companies to invest in key sectors like energy, IT, pharmaceutics and agriculture.
Hence, the correct option is (a).

24.

1. The Union Cabinet has given its approval for signing a Memorandum of Cooperation (MoC) in the field of cybersecurity between India and Japan.

2. It is aimed at enhancing cooperation in emerging technologies, protection of critical infrastructure, cyberspace and to mitigate threats to communication networks.

3. It will also strengthen the security of ICT infrastructure.
Hence, the correct option is (a).

25. 1st May is the International Workers' Day. International Workers' Day, also known as Labour Day in some countries and

often referred to as May Day, is a celebration of labourers and the working classes that is promoted by the international labour movement and occurs every year on May Day.
Hence, the correct option is (c).

26. May 21, the death anniversary of ex-prime minister of India, Shri Rajiv Gandhi is also observed as Anti Terrorism Day in India.
Hence, the correct option is (d).

27. Water vapor, water vapor or aqueous vapor is the gaseous phase of water. It is one state of water within the hydrosphere. Water vapor can be produced from the evaporation or boiling of liquid water or from the sublimation of ice. Unlike other forms of water, water vapor is invisible. Under typical atmospheric conditions, water vapor is continuously generated by evaporation and removed by condensation. It is less dense than air and triggers convection currents that can lead to clouds.
Hence, the correct option is (a).

28. It spilled 10.8 million US gallons (260,000 bbl) (or 37,000 metric tonnes) of crude oil over the next few days. It is considered to be one of the worst human-caused environmental disasters. The Valdez spill is the second largest in US waters, after the 2010 Deep water Horizon oil spill, in terms of volume released.
Hence, the correct option is (a).

29. Where a Proclamation of Emergency is in operation, the President may by order declare that the right to move any court for the enforcement of such of 1[the rights conferred by Part III (except articles 20 and 21)] as may be mentioned in the order and all proceedings pending in any court for the enforcement of the rights so mentioned shall remain suspended for the period during which the Proclamation is in force or for such shorter period as may be specified in the order.
Hence, the correct option is (a).

30. The correct chronological order of the formation of states as full states of Indian Union:
Nagaland on 1st December 1963.
Haryana on 1st November 1966.
Sikkim on 16th May 1975.
Arunachal Pradesh on 20th Feb 1987.
Hence, the correct option is (d).

31.

1. The Union Cabinet has approved the Railway Ministry's proposal for a revised cost estimate for the construction of the Kolkata East-West Metro Corridor project at ₹8,575 crores.

2. The 16.6km corridor will have 12 stations between Salt Lake Sector-V and Howrah Maidan.

3. The project will be implemented by a special purpose vehicle, Kolkata Metro Rail Corp. Ltd, set up under the railway ministry.Hence, the correct option is (c).

32. Sri Lanka got the status of Test playing country in 1981, and beat India in the 1979 World Cup. Before this they were champion of ICC non-test playing countries.
Hence, the correct option is (b).

33. Assume the total production of the first year as 1000, second year becomes 12000, third year 14400 and fourth year 17280.
Then,

0.2 ×17280 - 0.2 ×12000 = 1056
But this difference is given as 2640.
Hence, the value of production will be; 25000, 30000, 36000, and 43200 respectively for the 4 years.
Revenue = 125 × 0.4 × 30000 = 1500000.
Hence, the correct option is (a).

34. Assume the total production of the first year as 1000, second year becomes 12000, third year 14400 and fourth year 17280. Then,
0.2 ×17280 - 0.2 ×12000 = 1056

Bur this difference is given as 2640.
Hence, the value of production will be; 25000, 30000, 36000, and 43200 respectively for the 4 years.
Ratio of the number of units C produced in four year ,
= 0.2 ×25000 : 0.2 ×30000 : 0.2×36000 : 0.2×43200
250 : 300:360 :432 = 175 : 150 :180 :216
Hence, the correct option is (d).

35. Assume the total production of the first year as 1000, second year becomes 12000, third year 14400 and fourth year 17280.
Then,
0.2 ×17280 - 0.2 ×12000 = 1056
Bur this difference is given as 2640.
Hence, the value of production will be; 25000, 30000, 36000, and 43200 respectively for the 4 years.
Ratio of revenue generated in 2002,
= 2 × 3 : 4 × 5 : 2 × 7 : 2 × 8
= 6 : 20 : 14 : 16
= 3 : 10 : 7 : 8
Hence, the correct option is (d).

36. Assume the total production of the first year as 1000, second year becomes 12000, third year 14400 and fourth year 17280.
Then,
0.2 × 17280 - 0.2 ×12000 = 1056
Bur this difference is given as 2640.
Hence, the value of production will be; 25000, 30000, 36000, and 43200 respectively for the 4 years.

Growth rate of production = $\dfrac{(144-87.5)\times100}{87.5} = 65\%$ (approx)
Hence, the correct option is (d).

37. People who speak telugu $= 6\%$

People who speak hindi $= 18\%$

Percentage $= \dfrac{6}{18} \times 100$

$= 33\dfrac{1}{3}\%$

Hence, the correct option is (D).

38. Central angle $= 360 \times \dfrac{10}{100}$

$= 36°$

Hence, the correct option is (B).

39. As there is not given total population of India so data is inadequate to find Bengali speaking people.

Hence, the correct option is (D).

40. Hindi + Telugu = 18+6 = 24%

Hindi + Marathi = 18+14 = 32%

Malayalam + Punjabi = 11+17 = 28%

Punjabi + Hindi = 17+18 = 35%

So, Punjabi and Hindi speaking people are more in India.

Hence, the correct option is (D).

41. Concept:
We know that

$$P = \frac{V^2}{R}$$

Here P = Power, V = Voltage, R = Resistance
Calculation:

$$R = \frac{230^2}{100} = 529\Omega$$

Hence, the correct option is (a).

42. $(3 + j4)$ and $(3 - j4)$ are connected in parallel and this combination is in series with $\frac{17}{6}\Omega$ resistance.

Total impedance $(Z) = \frac{17}{6} + [(3 + j4) \parallel (3 - j4)]$

$$Z = \frac{17}{6} + \frac{(3+j4)(3-j4)}{3+j4+3-j4} = \frac{17}{6} + \frac{25}{6} = 7 + j0$$

Hence, the correct option is (a).

43. If the two coils are connected in series aiding, then L equation

$$= L_1 + L_2 + 2M$$

We know that

$$M = K\sqrt{L_1 L_2} = 0.5\sqrt{4 \times 9} = 3$$

Total inductance will be $= 4 + 9 + 2(3) = 19mH$
Hence, the correct option is (a).

44.

1. The input characteristics resemble the illuminated photo diode and the output characteristics resemble the forward biased diode

2. PN photodiodes are used in similar applications to other photodetectors, such as photoconductors, charge-coupled devices, and photomultiplier tubes

3. They are used to generate an output which is dependent upon the illumination or to change the state of circuitry.
   Hence, the correct option is (b).

45. Regenerative braking uses an energy recovery mechanism which slows down a vehicle by converting its kinetic energy into another form.

Important:

Regenerative braking: In this type braking back emf Eb is greater than the supply voltage V, which reverses the direction of the motor armature current. The motor begins to operate as an electric generator.

Dynamic braking: In this type of braking, the DC motor is disconnected from the supply and a braking resistor Rb is immediately connected across the armature. The motor will now work as a generator and produces the braking torque.

Plugging: In this method, the terminals of supply are reversed, as a result of the generator torque also reverses which resists the normal rotation of the motor and as a result the speed decreases. Hence, the correct option is (a).

46. Given that, deflection sensitivity (s) = 10 m/v
Deflection factor (D) is reciprocal of sensitivity.

$$D = \frac{1}{s} = \frac{1}{10} = 0.1 \text{ v/m}$$

Hence, the correct option is (b).

47. We know that
Rate of change of the flux $\propto$ frequency The rate of change of the flux within the coil will be increased due to the increase in frequency. Hence, the induced EMF is maximum in case of 1 amp 100 Hz supply source in the coil. Hence, the correct option is (b).

48. Appearance: The general appearance of an underground system is better as all the distribution lines are invisible.
Fault location and repairs: In general, there are little chances of faults in an underground system. However, if a fault does occur, it is difficult to locate and repair this system. On an overhead system, the conductors are visible and easily accessible so that fault locations and repairs can be easily made.
Initial cost: The underground system is more expensive due to the high cost of trenching, conduits, cables, manholes and other special equipment. The initial cost of an underground system may be five to ten times than that of an overhead system.
Hence, the correct option is (c).

49.

Function	code	Colour
single phase line		Red/Brown
single phase neutral		Black/Blue
single phase protective ground or earth		Green
Three phase line 1		Red
Three phase line 2		Yellow
Three phase line 3		Blue
Three phase neutral		Black
Three phase protective ground or earth		Green (or) Green Yellow

Hence, the correct option is (b).

50. In pure capacitive circuit, the current leads the voltage by 90°.
In series RC circuit, the current leads the voltage by an angle in between 0 to 90°.
In pure inductive circuit, the current lags the voltage by 90°.
In series RL circuit, the current lags the voltage by an angle in between 0 to 90°.
Hence, the correct option is (c).

51.

1. Most of the fractional horsepower motors have either plain or sleeve bearings.

2. Plain bearings and sleeve bearings (also referred to as bushings or journal bearings) are used to constrain, guide or reduce friction in rotary or linear applications.

3. They function via a sliding action instead of the rolling action used by ball, roller, and needle bearings.

4. Plain bearings and sleeve bearings are made from a variety of materials and are often self-lubricating to provide smooth operation and greater durability.

5. They consist of one part that is built up of many types of materials, layered and combined into a load carrying system.

6. Plain and sleeve bearings are often very inexpensive, compact, lightweight, and have a high load-carrying capacity.

Hence, the correct option is (d).

52. At low slip region (normal running range), the torque is proportional to slip. Hence, in the normal working region of the motor, the value of the slip is small. The torque slip curve is a straight line.

Torque $\propto$ slip

At the low-speed range, the torque is inversely proportional to slip which is shown in the figure.

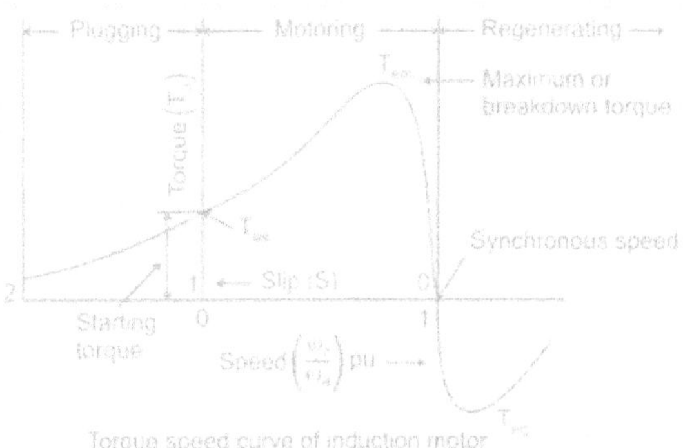

Torque speed curve of induction motor

In a three-phase induction motor, the developed torque is approximately directly proportional to slip in normal running range and inversely proportional to It in the low-speed range. Hence, the correct option is (a).

53. Resistance switching:

1. It is a method adopted for dampening the over-voltage transients due to current chopping.

2. In this method, a shunt resistance is connected across the contacts of the circuit breaker.

3. It reduces the rate of rising of re-striking voltage and the peak value of re-striking voltage.

4. It helps to reduce the voltage transient surge during current chopping and capacitive current breaking.

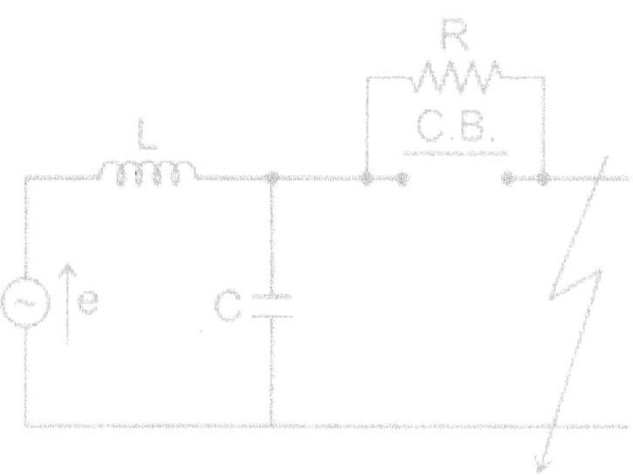

Hence, the correct option is (a).

54. Here, only R_L is variable hence for maximum power transfer occurs when the

$$R_L = \sqrt{R_s^2 + (X_s + X_c)^2}$$
$$R_L = \sqrt{2^2 + 1^2} = \sqrt{5}$$

Maximum power

$$P_{max} = \frac{V_s^2}{4R_L} = \frac{(20)^2}{4 \times \sqrt{5}} = 44.72W$$

Hence, the correct option is (c).

55. Need for composite systems:

1. 1 - φ AC system is preferable in the view of distribution cost and distribution voltage can be stepped up to high voltage with the use of transformers, which reduces the transmission losses

2. In DC system, DC series motors have most desirable features

3. In 3 – φ system, three phase induction motor has the advantage of automatic regenerative braking

4. So, it is necessary to combine the advantages of the DC/AC and 3-φ/1-φ systems; It leads to evolution of composite systems

Composite systems are of two types:

Single phase to DC system:

1. In this system, the advantages of both 1 – φ and DC systems are combined to get high voltage for distribution

2. High voltage distribution can be achieved through with single phase distribution networks

3. DC series motor is employed for producing the necessary propelling torque

4. Normal operating voltage employed of distribution is 25 kV at 50 Hz

5. This track electrification is used in India

Single phase to three phase system:

1. In this system, 1 – φ AC system is preferred for distribution network

2. Three phase induction motors are employed as traction motor

3. The voltage used for the distribution network is about 15 – 25 kV at 50 Hz
Hence, the correct option is (b).

56. An ideal rectifier should have:

1. Efficiency = 100%
2. AC components (V_{ac}) = 0
3. Transformer Utilization Factor = 1
4. Power Factor = 1
Hence, the correct option is (a).

57.

1. Split phase induction motors have low starting current and moderate starting torque.
2. So, these motors are used in fans, blowers, centrifugal pumps, washing machine, grinder, lathes, air conditioning fans, etc.
3. These motors are available in the size ranging from 0.05 kW to 0.5 kW.
Hence, the correct option is (c).

58. Given that, number of turns (N) = 100
Current (I) = 0.2 AMmf = NI = 100 × 0.2 = 20 Amp-turnsHence, the correct option is (a).

59. The electric drives possess the drawback of non-availability of various ratings.
Hence, the correct option is (c).

60. Windage losses refer to the losses sustained by a machine due to the resistance offered by air to the rotation of the shaft. Windage Losses occurs in electric rotating machines such as motors and generators.

Important Points:

Losses in DC machines:

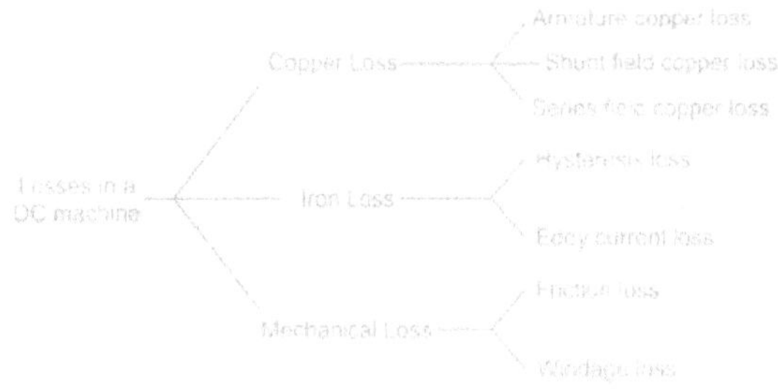

Hence, the correct option is (a).

61. Coefficient of utilization or utilization factor: It is defined as the ratio of a total number of lumens reaching the working plane to the total number of lumens emitting from the source.
Important Point:
Maintenance factor: It is defined as the ratio of illumination under normal working conditions to the illumination when everything is clean.
Its value is always less than 1, and it will be around 0.8. This is due to the accumulation of dust, dirt, and smoke on the lamps due to which they emit less light than that they emit when they are clean. Frequent cleaning of the lamp will improve the maintenance factor.

Depreciation factor: It is defined as the ratio of initial illumination to the ultimately maintained illumination on the working plane.

$$Depreciation\ factor\ =\ \frac{1}{maintenance\ factor}$$

Its value is always more than 1.
Hence, the correct option is (a).

62. Current through 10 resistor (using current division)
$$= \frac{2 \times 3}{3 + 3} = 1 amp$$
The voltage across 1 -ohm branch $= V_{th} = 1$ volt
$$R_{th} = 1 \parallel 5 = \frac{1 \times 5}{6} = \frac{5}{6} \Omega$$
(Replacing current source by its internal impedance i.e. open circuit)
Hence, the correct option is (d).

63. Starting torque: It is the torque developed by the motor when full voltage is applied to its stator winding.

Synchronous torque: It is the torque that acts on the shaft of a synchronous machine when the rotational speed of the rotor deviates from the synchronous speed and that keeps the machine in synchronism.

Pull-in torque:

1. A synchronous motor is started as an induction motor during starting condition and its speed below 2 to 5% of the synchronous speed
2. When the excitation (DC supply) to the field winding is applied, the motor pull into synchronism resulting stator and rotor magnetic field rotates at the same speed
3. The amount of torque requires for the synchronous motor to pull into synchronism is called as pull in torque

Pull-out torque:

1. It is maximum torque which the synchronous motor can develop without pulling out of step
2. When the synchronous motor is loaded, the rotor falls back by some angle a is called a load angle
3. The stator and rotor magnetic rotate at synchronous speed in spite of some load is applied on the rotor
4. The synchronous motor developed maximum torque when the rotor falls back by angle 90°
5. When the load increases beyond its maximum rating, the rotor steps out of synchronism and synchronous motor stop
Hence, the correct option is (a).

64. For a transformer, the iron loss can be found by open-circuit test and copper loss by short-circuit test

The open-circuit test on transformer is used to determine core losses in transformer and parameters of the shunt branch of the equivalent circuit of the transformer. Hence using the open circuit test, we can determine the magnetizing impedance.

The short circuit test on transformer is used to determine the copper loss in a transformer at full load and parameters of an approximate equivalent circuit of the transformer.
Hence, the correct option is (b).

65. Given:

Open circuit voltage $= V_{OC} = 24V$,

Short circuit current $= I_{SC} = 30A$

We know that

Resistance $= \dfrac{V_{OC}}{I_{SC}} = \dfrac{30}{24} = 1.2\Omega$

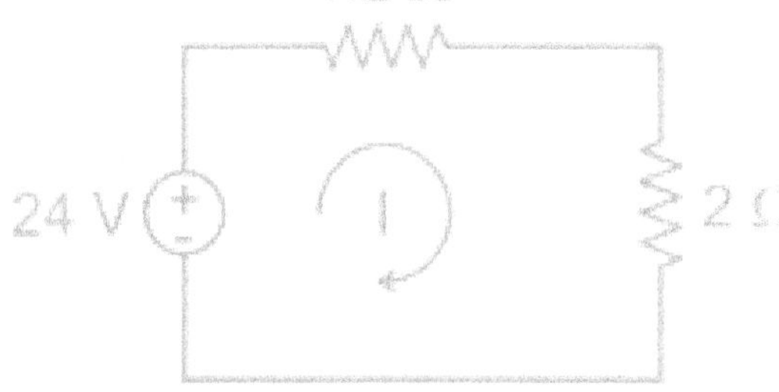

Current $I = \dfrac{V}{R} = \dfrac{24}{3.2} = 7.5A$

The power dissipated by the bulb is $= I^2 \times R = 7.5^2 \times 2 = 112.5W$

Hence, the correct option is (c).

66. Skin effect is the tendency of an alternating electric current to become distributed within a conductor such that the current density is largest near the surface of the conductor and decreases with greater depths in the conductor.

The electric current flows mainly at the skin of the conductor, between the outer surface and a level called the skin depth. The skin effect causes the effective resistance of the conductor to increase at higher frequencies where the skin depth is smaller, thus reducing the effective cross-section of the conductor.

Hence resistance in AC is greater than resistance in DC.
Hence, the correct option is (a).

67. Given:
$$L_1 = 4H \quad L_2 = 6H \quad M = 3H$$
Mutual inductance opposes the self-inductance
$$L = \dfrac{L_1 L_2 - M^2}{L_1 + L_2 + 2M} = \dfrac{4 \times 6 - 3^2}{4 + 6 + 2 \times 3} = 0.9375H$$

Important:
Mutual inductance assists the self-inductance
$$L = \dfrac{L_1 L_2 - M^2}{L_1 + L_2 - 2M}$$
Hence, the correct option is (a).

68. For satisfactory parallel operation of dc series generators and over the compound generator, it is necessary to connect the armatures of the two machines through a heavy copper bar, called the equalizing bar.

An equalizer bar has a low resistance conductor wire, which connects together the points in the armature winding which should be at the same potentials.

Important Points:

The functions of the equalizer bus are:

1. To cause the circulating current to flow within the armature winding itself, without letting them pass through the brushes.

2. To avoid unequal distribution of current at the brushes thereby helping to get sparkles commutation.

3. To save the brushes from handling the circulating currents.

4. To reduce the magnetic flux unbalance that cause the potential difference in various parallel paths.
   Hence, the correct option is (b).

69. The four band colour code is the most common variation. These resistors have two bands for the resistance value, one multiplier and one tolerance band

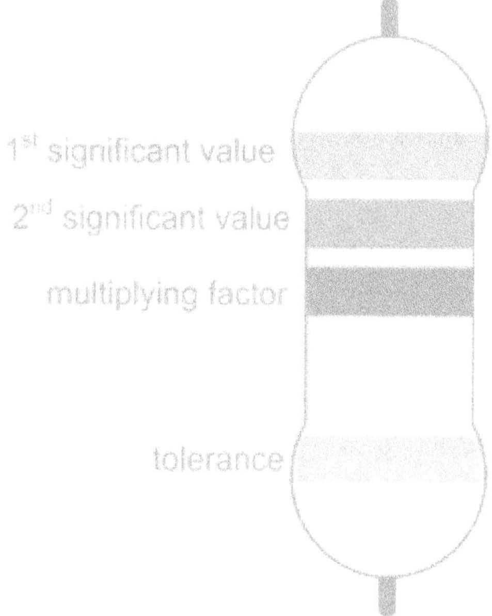

Hence, the correct option is (d).

70.

1. Common Mode Rejection Ratio (CMRR) is defined as the ratio of differential-mode gain to common-mode gain taken in magnitude

2. CMRR stands for Common Mode Rejection Ratio It is the ability of an operational amplifier to reject the common-mode signals at the input terminals

3. For practical differential amplimer, The Common Mode Rejection Ratio (CMMR) should be 80 to 100 dB
   Hence, the correct option is (a).

71. Concept:
Eddy current losses are given by
$$W_e = K_e f^2 B_m^2 t^2 v$$
Where $Ke =$ eddy current constant.
f is frequency
B_m is the flux density
t is thickness

v is volume

Here eddy current losses are directly proportional to the square of the thickness.

By reducing the thickness of laminations, the Eddy current losses in a transformer also get reduced.

Hence, the correct option is (a).

72. In an open device, the current through it is zero and the voltage is unknown

Important:

Short Circuit: It is an electrical circuit that allows a current to travel along an unintended path with zero or very low electrical impedance. This results in an excessive amount of current flowing into the circuit.

Ideally, it has zero resistance, hence high current will flow and no voltage drop across the terminals.

Open Circuit: It is a circuit where no current flows. Any circuit which does not have a return path to flow current is an open circuit.

It has infinite resistance, hence no current will flow.

Short circuit and open circuit can be represented as shown in the figure.

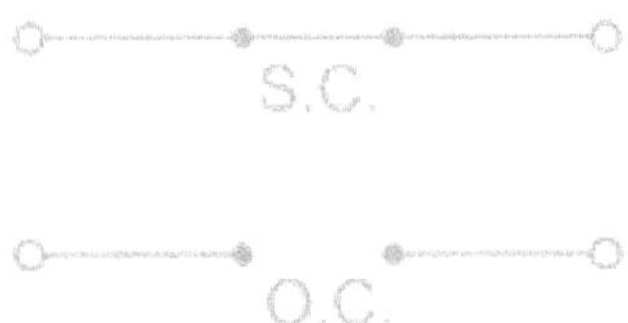

Hence, the correct option is (a).

73. Curie temperature: It is the temperature above which ferromagnetic materials lose their permanent magnetic field and the magnetism completely disappears.

The magnetic susceptibility decreases with an increase in temperature. So, the ferromagnetism decreases with rising temperature. It is maximum at absolute zero temperature and becomes zero at Curie temperature. Above this temperature, the ferromagnetic material behaves as paramagnetic substance.
Hence, the correct option is (a).

74. AC series motors are also known as the modified DC series motor as their construction is very similar to that of the DC series motor. If a DC series motor is operated on AC supply,

1. An AC supply will produce a unidirectional torque because the direction of both the currents (i.e. armature current and field current) reverses at the same time.

2. Due to the presence of alternating current, eddy currents are induced in the yoke and field cores which results in excessive heating of the yoke and field cores.

3. Due to the high inductance of the field and the armature circuit, the power factor would become very low.

4. There is sparking at the brushes of the DC series motor.

5. It has poor efficiency.
Hence, the correct option is (d).

75. Given: Quality factor $= 200$, Frequency $= 2MHz$, Inductance $= 100\mu H$

We know that

Quality factor $= \dfrac{\omega L}{R} = \left(\dfrac{2\pi f L}{R}\right)$

Here $f =$ Frequency, $L =$ Inductance of coil, $R =$ Resistance of coil

$$R = \left(\dfrac{2\pi \times 2\times10^6 \times 100\times10^{-6}}{200}\right) = 2\pi\Omega$$

Hence, the correct option is (a).

76. In case of failure of the prime mover of the generator and the excitation is present then generator draws power from the other parallel generator and starts working as a motor with the same direction and for this motor, the turbine is working as a load. Because of the huge mass of the turbine the motor draws a huge amount of current which damages the winding. It will absorb power from the bus bar i.e working at lagging power factor.
Hence, the correct option is (d).

77. Resonance in electric circuits is the phenomena, in which at a certain input voltage frequency the voltage and current drawn by the circuit are in phase.

In parallel resonant circuit at resonance frequency the impedance is maximum.

For parallel LC circuit

$$Y = j\omega C + \dfrac{1}{j\omega L}$$

$$Y = j\left(\omega C - \dfrac{1}{\omega L}\right)$$

At resonance

$$\omega = \dfrac{1}{\sqrt{LC}}$$

$$Y = j\left(\dfrac{1}{\sqrt{LC}}C - \dfrac{1}{\frac{1}{\sqrt{LC}}L}\right)$$

$$Y = j\left(\sqrt{\dfrac{C}{L}} - \sqrt{\dfrac{C}{L}}\right)$$

$$Y = 0$$

since $Y = 0, Z = \infty$
Hence, the correct option is (d).

78. Concept:

Real power (P) = VI cos φ
Reactive power (Q) = VI sin φ
Where, V = voltage
I = current
Cos φ = power factor
Calculation:
Given that, voltage (V) = 230
Current (I) = 350 mA = 0.35
Power factor (cos φ) = 0.75
Real power (P) = 230 × 0.35 × 0.75 = 60.375 watt
Hence, the correct option is (d).

79. Concept:
In a DC generator, generated emf is given by

$$E_g = V_t + I_a R_a$$

In a DC motor, back emf is given by

$$E_b = V - I_a R_a$$

Where, I_a is armature current

R_a is armature resistance

Calculation:

Armature current $(I_a) = 25A$

Armature resistance $(R_a) = 0.8 ohm$

Voltage $(V) = 200V$

$$E_b = V - I_a R_a = 200 - 25(0.8) = 180V$$

Hence, the correct option is (c).

80.

1. The trip circuit consists of a trip coil, battery and relay contacts

2. The relay contacts are the part of a trip circuit of a circuit breaker as shown in the figure

3. The trip circuit can operate on a.c. or d.c.

4. Trip coil activates the circuit breaker opening mechanism, making the circuit breaker open.

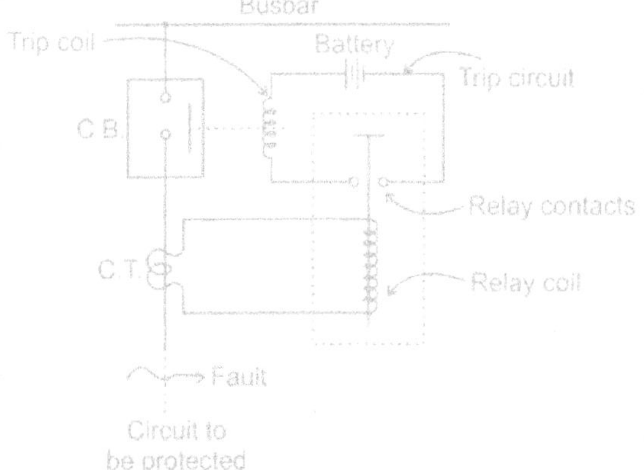

Hence, the correct option is (c).

81.

1. If a phase sequence indicator rotates clockwise for a phase sequence of RYB if the phase sequence is changed to BRY It will rotate clockwise only because there is no change in phase sequence.

2. The direction of AC motor can be reversed by interchanging any two of the three motor supply lines.

3. Let the phase sequence of the three-phase voltage applied to the stator winding is RYB.

4. If this sequence is changed to RBY, it is observed that the direction of rotation of the field is reversed i.e., the field rotates in the opposite direction.

5. However, the number of poles and the speed at which the magnetic field rotates remain unchanged.
   Hence, the correct option is (d).

82. Concept:

Phase angle in a series RLC circuit is given by

$$\phi = \tan^{-1}\frac{X}{R} = \cos^{-1}\frac{R}{Z}$$

Here, $X = X_L - X_C$

And $Z = \sqrt{R^2 + (X_L - X_C)^2}$

Where, R is resistance

X_L is inductive reactance

X_C is capacitive reactance

Calculation:

Given that, $R = 200, X_L = 350$ and $X_C = 150$

$$X = X_L - X_C = 350 - 150 = 200$$

$$\phi = \tan^{-1}\frac{X}{R} = \tan^{-1}\frac{200}{200} = 45°$$

Hence, the correct option is (c).

83.

EMF (Electro Motive Force)	Potential Difference
EMF is the maximum potential difference between the two electrodes of the cell when the circuit is open i.e. when no current is drawn from the cell.	Potential difference is the difference of potentials between any two points in a closed circuit.
It is independent of the resistance of the circuit as the circuit is open	It is proportional to the resistance between the two given points
The term EMF is used only for the source	It is measured between any two points of the circuit
It is greater than the potential difference between any two points in the circuit	It is greater than EMF when cell is being charged

Hence, the correct option is (c).

84.

1. The diode in which impurities are heavily doped is Tunnel diode.

2. Tunnel diode owing to heaving doping (typically 100 to several thousand times normal doping semiconductor diode) resulting in extremely small depletion layer width.

3. Due to this extremely thin depletion region width the charge carriers can "tunnel" through depletion region.
   Hence, the correct option is (c).

85. The distribution system is the electrical system between the sub-station fed by the transmission system and the consumer's meters. It generally consists of feeders, distributors and the service mains. The single line diagram of a typical low-tension distribution system is shown below.

Feeders:

1. A feeder is a conductor which connects the sub-station (or localised generating station) to the area where power is to be distributed

2. Generally, no tappings are taken from the feeder so that current in it remains the same throughout

3. The main consideration in the design of a feeder is the current carrying capacity

Distributor:

1. A distributor is a conductor from which tappings are taken for supply to the consumers. In the figure, AB, BC, CD and DA are the distributors

2. The current through a distributor is not constant because tappings are taken at various places along its length

3. While designing a distributor, voltage drop along its length is the main consideration since the statutory limit of voltage variations is ± 6% of the rated value at the consumers' terminals

Service mains: A service mains is generally a small cable which connects the distributor to the consumers' terminals.
Hence, the correct option is (d).

86. Given that, magnetic field strength (H) = 2×10^5 A-m^{-1}

Magnetic flux density, B = μH = $4\pi \times 10^{-7} \times 2 \times 10^5$ = 0.25 T
Hence, the correct option is (a).

87.

1. A potentiometer is an instrument designed to measure an unknown voltage by comparing it with the unknown voltage.

2. The known voltage may be supplied by a standard cell or any other known voltage reference source.

3. It makes use of a balance or null condition, no current flows and hence no power loss is consumed in the circuit.

4. Thus, the determination of voltage by a potentiometer is quite independent of the source resistance.

5. Measurements using comparison methods are capable of a high degree of accuracy because the result obtained does not depend upon the actual deflection of the pointer, as in the case of deflection methods.

6. Hence potentiometer is the best device to measure the true open circuit e.m.f. of a battery.
Hence, the correct option is (c).

88. Lightning arrester:

1. The device which is used for the protection of the equipment at the substations against travelling waves, such type of device is called lightning arrester or surge diverter

2. It diverts the abnormal high voltage to the ground without affecting the continuity of supply

3. It is connected between the line and earth, i.e., in parallel with the equipment to be protected at the substation

Characteristics are shown below.

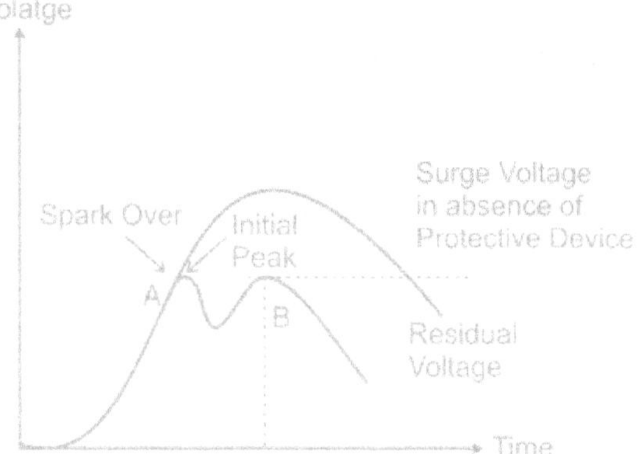

Voltage Characteristic

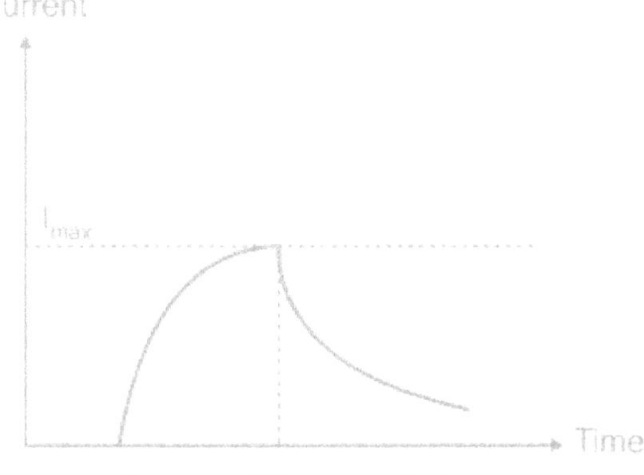

Current Characteristic
Hence, the correct option is (d).

89. The capacity of a battery is usually measured in amp-hours. This is a measure of the number of electrons that can be removed from the battery. The capacity is proportional to the size of the electrodes.
Anode acts as negative electrode; it is a material that undergoes oxidation during the cell discharge.
Cathode acts as positive electrode; It is a material that undergoes reduction during the cell discharge.
Hence, the correct option is (b).

90.

1. RMS voltage of a sinusoidal waveform is directly proportional to the peak voltage.
For a sinusoidal waveform, $V_{rms} = \dfrac{V_P}{\sqrt{2}}$

2. Multimeters measure average value of voltage and current of different waveforms.

3. The RMS value of a sinusoidal waveform gives half of the heating effect than a DC current of the same value.

4. The ratio of the RMS value of voltage to the maximum value of voltage is the same as the ratio of the RMS value of current to the maximum value of current.
Hence, the correct option is (d).

91. In series circuit, the current flowing through the circuit is same and the voltage is divided through all the elements in the circuit.

In parallel circuit, the voltage across each parallel branch is same and the current is divided between all the branches.

Thus, voltage divider is always a series circuit and current divider is always a parallel circuit.
Hence, the correct option is (b).

92.

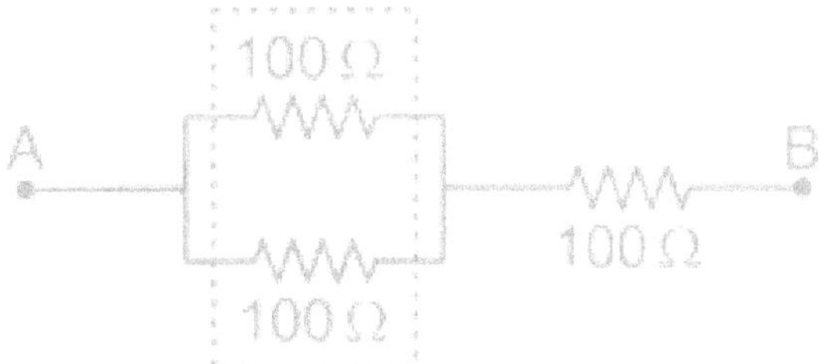

Two 100Ω resistors are connected in parallel

$$R_{100||100} = \frac{100 \times 100}{200} = 50\Omega$$

$$R_{AB} = 100 + 50 = 150\Omega$$

Two in parallel and one in series combinations is the best for replacing a 150 Ω resistor in a circuit using 100 Ω in the laboratory. Hence, the correct option is (b).

93. We know that

$$\beta = \frac{\alpha}{1-\alpha} = \frac{0.955}{1-.0995} = \frac{0.955}{0.005} = 199$$
$$I_{CEO} = (\beta + 1)I_{Co}$$
$$I_{CEO} = (199 + 1) \times 0.5 \times 10^{-6}$$
$$I_{CEO} = 100\mu A$$

Hence, the correct option is (a).

94. The filament used in bulb has positive temperature coefficient of resistance i.e. the resistance of the material increases with increase in temperature. Thus, the hot resistance of a bulb's filament is higher than its cold resistance.
Hence, the correct option is (c).

95. We known that
Power $= I^2 R$

$$I = \sqrt{\frac{P}{R}} = \sqrt{\frac{0.1}{100}} = 0.03162$$

Now milliammeter resistance $= 200$
∴ Power consumed $= I^2 R = 1 \times 10^{-3} \times 200 =$ $0.2mW$
Hence, the correct option is (a).

96. Impedance in the circuit is $Z = \sqrt{R^2 + X_C^2} = 50\Omega$

Current flows in the circuit $I = \frac{V}{Z} = \frac{100}{50} = 2A$

Power drawn $= I^2 R = 4 \times 40 = 160W$
Hence, the correct option is (b).

97. Concept:
Core loss $(P_C) = VI_C$
$I_C = I\cos\phi$
V is induced emf
I is current
ϕ is phase difference between induced emf and current
Calculation:
Given that, induced emf $(V) = 230V$
Current $(I) = 2A$
Phase difference $(\phi) = 60°$
$I_C = I\cos\phi = 2\cos60° = 1A$
Core loss $(P_c) = 230W$
Hence, the correct option is (c).

98. Drift currently density in a material can be given by
$$J = [?][?]E$$
$$= e(n\mu_n + p\mu_p)E$$
So, Drift current in semiconductors depends upon
1. Electric charge $(1.6 \times 10^{-19}C)$
2. Mobility of charge carriers
3. Electric Field
4. carrier concentration.
Hence, the correct option is (a).

99.

1. The Potier triangle determines the voltage regulation of the machines.
2. This method is also called a zero power factor (ZPF) method.
3. This method depends on the separation of the leakage reactance of armature and their effects.
4. The graph of the Potier triangle is shown in the figure below.
5. The triangle formed by the vertices a, b, c has shown below in the figure is called Potier triangle.
   Hence, the correct option is (d).

100. Concept:
Iron losses or core losses of the transformer includes both hysteresis and eddy current losses.
Hysteresis losses: These are due to the reversal of magnetization in the transformer core whenever it is subjected to alternating nature of magnetizing force.
$$W_h = \eta B_m^{1.6} f v$$
Where, $\eta = $ Steinmetz constant
$B_m = $ maximum flux density
$f = $ frequency of magnetization or supply frequency
$v = $ volume of the core

Eddy current losses: These are basically $I^2 R$ losses present in

the core due to the production of eddy current in the core.

$$W_h = \eta B_m^2 f^2 t^2$$

Where, η = Steinmetz constant

B_m = maximum flux density

f = frequency of magnetization or supply frequency

t = thickness of the core

maximum flux density (B_m) is directly proportional to the $\dfrac{V}{f}$ ratio.

$$B_m \propto \dfrac{V}{f}$$

Application:

At a constant $\dfrac{V}{f}$ ratio,

$$W_h \propto f, W_e \propto f^2$$

Now we can write the iron losses as,

$$W_i = W_h + W_e = Af + Af^2$$

By keeping the $\dfrac{V}{f}$ ratio constant and by operating the transformer at two different frequencies, we can separate the iron losses.

Hence, the correct option is (a).

101. Energy can neither be created nor destroyed, but it does change its form. And not all forms of energy are usable and it gets dissipated as heat energy and sound energy. Moreover, the current sources or energy such as fuels are non-renewable in nature and are rapidly consumed.

Hence, the correct option is (d).

102. An ideal source of energy should have higher calorific value, easy transportability, easy accessibility . These are the characterises of ideal source of energy.

Hence, the correct option is (d).

103. Fossile fuels were formed over million of years ago and there are only limited reserve. So they are non-renewable source of energy.

Hence, the correct option is (a).

104. The answer is dead organisms are transformed into petroleum and natural gas by absence of air. Because dead organisms are buried into the soil there will be no presence of air. Due to the heat and temperature present in the soil petroleum and natural gas are formed.

Hence, the correct option is (b).

105. Coal plants are the nation's top source of carbon dioxide emissions, the primary cause of global warming. Burning coal is also a leading cause of smog, ash, acid rain, and toxic air pollution.

Hence, the correct option is (d).

106. Water is required to produce steam. Thermal power plants are setup near the coal field and transmission of electricity is easy than transporting fuel.

Hence, the correct option is (c).

107. The working fluid is water in the liquid phase & steam in the gas phase. For fluid power, a working fluid is a gas or liquid that primarily transfers force, motion, or mechanical energy.

Hence, the correct option is (A).

108. Biogas has high calorific value and leave no residue, no smoke after burning and can be used for domestic purpose, running engins and in gas lanterns for illumination.

Hence, the correct option is (c).

109. In the absence of oxygen, anaerobic micro-organism decomposed the compound of cow- dung sturry to generate biogas.

Hence, the correct option is (b).

110. All are the factors that responsible for the blowing of wind. Wind is the movement of air, caused by the uneven heating of the Earth by the sun and the Earth's own rotation. Winds range from light breezes to natural hazards such as hurricanes and tornadoes. Wind is the movement of air caused by the uneven heating of the Earth by the sun.

Hence, the correct option is (d).

111. All the points given are the disadvantage age of using solar energy.

Disadvantages of Solar Energy

Cost:

The initial cost of purchasing a solar system is fairly high. This includes paying for solar panels, inverter, batteries, wiring, and for the installation.

Weather Dependent:

Although solar energy can still be collected during cloudy and rainy days, the efficiency of the solar system drops. Solar panels are dependent on sunlight to effectively gather solar energy. Therefore, a few cloudy, rainy days can have a noticeable effect on the energy system.

Solar Energy Storage Is Expensive:

Solar energy has to be used right away, or it can be stored in large batteries. These batteries, used in off-the-grid solar systems, can be charged during the day so that the energy is used at night. This is a good solution for using solar energy all day long but it is also quite expensive.

Uses a Lot of Space:

The more electricity you want to produce, the more solar panels you will need, as you want to collect as much sunlight as possible. Solar PV panels require a lot of space and some roofs are not big enough to fit the number of solar panels that you would like to have.

Associated with Pollution:

Although pollution related to solar energy systems is far less compared to other sources of energy, solar energy can be associated with pollution. Transportation and installation of solar systems have been associated with the emission of greenhouse gases. There are also some toxic materials and hazardous products used during the manufacturing process of solar photovoltaic systems, which can indirectly affect the environment.

Hence, the correct option is (d).

112. Solar cookers are devices that uses the sunlight as a source of heat to cook food. A simple solar cooker can reach a temperature just above the highest temperature of a thermometer. Most of the solar cookers can obtain the temperature from 85°C to 150°C.

Hence, the correct option is (b).

113. The reflector on the top of the solar cooker is used to focus the solar energy over the glass surface. The mirror reflects the heat energy in a confined area and increases the net input energy to the solar cooker.
Hence, the correct option is (c).

114. Special grade silicon is used for making solar cells. Monocrystalline solar cells are made from a very pure type of silicon, which makes them the most efficient material for converting sunlight into electricity. In addition, monocrystalline solar cells are also the most space-efficient.
Hence, the correct option is (b).

115. Silver is the metal which is used for connecting wires that connect solar cells in a solar panel, due to its large conductivity.
Hence, the correct option is (b).

116. A large number of solar cells connected together in a particular arrangement to deliver useful electrical power is called solar cell panel.
A solar panel, consisting of many photovoltaic cells. A solar panel, or solar module, is one component of a photovoltaic system. They are constructed out of a series of photovoltaic cells arranged into a panel. They come in a variety of rectangular shapes and are installed in combination to generate electricity.
Hence, the correct option is (c).

117. The energy produced by the surge of ocean water during high and low tides due to difference in sea level is called tidal energy.
Hence, the correct option is (b).

118. Difference in sea-levels due to tides during different times of day gives us tidal energy. Tidal energy is harnessed by constructing a dam across a narrow opening to the sea. A turbine fixed at the opening of the dam converts tidal energy to electricity.
Hence, the correct option is (a).

119. The waves are generated by a strong wind due to solar energy across the sea. Waves transmit energy, not water, and are commonly caused by the wind as it blows across the ocean, lakes, and rivers. Waves caused by the gravitational pull of the moon and the sun are called tides.
Hence, the correct option is (d).

120. Closed-cycle OTEC uses working fluids that are typically thought of as refrigerants such as ammonia or R-134a. These fluids have low boiling points, and are therefore suitable for powering the system's generator to generate electricity.
Hence, the correct option is (a).

Part - I

Q.1 Which of the following was conferred with GreenTech CSR India 2020 Award for its for outstanding achievements in promoting healthcare under its CSR programmes?
A. Tata Steel
B. Ashok Leyland
C. SAIL
D. Jindal Steel & Power Ltd

Q.2 Which of the following has approved the appointment of Mr. Vaibhav Karandikar as Chief Financial Officer and Key Managerial Personnel, in October 2020?
A. Abbott India Ltd
B. Sun Pharma
C. Glenmark Pharmaceuticals
D. Sanofi India

Q.3 Who was named the brand ambassador of India's first-ever badminton brand 'Transform' which was launched virtually in October 2020?
A. Ansal Yadav
B. Chetan Anand
C. Rahul Yadav
D. Saurabh Sharma

Q.4 Who has been roped in as the brand ambassador of Ubon in October 2020 to tap into the Southern market?
A. Rana Daggubati
B. Naga Chaitanya
C. Ram Charan
D. Allu Arjun

Q.5 Dinesh Kumar Khara has been appointed as the Chairman of which of the following banks in October 2020, for a period of three years?
A. State Bank of India
B. HDFC Bank
C. PNB
D. ICICI Bank

Q.6 Prasar Bharati has signed an MoU with which of the following to broadcast and promote new agriculture technology and innovations?
A. NASSCOM
B. IFFCO
C. QCA
D. NABARD

Q.7 In October 2020, the Ministry of Electronics and Information and Technology has cleared 16 proposals from domestic and international companies entailing an investment of how many rupees (in crores)?
A. 8000
B. 9000
C. 10000
D. 11000

Q.8 Who has been appointed to the post of Director General, BCAS, for a tenure up to his superannuation on February 29, 2024 or until further orders?
A. Arun Goel
B. M A Ganapathy
C. Om Prakash Gupta
D. Abhinav Kumar

Q.9 The sum of two numbers is 8 and their multiplication is 15 then what will be the value of the sum of the reciprocal of these numbers.
A. $\frac{8}{15}$
B. $\frac{15}{8}$
C. 23
D. 7

Q.10 The average marks obtained by 120 students in an exam is 35. If the average marks obtained by successful students is 39 and the average marks obtained by unsuccessful students is 15. Then what is the number of successful students?
A. 80
B. 110
C. 100
D. 90

Q.11 If $\frac{2a+b}{a+4b} = 3$ then find the value of $\frac{a+b}{a+2b} = ?$
A. $\frac{5}{9}$
B. $\frac{2}{7}$
C. $\frac{10}{9}$
D. $\frac{10}{7}$

Q.12 The length of the tangent drawn to a circle of radius 4 cm from a point 5 cm away from the centre of the circle is.
A. 3 cm
B. $4\sqrt{2}$ cm
C. $5\sqrt{2}$ cm
D. $3\sqrt{2}$ cm

Q.13 In $\triangle ABC$, D and E are points on AB and AC respectively such that DEBC divides the $\triangle ABC$ into two parts of equal areas. Then ratio of AD and BD is :
A. $1:1$
B. $1:\sqrt{2} - 1$
C. $1:\sqrt{2}$
D. $1:\sqrt{2} + 1$

Q.14 An amount of money appreciates to Rs. 7,000 after 4 years and to Rs. 10,000 after 8 years at a certain compound interest compounded annually. The initial amount of money was.
A. Rs. 4,700
B. Rs. 4,900
C. Rs. 4,100
D. Rs. 4,300

Q.15 There are 20% concentration of alcohol in 5 Lt. solution of alcohol and water. 2 Lt. of solution is replaced with 2 litre water. Find the concentration of alcohol in new solution.
A. 10%
B. 12%
C. 15%
D. 18%

Q.16 A man purchase a car for 1,35,000 and spent 25,000 on repairs. At what price was the car sold if he suffered 10% loss on it ?
A. 1,50,000
B. 1,76,000
C. 1,44,000
D. 1,21,500

Q.17 "e-Aksharayan" i.e. a software recently launched by Ministry of IT will enable and simplify...........?
A. Rural connectivity
B. 360 Degree 3D Tourism
C. Editing in scanned documents
D. Documentation in govt. offices and bank

Q.18 The state government will launch 'One farmer one transformer' scheme to curb electricity losses is______?
A. Goa
B. Maharashtra
C. Punjab
D. Rajasthan

Q.19 Ministry of Human Resource Development is planning to launch an ambitious ₹1.5 lakh crore project to improve the quality and accessibility of higher education over the next five years. What is the name of this project?

A. EQUIP Project   **B.** READ Project
C. HSTS Project   **D.** ANNA Project

Q.20 Which Bollywood personality has been felicitated by Council of European Chambers of Commerce (CEUCC) for promoting Children Rights?

A. Aamir Khan   **B.** Ajay Devgan
C. Anil Kapoor   **D.** Anupam Kher

Q.21 Which Bank launched the myApps application to boost digital payments?

A. SBI   **B.** HSBC Bank
C. HDFC   **D.** ICICI

Q.22 Which mini-UAV was selected by Indian Army for high-altitude surveillance?

A. AltiLite   **B.** SpyLite
C. HawkLite   **D.** EyeSkyLite

Q.23 Researchers of which institute developed an ultrasensitive quantum thermometer using graphene quantum dots, which can precisely measure between 27 degree C to −196 degree C?

A. CSIR, Chandigarh
B. University of Delhi
C. IIT Kanpur
D. Jamia Millia Islamia

Q.24 Which of the following is not considered to be a system software?

A. Compiler   **B.** Assembler
C. Interpreter   **D.** COBOL

Q.25 Direction : In the following questions a part of sentence Is bold. Below are given alternatives to the bold part at (A), (B) and (C), which may improve the sentence. Choose the correct alternative. In case no improvement , your answer is (D).
Everyday, **we usually had** lunch at 1.30 p.m.

A. we have had usually   **B.** we have usually
C. we usually have   **D.** No improvement

Q.26 Direction : In the following questions a part of sentence is bold. Below are given alternatives to the bold part at (A), (B) and (C), which may improve the sentence. Choose the correct alternative. In case no improvement , your answer is (D).

I gave to Sana the keys.

A. I gave   **B.** I gave to the
C. I gave the   **D.** No improvement

Q.27 Direction : In the following questions, some of the sentences have errors and some have none. Find out which part of the sentence has an error. The number of that part is your answer. If there is no error, the answer would be (D).
As an artist /(A) Raju is as good /(B) if not better than Ramesh. /(C) No error. /(D)

A. A   **B.** B   **C.** C   **D.** D

Q.28 Direction : In the following questions, some of the sentences have errors and some have none. Find out which part of the sentence has an error. The number of that part is your

answer. If there is no error, the answer would be (D).
He was (A)/ not in a position to state (B)/ the speed the ship travelled. (C)/ No error (D)

A. A   **B.** B   **C.** C   **D.** D

Q.29 Direction : In the following question, a sentence is given with a blank to be filled in with appropriate word(s). Some alternatives are suggested for each question. Choose the correct alternative from the given alternatives.
As a result of —— many unsuitable candidates were selected for the posts.

A. Neutrality   **B.** Favouritism
C. Tolerance   **D.** Weakness

Q.30 Direction : In the following questions, sentences are given with blanks to be filled in with an appropriate word (s) Some alternatives are suggested for each question. Choose the correct alternative out of the given alternatives as your answer.
London Mayor Boris Johnson has called for British immigration authorities to stop being ....in the neck to the Indian students.

A. A block   **B.** A pain
C. Preferred   **D.** Peck

Q.31 Direction : In the following questions out of the four/five alternatives, choose the one which is best express the meaning of the given word.

Clemency

A. Endeavour   **B.** Mercy
C. Seldom   **D.** Frequently

Q.32 Direction : In the following questions out of the four/five alternatives, choose the one which is best express the meaning of the given word.

Flout

A. Acceptable   **B.** Nervous
C. defy   **D.** irregular

Ques (33-36):Directions: The following bar chart gives the growth percentage in the number of households in the middle, upper-middle and high-income categories in the four regions for the period between 1987-88 and 1994-95.

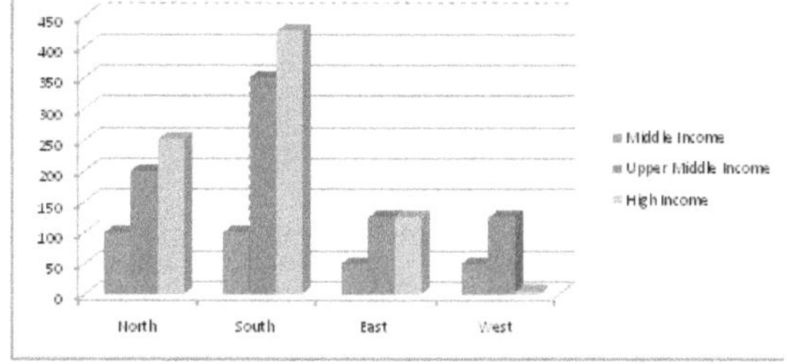

	No. of Households in $1987-88$ (In thousands)	Average Household Income $1987-88$	Growth in average income $1994-95$ over $1987-88$
Middle Income	40	Rs. 30,000	50%
Upper	10	Rs. 50,000	60%

Income			
High Income	5	Rs. 75,000	90%

Q.33 Which region showed the highest growth in a number of households in all the income categories for the period?

A. North　　　　　　　　B. South
C. West　　　　　　　　 D. None of these

Q.34 What was the total household income in the northern region for upper-middle-class?

A. Rs 50 lakh　　　　　　B. Rs 500 million
C. Rs 300 million　　　　 D. Cannot determined

Q.35 What is the percentage increase in the total number of households for the northern region (upper-middle) over the given period?

A. 100%　　B. 200%　　C. 240%　　D. 300%

Q.36 What was the average income of the high-income group in 1987-88?

A. Rs. 75,000　　　　　　B. Rs. 25,000
C. Rs. 2,25,000　　　　　D. Rs. 3,00,000

Ques (37-39):Directions: The proportion of male student and the proportion of vegetarian in a school are given below. The school has a total of 800 students, 80% of whom are in the Secondary Section and rest equally divided between Class 11 and 12.

	Male(M)	Vegetarian(V)
Class 12	40	Rs. 30,000
Class 11	10	Rs. 50,000
Total	5	Rs. 75,000

Q.37 What is the percentage of vegetarian students in class 12?
A. 40　　　　B. 45　　　　C. 50　　　　D. 55

Q.38 In class 12, twenty 25% of the vegetarian is male. What is the difference between a number of female vegetarian and male non-vegetarian?
A. 10　　　　B. 12　　　　C. 14　　　　D. 16

Q.39 What is the percentage of male students in the Secondary Section?
A. 40　　　　B. 45　　　　C. 50　　　　D. 55

Q.40 Directions: Study the table and answer the questions:
The table is given here

Year	English		Maths		Science		Social Science	
	High	Ave.	High	Ave.	High	Ave.	High	Ave.
2007	80	70	70	60	89	70	65	55
2008	82	65	85	62	95	64	66	58
2009	71	56	92	68	97	68	68	48
2010	75	52	91	64	92	75	77	58

What is the overall average of marks in the four subjects in the year 2009?
A. 63　　　　B. 64　　　　C. 65　　　　D. 60

Part - II

Q.41 A salient pole synchronous motor is running at no load. Its field current is switched off. The motor will _______
A. Come to stop
B. Continue to run at synchronous speed
C. Continue to run at a speed slightly more than the synchronous speed
D. Continue to run at a speed slightly less than the synchronous speed

Q.42 If the slip of an induction motor is 100% then what will its speed be?
A. Zero　　　　　　　　B. full load speed
C. half load speed　　　 D. quarter load speed

Q.43 No ceiling fan should be installed at height of less than
A. 2.5 m from the floor　　B. 5.5 m from the floor
C. 4.5 m from the floor　　D. 3.5 m from the floor

Q.44 For the circuit shown below, find the current (in A) produced by the 50 V battery.

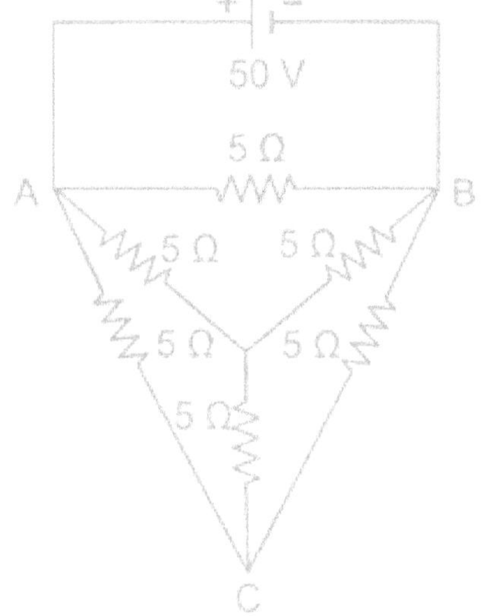

A. 10　　　　B. 20　　　　C. 3　　　　D. 40

Q.45 The expected value of voltage across a resistor is 80V. However, the measurement gives a value of 79.08V. The percentage error is _______.
A. 1.15%　　B. 1.25%　　C. 1%　　D. 0.15%

Q.46 What is the SI unit for magnetic moment?
A. Tesla　　　　　　　　B. Newton-meter/Tesla
C. Newton-meter　　　　D. Ampere/Tesla

Q.47 In heating the Ferro-magnetic materials by induction heating, heat is produced owing to
A. Flow of induced current through the charge
B. Hysteresis loss occurring below Curie temperature

C. Hysteresis loss as well as eddy current loss occurring in the charge

D. Any of the factors given in the options

Q.48 Potentiometer sensitivity can be increased by

A. Increasing the current in potentiometer wire

B. Increasing the length of potentiometer wire

C. Decreasing the length of potentiometer wire

D. Replacing the standard cell by a regulated power supply

Q.49 If the area of cross-section is reduced to half of its original value, then what will happen to the flux density?

A. Doubled
B. Halved
C. Remain same
D. One-fourth

Q.50 The voltage that appears across the breaker contact after the circuit breaker is opened is called.

A. Arc voltage
B. Restriking voltage
C. Recovery voltage
D. Surge voltage

Q.51 Which of the following statements regarding reluctance start motor is incorrect?

A. It is similar to repulsion motor

B. It is basically synchronous motor

C. So far as its basic working principle is concerned, it is similar to shaded pole motor

D. The air gap between the rotor and salient poles is non-uniform

Q.52 What is the power factor of the circuit when a current of 8 A flows in the ac circuit when 100 V dc is applied to it whereas it takes 125 V ac to produce the same current?

A. 0.8
B. 1.6
C. 1.25
D. None of these

Q.53 For a balanced load, the reactive power is measured by two wattmeter method with readings W_1 and W_2, the total reactive power is given by:

A. $(W_1 - W_2)$
B. $(W_1 + W_2)$
C. $\sqrt{3}\,(W_1 + W_2)$
D. $\sqrt{3}\,(W_1 - W_2)$

Q.54 The rectifier instrument is free from

A. Temperature error

B. Wave shape error

C. Frequency error

D. Both wave and frequency error

Q.55 The leakage current in the transistor (Ge)

A. Doubles for every 6° C rise in temperature

B. Doubles for every 10° C rise in temperature

C. Triples for every 6° C rise in temperature

D. Is independent of temperature

Q.56 An induction meter can handle current upto

A. 10 A
B. 30 A
C. 60 A
D. 100 A

Q.57 The Kirchhoff's current law as applied to ac circuit is defined as:

A. The algebraic sum of currents entering the node is equal to the algebraic sum of currents leaving the node.

B. The phasor sum of currents entering the node is equal to the phasor sum of current leaving the node.

C. The sum of the magnitude of currents at the node is equal to zero.

D. The total algebraic sum of currents at the node is equal to zero.

Q.58 Use of high permeability core in moving iron instrument helps in

A. Reducing size of meter

B. Increasing sensitivity

C. Reducing temperature error

D. Reducing losses

Q.59 In a ceiling fan employing capacitor run motor

A. secondary winding surrounds the primary winding

B. primary winding surrounds the secondary winding

C. bot are usual arrangements

D. None of the above

Q.60 To reverse the direction of rotation of a capacitor start motor while it is running, we should

A. disconnect the motor from the supply till it stops then reconnect it to supply with the reversed connection of main or auxiliary winding.

B. disconnect the motor from the supply and immediately reconnect it to supply with reversed connections of the main winding.

C. reverse the direction of connection of the auxiliary winding and after motor comes to rest then connect auxiliary winding to the supply.

D. reverse the direction of connections of the auxiliary winding and immediately connect it to supply.

Q.61 Which of the following method of induction motor is from the stator side?

A. By changing the applied voltage

B. By changing rheostat

C. By injecting emf

D. By cascading motors

Q.62 A power station has a maximum demand of 2 MW. The annual load factor is 40% and the plant capacity factor is 15%. What is the reserve capacity of the plant?

A. 1875 kW
B. 3750 kW
C. 6000 kW
D. 3333 kW

Q.63 Find the equivalent capacitance between the terminals a and b. all capacitance in µF:

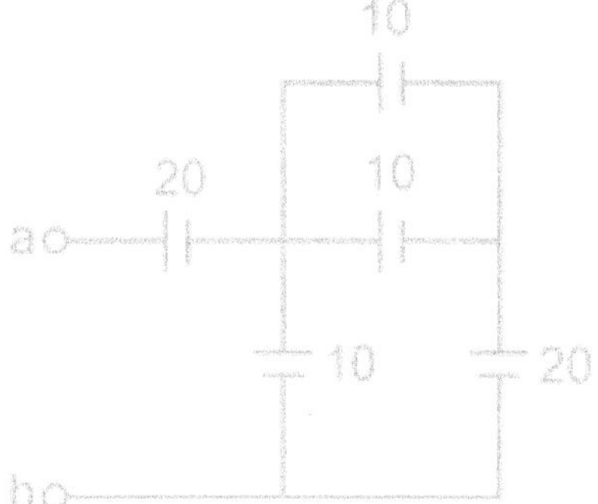

A. 15 μF   **B.** 10 μF   **C.** 5 μF   **D.** 25 μF

Q.64 In a Zener diode with high breakdown voltage
A.   Both P and N are heavily doped
B.   Both P and N are lightly doped
C.   Either P or N is lightly doped
D.   None of the above

Q.65 _______ is cause of failure to build up voltage.
A.   No residual magnetism
B.   Actual field connections
C.   Less resistance
D.   High field current

Q.66 The poorest voltage regulation of a transformer at full load is:
A.   At unity power factor
B.   At 0.8 lagging power factor
C.   At 0.8 leading power factor
D.   At 0.9 leading power factor

Q.67 For the same conductor length, same amount of power, same losses and same maximum voltage to earth, which system requires minimum conductor area?
A. Single-phase ac   **B.** 3 wire DC
C. 2-phase ac   **D.** 3 wire AC

Q.68 For the network shown below, the Norton's equivalent current across AB is given by:

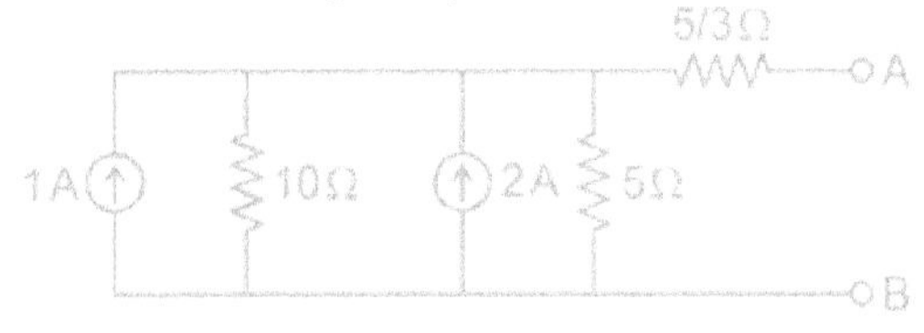

A. 1 A   **B.** 2 A   **C.** 3 A   **D.** 4 A

Q.69 The bridge method commonly used for measuring mutual inductance is:
A.   Heaviside Campbell bridge
B.   Schering bridge
C.   De Sauty bridge
D.   Wien bridge

Q.70 The carbon arc welding has the advantages of:
A.   Easy control of molten pool temperature simply by varying the arc length
B.   Easily adaptable to automation
C.   The excellent heat source for brazing, braze welding, soldering, etc
D.   All of the above

Q.71 In AC locomotives, squirrel cage induction motors are used, the method of speed control is:
A.   Pole changing method of speed control
B.   Frequency control method of speed control
C.   Cascade control method of speed control
D.   Slip control method of speed control

Q.72 Find the current I shown in the figure

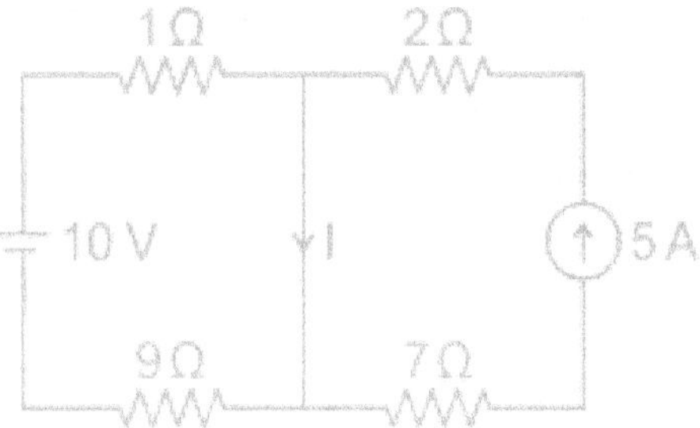

A. 5 A   **B.** 1 A   **C.** 0 A   **D.** 6 A

Q.73 Material used for making electric plug is
A. Porcelain   **B.** Bakelite
C. Rubber   **D.** China clay

Q.74 Which of the following is a paramagnetic material?
A. Magnesium   **B.** Soft iron
C. Hard iron   **D.** Nickel

Q.75 In armature control method, back emf (E_b) of DC motor is directly proportional to _______.
A.   Speed
B.   Number of armature conductor
C.   Flux
D.   Number of poles

Q.76 The lamp used in cinema projector is:
A.   Carbon arc lamp
B.   Tungsten filament lamp
C.   fluorescent lamp
D.   Sodium vapour lamp

Q.77 Which line separates stator and rotor copper losses in circle diagram of an induction motor?
A. Output line   **B.** Torque line
C. Input line   **D.** Power factor line

Q.78 If an induction type energy meter runs fast, it can be slowed by:
A.   Lag adjustment
B.   Light load adjustment
C.   Adjusting the position of braking magnet and making it come closer to the centre of the disc.
D.   Adjusting the position of braking magnet and making it move away from the centre of the disc.

Q.79 Suitable value of flux density for design of 250 kV transformer is
A. 1.1 T   **B.** 1.4 T   **C.** 1.6 T   **D.** 1.9 T

Q.80 Two incandescent bulbs of rating 230 V, 100 W and 230 V, 500 W are connected in parallel across the mains. As a result, what will happen?
A.   100 W bulb will glow brighter
B.   500 W bulb will glow brighter
C.   Both the bulbs will glow equally bright
D.   Both the bulbs will glow dim

Q.81 In two wattmeter method of measurement of a three-phase power of a balanced load, if both the wattmeters indicate the same reading, then the power factor of the load is-
A. 0.5 lagging
B. less than 0.5 lagging
C. unity
D. greater than 0.5 lagging

Q.82 A current wave starts at zero, rises instantaneously, then remains at a value of 20A for 10 sec., then decreases instantaneously, remaining at a value of — 10 A for 20 sec., and then repeats this cycle. The rms value of the wave is-
A. 22.36 A   B. 17.32 A   C. 8.165A   D. 14.14 A

Q.83 An AC voltage source with an internal impedance Z_1, is connected to a load of impedance Z_2. For maximum power transfer to the load, the condition is-
A. $Z_2 = Z_1$ B. $|Z_2| = |Z_1|$ C. $Z_2{}^* = Z_1$ D. $Z_2 = Z_1{}^*$

Q.84 The resonant frequency of the AC series circuit shown in figure given below, in Hz, is-

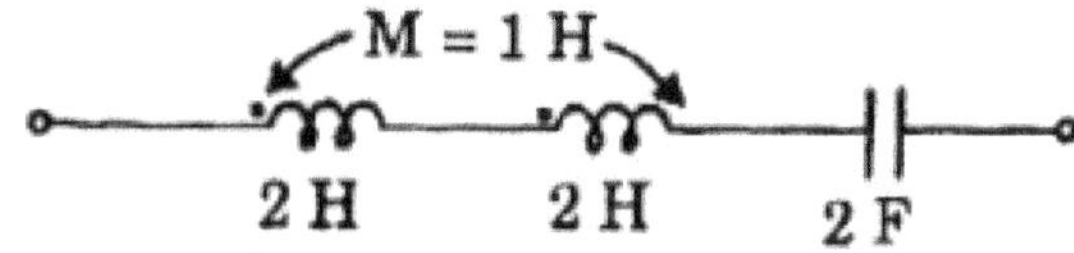

A. $\frac{1}{4\pi\sqrt{3}}$ B. $\frac{1}{4\pi\sqrt{2}}$ C. $\frac{1}{4\pi}$ D. $\frac{1}{2\pi\sqrt{10}}$

Q.85 If in an R-L-C series circuit the current lags the applied voltage by 60° then -
A. $Z_L - X_C = \frac{R}{\sqrt{3}}$
B. $X_L - X_C = \sqrt{3}R$
C. $X_L - X_C = R$
D. $X_L = X_C = R$

Q.86 A lossy capacitor with loss angle of 0.01 radian, draws a current of 0.5A when supplied at 1000V from a sinusoidal voltage source. The active power consumed by the capacitor is-
A. 5 W   B. 10 W   C. 2 W   D. 1 W

Q.87 For use in ac circuits, potential coil circuit of electrodynamic wattmeter should be purely-
A. resistive   B. inductive
C. capacitive   D. reactive

Q.88 The voltage wave given by v = 4 cos ωt produces a current wave i = 1.5 cos ωt – 2.598 sin ωt in a circuit. The current wave-
A. leads voltage wave by 60°
B. lags voltage wave by 60°
C. leads voltage wave by 30°
D. lags voltage wave by 30°

Q.89 The effective damping in D'Arsonval galvanometer is obtained by-
A. a shunt connected across moving coil
B. eddy current induced in metal discs
C. fluid friction
D. employing springs

Q.90 If θ represents deflection of pointer, the controlling torque in a spring -controlled indicating increment is proportional to-
A. θ B. θ^2 C. $\frac{1}{\theta}$ D. $\sin \theta$

Q.91 The range of a DC millimeters can be extended by using a-
A. low resistant in series
B. low resistance shunt
C. high resistance in series
D. high resistance shunt

Q.92 The response time of an indicating instrument is determined by its-
A. deflecting system
B. damping system
C. controlling system
D. support type to the moving system

Q.93 The ratio of the reading of two wattmeters connected to measure active power in a balanced 3-phase load is 2 : I. The power factor of the load is-
A. 0.866 lag   B. 0.866 lead
C. 0.866 lag or lead   D. None of the above

Q.94 The power input to a 3- phase, 50 Hz, 400 V, 4-pole induction motor is 60 kW and its stator losses are 1 kW. If this motor is running at 4% slip, the rotor copper loss is-
A. 1.18 kW   B. 2.36 kW   C. 0.18 kW   D. 0.36 kW

Q.95 In a transformer, the core loss is found to be 46 W at 50 Hz and is 80 W at 70 Hz, both losses being measured at the same peak flux density. The hysteresis loss and eddy current loss at 60 Hz is-
A. 11 W, 20 W   B. 30 W, 45 W
C. 16 W, 30 W   D. 22W, 40W

Q.96 Measurement of ______ is affected by the presence of thermo – emf in the measuring circuit.
A. high resistance   B. low resistance
C. capacitance   D. inductance

Q.97 A 220 V shunt motor develops a torque of 60 Nm at an armature current of 10 A. the torque developed when the armature current is 20 A, is-
A. 30 Nm   B. 240 Nm   C. 84 Nm   D. 120 Nm

Q.98 In a 3- phase synchronous generator, the stator winding is connected in star, because a delta connection would-
A. have circulating currents due to triplen harmonics
B. require low insulation and conductor material
C. require more insulation and conductor material
D. result in a short circuit

Q.99 A DC shunt generator builds up 230 V when driven in the clockwise direction. In case it is driven in anti-clockwise direction, other things remaining unchanged, then the voltage build-up is
A. Zero
B. 230 V with brush polarity same

C. Somewhat less than 230 V with brush polarity reversed

D. Somewhat less than 230 V with brush polarity same

Q.100 For cleat wiring and 250 volts supply, the cables will be placed _______apart centre to centre for single core cables-

A. 2.5 cm   **B.** 3 cm   **C.** 4 cm   **D.** 4.5 cm

Q.101 The working fluid in ocean thermal power plant is

A. Volatile liquid like ammonia

B. Petrol

C. Charcoal

D. Liquified petroleum gas

Q.102 Geothermal energy is

A. Heat energy in the interior of earth

B. energy of molten mars exists in the farm of magma inside the earth.

C. molten lava on the surface of earth

D. energy obtained from solar thermal electric plants

Q.103 A bulb has a power of 200W. What is the energy dissipated by it in 5 minutes?

A. 60J   **B.** 1000J   **C.** 60kJ   **D.** 1kJ

Q.104 In a hydropower plant

A. Potential energy possessed by stored water is converted into electricity

B. Kinetic energy possessed by stored water is converted into potential energy

C. Electricity is extracted from water

D. Water is converted into steam to produce electricity.

Q.105 Which is the ultimate source of energy?

A. Water   **B.** Sun

C. Uranium   **D.** Fossil fuels

Q.106 Which one of the following forms of energy leads to least environmental pollution in the process of its harnessing and utilisation?

A. Nuclear energy   **B.** Thermal energy

C. Solar energy   **D.** Geothermal energy

Q.107 Ocean thermal energy is due to

A. energy stored by waves in the ocean

B. temperature difference at different levels in the ocean

C. pressure difference at different levels in the ocean

D. tides arising out in the ocean

Q.108 The major problem in harnessing nuclear energy is how to

A. split nuclei?

B. sustain the reaction?

C. dispose off spent fuel safely?

D. convert nuclear energy into electrical energy?

Q.109 Which part of the solar cooker is responsible for the greenhouse effect?

A. Coating with black colour inside the box

B. Mirror

C. Glass sheet

D. Outer cover of the solar cooker

Q.110 The power generated in a windmill

A. is more in rainy season since damp air would mean more air mass hitting the blades

B. depends on the height of the tower

C. depends on wind velocity

D. can be increased by planting tall trees close to the tower

Q.111 Choose the correct statement

A. Sun can be taken as an inexhaustible source of energy

B. There is infinite storage of fossil fuel inside the earth

C. Hydro and wind energy plants are non-polluting

D. Waste from a nuclear power plant can be easily disposed off

Q.112 A good fuel should possess

A. high ignition temperature

B. moderate ignition temperature

C. high calorific value

D. both high calorific value and moderate ignition temperature

Q.113 The variety of coal which has the highest carbon content

A. Anthracite   **B.** Peat

C. Bituminous   **D.** Lignite

Q.114 Unit of calorific value of a substance is

A. Kcal   **B.** Joules   **C.** J kg   **D.** J/kg

Q.115 Biogas is formed in the

A. presence of air only

B. presence of water only

C. absence of air only

D. presence of water and absence of air

Q.116 Solar energy can be directly converted to elec-trical energy by which of the following de-vices?

A. solar cooker   **B.** solar heater

C. solar cell   **D.** solar geyser

Q.117 Which of the following is a disadvantage of most of the renewable energy sources?

A. Highly polluting

B. High waste disposal cost

C. Unreliable supply

D. High running cost

Q.118 Which of the following gases is the main con-stituent of natural gas?

A. Methane   **B.** Ethane   **C.** Propane   **D.** Butane

Q.119 Horizontal axis and vertical axis are the types of
____

A. Nuclear reactor   **B.** Wind mills

C. Biogas reactor   **D.** Solar cell

Q.120 A fuel cell, in order to produce electricity, burns
____

A. Helium

B. Nitrogen

C. Hydrogen

D. None of the mentioned

// Smart Answer Sheet //

Correct   Indicates percentage of students who answered questions correctly.

Skipped   Indicates percentage of students who skipped questions.

Q.	Ans.	Correct / Skipped	Q.	Ans.	Correct / Skipped	Q.	Ans.	Correct / Skipped	Q.	Ans.	Correct / Skipped	Q.	Ans.	Correct / Skipped
1	D	78.62 % / 10.51 %	17	C	82.99 % / 16.1 %	33	B	84.18 % / 12.83 %	49	A	77.35 % / 11.15 %	65	A	80.38 % / 17.23 %
2	D	78.17 % / 12.83 %	18	B	86.48 % / 13.38 %	34	D	80.77 % / 10.72 %	50	C	82.23 % / 16.63 %	66	B	77.16 % / 14.28 %
3	B	78.06 % / 13.57 %	19	A	78.93 % / 14.14 %	35	B	80.79 % / 16.65 %	51	A	89.47 % / 10.36 %	67	B	84.18 % / 14.49 %
4	A	77.4 % / 19.3 %	20	C	79.52 % / 11.85 %	36	A	81.79 % / 14.4 %	52	A	87.98 % / 11.63 %	68	B	88.7 % / 10.92 %
5	A	77.25 % / 11.08 %	21	C	78.15 % / 14.87 %	37	A	82.42 % / 12.21 %	53	D	84.95 % / 13.77 %	69	A	88.92 % / 10.31 %
6	B	87.58 % / 11.42 %	22	B	86.24 % / 13.15 %	38	D	84.56 % / 14.74 %	54	C	81.72 % / 18.08 %	70	D	84.04 % / 11.19 %
7	D	84.09 % / 11.27 %	23	D	79.85 % / 15.99 %	39	B	80.35 % / 19.01 %	55	B	82.59 % / 10.63 %	71	A	80.22 % / 13.01 %
8	B	89.05 % / 10.15 %	24	D	89.36 % / 10.03 %	40	D	79.87 % / 12.96 %	56	D	89.36 % / 10.2 %	72	D	87.48 % / 10.65 %
9	A	88.49 % / 11.0 %	25	C	88.65 % / 10.48 %	41	B	78.77 % / 15.03 %	57	B	82.5 % / 10.69 %	73	B	77.61 % / 19.34 %
10	C	87.79 % / 10.03 %	26	A	86.42 % / 12.45 %	42	A	78.89 % / 11.61 %	58	B	85.04 % / 13.15 %	74	A	85.65 % / 11.8 %
11	C	76.66 % / 15.63 %	27	B	76.65 % / 18.4 %	43	A	79.83 % / 17.72 %	59	A	89.68 % / 10.3 %	75	A	81.51 % / 14.19 %
12	A	87.9 % / 10.43 %	28	C	78.72 % / 19.24 %	44	B	89.31 % / 10.6 %	60	A	87.21 % / 11.87 %	76	A	81.99 % / 14.93 %
13	B	77.09 % / 15.39 %	29	B	86.76 % / 10.55 %	45	A	88.53 % / 11.09 %	61	A	89.76 % / 10.01 %	77	B	83.55 % / 10.68 %
14	B	82.75 % / 17.12 %	30	B	87.44 % / 10.81 %	46	B	76.71 % / 15.15 %	62	D	84.87 % / 11.77 %	78	D	85.77 % / 13.43 %
15	B	77.37 % / 19.14 %	31	B	80.84 % / 11.61 %	47	C	89.82 % / 10.01 %	63	B	80.91 % / 10.95 %	79	C	78.87 % / 21.02 %
16	C	78.57 % / 21.09 %	32	C	83.98 % / 11.81 %	48	B	85.97 % / 12.31 %	64	B	81.23 % / 12.04 %	80	B	84.24 % / 11.11 %

Q.	Ans.	Correct / Skipped		Q.	Ans.	Correct / Skipped		Q.	Ans.	Correct / Skipped		Q.	Ans.	Correct / Skipped		Q.	Ans.	Correct / Skipped
81	C	77.32 % 20.97 %		89	A	88.33 % 11.6 %		97	D	83.27 % 12.88 %		105	B	89.21 % 10.01 %		113	A	83.9 % 13.62 %
82	D	88.33 % 10.41 %		90	A	86.38 % 13.25 %		98	B	88.29 % 10.87 %		106	C	80.74 % 18.49 %		114	D	76.63 % 12.07 %
83	D	77.62 % 10.51 %		91	B	79.86 % 16.02 %		99	A	78.32 % 16.49 %		107	B	83.75 % 15.84 %		115	D	83.96 % 11.54 %
84	A	76.2 % 21.67 %		92	B	89.72 % 10.11 %		100	C	82.64 % 14.31 %		108	C	85.29 % 11.03 %		116	C	87.93 % 10.06 %
85	B	86.33 % 13.16 %		93	C	77.53 % 10.51 %		101	A	88.3 % 10.59 %		109	C	84.11 % 15.01 %		117	C	83.89 % 13.29 %
86	A	87.68 % 11.84 %		94	B	76.71 % 12.87 %		102	C	88.93 % 10.44 %		110	A	85.11 % 13.56 %		118	A	89.91 % 10.03 %
87	A	87.45 % 11.55 %		95	D	89.23 % 10.7 %		103	C	82.79 % 10.35 %		111	C	79.43 % 12.41 %		119	B	77.07 % 17.17 %
88	A	80.65 % 17.17 %		96	B	81.01 % 15.01 %		104	A	87.09 % 11.75 %		112	D	84.8 % 14.26 %		120	C	78.99 % 19.14 %

Performance Analysis

Avg. Score (%)	61.67%
Toppers Score (%)	65.83%
Your Score	

//Hints and Solutions//

1.

1. Jindal Steel & Power Ltd (JSPL) was conferred with GreenTech CSR India 2020 Award for its for outstanding achievements in promoting healthcare under its CSR programmes.

2. The Award was received by Chairperson of JSPL Foundation, Shallu Jindal, during the 7th CSR India Summit & Expo.

3. JSPL was declared the winner for this coveted award in the category of "Promotion of Health and Healthcare".
Hence, the correct option is (d).

2.

1. Drug major, Sanofi India has recently announced the Board of Directors of the Company at its meeting.

2. The approved the appointment of Mr Vaibhav Karandikar as Chief Financial Officer and Key Managerial Personnel.

3. He is a Chartered Accountant, a Company Secretary and a Cost Accountant with 25 years' experience across various domains in Finance.

4. He joined Sanofi in April 2007.
Hence, the correct option is (d).

3.

1. Commonwealth Games medallist shuttler Chetan Anand was named the brand ambassador of India's first-ever badminton brand 'Transform' which was launched virtually on 7th October 2020.

2. Anand is a former world no.10 and the men's singles bronze medal winner at the 2006 Melbourne CWG.

3. 'Transform' produces racquets, nylon shuttles, shoes, and apparels.
Hence, the correct option is (b).

4.

1. Gadget accessory and consumer electronics brand Ubon has roped in Rana Daggubati as its brand ambassador to tap into the Southern market.

2. With the association, the company aims to leverage the massive appeal the actor enjoys across the southern part of the country.

3. Rana is big-time tech-savvy and his philosophy inclines very well with Ubon's vision," the company said in a statement.
Hence, the correct option is (a).

5.

1. State Bank of India announced the appointment of Dinesh Kumar Khara, Managing Director, State Bank of India as Chairman, State Bank of India, for a period of three years.

2. Khara, one of the bank's four managing directors, replaces Rajnish Kumar, who is due to step down on October 7.

3. A state-run bank's appointment panel in August recommended Khara as the next chairman of SBI.
Hence, the correct option is (a).

6.

1. Prasar Bharati and Indian Farmers Fertilizer Cooperative Limited, IFFCO have signed an MoU to broadcast and promote new agriculture technology and innovations.

2. According to the agreement, DD Kisan will broadcast various innovative techniques being adopted in the agriculture field in easy language through 30 minutes program series for the benefit of farmers.

3. IFFCO is a Multi-state cooperative society engaged in the business of manufacturing and marketing of fertilisers.
Hence, the correct option is (b).

7.

1. The Ministry of Electronics and Information and Technology has cleared 16 proposals from domestic and international companies entailing an investment of 11000 crore rupees.

2. It is done under the production linked incentive, PLI scheme to manufacture mobile phones worth 10.5 lakh crore rupees over the next 5 years.

3. It will generate more than 2 lakh direct jobs.
Hence, the correct option is (d).

8.

1. The Appointments Committee of the Cabinet has approved the appointment of M A Ganapathy to the post of Director-General, BCAS, for a tenure up to his superannuation on February 29, 2024, or until further orders.

2. He is a 1986 batch IPS officer of Uttarakhand cadre.

3. The post of BCAS chief fell vacant after Rakesh Asthana was appointed as the Director-General of Border Security Force in August.
Hence, the correct option is (b).

9. $x + y = 8, xy = 15$
$$\frac{x+y}{xy} = \frac{1}{x} + \frac{1}{y} = \frac{8}{15}$$
Hence, the correct option is (a).

10. $(PASS \times 39) + (FAIL \times 15) = 120 \times 35$
$$P \times 39 + (120 - P) \times 15 = 120 \times 35$$
$$P39 + 120 \times 15 - 15P = 120 \times 35$$
$$24P = 120 \times 20$$
$$P = 100$$
Hence, the correct option is (c).

11. $\frac{2a+b}{a+4b} = 3$
$$\frac{a+b}{a+2b} = ?$$

$$\Rightarrow 2a + b = 3a + 12b$$
$$\Rightarrow a = -11b$$
$$\Rightarrow \frac{a}{b} = -11$$
$$\Rightarrow \frac{a+b}{a+2b} = \frac{\frac{a}{b}+1}{\frac{a}{b}+2} \Rightarrow \frac{-11+1}{-11+2} = \frac{10}{9}$$

Hence, the correct option is (c).

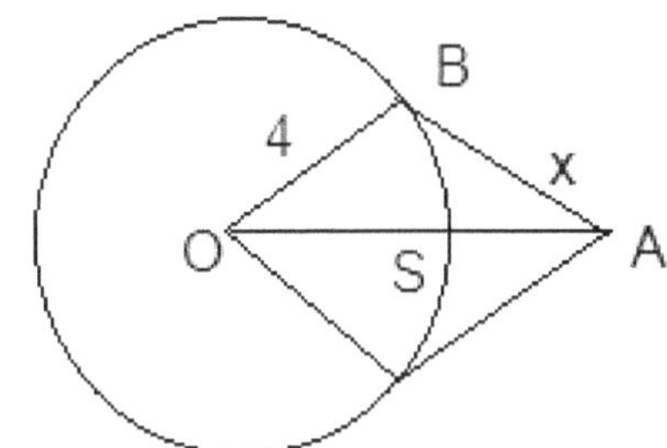

12.

$$AB = x = \sqrt{(OA)^2 - (OB)^2}$$
$$= \sqrt{25 - 16} = \sqrt{9} = 3$$

Hence, the correct option is (a).

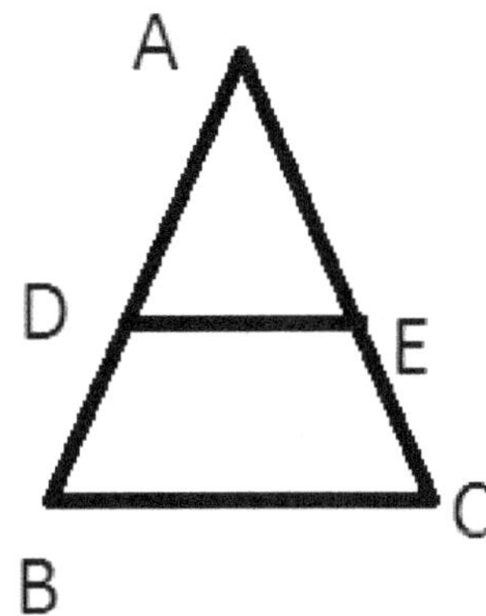

13.

we know that
$$\frac{\Delta ADE}{\Delta ABC} = \frac{1}{2} \text{ then } \left(\frac{AD}{AB}\right)^2 = \frac{1}{2}$$

here $\dfrac{AD}{AB} = \dfrac{1}{\sqrt{2}}$

$$\frac{AD}{AD+DB} = \frac{1}{\sqrt{2}}$$

So, $\dfrac{AD}{DB} = \dfrac{1}{\sqrt{2}-1}$

Hence, the correct option is (b).

14. Compound money in 4 years

$$7000 = x\left(1 + \frac{R}{100}\right)^4$$

Compound money in 8 years

$$10000 = x\left(1 + \frac{R}{100}\right)^8$$

$$\frac{10000}{x} = \left(\frac{7000}{x}\right)^2$$

$$x = \frac{7000 \times 7000}{10000} = 4900$$

Hence, the correct option is (b).

15. 3 liters after removing 2 liters solution Alcohol in solution $=$
$$3 \times \frac{20}{100} = \frac{3}{5}$$
So after adding 2 liters of water, it is 5 liters.

Alcohol also $= \dfrac{3}{5}$ liters of solution

Hence the concentration of alcohol $= \dfrac{\frac{3}{5}}{5} \times 100 = 12\%$

Hence, the correct option is (b).

16. Repairing cost $= 25000$
Total cost $= 1,60,000$

Selling price of car $= 1,60,000 \times \dfrac{90}{100} = 1,44,000$

Hence, the correct option is (c).

17. e-Aksharyan is a desktop software launched by Ministry of Information and Technology, for converting any scanned or printed Indian language documents into fully editable text. "e-Aksharayan" is an optical character recognition engine for Indian languages and can work for all 22 Indian languages.
Hence, the correct option is (c).

18. The Maharashtra government will launch 'One farmer one transformer' scheme from 15th August to curb electricity losses. Under this scheme, the state Government will provide electrical connection for high voltage distribution line to about two lakh farmers of the state.
Hence, the correct option is (b).

19. Ministry of Human Resource Development plans to launch an ambitious ₹1.5 lakh crore EQUIP project to improve the quality and accessibility of higher education over the next five years.
Hence, the correct option is (a).

20. Bollywood actor Anil Kapoor has been felicitated by Council of European Chambers of Commerce (CEUCC) in India and an European Union delegation as part of the 'Europe Day' celebrations in Mumbai on May 17.
Hence, the correct option is (c).

21. In a first, HDFC Bank launched the myApps application on 9 January 2020. The app aims to boost digital payments in India. The app will benefit urban local bodies, housing societies, local clubs and gymkhanas, and religious institutions.
Hence, the correct option is (c).

22. The Indian Army has selected SpyLite mini-UAV for high-altitude aerial surveillance. The SpyLite is built by Cyient Solutions & Systems (CSS), a joint venture between Cyient Ltd of India and BlueBird Aero Systems of Israel. SpyLite has an endurance of 4-5 hours and a maximum flight ceiling of 30,000 feet making it ideal for operations along the border with China as well as on the Siachen glacier.
Hence, the correct option is (b).

23. Researchers at Jamia Millia Islamia (New Delhi) have developed an ultrasensitive quantum thermometer using graphene quantum dots. The thermometer can precisely measure a wide range of temperature: 27 degree C to −196 degree C. The thermometer has high sensitivity when measuring different temperatures and can measure very minute (micro Kelvin) changes in temperature. The device can find widespread

applications in cryogenic temperature sensing.
Hence, the correct option is (d).

24. System software is a type of computer program that is designed to run a computer's hardware and application programs.Common Business-Oriented Language (COBOL) is a programming language similar to English that is widely used to develop business-oriented applications in the area of commercial data processing.
Hence, the correct option is (d).

25. Present tense shows what exits or happening now. It also denotes a habit which in this case is the timing of having lunch.
Hence, the correct option is (c).

26. 'to' is used to indicate directionality from one to another. Here no such thing is happening so 'to' is redundant here.
Hence, the correct option is (a).

27. Here, Raju is "(so/very)" good should be used. 'As' is superfluous here.
Hence, the correct option is (b).

28. the speed___ the ship travelled
something is missing here, such as 'at' or 'which'.
Hence, the correct option is (c).

29. Favouritism: the practice of giving unfair preferential treatment to one person or group at the expense of another.
Neutrality: absence of decided views, expression, or strong feeling.
Tolerance: the ability or willingness to tolerate the existence of opinions or behaviour that one dislikes or disagrees with.
the speed___ the ship travelled
something is missing here.... such as 'at' or 'which'.
Hence, the correct option is (b).

30. A pain in the neck = to be very annoying **(Idiom)**Hence, the correct option is (b).

31. Clemency - mercy; leniency.
Mercy - compassion or forgiveness shown towards someone whom it is within one's power to punish or harm.
Seldom - not often; rarely.
Endeavour - try hard to do or achieve something.
Hence, the correct option is (b).

32. Flout - openly disregard (a rule, law, or convention).
Defy - openly resist or refuse to obey.
Hence, the correct option is (c).

33. From the graph, it is clear that the southern region showed the highest growth in a number of households in all the income categories for the period.
Hence, the correct option is (b).

34. Region wise breakup is not available. hence, question cannot be answered.
Hence, the correct option is (d).

35. The percentage increase in the total number of households for the northern region for an upper-middle-income category is 200%.
Hence, the correct option is (b).

36. It is clear from the table average income is Rs. 75,000.
Hence, the correct option is (a).

37. Total Students = 800.
No. of students in secondary = 80% of 800 = 640.
Rest Students = 800 - 640 = 160.
Rest students are divided equally into class 12 and 11. So,
No. of students in class 12 = 160/2 = 80.
Now, total vegetarian = 53%
No. of Total vegetarian = 53% of 800 = 424.
55% of secondary students are vegetarian.
No. of vegetarian in secondary = 55% of 640 = 352.
No. vegetarian in 11 = 50% of 80 = 40
Thus, no. of vegetarian in 12,
= 424- 352 - 40 = 32.
Thus,
In class 12 total vegetarian = 32.
So, % of vegetarian = $(\dfrac{32}{80})$ 100 = 40%.
Hence, the correct option is (a).

38. Male vegetarian= 32-8 =24; Difference= 24-8=16.
Hence, the correct option is (d).

39. % of male students in secondary section,
$$= \left(\dfrac{288}{800}\right) 100 = 45\%$$
Hence, the correct option is (b).

40. Average in four subjects,
$$= \dfrac{(56 +68 +68 +48)}{4} = \dfrac{240}{4} = 60$$
Hence, the correct option is (d).

41. A salient pole synchronous motor is running at no load if Its field current is switched off. The motor will Continue to run at synchronous speed due to the presence of reluctance torque.

If the torque equations of salient pole synchronous motor are analysed, there is a term independent on field strength, which is nothing but reluctance torque.

$$P_s = \dfrac{EqV_s}{x_d}\sin\delta + \dfrac{V_s^2 x_d - x_q}{2x_d x_q}\sin 2\delta$$
Hence, the correct option is (b).

42. In the induction motor rotor always rotates speed less than synchronous speed.
The difference between the rotor speed (N) and the rotating magnetic flux speed (Ns) is called slip.
The induction motor slip is usually expressed as a percentage of synchronous speed (NS) and is represented by symbol S.
Mathematically, Percentage slip, % $S = \left[\dfrac{N_s - N}{N_s}\right] \times 100$

Or fractional slip, $S = \dfrac{N_s - N}{N_s}$

At start, $N = 0$, therefore, Slip, $S = \dfrac{N_s - 0}{N_s} = 1$

At synchronous speed, Slip, $S = \dfrac{N_s - N_s}{N_s} = 0$

Hence, the correct option is (a).

43. For safe operation, the fan's blades must hang at least 2.5 meter above the floor. For really high ceilings you'll want to use long downrods to lower the fan down to where people can feel

its breeze. The distance from the ceiling may need to be less when the ceilings are low because of safety concerns - a ceiling fast must be well above head height. That is, it must be at least 7' - 8' (210 - 240cm) above the floor.
Hence, the correct option is (a).

44. By using star to delta conversion, we can reduce the given circuit as follows.

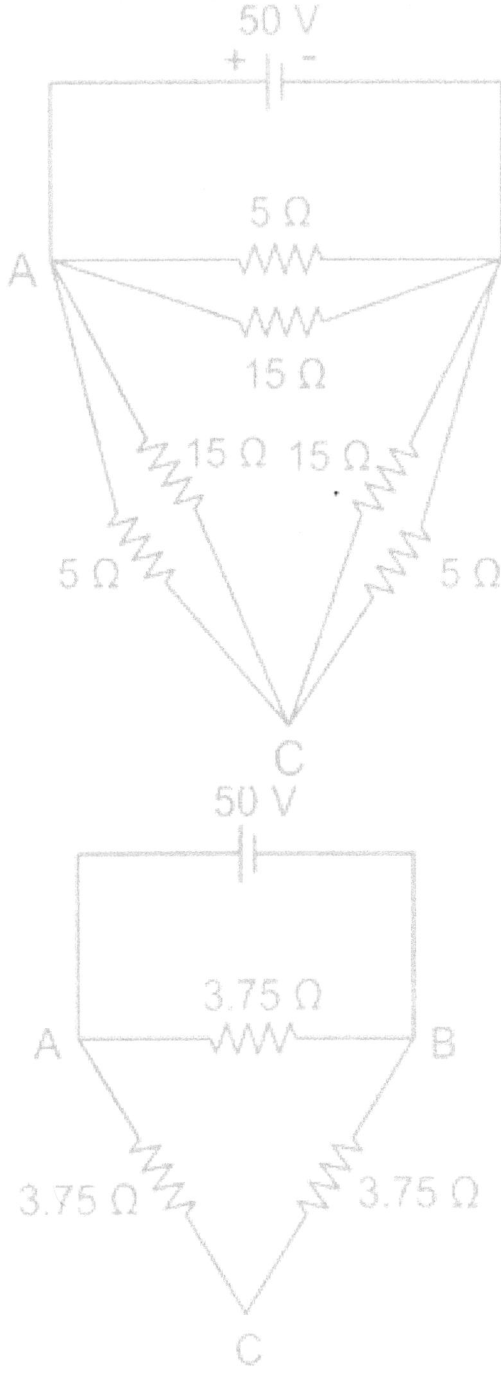

$$I_1 = \frac{50}{3.75} = 13.33A$$

$$I_2 = \frac{50}{7.5} = 6.66A$$

Total current $(I) = I_1 + I_2 = 20A$
Hence, the correct option is (b).

45. Concept:
Percentage error is given by,

$$\% \text{ error} = \frac{|A_m - A_t|}{A_t} \times 100$$

Where, A_m = measured value
A_t = true value
Calculation:
Given that, measured value $= 79.08V$
True value $= 80V$

$$\% \text{ error} = \frac{|A_m - A_t|}{A_t} \times 100$$

$$= \frac{|79.08 - 80|}{80} \times 100 = 1.15\%$$

Hence, the correct option is (a).

46. The SI unit for the magnetic moment Newton-meter/Tesla
Tesla is a unit of flux
Newton-meter is unit of torque
Important:
The magnetic moment of a magnet is a quantity that determines the torque it will experience in an external magnetic field.
It is considered to be a vector having a magnitude and direction.
The direction of the magnetic moment points from the South Pole to the North Pole of the magnet.
The magnetic field produced by the magnet is proportional to its magnetic moment.
Hence, the correct option is (b).

47.

1. Induction heating is the process of heating an electrically conducting object by electromagnetic induction, through heat generated in the object by eddy currents.

2. An induction heater consists of an electromagnet, and an electronic oscillator that passes a high-frequency alternating current (AC) through the electromagnet.

3. The rapidly alternating magnetic field penetrates the object, generating electric currents inside the conductor called eddy currents.

4. The eddy currents flowing through the resistance of the material heat it by Joule heating. In ferromagnetic materials like iron, heat may also be generated by magnetic hysteresis losses.
Hence, the correct option is (c).

48. Potentiometer is an instrument which is used to measure a known emf by comparison with known emf.
Sensitivity of potentiometer is the smallest potential difference can be measured using the potentiometer. It can be increased by decreasing its potential gradient. Thus, it can be increased by following methods.
1) By increasing length of the potentiometer wire as the length of the wire is directly proportional to resistance.
2) If the potentiometer wire is a fixed length, the potential gradient can be decreased by reducing the current in the circuit by varying rheostat.
Hence, the correct option is (b).

49. Magnetic flux density is the magnetic flux per unit area perpendicular to the direction of the magnetic force.
As flux density is inversely proportional to cross sectional area, it will get doubled by reducing area of cross section to half of its original value.
Hence, the correct option is (a).

50. Recovery Voltage: The RMS voltage that appears across the circuit breaker contacts after final arc interruption (when breaker opens) is called "recovery voltage"

Restriking Voltage: It may be defined as the voltages that appears across the breaking contact at the instant of arc extinction

Active Recovery Voltage: It may be defined as the instantaneous recovery voltage at the instant of arc extinction

Arc Voltage: It may be defined as the voltages that appears across the contact during the arcing period, when the current flow is maintained in the form of an arc. It assumes low value except for the point at which the voltage rises rapidly to a peak value and current reaches to zero. Hence, the correct option is (c).

51.

1. Reluctance start motor is a type of synchronous motor.
2. The reluctance motor has basically two main parts called stator and rotor.
3. The stator has a laminated construction, made up of stampings.
4. The stampings are slotted on its periphery to carry the winding called stator winding.
5. The stator carries only one winding and it is excited by single-phase AC supply.
6. The rotor has a particular shape. Due to its shape, the air gap between stator and rotor is not uniform.
7. Its working principle is similar to a shaded pole motor. Hence, the correct option is (a).

52. Power Factor is a ratio of the real power and apparent power flowing in the circuit.

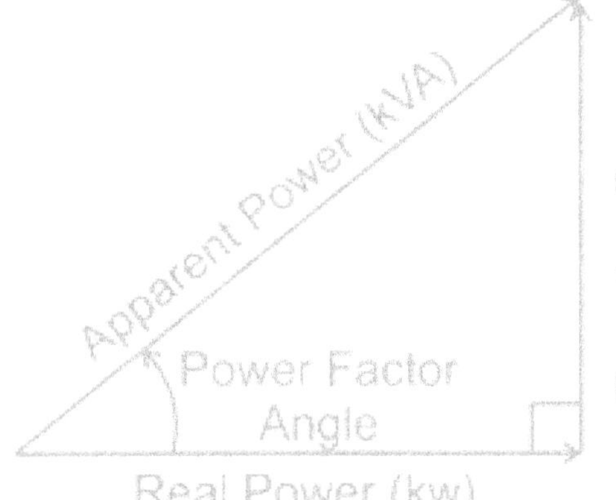

$$\text{Power factor} = \frac{\text{Real power}}{\text{Apparent power}} = \frac{R}{Z} = \frac{V_R}{V}$$

$$\cos\phi = \frac{100}{125} = 0.8$$

Important:
Active power (measured in Watt) is actual power or true power which does the useful work. (so, most of the equipment's which consume electricity or electric power are rated in terms of Watt or HP)
Reactive power (measured in Volt-Ampere- Reactive) is imaginary power which is required for the processes like energy conversion & energy storage. (so, the equipment's which generate only reactive power are rated in terms of VAr. e.g. capacitor banks for pf correction)
Apparent power (measured in terms of Volt-Ampere) is total power. And is combination of active and reactive powers.
Hence, the correct option is (a).

53. In two wattmeter method, the wattmeter readings are given by

$$W_1 = V_L I_L \cos(30 - \phi)$$
$$W_2 = V_L I_L \cos(30 + \phi)$$

Total power $= W_1 + W_2$

Reactive power $= \sqrt{3}(W_1 - W_2)$

Power factor $= \cos\phi$

Where $\phi = \tan^{-1}\left(\frac{\sqrt{3}(W_1 - W_2)}{(W_1 + W_2)}\right)$

Important Point:

p.f. angle (ϕ)	p.f. $(\cos\phi)$	W_1 $[V_L I_L \cos(30+\phi)]$	W_2 $[V_L I_L \cos(30-\phi)]$	$W = W_1 + W_2$ $[W =$]	Observation
0	1	$\frac{\sqrt{3}}{2}V_L I_L$	$\frac{\sqrt{3}}{2}V_L I_L$	$\sqrt{3}V_L I_L$	$W_1 = W_2$
30	0.866	$\frac{V_L I}{2}$	$V_L I_L$	$1.5V_L I_L$	$W_2 = 2W_1$
60	0.5	0	$\frac{\sqrt{3}}{2}V_L I_L$	$\frac{\sqrt{3}}{2}V_L I_L$	$W_1 = 0$
90	0	$\frac{-V_L I_L}{2}$	$\frac{V_L I_L}{2}$	0	$W_1 = -ve$ $W_2 = -ve$

Hence, the correct option is (d).

54. Effect of the waveform:

1. The rectifier type of instruments is calibrated in terms of r.m.s. values of sinusoidal currents and voltages
2. The markings on the instrument are 1.11 and 2.22 times of the average current for full wave and half wave rectification respectively
3. These instruments are subject to waveform errors as other waveforms may not have a form factor of 1.11 (in case of full wave rectifier) or 2.22 (in the case of half wave rectifier)
4. **Effect of Temperature Change:** The resistance of the rectifying element varies with the change in temperature. And this property of the rectifying component causes the error in the instruments.

Frequency Error: As PPMC instrument used in rectifier instruments, frequency error is absent.
Hence, the correct option is (c).

55. The leakage current in a transistor mainly depends on temperature and doubles for every 10°C rise in temperature. This leakage current dependence on temperature is responsible for thermal run-away in transistors.
Hence, the correct option is (b).

56.

1. Induction type of energy meter are universally used for measurement of energy in domestic and industrial A.C circuit.

2. The unit of electrical energy is kilowatt hour (KWh).

3. Induction type of energy meter used is based on the "electromagnetic induction" principle.

4. They are known as induction type instruments.

5. An induction meter can handle current up to 100 A.
    Hence, the correct option is (d).

57. KCL in DC circuits:

According to Kirchhoff's current law (KCL), the algebraic sum of the electric currents meeting at a common point is zero. I.e. the sum of currents entering a node is equal to the sum of currents leaving the node. It is based on the conservation of charge.

KCL in AC circuits:

The Kirchhoff's current law as applied to the ac circuit is defined as the phasor sum of currents entering the node is equal to the phasor sum of currents leaving the node.
Hence, the correct option is (b).

58. High permeability core in MI instrument helps in reducing size of instrument and increase sensitivity. It is the ability of a magnetic material to support magnetic field development.
Hence, the correct option is (b).

59.

1. A capacitor start capacitor run motor is used in a ceiling fan

2. It essentially consists of a running winding and a starting winding

3. The capacitor is connected in series with the starting winding to make it start

4. Secondary winding surrounds the primary winding and at starting these both are connected in parallel.
    Hence, the correct option is (a).

60. The direction of rotation of a capacitor start motor can be reversed by reversing the connection of the main winding or auxiliary winding.

To reverse the direction of rotation of a capacitor start motor while it is running, we should disconnect the motor from the supply till it stops then reconnect it to supply with the reversed connection of main or auxiliary winding.
Hence, the correct option is (a).

61. The speed control of three-phase induction motor from the stator side are classified as:

1. $\dfrac{V}{f}$ control or frequency control

2. Changing the number of stator poles

3. Controlling supply voltage

4. Adding rheostat in the stator circuit

The speed controls of three-phase induction motor from rotor side are classified as:

1. Adding external resistance on the rotor side

2. Cascade control method

3. Injecting slip frequency emf into rotor side
    Hence, the correct option is (a).

62. Plant capacity factor

$$= \frac{\text{Peak load}}{\text{Plant capacity}} \times \text{load factor}$$

$$0.15 = \frac{2}{\text{Plant capacity}} \times 0.4$$

∴ Plant capacity $= 5.33 MW$

∴ Reserve capacity

$=$ Plant capacity - Peak load

$= 5.333 - 2 = 3333 kW$

Hence, the correct option is (d).

63.

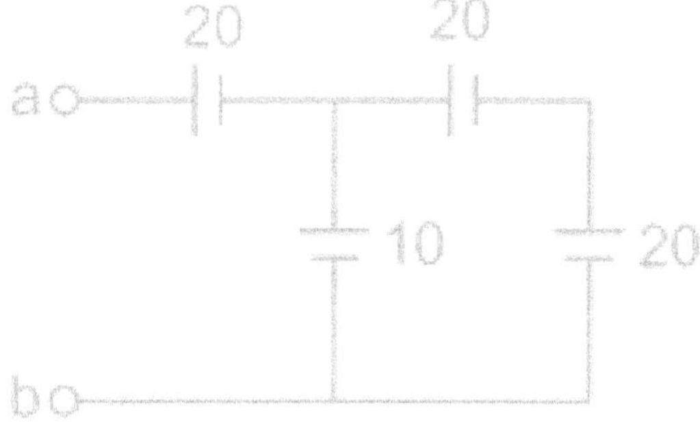

$$\frac{20\times20}{20+20} = 10$$

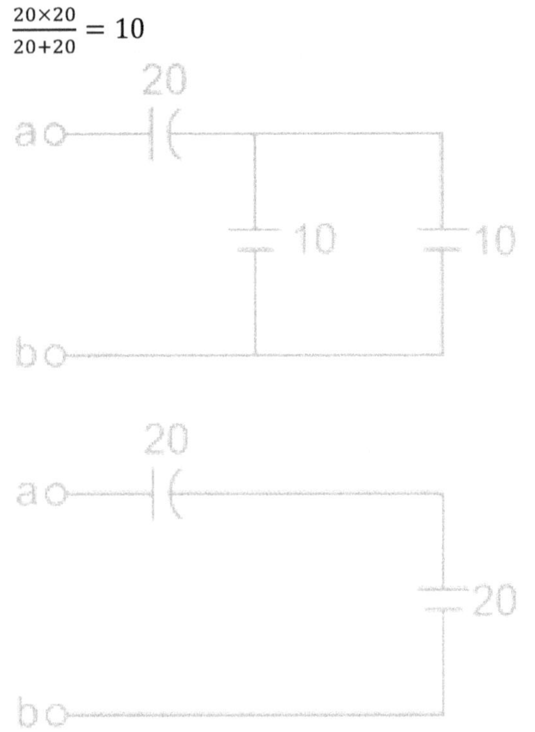

$$E_{ab} = \frac{20\times20}{20+20} = 10\mu F$$

Hence, the correct option is (b).

64. This type of breakdown occurs at the reverse bias voltage above 8 V and higher. It occurs for lightly doped diode with large breakdown voltage. As minority charge carriers (electrons) flow across the device, they tend to collide with the electrons in the covalent bond and cause the covalent bond to disrupt.
Hence, the correct option is (b).

65. Conditions to build up the voltage in shunt generator:

1. The shunt winding should have a residual magnetic field.

2. The direction of the shunt winding and armature winding should be in such a way that flux generated by them should aid together.

3. The shunt winding should have critical winding resistance.

Voltage building in shunt generator:

When the armature is rotated, the residual flux in the field winding will induce a small voltage in the armature. The induced voltage in armature generates a flux and it will aid with field flux and the net flux will increase further. This process will be repeating until the actual terminal voltage is reached.

This process is restricted by the saturation of the iron core. Once the terminal voltage is reached then the winding will get saturated and hence there won't be any further increase in flux, also the voltage gets constant.
Hence, the correct option is (a).

66. Voltage regulation is the change in secondary terminal voltage from no load to full load at a specific power factor of

load and the change is expressed in percentage.
E_2 = no-load secondary voltage
V_2 = Full load secondary voltage
Voltage regulation for the transformer is given by the ratio of change in secondary terminal voltage from no load to full load to no load secondary voltage.

$$\text{Voltage regulation } = \frac{E_2 - V_2}{E_2}$$

It can also be expressed as,

$$\text{Regulation } = \frac{I_2 R_{02}\cos\phi_2 \pm I_2 X_{02}\sin\phi_2}{E_2}$$

+ sign is used for lagging loads and
ve sign is used for leading loads

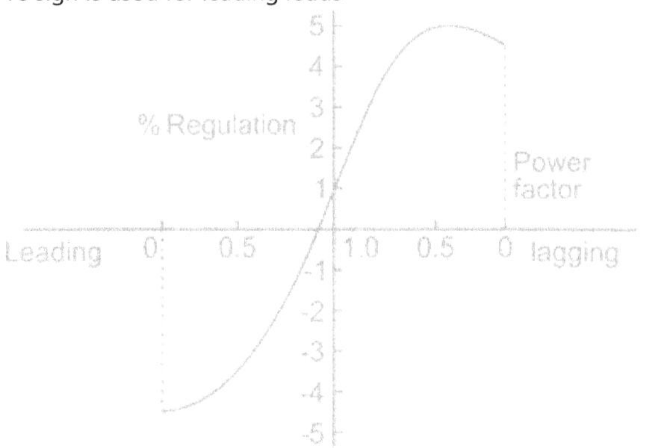

From the above graph, the poorest voltage regulation of a transformer at full load is at 0.8 lagging power factor.
Hence, the correct option is (b).

67.

1. For the same conductor length, same amount of power, same losses and same maximum voltage to earth, 3 wire DC system requires minimum conductor area.

2. For transmitting the same amount of power at the same voltage, a three-phase transmission line requires less conductor material than a single-phase line. The three-phase transmission system is so cheaper.

3. For a given amount of power transmitted through a system, the three-phase system requires conductors with a smaller cross-sectional area. This means a saving of copper and thus the original installation costs are less.

Important Point:

Below is given the table which shows the ratio of conductor-material in any system compared with that in the corresponding 2-wire DC system. Cos φ is the power factor in an AC system.

System	Same maximum voltage to earth	Same maximum voltage between conductors
DC system: Two wire	1	1
DC:Two wire mid-point earthed	0.25	1
DC: 3 wire	0.3125	1.25

Single phase:2 wire	$\dfrac{2}{\cos 2\phi}$	$\dfrac{2}{\cos 2\phi}$
Single phase:2 wire mid-point earthed	$\dfrac{0.5}{\cos 2\phi}$	$\dfrac{2}{\cos 2\phi}$
Single phase:3 wire	$\dfrac{0.625}{\cos 2\phi}$	$\dfrac{2.5}{\cos 2\phi}$
2-phase:4 wire	$\dfrac{0.5}{\cos 2\phi}$	$\dfrac{2}{\cos 2\phi}$
2-phase:3 wire	$\dfrac{1.457}{\cos 2\phi}$	$\dfrac{2.914}{\cos 2\phi}$
3-phase:4 wire	$\dfrac{0.5}{\cos 2\phi}$	$\dfrac{1.5}{\cos 2\phi}$
3-phase:3 wire	$\dfrac{0.583}{\cos 2\phi}$	$\dfrac{1.75}{\cos 2\phi}$

Hence, the correct option is (b).

68. Norton's equivalent current is nothing but the short circuit current flows through the terminals A and B.

Let the short circuit current be I_{sc}. The circuit can be reduced as,

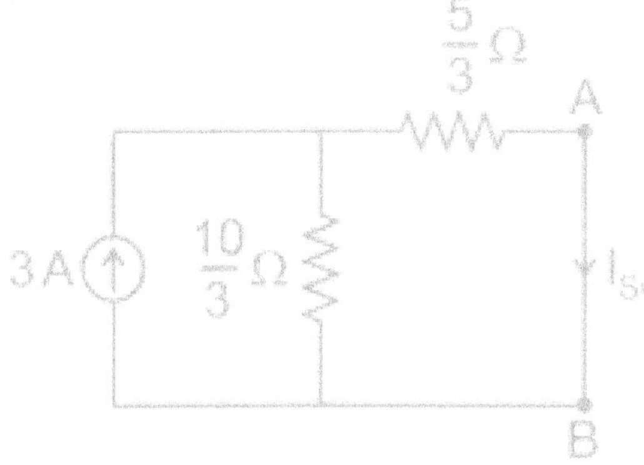

By using current division rule,

$$I_{sc} = 3\left(\frac{\frac{10}{3}}{\frac{10}{3}+\frac{5}{3}}\right) = 3 \times \frac{10}{15} = 2A$$

Hence, the correct option is (b).

69.

1. Heaviside bridge is used to measure the mutual inductance.

2. Maxwell's inductance capacitance bridge is used to measure the inductance of high-quality factor coils.

3. Hay's bridge is used to measure the inductance of high-quality factor coils.

4. Anderson bridge is used to measure the inductance.

Important Point

Heaviside bridge:

1. This bridge uses mutual inductance to measure self-inductance over a wide range.

2. The bridge which measures the unknown mutual inductance regarding mutual inductance such type of bridge is known as the Campbell bridge.

3. The mutual inductance is the phenomenon in which the variation of current in one coil induces the current in the nearer coil.

4. The bridge also used for measuring the frequency by adjusting the mutual inductance until the null point is not obtained.

Hence, the correct option is (a).

70. Advantages of carbon arc welding:

1. The heat developed during the welding can be easily controlled by adjusting the length of the arc.

2. It is quite clean, simple, and less expensive when compared to other welding processes.

3. Both the ferrous and non-ferrous metals can be welded.

4. Easily adaptable to automation.

Disadvantages of carbon arc welding:

1. Input current required in this welding, for the workpiece to raise its temperature to welding temperature, is more.

2. In case of ferrous metal, there is a chance of disintegrating the carbon at high temperature and transfer to the weld, which causes weld deposit to be harder and brittle.

3. A separate filler rod has to be used if any filler metal is required.

Hence, the correct option is (d).

71. The speed of the induction motor can be controlled by the following methods:

1) $\dfrac{V}{f}$ control (or) frequency control.

2) Changing the number of stator poles.

3) Controlling supply voltage.

4) Changing winding resistance by adding rheostat in the stator circuit.

In AC locomotives, pole changing method of speed control is used for squirrel cage induction motors.

Important Points:

Rheostatic control is the simplest but the least efficient method of speed control of 3-phase induction motors. This method of speed control is employed in light locomotives and motor coaches where a single economical speed is sufficient and energy consumption is of no importance.

Pole changing control is the simplest of the multi-speed control methods. This method has the advantage of simplicity, good speed regulation for each setting, high operation efficiency, and moderate first cost and maintenance. The choice of the number of poles on a pole-changing winding is in the ratio of 2: 1, 3: 2, 4: 3.

Hence, the correct option is (a).

72. Apply superposition theorem:

Consider 10 V source and open the current source

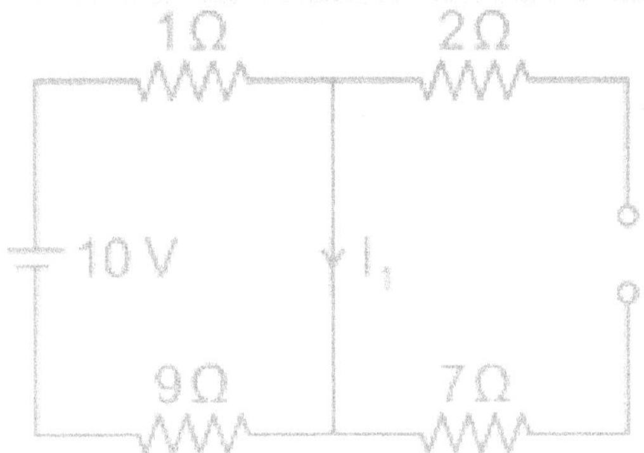

$$I_1 = \frac{10}{10} = 1A$$

Now consider current source and inactive the voltage source

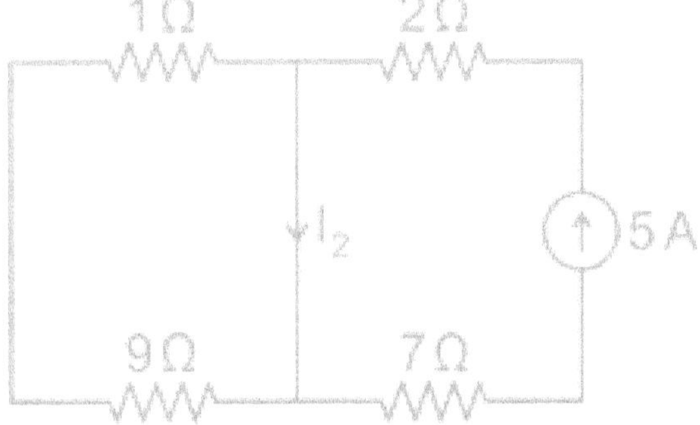

$$I_2 = 5A$$

∴ Total current $I = I_1 + I_2 = 1 + 5 = 6A$

Hence, the correct option is (d).

73. Bakelite is used for making electric plug because it is a rigid thermosetting plastic that is highly heat resistant. Once cured during the compression moulding process, it cannot be melted or recycled.

Hence, the correct option is (b).

74. Paramagnetic materials

1. Small, positive susceptibility to magnetic fields.

2. These materials are slightly attracted by a magnetic field.

3. Paramagnetic properties are due to the presence of some unpaired electrons, and from the realignment of the electron paths caused by the external magnetic field.

4. Paramagnetic materials include magnesium, molybdenum, lithium, and tantalum.

Important:

Ferromagnetic materials

1. Have a large, positive susceptibility to an external magnetic field.

2. They exhibit a strong attraction to magnetic fields and can retain their magnetic properties after the external field has been removed.

3. Ferromagnetic materials have some unpaired electrons, so their atoms have a net magnetic moment.

4. Iron, nickel, and cobalt are examples of ferromagnetic materials.

Diamagnetic materials

1. Weak, negative susceptibility to magnetic fields.

2. Diamagnetic materials are slightly repelled by a magnetic field.

3. All the electrons are paired so there is no permanent net magnetic moment per atom.

4. Most elements in the periodic table, including copper, silver, and gold, are diamagnetic.

Hence, the correct option is (a).

75. An armature control method is used in the DC shunt motor.

In a DC motor, the back emf is directly proportional to speed and flux.

$E_b \propto N\varphi$

Where N is speed and φ is flux.

In a DC shunt motor, flux is constant.

So, the back emf is directly proportional to speed.

Important Point:

Armature resistance control:

We know that,

$$N \propto \frac{E_b}{\phi}$$

$$N \propto \frac{V - I_a(R_a + R)}{\phi}$$

We can control the speed by increasing armature resistance. This method gives only below base speeds. This method is a constant torque and variable power drive.

Field control method:

We know that,

$$N \propto \frac{E_b}{\phi}$$

$$N \propto \frac{V - I_a R_a}{\phi}$$

By varying flux, we can increase the speed more than its base speed. This method is constant power and variable torque drive. The characteristics are shown below

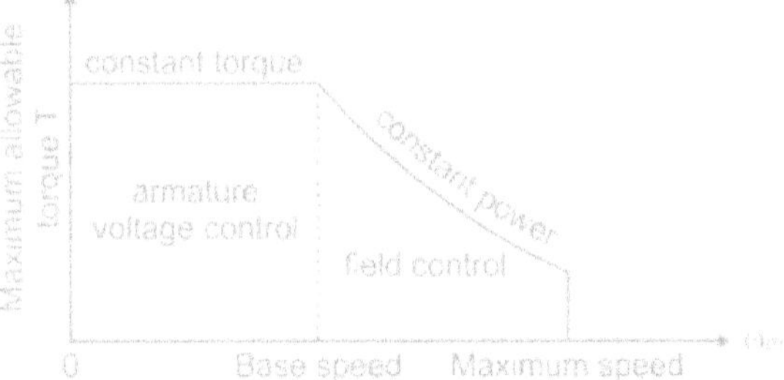

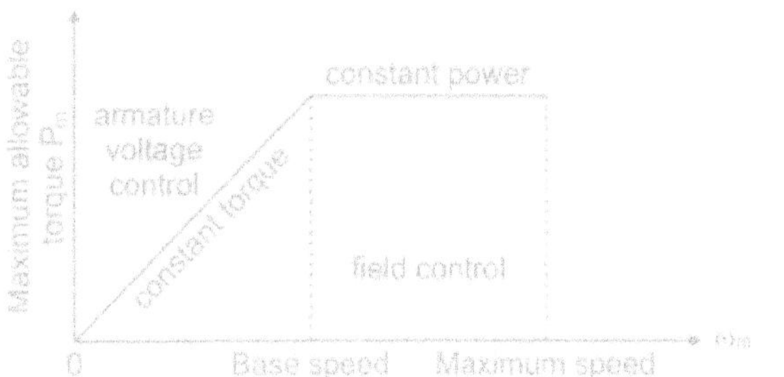

Hence, the correct option is (a).

76.

Lamp	Application
Neon discharge lamp	Used as night lamps and as an indicator lamps and used for the determination of the polarity of DC mains and for advertising purpose
Sodium vapor lamp	Used for highway and street lighting, parks, railway yards, general outdoor lighting
Mercury vapor lamp	Industrial lighting, ports, shopping centres, railway yards
Carbon arc lamp	Cinema projector, search light and flash camera

Hence, the correct option is (a).

77. Circle Diagram:

1. It is the diagrammatic representation of the performance of the induction motor.

2. It provides information about the power output, losses and the efficiency of the induction motor.

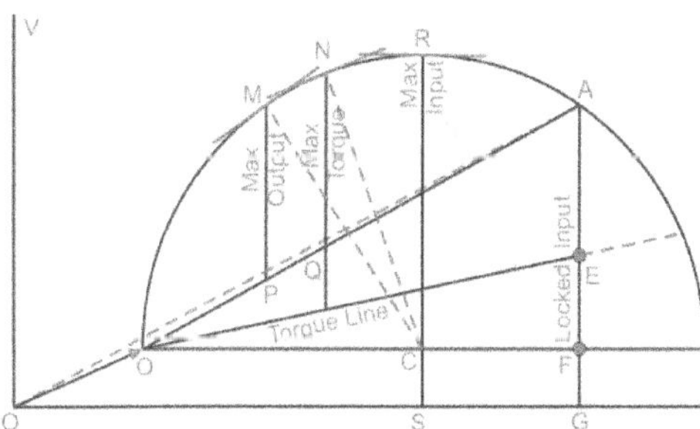

Significance of lines on the Circle Diagram:

Input line: The vertical distance between any point on the circle and the input line represent the input power.

Output line: The vertical distance between any point on the circle and the output line represents the output power.

Air gap power line: This line represents the air gap power. This line is also known as a torque line. It separates stator and rotor copper losses in the circle diagram.
Hence, the correct option is (b).

78. The breaking torque is given by

$$T_B \propto N\phi_m^2 d$$

$\therefore N \propto \dfrac{1}{d}$ i.e speed of disc is inverse relation with the position of spindle from the permanent magnet.
If an induction type energy meter runs fast, it can be slowed by

adjusting the position of braking magnet and making it move away from the centre of the disc.
Hence, the correct option is (d).

79. The values of maximum flux density for different transformers are as follows:

For hot rolled silicon steel:

1. Distribution transformer – 1.1 to 1.35 T
2. Power transformer – 1.25 to 1.45 T

For CRGO core:

1. Up to 132 kV – 1.55 T
2. For 275 kV – 1.6 T
3. For 400 kV and generation transformer – 1.7 to 1.75 T
   Hence, the correct option is (c).

80.

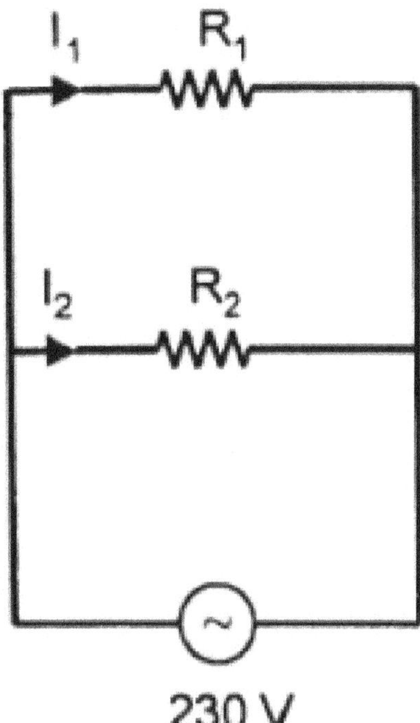

In a parallel connection, the voltage across each element is the same. So when 100W bulb and 500W bulb are connected in parallel, the voltage across them will be the same (230 V in the given case). To find which bulb will glow brighter we need to find the power dissipation across each of them. From the relation

$$P = \frac{V_2}{R}$$

$$R_{100} = \frac{230^2}{100} = 529 \Omega$$

$$R_{500} = \frac{230^2}{500} = 105.8 \Omega$$

Since the voltage is the same we can say that power dissipation will be higher for the bulb with lower resistance i.e. 500W bulb. Therefore 500-watt bulb will glow brighter.
Hence, the correct option is (b).

81. $\phi = \tan^{-1}\sqrt{3}\left(\frac{W_1 - W_2}{W_1 W_2}\right)$

$\phi = \tan^{-1}\sqrt{3}\left(\frac{W_1 - W_2}{W_1 W_2}\right) = 0$

$= \cos\phi = \cos0° = 1$

Hence, the correct option is (c).

82.

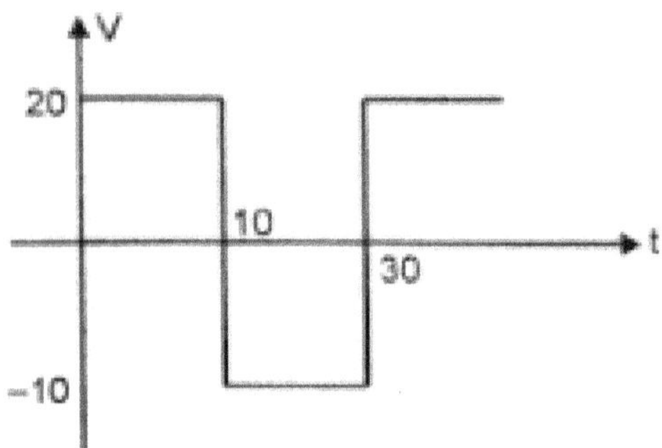

RMS Value of the current of the sine wave is

$I = \sqrt{\text{Mean value of } I^2}$

$I = \sqrt{\frac{I_1^2 + I_2^2 + \cdots\cdots I_n^2}{n}}$

$= \sqrt{\frac{20^2(10+0)+(-10)^2(30-10)}{10+20}}$

$= 14.14A$

Hence, the correct option is (d).

83. For maximum power transfer, input Impedance must be equal to the conjugate of output Impedance.

As we know that the impedance of input is something to which a signal is applied to measure of how much power that input will tend to draw (from a given output voltage). This impedance is known as the load impedance.

Therefore $Z_2 = Z_1{}^*$

Hence, the correct option is (d).

84. $L_{eq} = L_1 L_2 2M$

$= 222 = 64$

$f = \frac{1}{2\pi\sqrt{L_{eq}C}} = \frac{1}{2\pi\sqrt{6\times2}} = \frac{1}{4\pi\sqrt{3}}Hz$

Hence, the correct option is (a).

85. $\tan\phi = \frac{X_L - X_C}{R}$

$\Rightarrow X_L - X_C = (\tan60°)R = R\sqrt{3}$

Hence, the correct option is (b).

86. Active power consumed = P = VI tan φ

1000 × 0.5 × 0.01 = 5W

Hence, the correct option is (a).

87. Electrodynamic Wattmeter consists of a pair of fixed coils, known as current coils, and a movable coil is known as the potential coil. The fixed coils are made up of a few turns of a comparatively large conductor. The potential coil consists of many turns of fine wire. The current coils are connected in series

with the circuit, while the potential coil is connected in parallel.

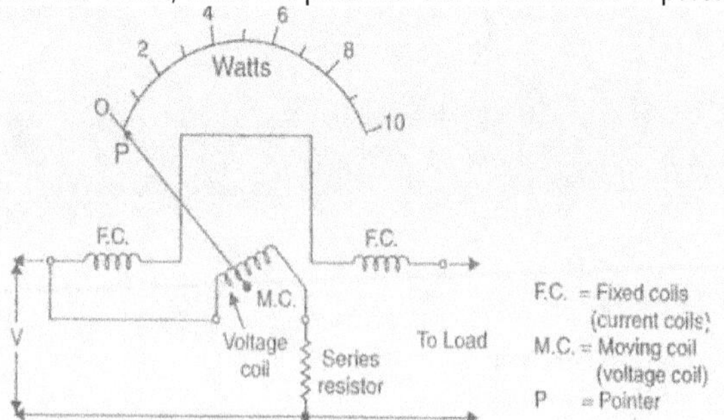

When line current flows through the current coil of a wattmeter, a field is set up around the coil. Since for AC power, current and voltage may not be in phase, owing to the delaying effects of circuit inductance or capacitance. Therefore the potential coil of the wattmeter generally has a high-resistance resistor connected in series with it. This is for the purpose of making the potential-coil circuit of the meter as purely resistive as possible. As a result, current in the potential circuit is practically in phase with line voltage. Hence, the correct option is (a).

88. Given,

$V = 4\cos\omega t$

$i = 1.5\cos\omega t - 2.598 \sin \omega t$

$= 1.5\cos\omega t + 2.598\sin\left(\omega t + \frac{\pi}{2}\right)$

$Or\ I = l_a(\cos\omega t + \theta)$

Where I_a is amplitude or peak value of current which is given as

$I_a = \sqrt{a^2 + b^2 + 2ab\cos\phi}$

$I_a =$

$\sqrt{1.5^2 + (2.598)^2 + 2 \times 1.5 \times 2.598 \times \cos\left(\frac{\pi}{2}\right)}$

$= 3$

$\tan\theta = \frac{2.598}{1.5} = 60°$

So, $i = 3\cos(\omega t + 60°)$

& $V = 4\cos(\omega t)$

So, Current leads voltage by $60°$.

Hence, the correct option is (a).

89. The use of D-Arsonval galvanometer very common in the variety of measuring instrument. The galvanometer is basically used in an instrument for detecting the presence of small voltages or currents in a circuit or to indicate zero current in applications lilts bridge circuits. Thus galvanometer has to be very much sensitive.

Damping: The damping is eddy current damping. The eddy currents developed in the metal former on which coil is mounted, are responsible to produce damping torque. For effective damping, low resistance is connected across the galvanometer terminals. By adjusting the value of this resistance damping can be changed and critical damping can be achieved.

Hence, the correct option is (a).

90. Spring Control Method

The springs used in measuring instruments for providing the

controlling torque must have the following properties.

1. These should be of non-magnetic material.
2. Specific resistance should be low.
3. Resistance temperature coefficient should be low.
4. These should not be affected much by mechanical fatigue.

Phosphor Bronze is the most suitable for the springs of an indicating instrument as it satisfies most of the above properties. In this method, two spiral hair springs are used and spiralled in opposite direction. The use of two springs also avoids error due to temperature variations. One end of both the springs are attached to the body of the instrument and another end is attached to the moving system.

When the instrument is not in use, the two springs are in their natural position without any tension or compression(deflecting torque = Controlling Torque). When the instrument is connected to the circuit for the measurement, deflecting torque acts and the pointer moves on the calibrated scale. One of the springs is unwound while the other gets twisted. The resultant movement in the springs provides the controlling torque.
More the deflection more is the twist and hence greater will be the controlling torque. Thus the controlling torque is directly proportional to the deflection of the moving system, i.e.,
Tc ∝ θ

And it is also clear that the pointer comes to rest when controlling torque becomes numerically equal to deflecting torque i.e

Tc = Td

But the deflection or the deflection torque depends upon the current flowing through it, hence

I ∝ θ

Hence, the correct option is (a).

91. The Range of DC milliammeter can be extended by using resistance in parallel.The shunts are low resistances used in ammeters for range extension. The shunt is made of Manganin or Constantan depending on whether it is used for DC or AC.

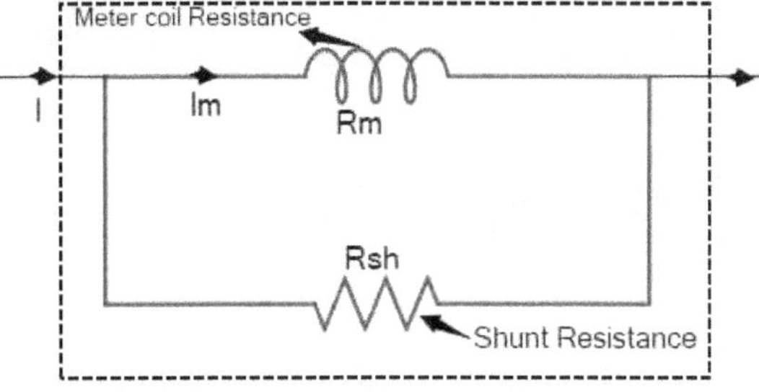

Milli Ammeter

With I_m as the current flow through the meter capable of producing the maximum deflection, precautions are to be taken to ensure that the current through the meter coil is limited to I_m. However, when the current to be measured is large, the alternative path is provided via, the low resistance shunt R_{sh}.
Hence, the correct option is (b).

92. Damping system decides the time response of an indicating instrument. Torque/Weight ration of an instrument decides the sensitivity of an indicating instrument. It should be high for high sensitivity of the instrument. An indicating instrument is more sensitive if its torque to weight ratio is of the order of unity. Hence, the correct option is (b).

93. The power factor of the load is given as
$$\cos\phi = \text{costan}^{-1}\sqrt{3}\left(\frac{W_1 - W_2}{W_1 W_2}\right)$$
As $W_1 = 2W_2$
$$\cos\phi = \text{costan}^{-1}\frac{\sqrt{3}}{3} = \cos\frac{\pi}{6} = 0.866 \text{ (leading)}$$
For $W_2 = 2W_1$
$$\cos\phi = -0.866 \text{ (lagging)}$$
Hence, the correct option is (c).

94. Air gap power P_g
$$P_g = P_{\text{input}} - \text{stator Loss}$$
$$P_g = 60 - 1 = 59 \ kW$$
Rotor copper loss = $S \times P_g$
$$= 0.04 \times 59 = 2.36 \ kW$$
Hence, the correct option is (b).

95. Core loss = Eddy current loss + Hysteresis loss
= $K_e f^2 + K_c f$
At 50 Hz, Pc = 46 watt
$46 = K_e (50)^2 + K_h \times 50$.......... (1)
At 70 Hz, Pc = 80 watt
$70 = K_e (70)^2 + K_h \times 70$.............. (2)
From equation (1) and (2),
$K_e = 0.0111$
$K_h = 0.363$
Now at 60 Hz,
$P_e = K_e \times 602$
= $0.0111 \times 3600 = 39.96 \cong 40$ Watt
$P_h = 0.36306 \times 60$
= $21.78 \cong 22$ Watt
Hence, the correct option is (d).

96. In the galvanometer circuit, the dissimilar metals come in contact and generate the thermal e.m.f.s . Such thermal e.m.f.s may cause affected while measuring low-value resistances. To prevent this, more sensitive galvanometers having copper coils and copper suspension systems are used.
Hence, the correct option is (b).

97. $T = K_1\phi I_a$
$$\frac{T_1}{T_2} = \frac{I_{a2}}{I_{a1}}$$
[ϕ is constant for DC shunt motor]
$$\Rightarrow T_2 = T_1 \times \frac{I_{a2}}{I_{a1}} = 60 \times \frac{20}{10} = 120 \text{ N-m}$$
Hence, the correct option is (d).

98. Alternators are connected primarily in the star to achieve the following motives:

1. The phase voltages in star connection is 57.7 % of the line voltages, i.e. the armature winding in star connection is less exposed to voltage as compared to

the delta connection which in turn prove more economic if we consider insulation, breakdown strength, the requirement of conductor material

2. **Easy protection:** Neutral grounding is necessary to allow zero sequence currents to flow to the ground in case of a fault.

3. **Elimination of harmonics:** Star connection facilitates a neutral connection which is instrumental in eliminating triple harmonics.

4. **No circulating currents:** In star connection, we don't have circulating parasitic currents like in Delta which lead to heating losses.
   Hence, the correct option is (b).

99. In case of DC shunt generator if we reverse the rotation there is no voltage build up.When we rotate the generator in reverse direction, flux due to residual magnetism will be cancelled out and hence generator will not get sufficient initial flux for emf build up.Hence, the correct option is (a).

100. For cleat wiring and 250 volt supply the cables will be placed (standard value) 4 cm apart from center to center for single are cable.

This type of wiring is not used practical for permanent wiring and is only suitable for temporary wiring purposes such as for marriages with advantages of saving labor and overall cost.

The cleat should be provided every 60 cm to avoid sag in the cables. Sharp bends should be avoided in the wiring and the spacing between the cleats should be reduced to prevent the touching of the wall and sagging.
Hence, the correct option is (c).

101. Closed-cycle OTEC uses working fluids that are typically thought of as refrigerants such as **ammonia** or R-134a. These fluids have low boiling points, and are therefore suitable for powering the system's generator to generate electricity.
Hence, the correct option is (a).

102. The heat energy trapped in a certain region of earth's crust is called geo thermal energy.
Magma heats nearby rocks and underground aquifers. Hot water can be released through geysers, hot springs, steam vents, underwater hydrothermal vents, and mud pots. These are all sources of geothermal energy. Their heat can be captured and used directly for heat, or their steam can be used to generate electricity.
Hence, the correct option is (c).

103. Here,

Power = 200w and time = 5min.

$E = P \times t$

$E = 200 \times 5$

$= 1000Wmin$

$= 60000Ws$

$= 60000J$

$= 60kJ$

Hence, the correct option is (C).

104. The stored water behind the dam has a potential energy which charges into the kinetic energy of falling water. This kinetic energy is utilized to rotate the turbine to produce electricity. Hence, the correct option is (a).

105. The sun is considered the primary energy source since it is the source of nearly all the earth's energy. Plants produce food using sunlight, and the food we get from plants and animals also has its primary sunlight source.
Hence, the correct option is (b).

106. Solar energy leads to least environmental pollution in the process of its harnessing and utilization because it doesn't emit harmful gases in the environment. In case of nuclear energy, the major concerns of pollution are while storage and disposal of spent fuels where there is always a risk of leakage of radiation.
Hence, the correct option is (c).

107. Energy of warm surface water used to vaporise the low boiling point liquid ammonia. This vapours at high pressure is used to strin the turbines to generate electricity. Deep ocean cold water again condenses the used vapour into liquid.
Ocean Thermal Energy Conversion (OTEC) uses the temperature difference between cooler deep and warmer shallow or surface ocean water to run a heat engine and produce useful work, usually in the form of electricity.
Hence, the correct option is (b).

108. The waste product obtained from nuclear power plant is highly radioactive material and harmful for human beings and environment.
Major problem in harnessing nuclear energy is ,how to dispose its residue which is highly radioactive in nature. It requires proper waste disposal mechanism.
Hence, the correct option is (c).

109. In a solar cooker the glass sheet prevents the thermal radiation of the sun light from going out of the box,causing green house effect.
Hence, the correct option is (c).

110. Power generated in a windmill depends on the velocity of the wind. More is the velocity $\rightarrow$ more will be the velocity of the windmills thereby generating more power.
Hence, the correct option is (a).

111. Fossil fuels inside the earth are present in very limited amount. Hydro and wind energy plants run with the help of air and do not cause any pollution. A larger amount of potential energy is converted into kinetic energy due to which more electric power will be obtained.
Hence, the correct option is (c).

112. Ideal fuel should have a proper ignition temperature, so that it can be burned easily. The ignition temperature of an ideal fuel should neither be too low nor too high. If the ignition temperature of the fuel is very low, then the fuel will catch fire too easily and hence it will be very unsafe to use it.
Hence, the correct option is (d).

113. Anthracite: The highest rank of coal. It is a hard, brittle, and black lustrous coal, often referred to as hard coal, containing a high percentage of fixed carbon and a low percentage of volatile

matter.
Hence, the correct option is (a).

114. Calorific value provides the amount of energy that is released when a fuel or material undergoes the process of combustion. It is usually a measure of energy. The SI unit (international system of units) of calorific value is Joule/Kg or Kilo Joule/Kg.
Hence, the correct option is (d).

115. Biogas is a type of biofuel that is naturally produced from the decomposition of organic waste. When organic matter, such as food scraps and animal waste, break down in an anaerobic environment (an environment absent of oxygen) they release a blend of gases, primarily methane and carbon dioxide.
Hence, the correct option is (d).

116. A solar cell, or photovoltaic cell, is an electrical device that converts the energy of light(sun) directly into electricity by the photovoltaic effect.
Hence, the correct option is (c).

117. Energy- abundant, versatile, reliable, portable, and affordable, fossil fuels provide over 80 percent of the worlds energy because they are superior to the current alternatives, Disadvantage of most of the renewable energy sources is its unreliable supply.
Hence, the correct option is (c).

118. Naturally occurring mixture of a hydrocarbon gas with methane being the primary constituent is called natural gas. Other gases found in minute traces are hydrogen, hydrogen sulphide, nitrogen, carbon monoxide and carbon dioxide.
Hence, the correct option is (a).

119. Horizontal axis means the rotating axis of the wind turbine is horizontal, or parallel with the ground. With vertical axis wind turbines the rotational axis of the turbine stands vertical or perpendicular to the ground.Hence, the correct option is (b).

120. A fuel cell, in order to produce electricity, burns Hydrogen. A fuel cell is nothing but a reaction in which hydrogen bonds in the presence of oxygen to produce water.
This results in the production of a large amount of heat which is converted into electricity.
This electricity is then make to run in a closed circuit resulting in the production of current and running of appliance- a fuel cell is a modern cell which is developed to produce electricity without causing any damage to the exhaustible natural resources.
Hence, the correct option is (c).

Part - I

Q.1 Out of the four alternatives, choose the one which best expresses the meaning of the given word.
Voracious.

A. Quick   **B.** Angry   **C.** Hungry   **D.** Wild

Q.2 Direction : In the following questions, choose the word opposite in meaning to the given word.
Unsullied

A. paper   **B.** soggy   **C.** tarnished   **D.** swarthy

Q.3 Find the correctly spelt word.

A. Vaudville   **B.** Vawdville

C. Vaudeville   **D.** Vaudiville

Q.4 Direction : In the following question, a sentence is given with a blank to be filled in with appropriate word(s). Some alternatives are suggested for each question. Choose the correct alternative from the given alternatives.
Manya is disgusted _____ the habit of her husband.

A. at   **B.** on   **C.** of   **D.** with

Q.5 In the following question, a sentence is given with a blank to be filled in with appropriate word(s). Some alternatives are suggested for each question. Choose the correct alternative from the given alternatives.
At times he gets very angry, and then no one can _____ him.

A. prevent   **B.** humour   **C.** mollify   **D.** satisfy

Q.6 Direction : In the following questions, four alternatives are given for the meaning of the given Idiom/Phrase. Choose the alternative which best express the meaning of the Idiom/Phrase.
Barking up the wrong tree.

A. Scolding the one who is innocent.

B. Expecting a favour from a heartless person.

C. Looking in the wrong place.

D. Requesting but in an arrogant manner.

Q.7 In the following questions, four alternatives are given for the meaning of the given Idiom/Phrase. Choose the alternative which best express the meaning of the Idiom/Phrase.
To keeps one's temper

A. To become hungry

B. To preserve ones energy

C. To be aloof from

D. To be in good mood

Q.8 Direction : In the following questions out of the four alternatives, choose the one which is best express the meaning of the given word.
SPLENETIC

A. Enfranchise   **B.** Waspish

C. Bulwark   **D.** Blare

Q.9 The Editor of 'Young India' and 'Harijan' was-

A. Nehru

B. Ambedkar

C. Mahatma Gandhi

D. Subash Chandra Bose

Q.10 A Presidential Ordinance can remain in force-

A. For Three months   **B.** For six months

C. For nine months   **D.** Indefinitely

Q.11 Who said that Directive principles of state policy are just like 'a cheque payable by the bank concerned at its convenience.'

A. Pandit Nehru   **B.** K. T. Shah

C. B. R. Ambedkar   **D.** N. G. Ranga

Q.12 India making 'Double Taxation Avoidance Agreements' (DTAA) with other countries for the promotion of:

A. Bilateral trade

B. External commercial borrowings

C. Foreign direct investments

D. Foreign institutional investment

Q.13 What is used to identify whether a data word has an odd or even number of 1's ?

A. Sign bit   **B.** Zero bit

C. Parity bit   **D.** Carry bit

Q.14 'Shock–absorbers' are usually made of steel as it:

A. is not brittle

B. has lower elasticity

C. has higher elasticity

D. has no ductile property

Q.15 The pH of human blood is

A. 7.2   **B.** 7.8   **C.** 6.6   **D.** 7.4

Q.16 BT seed is associated with:-

A. Rice   **B.** Wheat

C. Cotton   **D.** Oil seeds

Q.17 The expense of placing the mat on the floor is Rs. 759. If the length is shortened by 6m, then the expense would be Rs.561.Find the rate of the mat per metre (If the breadth of the floor is same as the breadth mat).

A. Rs.21 per metre   **B.** Rs.23 per metre

C. Rs.45 per metre   **D.** Rs.33 per metre

Q.18 One bacteria splits into eight bacteria of the next generation. But due to environment, only 50% of one generation can produce the next generation. If the seventh generation number is 4096 million, what is the number in first generation?

A. 1 million   **B.** 2 million   **C.** 4 million   **D.** 8 million

Q.19 If $\dfrac{p}{b-c} = \dfrac{q}{c-a} = \dfrac{r}{a-b}$, then $p + q + r = ?$

A. 0   **B.** 1   **C.** -1 **D.** 2

Q.20 A sum was put at S.I. at a certain rate for 6 years. Had it been put at 4% higher rate, it would have fetched Rs. 960 more. The sum was:

A. Rs. 3000   **B.** Rs. 3500   **C.** Rs. 4000   **D.** Rs. 4500

Q.21 If $a + b + c = 2s$, then $\dfrac{(s-a)^2+(s-b)^2+(s-c)^2+s^2}{a^2+b^2+c^2}$ is equal to :

A. $a^2+b^2+c^2$ **B.** 0

C. 1   **D.** 2

Q.22 The number of prime factor is $(8)^{20} \times (15)^{24} \times (7)^{15}$ is :-

A. 59   **B.** 98   **C.** 123   **D.** 138

Q.23 66 cubic centimetres of silver is drawn into a wire 1 mm in diameter. The length of the wire in metres will be:

A. 72   **B.** 90   **C.** 84   **D.** 66

Q.24 If $\dfrac{\sin\theta+\cos\theta}{\sin\theta-\cos\theta} = \dfrac{5}{4}$, then value of $\dfrac{\tan^2\theta+1}{\tan^2\theta-1}$

A. 1   **B.** $\dfrac{40}{41}$ **C.** $\dfrac{41}{40}$ **D.** 0

Q.25 Here are some words translated from an artificial language.
gorblflur means fan belt
pixngorbl means ceiling fan
arthtusl means tile roof
Which word could mean "ceiling tile"?

A. gorbltusl   **B.** flurgorbl   **C.** arthflur   **D.** pixnarth

Q.26 In these series, you will be looking at both the letter pattern and the number pattern. Fill the blank in the middle of the series or end of the series.

SCD, TEF, UGH, ___, WKL

A. CMN   **B.** UJI   **C.** VIJ   **D.** IJT

Q.27 In the following question, select the related number from the given alternatives.

24 : 71 :: 42 : ___

A. 123   **B.** 124   **C.** 125   **D.** 156

Q.28 Each of the following questions contains a small paragraph followed by a question on it. Read each paragraph carefully and answer the question given below it.

The attainment of individual and organisational goals is mutually interdependent and linked by a common denominator - employee work motivation. Organisational members are motivated to satisfy their personal goals, and they contribute their efforts to the attainment of organisational objectives as means of achieving these personal goals.

The passage best supports the statement that motivation -

A. encourages an individual to give priority to personal goals over organisational goals.

B. is crucial for the survival of an individual and organisation.

C. is the product of an individual's physical and mental energy.

D. is the external force which induces an individual to contribute his efforts.

Ques (29-32):Directions: Tech Vinayak software company before selling a package to its clients, follows the given schedule.

Month	Stage	cost (Rs '000 per month)
1 – 2	Specification	40
3 – 4	Design	20
5 – 8	coding	10
9 – 10	Testing	15
11 – 15	Maintenance	10

Month	1	2	3	4	5	6	7	8	9	10	11	12	13
Number of people employed	2	3	4	3	4	5	5	4	4	1	3	3	1

Q.29 Due to overrun in design, the stage took 3 months, i.e., months 3, 4 and 5. the number of people working on design in the fifth month was 5. Calculate the percentage change in cost incurred in the fifth month. (Due to improvement in Coding technique, this stage was completed in month 6-8 only.)

A. 150%   **B.** 225%   **C.** 270%   **D.** 240%

Q.30 With reference to the previous question, what is the cost incurred in the new Coding stage ? (Under new technique 4 people work in the sixth month and 5 in the eighth).

A. Rs. 1,40,000   **B.** Rs. 1,50,000
C. Rs. 1,60,000   **D.** Rs. 1,90,000

Q.31 What is the difference in cost between the old and new techniques ?

A. Rs. 30,000   **B.** Rs. 60,000
C. Rs. 70,000   **D.** Rs. 40,000

Q.32 Under the new technique, which stage of software development is most expensive.

A. Testing   **B.** Specification
C. Coding   **D.** Design

Q.33 Pravasi Bhartiya Kendra has been renamed after which late Union Minister?

A. Sushma Swaraj

B. Atal Bihari Vajpayee
C. Arun Jaitley
D. Manohar Parrikar

Q.34 President Ram Nath Kovind presented the President's Colour to which military unit?
A. INS Vikrant
B. INS Satlej
C. INS Shivaji
D. INS Shivalik

Q.35 Which state government has approved a five day week for government employees?
A. Uttar Pradesh
B. Rajasthan
C. Maharashtra
D. Madhya Pradesh

Q.36 Which state's Chief Minister has launched 'Anganphou Hunba' programme?
A. Meghalaya
B. Manipur
C. Assam
D. Nagaland

Q.37 When is World Radio Day celebrated every year?
A. 11th February
B. 12th February
C. 13th February
D. 14th February

Q.38 When National Women's Day of India is celebrated in the country?
A. 10th February
B. 11th February
C. 12th February
D. 13th February

Q.39 What is the name of world's oldest person who was officially confirmed as the oldest living man by the Guinness World Records on February 12, 2020?
A. Chitetsu Watanabe
B. Chi Hun Saan
C. John Barracks
D. Dai Nippon Meiji

Q.40 Where is the world's biggest cricket stadium being constructed that will be inaugurated by the US President Donald Trump in February 2020?
A. New York
B. Gujarat
C. Sydney
D. Barcelona

Part - II

Q.41 PVC is preferred over VIR in extreme environments such as in cement/chemical factory. This is because
A. PVC is inert to oxygen and almost inert to oils and too many alkaline and acids
B. PVC is less costly
C. of good mechanical properties of PVC
D. All of the above

Q.42 Galvanizing is a process of applying a layer of zinc on a metal surface. It is also known as:-
A. Hot dip galvanization
B. Anodizing
C. Electroplating
D. Cathodizing

Q.43 The moderator used in fast breeder reactor is:
A. Heavy water
B. Graphite
C. Ordinary water
D. Any of these

Q.44 Belt conveyors offer:
A. High starting torque
B. Medium starting torque
C. Low starting torque
D. Zero starting torque

Q.45 The S.I. unit of Electric Field is:-
A. NC^{-2}
B. NC^{-1}
C. NC^{-3}
D. None of These

Q.46 Four wires of the same material, same cross-section area and the same length, when connected in parallel, give effective resistance of 0.25 ohm. If these four wires are connected in series, then the effective resistance will be:
A. 4 ohm
B. 1 ohm
C. 2 ohm
D. 0.50 ohm

Q.47 Which of the following is a passive component?
A. semiconductor devices
B. vacuum tube devices
C. capacitors
D. All of these

Q.48 What is the function of rheostat in the circuit?
A. It limits the current
B. It increases the current
C. It makes the current constant in the circuit
D. It increases the voltage

Q.49 Which of the following statements regarding a shell-type transformer is incorrect?
A. It provides a shorter magnetic path
B. Magnetizing current is lesser as compared to the core type
C. Natural cooling is quite good
D. It gives better support against electromagnetic forces between the current-carrying transformer

Q.50 In an impedance relay, fault current is maximum if fault occurs near the________.
A. Relay
B. Center of the line
C. Transformer
D. None of these

Q.51 $(23)_8 + (67)_8$ is:
A. $(90)_8$
B. $(112)_8$
C. $(1101)_8$
D. $(111)_8$

Q.52 Which of the following is different from others?
A. Spot welding
B. Seam welding
C. Butt welding
D. Argon arc welding

Q.53 Salient pole generators are used in hydro power plant, because____________________.
A. Salient pole machines are suitable to run at low speed.
B. Salient pole machines are suitable to run at high speed.
C. Salient pole machines are more stable.
D. Salient pole machines are water cooled.

Q.54 If three resistors R_1 = 2 kΩ, R_2 = 4 kΩ and R_3 = 6 kΩ are connected in series across a 12V Battery then the voltage across R_2 is ______.
A. 4 V
B. 8 V
C. 12 V
D. 16 V

Q.55 The resistance of a conductor is directly proportional to:

A. Its area of cross-section

B. density

C. melting point

D. length

Q.56 What is the capacitance when a capacitor carries a charge of 0.6 C at 30 V?

A. 2 F

B. 0.2 F

C. 0.02 F

D. None of these

Q.57 The main consideration in designing feeders is:-

A. Current carrying capacity

B. Voltage drop

C. Resistance

D. Transmission voltage

Q.58 A strong magnetic field is applied on a stationary electron. Then the electron:

A. moves opposite to the direction of the field.

B. moves in the direction of the field.

C. remained stationary.

D. moves perpendicular to the direction of the field.

Q.59 Boost charge is given to:-

A. Dead battery

B. Battery in danger of becoming over-discharged during a working shift

C. Fully charged battery

D. Completely discharged battery

Q.60 The Thevenin equivalent for the network of the figure is:

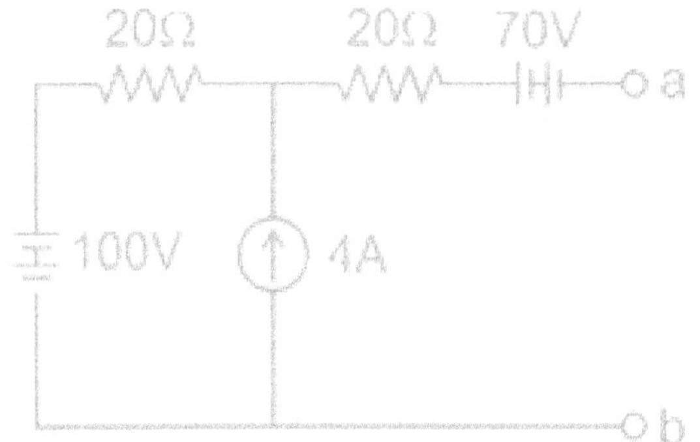

A. 110 V, 10Ω

B. 110 V, 40Ω

C. 30 V, 40Ω

D. 30 V, 10Ω

Q.61 Major insulation in a transformer is the insulation between the:

A. LV winding and core

B. LV winding and HV winding

C. Turns of the windings

D. Both (a) and (b)

Q.62 Leclanche cell is most suited for:

A. Continuous use

B. Large current requirements

C. Intermittent use

D. Large voltage requirements

Q.63 A certain network consists of two ideal voltage sources and a large number of ideal resistors. The power consumed in one of the resistors is 4 W when either of the two sources is active and the other is replaced by a short circuit. The power consumed by the same resistor, when both the sources are simultaneously active, would be:

A. Zero or 16 W

B. 4 W or 8 W

C. Zero or 8 W

D. 8 W or 16 W

Q.64 A fuse wire is inserted in :-

A. May be connected in any line

B. In the earth wire

C. In the neutral wire

D. Live wire

Q.65 A 680 Ω load resistor R_L, is connected across a constant current source of 1.0 A. The internal source resistance, R_S, is 12 k Ω. The load current through R_L is:-

A. 0.2 A

B. 1.2 A

C. 1.14 mA

D. 0.94 A

Q.66 Which instrument is used for measuring electric potential?

A. ammeter

B. voltmeter

C. potentiometer

D. galvanometer

Q.67 The level of illumination on a surface least depends on

A. Ambient temperature

B. Candle power of the source

C. Distance of the source

D. Type of reflector used

Q.68 How many relays are used to detect interphase fault of a three-line system?

A. One

B. Two

C. Three

D. Six

Q.69 In the majority of instruments, damping is provided by:-

A. fluid friction

B. spring

C. eddy currents

D. All of these

Q.70 A transformer Is a ________ devlce.

A. Active

B. Passive

C. Unilateral

D. None of these

Q.71 Reduced voltage starter can be used with:

A. Slip ring motor only but not with squirrel cage induction motor

B. Squirrel cage induction motor only but not with slip ring motor

C. Squirrel cage as well as slip ring induction motor

D. None of the above

Q.72 In a primary cell, the local action can be rectified by:

A. Charging the cell

B. Amalgamating the zinc electrode with mercury

C. Using a cell for few minutes only

D. Making a dry cell

Q.73 A stationary alternator should not be connected to a live busbar because of it:

A. will get short-circuited

B. will disturb generated e.m.fs of other alternators connected in parallel

C. is likely to run as a synchronous motor

D. will decrease busbar voltage though momentarily

Q.74 In a single-phase induction motor, the motor speed on no load is:

A. Almost equal to its synchronous speed

B. Less than its synchronous speed

C. Greater than synchronous speed

D. None of these

Q.75 Earth electrode used in plate earthing is a ______.

A. Plate   **B.** Pipe   **C.** Rod   **D.** Grid

Q.76 Two spheres of radii R_1 and R_2 ($R_2 > R_1$) are connected by a conducting wire. Each of the spheres has been given a charge q. Now:

A. Sphere of radius R_1 will have greater potential

B. Sphere of radius R_2 will have greater potential

C. Potential of both the spheres will be equal

D. Sphere of radius R_1 will have zero potential

Q.77 The thermal resistance between junction and the SCR (θ_{jc}) has the unit:

A. $\Omega/°C$ **B.** W/Ω **C.** $°C/W$ **D.** $\Omega W/°C$

Q.78 In any bilateral network, if a source of e.m.f. E in any branch produces a current I in any other branch, then same e.m.f. acting in the second branch would produce the same current I in the first branch. This statement is associated with

A. Compensation theorem

B. Reciprocity theorem

C. Superposition theorem

D. None of the above

Q.79 An electric heater is connected to the voltage supply. After few seconds, current gets its steady value then its initial current will be:

A. equal to its steady current

B. slightly higher than its steady current

C. zero

D. slightly less than its steady current

Q.80 The motor best suited for DC traction is:

A. DC shunt motor

B. DC differentially compounded motor

C. DC series motor

D. Stepper motor

Q.81 If the collector current changes 2 mA to 3 mA in a transistor when collector-emitter voltage is increased from 2 V to 10 V, find the output resistance.

A. 2 kΩ   **B.** 4 kΩ   **C.** 6 kΩ   **D.** 8 kΩ

Q.82 Find the rms current in a capacitor of 0.1 µF, when an AC voltage of 5 V and frequency of 5 kHz is applied to it.

A. 1.57 mA   **B.** 15.71 mA

C. 12.57 mA   **D.** 25.32 mA

Q.83 An alternator with higher value of SCR has:

A. Poor voltage regulation and lower stability limit

B. Better voltage regulation and higher stability limit

C. poor voltage regulation and higher stability

D. Better voltage regulation and lower stability limit

Q.84 With the rise in temperature, the insulation resistivity:

A. Reduces exponentially

B. Reduces linearly

C. Increases linearly

D. Remains same

Q.85 What is the composition of the alloy 'Kanthal' (used as a heating element in electrical heating systems)?

A. Chromium, aluminum, nickel

B. Chromium, aluminium, iron

C. Chromium, copper, cobalt

D. Chromium, aluminium, cobalt, iron

Q.86 Potentiometer method is used for the measurement of:

A. Low C   **B.** High R

C. Low R   **D.** Medium R

Q.87 The equivalent ______ is the sum of individual ______ for a parallel circuit.

A. Conductance, Conductance

B. Conductance, Resistance

C. Resistance, Conductance

D. Conductance, Substance

Q.88 In the series combination of two or more than two resistances:

A. neither current nor voltage through each resistance is same.

B. both current and voltage through each resistance are same.

C. the current through each resistance is same.

D. the voltage through each resistance is same.

Q.89 The efficiency of a transmission line is:

A. Independent of load

B. Increase with decrease in load p.f.

C. Increase with the increase in load p.f.

D. Decrease with the increase in load p.f.

Q.90 In parallel combination of n cells, we obtain:

A. more voltage   **B.** more current

C. less voltage   **D.** less current

Q.91 Which of the following power stations will take least time in starting from cold condition to full load operation?

A. Nuclear power plant   **B.** Steam power plant

C. Gas turbine plant   **D.** Hydro power plant

Q.92 The following system is used in connections of various lamps and appliances in parallel. Identify the system.

A. Gain-in-system   **B.** Loop-in-system

C. Voltage-in-system   **D.** Parallel-in-system

Q.93 In a Wheatstone bridge if the battery and galvanometer are interchanged then the deflection in galvanometer will:

A. change in previous direction
B. not change
C. change in opposite direction
D. none of these.

Q.94 Two parallel wires separated by a distance 'd' are carrying a DC current 'I' in the same direction. The magnetic field along a line running parallel to these wires and midway between them _________.

A. depends upon I
B. is zero
C. depends upon d
D. depends upon the permeability of the medium between the wires

Q.95 When a magnet is in motion relative to a coil the induced e.m.f. does not depend upon:

A. resistance of the coil
B. motion of the magnet
C. number of turns of the coil
D. pole strength of the magnet

Q.96 Main reason for break point in the load characteristic of a dc generator is:-

A. Ohmic drop
B. Armature reaction
C. Both (1) and (2)
D. None of these

Q.97 The device which acts like an NPN and a PNP transistor base to collector and emitter to base is:

A. Triac
B. UJT
C. Diac
D. SCR

Q.98 Hysteresis loss least depends on:-

A. Volume of material
B. Frequency
C. Steinmetz coefficient of material
D. Ambient temperature

Q.99 Which of the following materials has a large number of free electrons in it?

A. Insulators
B. Semiconductors
C. Conductors
D. Resistors

Q.100 The cross-section of conductors for large size DC machines are:-

A. Circular
B. Rectangular
C. Triangular
D. Trapezoidal

Q.101 When a metal conductor connected to left gap of a meter bridge is heated, the balancing point:

A. shifts towards right
B. shifts towards left
C. remains unchanged
D. remains at zero

Q.102 The angle of deviation of the normal to the surface from the local meridian is called as ________.

A. Surface azimuth angle
B. Solar azimuth angle
C. Solar altitude
D. Hour angle

Q.103 The angle being measured from a plane and which is equal to angle between the beam of rays and normal to the plane is called _________.

A. Incident angle
B. Azimuth angle
C. Hour angle
D. Declination

Q.104 The vector sum of the components along the line normal of the titled surface in a direction normal to the tilted surface is called as_________.

A. Solar intensity
B. Declination
C. Incident angle
D. Hour angle

Q.105 The time from sunrise to sunset is termed as _____________.

A. Slope
B. Day length
C. Local solar time
D. Solar intensity

Q.106 Which of the following states is well known for terrace cultivation?

A. Punjab
B. Haryana
C. Uttar Pradesh
D. Uttarakhand

Q.107 How much would be the angle of declination on DECEMBER 21 at 0900 h (LAT). The collector s located in New Delhi (28°35'N, 77°12'E) and is tilted at an angle of 36° with the horizontal and is pointing south?

A. -44.28 °
B. -28.92 °
C. -23.45 °
D. -42.22 °

Q.108 Which of the following I-V graph represents ohmic conductors?

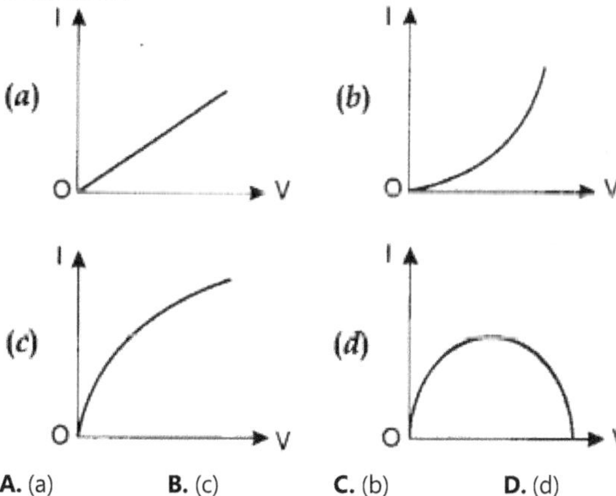

A. (a)
B. (c)
C. (b)
D. (d)

Q.109 When a magnetic compass needle is carried nearby to a straight wire carrying current, then:

(I) the straight wire cause a noticeable deflection in the compass needle.

(II) the alignment of the needle is tangential to an imaginary circle with straight wire as its centre and has a plane perpendicular to the wire.

A. both (I) and (II) are correct
B. (I) is correct
C. (II) is correct
D. neither (I) nor (II) is correct

Q.110 When the sun is directly on the top of head, it as referred to ________.

A. Zenith
B. Azimuth

C. Declination   **D.** Hour angle

Q.111 Path length of radiation through the atmosphere to the length of path when the sun is at zenith is called __________.

A. Declination   **B.** Air mass

C. Azimuth   **D.** Solar Constant

Q.112 In half-wave rectification, what is the output frequency if the input frequency is 50 Hz. What is the output frequency of a full-wave rectifier for the same input frequency?

A. 100 Hz   **B.** 50 Hz

C. 2 Hz   **D.** none of these

Q.113 Angle made by radial line joining the location to the centre of the earth with the projection of the line on the equatorial plane is called ________.

A. Latitude   **B.** Zenith angle

C. Hour angle   **D.** Declination

Q.114 Angular distance of sun's rays north or south of the equator is called ______.

A. Declination   **B.** Hour angle

C. Latitude   **D.** Air mass

Q.115 By which of the following symbol is solar Declination denoted by __________.

A. δ **B.** ρ **C.** Δ **D.** γ

Q.116 The angle through which the earth must turn to bring the meridian of a point directly in sun's rays is called ________.

A. Hour angle   **B.** Declination

C. Latitude   **D.** Air mass

Q.117 Solar Altitude is also called as ______.

A. Declination   **B.** Altitude angle

C. Zenith angle   **D.** Azimuth angle

Q.118 The angle between the sun's rays and a line perpendicular to the horizontal plane through angle the beam of the sun and vertical is called ________.

A. Solar Azimuth angle

B. Zenith angle

C. Altitude angle

D. Declination

Q.119 The solar angle in degrees along the horizon east or west of north or it is the horizontal angle measured from north to the horizontal projection of sun's rays is called ________.

A. Solar azimuth angle   **B.** Zenith angle

C. Altitude angle   **D.** Declination

Q.120 Angle made by plane surface with horizontal is called ________.

A. Slope   **B.** Altitude angle

C. Zenith angle   **D.** Hour Angle

// Smart Answer Sheet //

Correct — Indicates percentage of students who answered questions correctly.

Skipped — Indicates percentage of students who skipped questions.

Q.	Ans.	Correct	Skipped
1	C	82.09 %	10.67 %
2	C	79.26 %	19.84 %
3	C	84.19 %	11.98 %
4	A	84.54 %	12.26 %
5	C	76.06 %	21.36 %
6	C	78.13 %	20.1 %
7	D	80.39 %	13.36 %
8	B	89.83 %	10.12 %
9	C	76.56 %	10.17 %
10	B	81.24 %	17.75 %
11	B	79.71 %	13.67 %
12	A	81.06 %	18.12 %
13	C	89.67 %	10.26 %
14	C	79.19 %	15.36 %
15	D	80.69 %	10.3 %
16	C	84.78 %	13.67 %
17	D	81.2 %	10.73 %
18	A	80.27 %	16.42 %
19	A	81.01 %	14.68 %
20	C	79.23 %	11.53 %
21	C	88.58 %	11.25 %
22	C	89.61 %	10.37 %
23	C	78.93 %	15.07 %
24	C	81.57 %	11.17 %
25	D	79.97 %	16.19 %
26	C	80.18 %	19.4 %
27	C	82.09 %	17.67 %
28	A	76.44 %	20.09 %
29	A	77.61 %	11.92 %
30	D	82.98 %	11.37 %
31	B	79.48 %	15.38 %
32	B	87.84 %	10.42 %
33	A	81.26 %	16.4 %
34	C	81.47 %	16.69 %
35	C	84.18 %	14.61 %
36	B	76.07 %	11.3 %
37	C	76.36 %	13.23 %
38	D	81.84 %	16.81 %
39	A	79.6 %	19.61 %
40	B	78.54 %	14.99 %
41	A	85.12 %	10.26 %
42	A	86.79 %	12.76 %
43	D	79.47 %	17.62 %
44	A	81.62 %	17.82 %
45	B	83.64 %	15.64 %
46	A	77.86 %	20.76 %
47	C	87.75 %	11.98 %
48	A	79.28 %	17.35 %
49	C	82.32 %	14.08 %
50	A	88.52 %	10.7 %
51	B	82.82 %	13.94 %
52	D	80.39 %	19.01 %
53	A	81.96 %	14.37 %
54	A	79.88 %	15.28 %
55	D	77.22 %	15.91 %
56	C	80.41 %	11.47 %
57	A	76.06 %	10.15 %
58	C	81.31 %	13.78 %
59	B	88.05 %	10.39 %
60	B	84.66 %	14.57 %
61	D	83.43 %	16.09 %
62	C	76.18 %	10.69 %
63	A	78.27 %	10.68 %
64	D	87.23 %	12.57 %
65	D	88.53 %	10.71 %
66	B	82.67 %	16.74 %
67	A	88.33 %	10.95 %
68	C	80.57 %	16.99 %
69	C	78.36 %	19.47 %
70	B	77.96 %	15.88 %
71	C	78.69 %	20.75 %
72	B	79.0 %	18.31 %
73	A	76.9 %	18.28 %
74	A	86.83 %	11.94 %
75	A	89.18 %	10.81 %
76	C	84.63 %	13.43 %
77	C	83.59 %	15.49 %
78	B	80.93 %	10.08 %
79	B	76.43 %	11.19 %
80	C	89.1 %	10.07 %

Q.	Ans.	Correct
		Skipped
81	D	86.52 %
		13.23 %
82	B	79.91 %
		12.43 %
83	B	86.51 %
		11.93 %
84	B	87.64 %
		11.72 %
85	B	88.81 %
		10.8 %
86	C	79.64 %
		19.73 %
87	A	79.77 %
		10.71 %
88	C	80.67 %
		11.05 %

Q.	Ans.	Correct
		Skipped
89	C	76.29 %
		16.41 %
90	B	77.4 %
		17.72 %
91	D	86.91 %
		12.09 %
92	B	85.18 %
		12.76 %
93	B	86.99 %
		10.47 %
94	B	77.23 %
		19.36 %
95	A	89.27 %
		10.39 %
96	B	82.69 %
		10.96 %

Q.	Ans.	Correct
		Skipped
97	D	87.67 %
		11.75 %
98	D	78.35 %
		14.34 %
99	C	84.79 %
		12.33 %
100	B	85.68 %
		10.59 %
101	A	86.87 %
		10.79 %
102	A	81.8 %
		14.44 %
103	A	87.68 %
		10.33 %
104	A	80.55 %
		19.35 %

Q.	Ans.	Correct
		Skipped
105	B	81.93 %
		13.91 %
106	D	79.48 %
		17.79 %
107	C	84.6 %
		12.07 %
108	A	78.26 %
		12.9 %
109	A	86.44 %
		12.18 %
110	A	76.33 %
		20.43 %
111	B	81.56 %
		14.11 %
112	A	87.42 %
		10.81 %

Q.	Ans.	Correct
		Skipped
113	A	88.78 %
		10.09 %
114	A	79.4 %
		13.47 %
115	A	86.85 %
		11.71 %
116	A	76.84 %
		14.01 %
117	B	76.47 %
		16.32 %
118	B	85.8 %
		13.94 %
119	A	79.53 %
		10.77 %
120	A	80.45 %
		18.44 %

Performance Analysis	
Avg. Score (%)	36.67%
Toppers Score (%)	62.5%
Your Score	

//Hints and Solutions//

1. 'Voracious' means very eager for something, especially for food. E.g:- He has a voracious appetite. 'Quick' means fast. 'Angry' means annoyed or upset with something or something. 'Hungry' means wanting food. 'Wild' means not controlled.

Hence, the correct option is (c).

2. Unsullied

opposite : tarnished

Similarly:- swarthy, soggy, paper

Hence, the correct option is (c).

3. Correct Spelling is Vaudeville.

Vaudeville, a farce with music. In the United States the term connotes a light entertainment popular from the mid-1890s until the early 1930s that consisted of 10 to 15 individual unrelated acts, featuring magicians, acrobats, comedians, trained animals, jugglers, singers, and dancers.

Hence, the correct option is (c).

4. disgusted at=Very unhappy or disappointed with someone or something.

Manya is disgusted at the habit of her husband.

Hence, the correct option is (a).

5. Mollify: appease the anger or anxiety of (someone).

At times he gets very angry, and then no one can mollify him.

Hence, the correct option is (c).

6. Barking up the wrong tree mean that looking in the wrong place.

Hence, the correct option is (c).

7. Definition of keep one's temper : to not become angry, begin shouting, etc. He was upset but kept his temper.

Hence, the correct option is (d).

8. SPLENETIC mean that Waspish.

Waspish definition: A waspish remark or sense of humour is sharp and critical .

Hence, the correct option is (b).

9. Gandhiji was the editor of three English weeklies, namely Indian Opinion (in South Africa during 1903-1915), Young India (1919- 1931), and Harijan (1933-1942 and 1946-January 1948).

Hence, the correct option is (c).

10. President can issue ordinance when one of the houses of the Parliament is not in session. The maximum validity of an ordinance is 6 months and 6 weeks. An ordinance will expire after 6 weeks once both houses of the Parliament are in session.

Hence, the correct option is (b).

11. K.T. Shah described the Directive Principles of State Policy as 'a cheque payable by the bank concerned at its convenience.'

Hence, the correct option is (b).

12. The Double Tax Avoidance Agreements (DTAA) is essentially bilateral agreements entered into between two countries, in our case, between India and another foreign state. The basic objective is to avoid, taxation of income in both the countries (i.e. Double taxation of same income) and to promote and foster economic trade and investment between the two countries. Its key objective is that tax-payers in these countries can avoid being taxed twice for the same income. A DTAA applies in cases where a tax-payer resides in one country and earns income in another.Its key objective is that tax-payers in these countries can avoid being taxed twice for the same income. A DTAA applies in cases where a tax-payer resides in one country and earns income in another.

Hence, the correct option is (a).

13. A parity bit, or check bit is a bit added to the end of a string of binary code that indicates whether the number of bits in the string with the value one is even or odd. Parity bits are used as the simplest form of error detecting code.

Hence, the correct option is (c).

14. A shock absorber is a mechanical device designed to smooth out or damp shock impulse, and dissipate kinetic energy. Steel is an alloy made by combining iron and other elements, the most common of these being carbon. When carbon is used, its content in the steel is between 0.2% and 2.1% by weight, depending on the grade. Varying the amount of alloying elements and the form of their presence in the steel (solute elements, precipitated phase) controls qualities such as the higher elasticity, hardness, ductility, and tensile strength of the resulting steel.

Hence, the correct option is (c).

15. Blood is normally slightly basic, with a normal pH range of **7.35 to 7.45**.

Hence, the correct option is (d).

16. The cotton incorporated the cry1Ac gene from the soil bacterium Bacillus thuringiensis (Bt), making the cotton toxic to bollworms. It is a cheaper alternative to Bt cotton hybrid seed. Bt cotton is a genetically modified cotton. It is produced by a company called Mansanto.

Hence, the correct option is (c).

17. The expense of the floor mat = Rs. 759

Expense after shorting 6m= Rs. 561

therefore, expense of 6 m = 759-561=198

So cost of mat per meter $= \dfrac{198}{6} = Rs.\,33$ per metre.

Hence, the correct option is (d).

18. Let there be x bacteria in first generation.

Due to environment 50% i.e. would be able to produce the next generation. And they will give rise to 4x bacteria.

likewise, able to produce the next generation and they will give rise to 4(4x)= 16x bacteria. on the basis of the pattern we find that a G.P. will be formed as x, 4x, 16x, 64x........

seventh generation number = ar^{n-1}

4096 = x(4)^6

$x = \dfrac{4096}{4^6}$

= 1 million

Hence, the correct option is (a).

19. $\dfrac{p}{b-c} = \dfrac{q}{c-a} = \dfrac{r}{a-b}$

$\dfrac{p}{b-c} = \dfrac{q}{c-a} = \dfrac{r}{a-b} = k$

$p = k(b-c), q = k(c-a), r = k(a-b)$

$\Rightarrow p = kb - kc, q = kc - ka, r = ka - kb$

$p + q + r = kb - kc + kc - ka + ka - kb = 0$

Hence, the correct option is (a).

20. Let the Principal be Rs. P and Ratebe R\%.
According to the question,

$\dfrac{P\times(R+4)\times6}{100} - \dfrac{P\times R\times6}{100} = 960$

$\dfrac{24P}{100} = 960$

$\therefore P = Rs.\ 4000$

Hence, the correct option is (c).

21. $= \dfrac{(s-a)^2+(s-b)^2+(s-c)^2+s^2}{a^2+b^2+c^2}$

$= \dfrac{s^2-2sa+a^2+s^2+b^2-2sb+s^2-2sc+c^2+s^2}{a^2+b^2+c^2}$

$= \dfrac{4s^2+a^2+b^2+c^2-2s(a+b+c)}{a^2+b^2+c^2}$

$= \dfrac{4s^2+a^2+b^2+c^2-4s^2}{a^2+b^2+c^2} => 1$

Hence, the correct option is (c).

22. $(8)^{20} \times (15)^{24} \times (7)^{15}$

$= 2^{60} \times 3^{24} \times 5^{24} \times 7^{15}$

Total number of prime factors $= 60 + 24 + 24 + 15 =>$ 123

Hence, the correct option is (c).

23. Let the length of the wire be h.

Radius $= \dfrac{1}{2}mm = \dfrac{1}{20}cm.$ Then

$\Rightarrow \dfrac{22}{7} \times \dfrac{1}{20} \times \dfrac{1}{20} \times h = 66$

$\Rightarrow h = \left(\dfrac{66\times20\times20\times7}{22}\right) = 8400cm$

$= 84m$

Hence, the correct option is (c).

24. $\dfrac{\sin\theta+\cos\theta}{\sin\theta-\cos\theta} = \dfrac{5}{4}$

$\Rightarrow \dfrac{\cos\theta\left(\frac{\sin\theta}{\cos\theta}+1\right)}{\cos\theta\left(\frac{\sin\theta}{\cos\theta}-1\right)} = \dfrac{5}{4}$

$\Rightarrow \dfrac{\tan\theta+1}{\tan\theta-1} = \dfrac{5}{4}$

$\Rightarrow \dfrac{2\tan\theta}{2} = \dfrac{5+4}{5-4}$ (By componendo and dividendo)

$\tan\theta = 9$

$\therefore \dfrac{\tan^2\theta+1}{\tan^2\theta-1} = \dfrac{81+1}{81-1}$

$= \dfrac{82}{80} => \dfrac{41}{40}$

Hence, the correct option is (c).

25. Gorbl means fan; flur means belt; pixn means ceiling; arth means tile; and tusl means roof. Therefore, pixnarth is the correct choice.

Hence, the correct option is (d).

26. There are two alphabetical series here. The first series is with the first letters only: STUVW. The second series involves the remaining letters: CD, EF, GH, IJ, KL.

Hence, the correct option is (c).

27. The pattern follows as:

24 → 24 × 3 − 1 = 71

Similarly,

42 → 42 × 3 − 1 = 125

So, the correct answer is 125.

Hence, the correct option is (C).

28. The passage best supports the statement that motivation is encourages an individual to give priority to personal goals over organisational goals.

Hence, the correct option is (a).

29. % change in the cost incurred in the fifth month,

$= \dfrac{100000-40000}{40000} \times$

$= 1.5 \times 100$

$= 150\%$

Hence, the correct option is (a).

30. In new technique 5 people working in 5th month, 4 in 6th 5 in 7th and 5 in 8th.

Total people working in this period = 19.

Each get paid Rs. 10000, then total cost = Rs. 1,90,000.

Hence, the correct option is (d).

31. Difference between old and new technique,

= 190000 - 130000 = Rs. 60,000.

Hence, the correct option is (d).

32. Number of people in one and two months is (2+3).

So, Rs. 40000 ✕ (2+3)

Cost incurred in specification stage, = Rs. 200000, which is maximum cost.

Hence, the correct option is (b).

33. Indian External Affairs Ministry announced on February 13, 2020 that the Pravasi Bhartiya Kendra has been renamed as Sushma Swaraj Bhawan to commemorate the late leader's invaluable service to Indian diplomacy.

Hence, the correct option is (a).

34. INS Shivaji was presented with the President's Colour by President Ram Nath Kovind on February 13, 2020. The President's colour is the highest honour bestowed upon any Indian military unit.

Hence, the correct option is (c).

35. The Maharashtra cabinet has approved a five-day working week plan for all government employees.

Hence, the correct option is (c).

36. Manipur's Chief Minister N Biren Singh launched 'Anganphou Hunba' programme on February 13, 2020. The state government has prepared a 260-crore rupee project to provide irrigation water to places having adequate arable land and large number of farmers.

Hence, the correct option is (b).

37. World Radio Day is observed every year on February 13 across the globe. This day highlights importance and value of radio. It was first celebrated by the UNESCO on February 13.

Hence, the correct option is (c).

38. National Women's Day is celebrated every year on February 13 in India. It is celebrated on the occasion of Sarojini Naidu's birthday. This year, India is observing her 141st birth anniversary.

Hence, the correct option is (d).

39. The Guinness World Records recently announced Chitetsu Watanabe, a Japanese man, as the oldest living man on the earth. His age is 112 years and 344 days as of February 12. He was born on March 5, 1907, in Niigata, Japan.

Hence, the correct option is (a).

40. World's biggest cricket stadium is under construction at Motera, Gujarat. It will be known as Sardar Patel Cricket Stadium. Till date, Melbourne Cricket Stadium is considered as the largest cricket stadium in the world.

41. Conduit wiring system consists of either VIR (Vulcanized Indian Rubber) or PVC (Poly Vinyl Chloride) cables taken through tubes or pipes and terminated at the outlets or switches/sockets.

PVC conduits are resistant to acids, alkalis, oil and moisture; they can be buried in lime or cement plaster without ill effects. PVC is preferred over VIR in extreme environments such as in cement/chemical factory

Hence, the correct option is (a).

42. Galvanization is the process of depositing a protective layer of zinc on iron or steel to avoid rusting. The most commonly used method of galvanization is **hot dip galvanizing**, in which iron or steel units are submerged in a molten zinc bath.

Anodizing is the process of deposition of oxide film on a metal surface is known as anodizing and oxidation.

Electroplating is defined as the deposition of metal over any metallic or non-metallic surfaces.

Hence, the correct option is (a).

43. A breeder reactor is a nuclear reactor that generates more fissile material than it consumes. These devices achieve this because their neutron economy is high enough to breed more fissile fuel than they use from the fertile material, such as uranium-238 or thorium-232. We can use heavy water, graphite and ordinary water as a moderator in the fast breeder reactor.

Hence, the correct option is (d).

44. Conveyor belts are used power plant industries as well as in any assembly line.

Huge load is driven by the conveyor belt so the motor needs very high starting torque greater than their running torque.

Hence, the correct option is (a).

45. Electric field is force per unit positive charge.

$$E = \frac{Force\,[F]}{charge\,[q]}$$

Hence, SI unit of electric field is NC⁻¹

Hence, the correct option is (b).

46. The effective resistance of four same wires will be 0.25 Ω when each resistance having a resistance of 1 Ω.

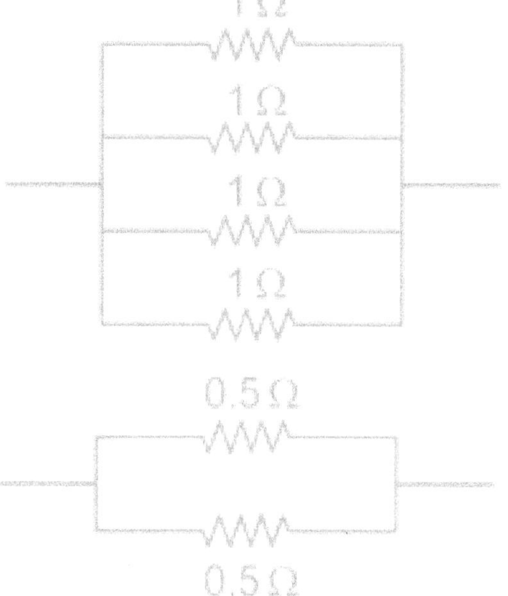

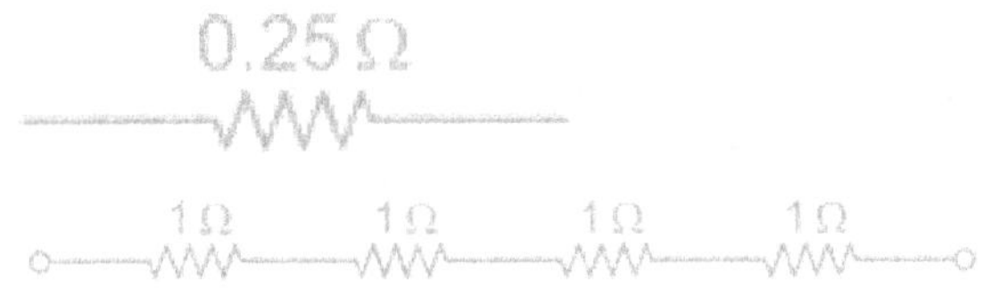

Total resistance = 1 + 1 + 1 + 1 = 4 Ω

Hence, the correct option is (a).

47. Passive Element:-

The element which receives or absorbs energy and then either converts it into heat (R) or stored it in an electric (C) or magnetic (L) field is called passive element.

Do not need any form of electrical power to operate.

Not able to control the flow of charge.

Cannot amplify, oscillate, or generate an electrical signal.

Used for energy storage, discharge, oscillating, filtering and phase shifting applications.

Examples: Resistor, inductor, capacitor.

Hence, the correct option is (c).

48. A rheostat is a variable resistor. By changing the resistance you can control the current flowing through it. This can then be used to control downstream devices like transistors or lamps.

Hence, the correct option is (a).

49. Shell type transformer provides a shorter magnetic path when compared to the core type.

In shell-type transformer leakage, flux and magnetizing current are lesser than core type, and power transfer capability is more.

In core type and cylinder type transformer have batter cooling since more surface exposed to the atmosphere but in shell type transformer cooling is not very effective because less surface area exposed in the atmosphere.

It gives better support against electromagnetic forces between the current-carrying transformer.

Hence, the correct option is (c).

50. In impedance relay, there is one voltage element fed from potential transformer and a current element fed from current transformer of the system.

The deflecting torque is produced by secondary current of CT and restoring torque is produced by voltage of potential transformer.

In normal operating condition, restoring torque is more than deflecting torque, hence relay will not operate.

But in faulty condition, the current becomes quite large whereas voltage becomes less.

Consequently, deflecting torque becomes more than restoring torque and dynamic parts of the relay starts moving which ultimately close the No contact of relay.

Hence clearly operation or working principle of distance relay depends upon the ratio of system voltage and current.

As the ratio of voltage to current is nothing but impedance so a distance relay is also known as impedance relay.

As the impedance of a transmission line is directly proportional to its length, the impedance will be less if fault occurs near the relay, thus, fault current is maximum at this condition.

Hence, the correct option is (a).

51. To add

23 + 67 in octal

Add LSB

$(3)_8 + (7)_8 = 10$ is not valid in octal

Convert to octal

$10 \rightarrow (12)_8$

LSB of result $\rightarrow 2$ .... (1)

Carry $\rightarrow 1$

Add MSB with carry

$1 + 2 + 6 = 9$

Convert to octal

$9 \rightarrow (11)_8$ .... (2)

From 1 and 2

$(23)_8 + (67)_8 = (112)_8$

Hence, the correct option is (b).

52. Spot welding, seam welding, butt welding are the types of resistance welding whereas argon arc welding is a type of arc welding. The classification electrical welding is shown below.

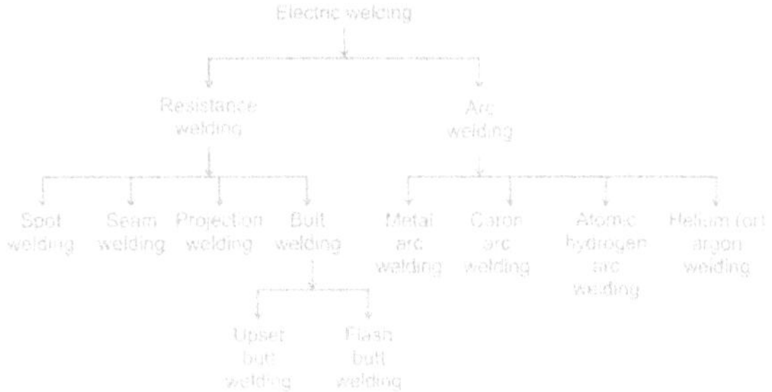

Hence, the correct option is (d).

53. Low speed motors are used in hydro power plant. Salient pole machines are suitable to run at low speed. Hence salient pole generators are used in hydro power plants.

Hence, the correct option is (a).

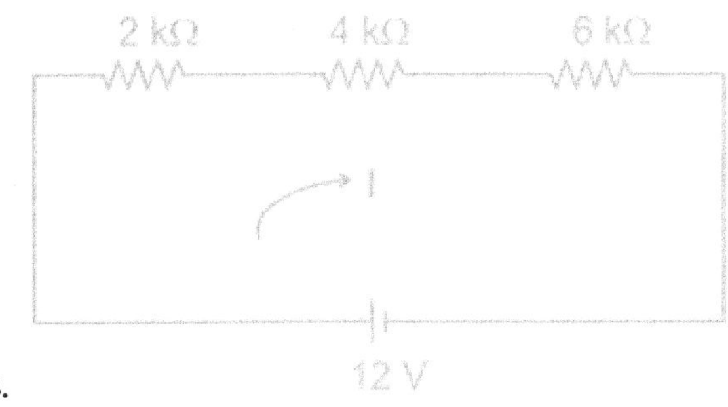

54.

Current in the circuit is, $I = \dfrac{12}{2+4+6} = 1$ mA

Voltage across resistor $R_2 = IR_2 = 1 \times 4 = 4$ V

Hence, the correct option is (a).

55. The resistance of a wire is directly proportional to its length and inversely proportional to its cross-sectional area. Resistance also depends on the material of the conductor.

Hence, the correct option is (d).

56. Given:

Q = 0.6, V = 30 V

The capacitance of conductors will be given by:-

$$C = \dfrac{Q}{V}$$

Where C is the capacitance in Farads.

Q is the charge in Coulombs.

V is the voltage in volts.

$$C = \dfrac{0.6}{30} = 0.02 \text{ F}$$

Hence, the correct option is (c).

57. Feeders are the conductors which have a large current carrying capacity.

Feeders connect the substation to the area where power is to be finally distributed to the consumers.

It feeds power to end distributor.

Hence, the correct option is (c).

58. A strong magnetic field is applied on a stationary electron. Then the electron remains stationary because magnetic force act on moving charge.

Hence, the correct option is (c).

59. Boost charging involves a high current for short period of time to charge the battery.

It is generally used when the battery has been discharged heavily.

Boost charge is given to a battery in danger of becoming over-discharged during a working shift.

Hence, the correct option is (b).

60. To find Thevenin equivalent we need to find Thevenin's voltage and resistance.

To find Thevenin's voltage, we need to find open circuit voltage across the terminals a and b

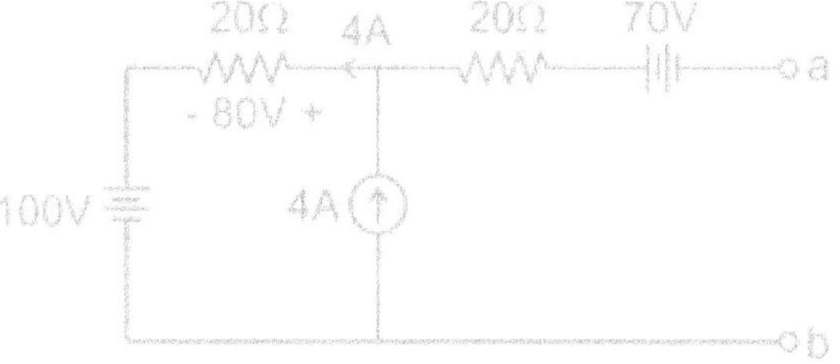

By applying KVL,

$-100 - 80 + 70 + V_{ab} = 0$

$\Rightarrow V_{ab} = V_{th} = 110$ V

To find Thevenin's resistance, we need to find the equivalent resistance across ab by replacing the independent sources with their internal resistances.

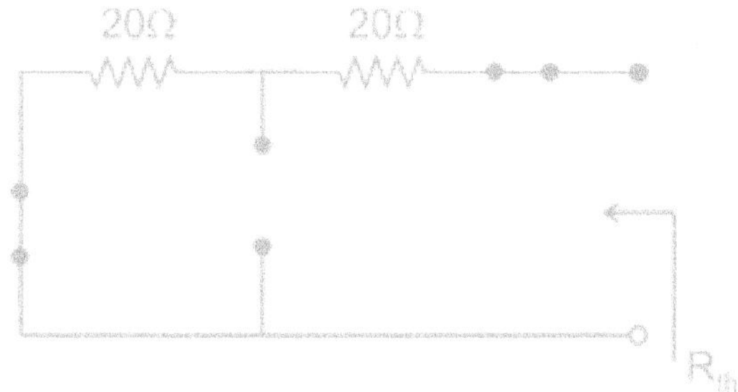

$R_{th} = 20 + 20 = 40 \ \Omega$.

Hence, the correct option is (b).

61. Transformer insulation is provided between core and LV winding, LV winding and HV winding.

Due to high voltage surges, every electrical equipment must be provided with proper insulation. Otherwise the equipment may get damaged.

Generally both HV and LV windings are placed on the same limb of the transformer to avoid short-circuits, insulation is placed.

Hence, the correct option is (d).

62. Leclanche cell is an instant emf supplying device.

A cell once discharged fully cannot be recharged again.

It is cheap in cost.

It is portable.

It is suitable for intermittent uses such as bell, telephone, telegraphy etc.

Hence, the correct option is (c).

63. Concept:

Let the resistance in a circuit is R and there are two independent sources.

Let the current I_1 is current flows through the resistor R when only one source is active and I_2 is the current flow through the resistor R when only the other source is active.

Power consumed by R when the first source active is

$$P_1 = I_1^2 R \Rightarrow I_1 = \sqrt{\frac{P_1}{R}}$$

Power consumed by R when second source active is

$$P_2 = I_2^2 R \Rightarrow I_2 = \sqrt{\frac{P_2}{R}}$$

By using superposition theorem, the current flows in through resistor $R = I_1 \pm I_2$

Now, the power consumed by resistor $R, P = (I_1 \pm I_2)^2 R$

$$P = \left(\sqrt{\frac{P_1}{R}} + \sqrt{\frac{P_2}{R}}\right)^2 R$$
$$= \left(\sqrt{P_1} \pm \sqrt{P_2}\right)^2$$

Calculation:

Given that,

$$P_1 = P_2 = 4W$$

By using superposition theorem, $P = \left(\sqrt{P_1} \pm \sqrt{P_2}\right)^2$

$$P = \left(\sqrt{4} \pm \sqrt{4}\right)^2 = 0 \text{ or } 16W$$

Hence, the correct option is (a).

64. Fuse wire is inserted in live **wire** because it is a safety device used to protect electrical appliances from short circuit and overloading.

Hence, the correct option is (d).

65. $I_L = I_S \times \dfrac{R_S}{R_S + R_L}$

$$I_L = 1.0 \left(\frac{12}{12 + 0.68}\right) = 0.94\ A$$

Hence, the correct option is (d).

66. Measuring Voltage with a Voltmeter

A voltmeter is connected in parallel with whatever device it is measuring. A parallel connection is used because objects in parallel experience the same potential difference.

Hence, the correct option is (b).

67. The illumination (E) of a surface depends upon the following factors.

E is directly proportional to the luminous intensity (I) of the source or candle power of the source. i.e. E ∝ I

Inverse square law: The illumination of a surface is inversely proportional to the square of the distance of the surface from the source, in other words, E ∝ $\dfrac{1}{r^2}$

Lambert's cosine law: According to this law, E is directly proportional to the cosine of the angle made by the normal to the illuminated surface with the direction of the incident flux

It is least dependent on ambient temperature

Hence, the correct option is (a).

68. Three relays are used to detect interphase fault of a three-line system because we use 2 relay for 2 phase and 1 relay between phase and earth known as EFR (earth fault relay).

A relay is an automatic device which senses an abnormal condition of the electrical circuit and closes its contacts.

Hence, the correct option is (c).

69. The deflecting torque is used for deflection, the controlling torque acts opposite to the deflecting torque. So before coming to rest the pointer always oscillates due to inertia, so to bring the pointer rest within a short time by reducing oscillations, we use damping torque without effecting controlling torque (or) inertia.

The following mechanism can be used for producing damping torque.

1. Air friction damping

2. Fluid friction damping

3. Eddy current damping

The damping device should be such that it produces a damping torque only while the moving system is in motion. To be effective the damping torque should be proportional to the velocity of the moving current but independent of operating current.

In the majority of instruments, damping is provided by eddy current damping.

Eddy current damping:

When a conductor moves in a magnetic field an emf is induced in it and if a closed path is provided, a current (known as eddy current) flows.

This current interacts with the magnetic field to produce an electromagnet torque which opposes the motion.

This torque is proportional to the strength of the magnetic field and the current produced.

Hence, the correct option is (c).

70. A passive component is an electronic component which can only receive energy, which it can either dissipate, absorb or store it in an electric field or a magnetic field**.**

Example: Resistors, Inductors, Capacitors, **Transformers**

Hence, the correct option is (b).

71. Reduced Voltage Starters are needed to avoid overloading the power distribution system and to avoid unnecessary wear and tear on equipment by reducing starting torque. These are used on all types of AC and DC motors.

Types of reduced voltage starter methods:
Series resistance or reactor method

Auto transformer method

Star delta method

All these methods can be used with both squirrel cage as well as slip ring induction motor.

Hence, the correct option is (c).

72. Local action: Normally, zinc consists of many impurities such as copper iron etc. When a zinc rod is used as an electrode in a primary cell, its circuit becomes complete even current is set up from zinc to copper or iron particles. In this way, it causes a loss of zinc and electrical power; this action is known as local action.

In order to minimise the local action, an amalgamating the zinc rod is used i.e. coating the rod with mercury.

Hence, the correct option is (b).

73. It is not a practice to connect a stationary alternator to a live busbar.

Under a stationary condition, the emf induced in stator winding is zero. If such an alternator is connected to a live bus bar, there is always a danger of short circuit as armature resistance is negligible, and reactance is zero (frequency is zero).

Hence, the correct option is (a).

74. In single-phase induction motor,

The motor speed on no load is almost equal to its synchronous speed.

At loading condition, the power factor is 0.6 – 0.8 lagging.

At no-load condition, the power factor is 0.2-0.3 lagging.

Hence, the correct option is (a).

75. In plate earthing, a copper plate or galvanized plate is buried in an earth pit below ground level. The plate electrode connects the electrical conductors to the earth.

Hence, the correct option is (a).

76. Two spheres of radii R_1 and R_2 ($R_2 > R_1$) are connected by a conducting wire. Each of the spheres has been given a charge q. Now **Potential of both the spheres will be equal** because of both sphere has the same charge.

Flowing of charge does not depend upon the charge amount or size of the two bodies.

If there is an electric potential difference there will be a flow of charge, if no potential difference, there will not be a flow of charge i.e. current flow is not possible.

Thus, in all electrical circuits when the current flows, it means there is an electrical potential difference between two points.

Hence, the correct option is (c).

77. Thermal resistance always has the unit degree temperature per watt (°C/W).

Thermal resistance always has the unit degree temperature per watt.

Hence, the correct option is (c).

78. Reciprocity theorem states that in any branch of a network, the current (I) due to a single source of voltage (V) elsewhere in the network is equal to the current through the branch in which the source was originally placed when the source is placed in the branch in which the current (I) was originally obtained.

It is applicable for only single source networks.

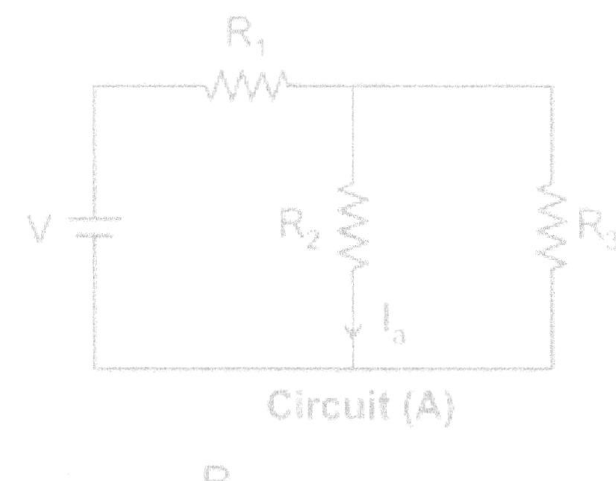

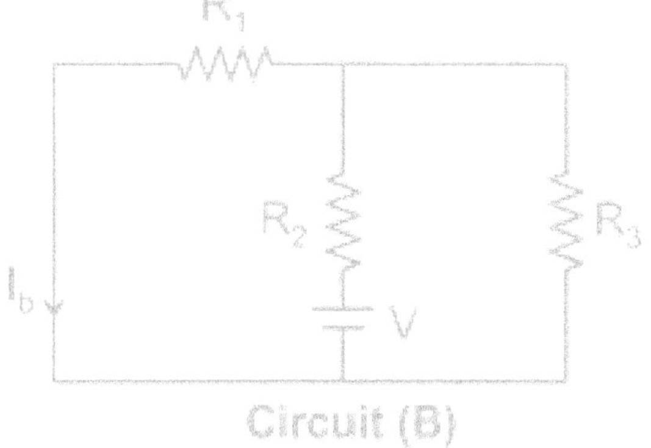

In the circuit (a), the value I_a is obtained for a voltage source V. According to reciprocity theorem, this current is equivalent to I_b in circuit B.

Hence, the correct option is (b).

79. An electric heater is connected to the voltage supply. After few seconds, current gets its steady value then its initial current will be slightly higher than its steady current.

Hence, the correct option is (b).

80. DC series motor is best suited for DC traction, as it provides high starting torque and easy speed control which is primary requirement of DC traction.

Hence, the correct option is (c).

81. Concept:

In a transistor, dynamic output resistance is given by

$$r_0 = \frac{\Delta V_{CE}}{\Delta I_C}$$

Where r_0 = output resistance

ΔV_{CE} = change in collector- emitter voltage

ΔI_C = change in collector current

Calculation:

ΔV_{CE} = change in collector- emitter voltage = 10 – 2 = 8 V

ΔI_C = change in collector current = 3 – 2 = 1 mA

$$r0 = \frac{8}{1 \times 10^{-3}}$$

= 8 kΩ

Hence, the correct option is (d).

82. Rms current in capacitor is given by,

$I_{rms} = V \omega C$

Where V = voltage across capacitor

C = 0.1 μf

f = 5 kHz

$\omega = 2 \pi f$

now, $I_{rms} = 5 \times 2 \times \pi \times 5 \times 10^3 \times 0.1 \times 10^{-6}$

= 15.71 mA

Hence, the correct option is (b).

83. A synchronous machine with the high value of SCR **had a better voltage regulation and improved steady state stability limit**, but the short circuit fault current in the armature is high. It also affects the size and cost of the machine.

Hence, the correct option is (b).

84. When the temperature is increased, the atoms of the material vibrate, and it makes the valence electrons present in the valence band to shift to the conduction band

This in turn increases the conductivity of the material; When the conductivity of the material increases, it means that the resistivity decreases and so the current flow increases; Thus, some insulators at room temperatures changes to conductors at high temperature.

Hence, the correct option is (b).

85. Kanthal is a type of iron-chromium-aluminium (FeCrAl) alloys used in a wide range of resistance and high-temperature applications. Kanthal FeCrAl alloys consist of mainly iron, chromium (20–30%) and aluminium (4–7.5 %).

Hence, the correct option is (b).

86. Potentiometer method is used for the measurement of low resistance.

This method uses a volt-ratio box to measure the unknown resistance.

It is based on comparison method.

The volt-ratio box gives the accurate result of measure voltage.

Hence, the correct option is (c).

87. The equivalent **conductance** is the sum of individual **conductance** for a parallel circuit which is shown in the figure.

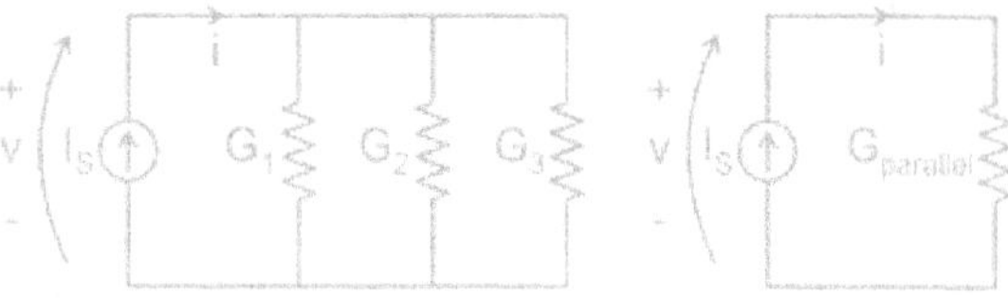

Hence, the correct option is (a).

88. In the series combination of two or more than two resistances the current through each resistance is same.

Hence, the correct option is (c).

89. The efficiency of a transmission line is increase with the increase in load p.f.

Efficiency also increases when we increase the transmission voltage as I^2R losses decreases.

Hence, the correct option is (b).

90. In parallel combination of cells the voltage across the terminals is same and resistance is minimum. Therefore from V=IR. The current drawn from cell combination will be more.

Hence, the correct option is (b).

91. The hydroelectric power plant will take least time of about 5-10 minutes in starting from cold conditions to full load operation. Hence these plants used to supply the peak load of the system.

Nuclear power plant takes about 12 to 16 hours to start producing electricity.

Hence, the correct option is (d).

92. Loop-in or Looping System:

In this method of wiring, lamps and other appliances are connected in parallel so that each of the appliances can be controlled individually.

When a connection is required at a light or switch, the feed conductor is looped in by bringing it directly to the terminal and then carrying it forward again to the next point to be fed.

The switch and light feeds are carried round the circuit in a series of loops from one point to another until the last on the circuit is reached.

The phase or line conductors are looped either in switchboard or box and neutrals are looped either in switchboard or from light or fan. Line or phase should never be looped from light or fan.

Hence, the correct option is (b).

93. The changed configuration is still a wheat stone bridge hence there will be no change in deflection.

Hence, the correct option is (b).

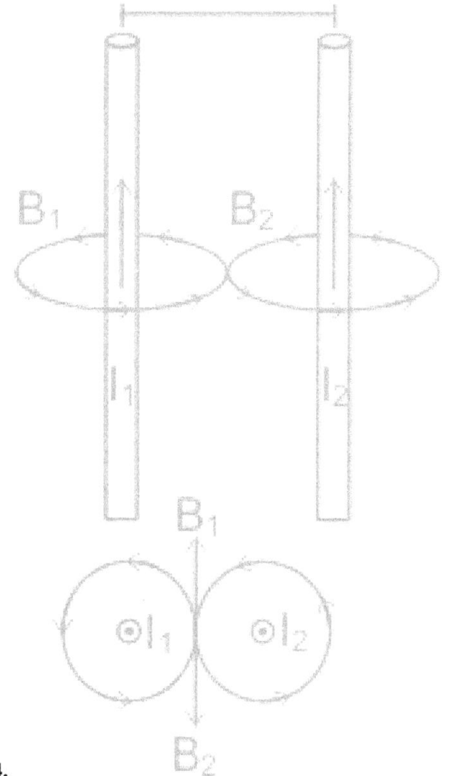

94.

Formulae for magnetic field B is given by B = $\dfrac{\mu(I_1 - I_2)}{2\pi d}$

Here in the question, I_1 is equal to I_2 so B becomes zero.

Hence, the correct option is (b).

95. When a magnet is in motion relative to a coil, the induced e.m.f. is depend on the following three factors.

The number of turns of wire in the coil: By increasing the number of individual conductors cutting through the magnetic field, the emf can be increased. The amount of induced emf produced will be the sum of all the individual loops of the coil.

The speed of the relative motion between the coil and the magnet: If the same coil of wire passed through the same magnetic field but its speed or velocity is increased, the wire will cut the lines of flux at a faster rate so more induced emf would be produced.

The strength of the magnetic field: If the same coil of wire is moved at the same speed through a stronger magnetic field, there will be more emf produced because there are more lines of force to cut.

The induced emf is independent of resistance of the coil.

Hence, the correct option is (a).

96. The armature reaction is the effect of armature field on the main field.

The armature field is produced by the armature conductors when current flows through them.

The main field is produced by the magnetic poles.

The armature flux causes two effects on the main field flux.

It distorts the main field flux and reduces the magnitude of the main field flux.

Hence, the correct option is (b).

97. An SCR – Silicon controlled rectifier is 4 layered solid-state current controlling device. It has PNPN or NPNP structure with three P-N junctions and three terminals.

The operation of SCR is similar to a PNP and NPN transistors connected base to collector and emitter to base.

Hence, the correct option is (d).

98. Hysteresis loss least depends on ambient temperature.

The hysteresis and eddy current losses vary linearly with temperature between 40 °C to 100 °C.

Varying rates of hysteresis and eddy current losses with the temperature are different and fluctuate with flux density and frequency.

Hence, the correct option is (d).

99. The substances which have many free electrons and offer very low resistance are called conductors.

The substances which cannot pass a current under normal conditions are known as insulators. The resistance of an insulator is usually high. Insulators have no free electrons.

Hence, the correct option is (c).

100. Pole cross section i.e. circular or rectangular is the guiding factor to control mean turn length and weight or cost of copper in case of field winding.

Circular pole cross section gives smallest length of mean turn length and weight of copper. At the same time, it necessitates the solid structure.

Rectangular pole cross section contributes in larger mean turn length and weight of copper; At the same time gives facility to use laminated structure with reduces the production cost.

Hence, the correct option is (b).

101. When a metal conductor connected to left gap of a meter bridge is heated, the balancing point shifts towards right.

Hence, the correct option is (a).

102. Surface azimuth angle is the angle of deviation of the normal to the surface from the local meridian, the zero point being south, east positive and west negative. And surface azimuth is different where it is an angle on a horizontal plane between the normal to a vertical surface and the north-south direction line.

Hence, the correct option is (a).

103. The angle being measured from a plane and which is equal to angle between the beam of rays and normal to the plane is called as incident angle. And it is denoted by Greek letter θ

(Theta). The angle of incidence (θ) is the angle between the sun's rays irradiated on a surface and the line normal to this surface.

Hence, the correct option is (a).

104. The solar intensity at a direction normal to the tilted surface is the vector sum of the components along the line normal of the tilted surface. And is given by formula,

I_{Σ} = IDN cosθ$_{\Sigma}$

Where IDN = solar intensity irradiated on a surface normal to the sun's rays.

Hence, the correct option is (a).

105. The time from sunrise to sunset is termed as day length. On earth, daytime is roughly the period of the day during which any given point in the world experiences natural illumination from especially direct sunlight. Daytime occurs when the sun appears above the local horizon, that is, anywhere on the globe's hemisphere facing the Sun. During daytime, an observer sees indirect sunlight while in the shade, which includes cloud cover.

Hence, the correct option is (b).

106. Uttarakhand is famous for terrace cultivation. In agriculture, a terrace is a leveled section of a hilly cultivated area designed as a method of soil conservation to slow or prevent the rapid surface runoff. Terraced farming helps to prevent free flow of water.

Hence, the correct option is (D).

107. In the case $Y = 0°$, on December $21, n = 355$

Angle of declination, $\delta = 23.45 \sin\left[\dfrac{360}{365} \times (284 + n)\right]$

$$\delta = 23.45\sin\left[\dfrac{360}{365} \times (284 + 355)\right]$$
$$\delta = -23.45°$$

Hence, the correct option is (c).

108. Ohm's law I= $\dfrac{V}{R}$ is an equation of straight line. I-V characteristics for ohmic conductors is also straight line.

Hence, the correct option is (a).

109. When a magnetic compass needle is carried nearby to a straight wire carrying current, then the straight wire cause a noticeable deflection in the compass needle. The alignment of the needle is tangential to an imaginary circle with straight wire as its centre and has a plane perpendicular to the wire.

Hence, the correct option is (a).

110. When the sun is directly on the top of the head, it is referred to as sun at zenith. The zenith is an imaginary point directly "above" a particular location, on the imaginary celestial sphere. The zenith is the "highest" point on the celestial sphere.

Hence, the correct option is (a).

111. Path length of radiation through the atmosphere to the length of path when the sun is at zenith is called Air mass.

Air mass, m = Cos (altitude angle), except for very low solar altitude angles.

m = 1; When the sun is at the zenith

m = 2; When zenith angle is 60°

m = 3; sec (θz) for m>3.

Hence, the correct option is (b).

112. For a half-wave rectifier, the output frequency is equal to the input frequency, in this case, the output frequency of the half-wave rectifier is 50 Hz.

On the other hand, the output frequency for a full-wave rectifier is twice the input frequency.

Therefore, the output frequency is 2 × 50 = 100 Hz.

Hence, the correct option is (a).

113. Angle made by radial line joining the location to the centre of the earth with the projection of the line on the equatorial plane is called latitude. And it is denoted by φl. It is also given by the angular distance north or south of the equator measured from the centre of the earth.

Hence, the correct option is (a).

114. Declination is the angular distance of sun's rays north or south of the equator. It is the angle between the line extending from the centre of the sun to the centre of the earth and the projection of this line upon earth's equatorial plane.

Hence, the correct option is (a).

115. Solar declination is denoted by Greek letter δ (DELTA). Solar declination is the angle between the earth-sun line and the equatorial plane. Solar declination varies throughout the year.

Hence, the correct option is (a).

116. The angle through which the earth must turn to bring the meridian of a point directly in sun's rays is called Hour angle. And it is denoted by Greek letter ω (OMEGA). It is measured from noon based on the solar local time (LST).

Hence, the correct option is (a).

117. The vertical angle between the projection of the sun's rays on the horizontal plane and the direction of sun's rays passing through the point s called solar altitude and is also referred to altitude angle and is denoted by Greek letter α (ALPHA).

Hence, the correct option is (b).

118. The angle between the sun's rays and a line perpendicular to the horizontal plane through angle measured from the north to the horizontal projection of rays is called zenith angle. And it is denoted by θ$_z$.

Hence, the correct option is (b).

119. The solar angle in degrees along the horizon east or west of north or it is the horizontal angle measured from north to the horizontal projection of sun's rays is called solar azimuth angle. And it is denoted by Greek letter γs (GAMMA).

Hence, the correct option is (a).

120. The slope is the angle made by the plane surfaces with the horizontal. It is considered positive for surfaces slopping towards

the south and negative for surface slopping towards the north.
Different types of measurements are calculated by slopes.

Hence, the correct option is (a).

Mock Test 08

Part - I

Q.1 Direction : In the following questions, choose the word opposite in meaning to the given word.
EFFEMINACY

A. Aggressiveness   **B.** Attractiveness
C. Manliness   **D.** Boorishness

Q.2 Direction : In the following questions, choose the word opposite in meaning to the given word.
Convulsion

A. Cramp   **B.** Shaking   **C.** Restful   **D.** Disaster

Q.3 Direction : In the following questions out of the four alternatives, choose the one which is best express the meaning of the given word.
Pejorative

A. Right   **B.** Discussion
C. Derogatory   **D.** Complimentary

Q.4 Direction : In the following questions out of the four alternatives, choose the one which is best express the meaning of the given word.
Barbarous

A. Refined   **B.** Polite   **C.** Crude   **D.** Civilized

Q.5 Direction : In the following questions, four alternatives are given for the meaning of the given Idiom/Phrase. Choose the alternative which best express the meaning of the Idiom/Phrase.
Every inch a gentleman

A. Somewhat   **B.** Partly
C. Entirely   **D.** Calculatively

Q.6 In the following questions, four alternatives are given for the meaning of the given Idiom/Phrase. Choose the alternative which best express the meaning of the Idiom/Phrase.
Gall and wormwood

A. A problem   **B.** Hateful
C. Useless   **D.** Hard to digest

Q.7 Direction : In the following questions, out of the given alternatives, choose the one which can be substituted for the given words/sentence.
A stand having three legs

A. Triptan   **B.** Tripod   **C.** Thriver   **D.** Tricot

Q.8 Direction : In the following questions, out of the given alternatives, choose the one which can be substituted for the given words/sentence.
Loss of speech due to medical problem

A. Anorexia   **B.** Anosmia
C. Aphasia   **D.** Hypogeusia

Q.9 P and Q undertook to do a work for Rs 7200. P alone could do it in 20 days and Q alone in 12 days. With the assistance of R they finished the work in 5 days. What is the share (in Rs) of R?

A. 1800   **B.** 2400   **C.** 2800   **D.** 2600

Q.10 If a saree is sold for Rs 1900 the seller will face 5% loss, at what price (in Rs) should he sell the saree to gain 15% profit?

A. 2200   **B.** 2400   **C.** 2500   **D.** 2300

Q.11 The ratio of two numbers is 5: 11. If both numbers are increased by 10, the ratio becomes 7:13. What is the sum of the two numbers?

A. 56   **B.** 32   **C.** 48   **D.** 80

Q.12 If the sum of five consecutive positive integers is 40, then the average of first and last integers is-

A. 6   **B.** 8   **C.** 9   **D.** 10

Q.13 Sanjay and Suresh started driving from two opposite points 300 km apart. The speed of Suresh's car is 60 kmph while Sanjay is two-third, as fast as Suresh. If they start at the same time, after how much time will they meet each other for the first time?

A. 15 hr   **B.** 7.5 hr   **C.** 5 hr   **D.** 3 hr

Q.14 If the cost price of 10 articles is equal to the selling price of 15 articles, then what is the loss percentage?

A. 25%   **B.** 50%   **C.** 33.33%   **D.** 20%

Q.15 The compound interest earned in two years at 12% per annum is Rs 10176. What is the sum (in Rs) invested?

A. 50000   **B.** 60000   **C.** 40000   **D.** 80000

Q.16 A shopkeeper allows two successive discounts of 35% and 15% on selling an article. If he gets Rs 221 for the article, then what is the marked price (in Rs) of the article?

A. 400   **B.** 420   **C.** 380   **D.** 450

Q.17 The law of multiple proportion was discovered by whom?

A. John Dalton   **B.** Robert Brown
C. Joseph Proust   **D.** James Chadwick

Q.18 Which of the following is necessary for Blood clotting in humans?

A. Vitamin A   **B.** Vitamin K
C. Vitamin C   **D.** Vitamin E

Q.19 The plant organelles which can trip sunlight are:-

A. Chlorophyll only
B. Chloroplasts only
C. Mitochondria only
D. Mitochondria and Chloroplasts

Q.20 What is the process by which autotrophs take in substances from the outside and convert them into stored form of energy?

A. Respiration
B. Photosynthesis
C. Ingestion
D. Transpiration

Q.21 'Khajuraho' group of monuments can be found in:
A. Maharashtra
B. Bihar
C. Madhya Pradesh
D. Gujarat

Q.22 Which of the following contains the World's largest area of mangrove forests?
A. Namdapha National Park
B. Rann of Kutch
C. Balphakram National Park
D. Sundarbans

Q.23 Which of the following is world's first country to have cashless economy?
A. Canada **B.** Sweden **C.** France **D.** Belgium

Q.24 73rd Constitutional Amendment Act gave Constitutional recognition to panchayats by adding _______.
A. Part VIII **B.** Part IX **C.** Part X **D.** Part XI

Ques (25-28):Study the following table and answer the questions based on it. Expenditures of a Company (in Lakh Rupees) per Annum Over the given Years.

| Year | Item of Expenditure | | | | | |
	Salary	Fuel and Transport	Bonus	Interest on Loans	Taxes
1998	288	98	3.00	23.4	83
1999	342	112	2.52	32.5	108
2000	324	101	3.84	41.6	74
2001	336	133	3.68	36.4	88
2002	420	142	3.96	49.4	98

Q.25
What is the average amount of interest per year which the company had to pay during this period?
A. Rs. 32.43 lakhs
B. Rs. 33.72 lakhs
C. Rs. 34.18 lakhs
D. Rs. 36.66 lakhs

Q.26 The total amount of bonus paid by the company during the given period is approximately what percent of the total amount of salary paid during this period?
A. 0.1% **B.** 0.5% **C.** 1% **D.** 1.25%

Q.27 Total expenditure on all these items in 1998 was approximately what percent of the total expenditure in 2002?
A. 62% **B.** 66% **C.** 69% **D.** 71%

Q.28 The total expenditure of the company over these items during the year 2000 is?
A. Rs. 544.44 lakhs
B. Rs. 501.11 lakhs
C. Rs. 446.46 lakhs
D. Rs. 478.87 lakhs

Ques (29-32):The following pie-chart shows the percentage distribution of the expenditure incurred in publishing a book. Study the pie-chart and the answer the questions based on it.

Various Expenditures (in percentage) Incurred in Publishing a Book

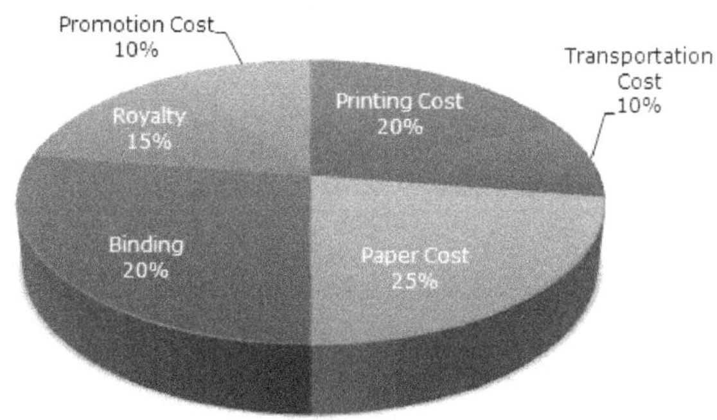

Q.29
If for a certain quantity of books, the publisher has to pay Rs. 30,600 as printing cost, then what will be amount of royalty to be paid for these books?
A. Rs. 19,450
B. Rs. 21,200
C. Rs. 22,950
D. Rs. 26,150

Q.30
What is the central angle of the sector corresponding to the expenditure incurred on Royalty?
A. 15° **B.** 24° **C.** 54° **D.** 48°

Q.31
The price of the book is marked 20% above the C.P. If the marked price of the book is Rs. 180, then what is the cost of the paper used in a single copy of the book?
A. Rs. 36
B. Rs. 37.50
C. Rs. 42
D. Rs. 44.25

Q.32 If 5500 copies are published and the transportation cost on them amounts to Rs. 82500, then what should be the selling price of the book so that the publisher can earn a profit of 25%?
A. Rs. 187.50
B. Rs. 191.50
C. Rs. 175
D. Rs. 180

Q.33 Who won 17th NBA Championship?
A. Indiana Pacers
B. Miami Heat
C. Los Angeles Lakers
D. Orlando Magic

Q.34 Who won the Eifel Grand Prix in Germany?
A. Max Versteppen
B. Gautam Gambhir
C. Valteri Bottas
D. Lewis Hamilton

Q.35 When is World Unani Day celebrated?
A. February 11th
B. February 10th
C. February 8th
D. February 12th

Q.36 Which state government recently launched Mukhyamantri Pariwar Smridhi Scheme?
A. Punjab
B. Bihar

C. Haryana   **D.** Uttar Pradesh

Q.37 Which state government has announced to ban CFL and filament bulbs from November 2020?
A. Madhya Pradesh   **B.** Rajasthan
C. West Bengal   **D.** Kerala

Q.38 When is world pulses day observed every year across the globe?
A. 8th February   **B.** 9th February
C. 10th February   **D.** 11th February

Q.39 What was India's rank in CRI Index released by Oxfam?
A. 1   **B.** 129   **C.** 9   **D.** 76

Q.40 Which country revealed that it has 'neutralised' 101 Syrian troops?
A. Turkey   **B.** US   **C.** Israel   **D.** Iran

Part - II

Q.41 The inductors of value L_1 and L_2 are coupled by mutual inductance M. By interconnection of the elements one can obtain the maximum inductance of:
A. $L_1 + L_2 - M$ **B.** $L_1 + L_2$
C. $L_1 + L_2 + M$ **D.** $L_1 + L_2 + 2M$

Q.42 The no-load power factor of a transformer is approximately:
A. 0   **B.** 0.2   **C.** 0.7   **D.** 1

Q.43 For network shown in the given figure, the current in the 2 Ω resistor would be:

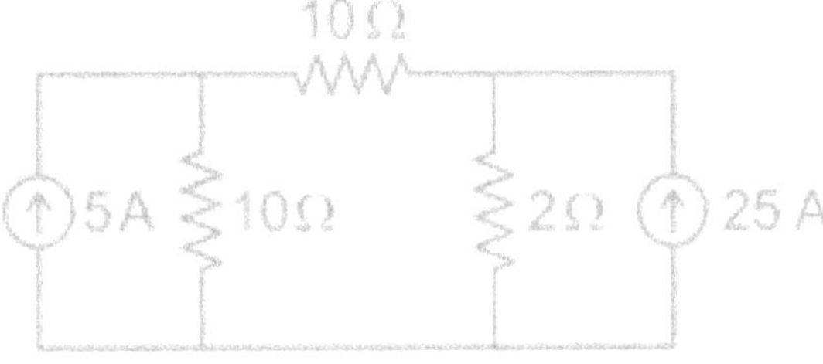

A. 5 A   **B.** 20 A   **C.** 25 A   **D.** 30 A

Q.44 Maximum work that could be secured by expanding the gas over a given pressure range is the _________ work.
A. Isothermal   **B.** Adiabatic
C. Isentropic   **D.** None of these

Q.45 The Norton current for the circuit shown below is

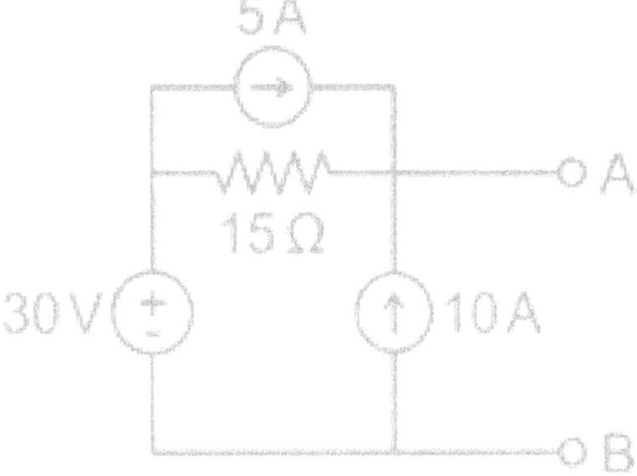

A. 10 A   **B.** 17 A   **C.** 20 A   **D.** 25 A

Q.46 Which of the following are environment-friendly particles?
A. Carrying cloth bags to put purchases in while shopping
B. Switching off unnecessary lights and fans
C. Walking to school instead of getting your mother to drop you on her scooter
D. All of the above

Q.47 In case of two alternators running in parallel and perfectly synchronized, the synchronizing power is:-
A. zero   **B.** positive
C. negative   **D.** ideally infinite

Q.48 The gate voltage in a JFET at which drain current becomes zero is called:-
A. Pinch-off voltage   **B.** Saturation voltage
C. Active voltage   **D.** Cut-off voltage

Q.49 The motor used in ceiling fan is _______.
A. Split phase motor   **B.** Capacitor run motor
C. Shaded pole motor   **D.** AC series motor

Q.50 In an R, L, C series circuit impedance Z in equal to:
A. $\sqrt{R_2 + (X_L - X_C)^2}$
B. $\sqrt{R^2 - (X_L - X_C)^2}$
C. $\sqrt{R^2 + X_L{}^2}$
D. $\sqrt{R^2 + X_C{}^2}$

Q.51 Which of the following is the disadvantage of electric traction over other systems of traction?
A. Short time power failure interrupts traffic for hours
B. High capital outlay in fixed installations beside route limitation
C. Interference with communication lines
D. All of the above

Q.52 A current divider is always a _______.
A. series-parallel circuit
B. series circuit
C. parallel circuit
D. bridge circuit

Q.53 Thevenin equivalent resistance of the given circuit is:

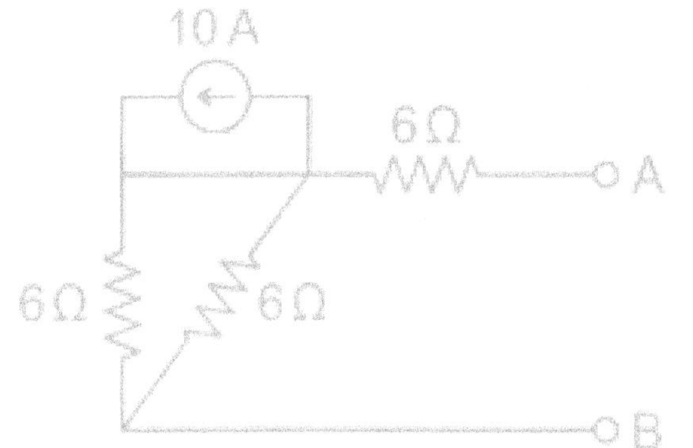

A. 18 Ω   **B.** 6 Ω   **C.** 9 Ω   **D.** 12 Ω

Q.54 Maximum temperature limit for class F insulation is:

A. 105°   **B.** 120°   **C.** 130°   **D.** 155°

Q.55 The leakage resistance of a 100 km long cable is 1mΩ. For a length of 50 km, the resistance will be:

A. 2 mΩ   **B.** 1 mΩ   **C.** 4 mΩ   **D.** 0.6 mΩ

Q.56 The noise factor of an ideal amplifier is ______.

A. 0 dB   **B.** 1.2 dB   **C.** 0.1 dB   **D.** 10 dB

Q.57 Regulating transformers are used power systems for control of:

A. voltage   **B.** power factor
C. power flow   **D.** all of these

Q.58 Which of the following inductor has minimum eddy current loss?

A. Ferrite core inductor
B. Iron core inductor
C. Air core inductor
D. All these

Q.59 The best location of the power factor improving device to be installed in the transmission line is at:

A. The receiving end   **B.** The sending end
C. Middle of the line   **D.** Any place

Q.60 Arc heating occurs when the air between electrodes of opposite polarity becomes:

A. Moistened   **B.** Dry
C. Ionized   **D.** None of the above

Q.61 The phase difference between displacement and acceleration of a particle in a simple harmonic motion is:

A. 3π rad   **B.** zero   **C.** π rad   **D.** 2π rad

Q.62 A sinusoidal ac has a frequency of 50 Hz and a peak value of 20 A. Starting from zero, how long will it take the current to reach 10 A for the first time?

A. $\frac{1}{300}$ s   **B.** $\frac{1}{600}$ s   **C.** $\frac{1}{400}$ s   **D.** $\frac{1}{60}$ s

Q.63 In a Brush Less DC (BLDC) motor, the construction of motor is similar to:

A. Stepper   **B.** Universal motor
C. DC motor   **D.** Synchronous motor

Q.64 Light load adjustment for induction type energy meter is usually done at:

A.   10% of full load current
B.   5% of full load current
C.   50% of full load current
D.   1% of full load current

Q.65 Two wattmeters are used to measure the power in a three-phase balanced load. The wattmeter readings are 8.2 kW and 7.5 kW. The active power will be:

A. 61.5 W   **B.** 0.997 W   **C.** 0.7 W   **D.** 15.7 W

Q.66 Relative error is same as:

A.   Ratio of absolute error and true value
B.   Absolute error
C.   True error
D.   None of the above

Q.67 Single-phase induction motors are ______ motors.

A.   self-start
B.   capacitor-start
C.   capacitor-start capacitor-run
D.   Both capacitor-start and capacitor-start capacitor-run

Q.68 Which of the following is NOT true about A.C. power transmission?

A.   Power can be generated at high voltage
B.   Voltages can be easily stepped-up and down
C.   Less loss of power during transmission
D.   Effective resistance during transmission is low

Q.69 In the P-N junction, the barrier voltage:

A.   decreases with increases in temperature
B.   increases with increases in temperature
C.   decreases with decreases in temperature
D.   in independent of temperature

Q.70 The dependent current source shown in figure

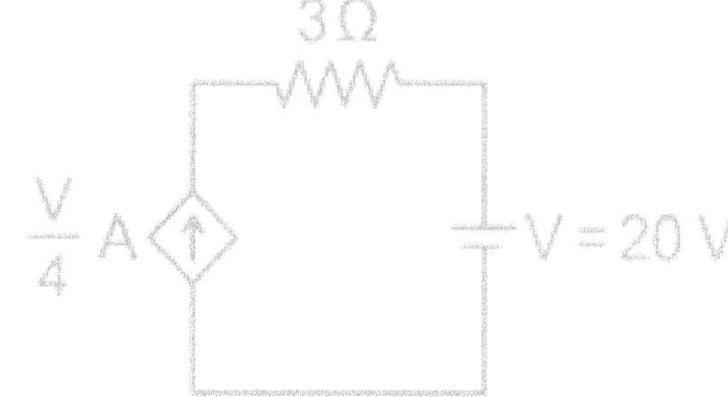

A. Delivers 70 W   **B.** Absorb 70 W
C. Delivers 175 W   **D.** Absorbs 175 W

Q.71 Which of the following is NOT a property of good conductor of electricity?

A.   Low resistance
B.   High electrical conductivity
C.   Low specific gravity
D.   Low tensile strength

Q.72 For the below circuit, if the current I = 3 A and 1.5 A for R_L = 0 and 2 Ω respectively, then what is the value of I for R_L = I Ω?

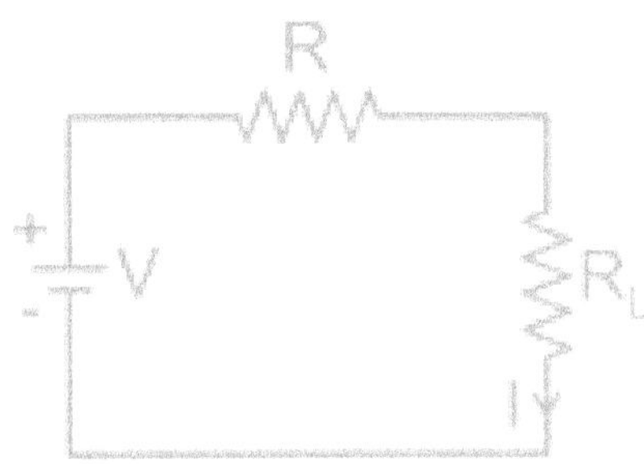

A. 0.5 A　　**B.** 1.0 A　　**C.** 2.0 A　　**D.** 3.0 A

Q.73 The _______ should be capable of supplying current enough to charge and discharge the deflection plate capacitor.
A. Vertical amplifier
B. Horizontal amplifier
C. Anode
D. Signal generator

Q.74 The effect of cross-magnetizing field in an alternator may be reduced by:
A. Shifting the brush positions
B. Using interpoles
C. Using a magnetizing pole
D. None of these

Q.75 What is the total charge of capacitor when 300 V is applied across a series combination of 10 μF and 10 μF?
A. 100 μC
B. 1500 μC
C. 10 μC
D. None of these

Q.76 Read the assertion and reason both carefully, choose the correct option:-
Assertion (A): If the voltages across R, L and C elements connected in series in an ac circuit are 300 V, 100 V and 500 V respectively, the total voltage applied will be 500 V.
Reason (R): The applied voltage in LCR series circuit is equal to the maximum voltage existing across any of these elements.
A. Both A and R are true, and R is the correct explanation of A
B. Both A and R are true, but R is not a correct explanation of A
C. A is true, but R is false
D. A is false, but R is false

Q.77 A sinusoidal voltage V(t) = 200 sinωt is applied to a series LCR circuit with L = 10 mH, C = 100 nF and R = 20 Ω. Find the amplitude of current at resonance
A. 10 A　　**B.** 20 A　　**C.** 15 A　　**D.** 25 A

Q.78 The daily energy produced in a thermal power station is 720 MWh at a load factor of 0.6. What is the maximum demand of the station?
A. 50 MW　　**B.** 30 MW　　**C.** 72 MW　　**D.** 720 MW

Q.79 An alternating (ac) quantity (voltage current or power) is defined as the one which changes its _____ as well as ____ with respect to time.
A. Value, direction
B. Phase, polarity
C. Value, phase
D. None of these

Q.80 The current flowing through armature of a dc motor is:
A. Pulsating
B. DC
C. AC
D. None of these

Q.81 Transmission lines transposed to _______.
A. Reduce the copper loss
B. Reduce skin effect
C. Prevent interference with neighbouring telephone lines
D. Prevent short-circuit between any two lines

Q.82 Which of the following is not true about voltage source?
A. Source resistance (R_S) is typically low
B. Load resistance is greater than 100 R_S
C. Load voltage is constant
D. Load current is constant and independent of load resistance

Q.83 In a balanced 3ø system, the zero phase sequence currents are:
A. maximum
B. minimum
C. zero
D. varying

Q.84 A BJT is a current controlled device because its output characteristics are determined by the____.
A. Input voltage
B. Output current
C. Input current
D. Field

Q.85 The purpose of interpoles in dc machines is to nullify:
A. the demagnetizing effect of armature MMF
B. the cross-magnetizing effect of armature MMF
C. the reactance voltage
D. both the cross-magnetizing MMF and the reactance voltage

Q.86 When the strength of current in 2 H inductor changes at a rate of 4 A/sec, what is the voltage across it?
A. 8 V
B. 2 V
C. 0.5 V
D. None of these

Q.87 ___________refers to all the energy used to perform an action, manufacture something or simply inhabit a building.
A. energy cost
B. energy efficiency
C. energy saving
D. energy consumption

Q.88 Which of the following statement is true?
A. ESCOs are usually companies that provide a complete energy project service, from assessment to design to construction or installation, along with engineering and project management services, and financing.
B. Energy efficiency projects generate incremental cost savings as similar to incremental revenues from the sale of outputs.
C. ESCOs are "bankers" in the narrow sense
D. Taxes, using the crucial tax rate applied to positive (i.e. increasing taxes) or negative (i.e. decreasing taxes) Net

Present Value.

Q.89 _____________, is key to the successful involvement of an ESCO in performance contracting where energy cost savings are being guaranteed.

A. Macro economic

B. Micro economic

C. Monitoring and verification

D. Cash Flows

Q.90 The solids which have negative temperature coefficient of resistance are :

A. insulators only

B. insulators and semiconductors

C. metals

D. semiconductors only

Q.91 ESCOs mean:-

A. Energy Service Companies

B. Escort Service Companies

C. Efficiency Service Companies

D. Energy Social Correlation

Q.92 Match the following:

1. Micro factors	a. "annual return"
2. sensitivity analysis	b. Depreciation
3. Return on Investment expresses the	c. Capital structure
4. Cost Calculation	d." what if"

A. 1-d, 2-a, 3-b, 4-c   **B.** 1-b, 2-c, 3-d, 4-a

C. 1-c, 2-d, 3-a, 4-b   **D.** 1-d, 2-c, 3-b, 4-a

Q.93 Frequencies in the UHF range normally propagate by means of :

A. Surface Waves   **B.** Ground Waves

C. Space Waves   **D.** Sky Waves

Q.94 Financing option for in-house energy management is:

A. by retaining a proportion of the savings achieved

B. changes in interest rates

C. costs of debt, equity

D. simple payback

Q.95 It is essential to keep a careful watch on the organisation's maintenance policy and practices in order to protect any investment already made in reducing your organisation's ___________.

A. energy cost   **B.** energy consumption

C. energy efficiency   **D.** energy saving

Q.96 ROI must always be ___________ than cost of money (interest rate); the greater the return on investment better is the investment.

A. lower   **B.** medium

C. higher   **D.** decreasing

Q.97 Is it necessary for a transmitting antenna to be at the same height as that of the receiving antenna for line-of-sight communication? A TV transmitting antenna is 81m tall. How much service area can it cover if the receiving antenna is at the ground level?

A. 3256 km^2 **B.** 2256 km^2

C. 3206 km^2 **D.** none of these

Q.98 A closely wound solenoid of 800 turns and area of cross-section 2.5×10^{-4} m^2 carries a current of 3.0 A. Explain the sense in which the solenoid acts like a bar magnet. What is its associated magnetic moment?

A. 0.6 JT^{-1} **B.** 0.7 JT^{-1}

C. 0.9 JT^{-1} **D.** None of these

Q.99 Radioactive isotope has a half-life of T years. How long will it take the activity to reduce to 3.125%.

A. 7T years   **B.** 6T years

C. 5T years   **D.** None of these

Q.100 _______ also show the dependency relationships between activities and current schedule status.

A. Technical Design   **B.** PERT

C. CPM   **D.** Gantt chart

Q.101 ___________ is the basic processes that should be performed to get the project started.

A. Planning   **B.** Executing

C. Initiating   **D.** Closing out

Q.102 An elevator is moving down with an uniform speed of 8 m s^{-1} and a bolt of mass 0.4 kg falls from the ceiling. It hits the elevator's floor and does not rebound. The length of the elevator is 3 m. Find the heat produced during the impact.

A. 1.76 J   **B.** 11 J   **C.** 12.76 J   **D.** 11.76 J

Q.103 What is the magnitude of magnetic force per unit length on a wire carrying a current of 8 A and making an angle of 30° with the direction of a uniform magnetic field of 0.15 T?

A. 0.6 Nm^{-1} **B.** 0.7 Nm^{-1}

C. 0.9 Nm^{-1} **D.** None of these

Q.104 A proactive report generated by project planner software can really help the ___________ to know whether the tasks are progressing as per the plan.

A. finance manager   **B.** project manager

C. auditor   **D.** general manager

Q.105 Which of the following is false?

A. Henry Gantt developed the Gantt Chart.

B. The contractor provides the financing and is paid an agreed fraction of actual savings as they are achieved. This payment is used to pay down the debt costs of equipment and/or services.

C. A finance manager's success is measured by the amount of cost optimisation done for a project.

D. CPM (Critical Path Method) models the activities and events of a project as a network.

Q.106 A square coil of side 10 cm consists of 20 turns and carries a current of 12 A. The coil is suspended vertically and the normal to the plane of the coil makes an angle of 30° with the direction of a uniform the horizontal magnetic field of magnitude 0.80 T. What is the magnitude of torque experienced by the coil?

A. 0.56 Nm   **B.** 0.76 Nm   **C.** 1 Nm   **D.** 0.96 Nm

Q.107 A critical feature of M&T is to understand what drives
__________.

A. energy cost
B. energy efficiency
C. energy saving
D. energy consumption

Q.108 Energy monitoring and targeting is built on the principle of _____________.

A. "you cant manage what you do measure".
B. "you cannot manage what you do not measure".
C. "production can be reduced to achieve reduced energy consumption".
D. "consumption of energy is proportional to production rate".

Q.109 Which of the following is not an example of a bio-mass energy source?

A. Wood
B. Gobar-gas
C. Nuclear energy
D. Coal

Q.110 Which of the following is false?

A. With the rapid progress in instrumentation and online computerisation, it has become quite easy to collect data and also compare quickly to take appropriate steps for performance improvement.
B. A better appreciation of variations is almost always obtained from a table of numbers, rather than from a visual presentation.
C. Electricity bills and other fuel bills should be collected periodically and analysed.
D. Equipment level information can be obtained from nameplate data, run-time and schedule information, sub-metered data on specific energy consuming equipment.

Q.111 How much energy is given to each coulomb of charge passing through a 6 V battery?

A. 6 J   **B.** 5 J   **C.** 3 J   **D.** 4 J

Q.112 CUSUM means

A. Cumbersome
B. Cumulative sum
C. Calculated sum
D. Cross sum

Q.113 A CUSUM graph follows a trend and shows the random fluctuation of energy consumption and should oscillate around __________.

A. 1,000   **B.** 100   **C.** 10   **D.** 0

Q.114 An electric iron of resistance 20 Ω takes a current of 5 A. Calculate the heat developed in 30 s.

A. 0.5×10^4 J
B. 1.5×10^3 J
C. 1.5×10^4 J
D. None of these

Q.115 From rest, a car accelerated at 8 m/s^2 for 10 seconds. What is the position of the car at the end of the 10 seconds?

A. 400 m
B. 200 m
C. 300 m
D. none of these

Q.116 Graph generally provide an effective means of developing the energy-production relationships, which explain what is going on in the plant.

A. Texts   **B.** Tables   **C.** Graphs   **D.** Visuals

Q.117 Where has India launched the state-of-the-art Solar Electrification Project?

A. Agaween village
B. Libya
C. Egypt
D. Both A and C

Q.118 Which of the following is/are the new scheme(s) launched for the powerloom sector?

A. Pradhan Mantri Credit Scheme for powerloom weavers
B. Solar energy scheme for powerlooms
C. Both the above
D. None of the above

Q.119 An electric heater of resistance 8 Ω draws 15 A from the service mains 2 hours. Calculate the rate at which heat is developed in the heater.

A. 1800 J/s
B. 1900 J/s
C. 1700 J/s
D. None of the above

Q.120 India is likely to export nearly one-fifth less cotton than previously estimated as _____ have eaten into the country output.

A. Termites
B. Green Earthworms
C. Bacteria
D. Pink Bollworms

// Smart Answer Sheet //

Correct — Indicates percentage of students who answered questions correctly.

Skipped — Indicates percentage of students who skipped questions.

Q.	Ans.	Correct	Skipped
1	C	81.59 %	17.8 %
2	C	85.16 %	13.01 %
3	C	89.67 %	10.04 %
4	C	82.1 %	15.5 %
5	C	85.14 %	10.81 %
6	B	79.7 %	19.25 %
7	B	85.13 %	13.06 %
8	C	78.08 %	15.71 %
9	B	87.92 %	11.6 %
10	D	87.71 %	12.14 %
11	D	88.99 %	10.47 %
12	B	84.6 %	11.08 %
13	D	89.46 %	10.3 %
14	C	86.98 %	10.21 %
15	C	83.93 %	12.27 %
16	A	80.26 %	14.58 %
17	A	85.08 %	14.47 %
18	B	81.7 %	10.71 %
19	B	81.08 %	10.99 %
20	B	89.5 %	10.19 %
21	C	87.0 %	12.5 %
22	D	81.19 %	16.86 %
23	B	87.96 %	11.81 %
24	B	81.62 %	14.47 %
25	D	83.49 %	16.17 %
26	C	79.55 %	20.06 %
27	C	78.9 %	16.86 %
28	A	86.31 %	12.4 %
29	C	81.95 %	15.11 %
30	C	82.01 %	16.05 %
31	B	79.67 %	11.65 %
32	A	85.08 %	13.9 %
33	C	77.46 %	14.48 %
34	D	88.79 %	10.56 %
35	A	79.68 %	20.11 %
36	C	86.81 %	11.43 %
37	D	82.41 %	10.28 %
38	C	76.1 %	23.88 %
39	B	87.78 %	11.81 %
40	A	83.48 %	12.22 %
41	D	86.13 %	10.99 %
42	B	83.31 %	16.56 %
43	C	84.82 %	12.49 %
44	A	89.2 %	10.34 %
45	B	76.21 %	17.33 %
46	D	80.22 %	13.37 %
47	A	84.36 %	11.9 %
48	A	80.42 %	15.61 %
49	B	80.73 %	12.76 %
50	A	80.0 %	12.19 %
51	D	86.97 %	12.25 %
52	C	89.81 %	10.06 %
53	C	87.42 %	11.02 %
54	D	77.14 %	21.3 %
55	A	77.01 %	13.24 %
56	A	85.53 %	11.99 %
57	D	78.27 %	14.68 %
58	C	78.72 %	19.17 %
59	A	85.3 %	12.01 %
60	C	88.46 %	10.16 %
61	C	89.25 %	10.74 %
62	B	89.99 %	10.0 %
63	D	77.45 %	12.82 %
64	B	81.72 %	17.76 %
65	D	76.26 %	13.39 %
66	A	82.66 %	13.78 %
67	D	78.69 %	21.0 %
68	D	80.48 %	14.06 %
69	A	79.22 %	19.8 %
70	C	84.59 %	15.24 %
71	D	82.0 %	15.53 %
72	C	87.78 %	11.38 %
73	A	76.26 %	19.01 %
74	A	76.34 %	22.28 %
75	B	83.74 %	12.56 %
76	C	81.27 %	16.32 %
77	A	80.1 %	14.39 %
78	A	76.02 %	12.63 %
79	A	78.99 %	20.18 %
80	C	87.13 %	11.77 %

Q.	Ans.	Correct / Skipped	Q.	Ans.	Correct / Skipped	Q.	Ans.	Correct / Skipped	Q.	Ans.	Correct / Skipped	Q.	Ans.	Correct / Skipped
81	C	86.03 % / 11.79 %	89	C	81.85 % / 15.11 %	97	A	81.67 % / 11.64 %	105	C	88.81 % / 10.65 %	113	D	83.11 % / 12.46 %
82	D	76.76 % / 12.48 %	90	B	76.43 % / 20.96 %	98	A	86.92 % / 12.03 %	106	D	82.42 % / 15.82 %	114	C	82.41 % / 12.07 %
83	C	83.41 % / 12.29 %	91	A	80.39 % / 11.64 %	99	C	81.44 % / 15.25 %	107	D	77.18 % / 18.02 %	115	A	79.68 % / 17.08 %
84	C	88.91 % / 10.38 %	92	C	86.06 % / 13.62 %	100	D	80.77 % / 10.54 %	108	B	85.06 % / 12.73 %	116	C	83.78 % / 10.15 %
85	D	85.43 % / 10.31 %	93	C	87.93 % / 11.85 %	101	C	87.73 % / 11.79 %	109	C	87.41 % / 10.78 %	117	D	81.51 % / 17.87 %
86	A	82.74 % / 15.27 %	94	A	76.16 % / 15.01 %	102	D	76.76 % / 14.99 %	110	B	77.56 % / 20.17 %	118	C	78.13 % / 11.88 %
87	D	88.83 % / 11.01 %	95	B	85.76 % / 13.65 %	103	A	85.22 % / 12.8 %	111	A	85.98 % / 11.91 %	119	A	76.62 % / 21.36 %
88	A	87.9 % / 11.44 %	96	C	77.24 % / 18.53 %	104	B	81.47 % / 12.61 %	112	B	76.52 % / 15.02 %	120	D	89.02 % / 10.05 %

Performance Analysis

Avg. Score (%)	50.0%
Toppers Score (%)	56.67%
Your Score	

//Hints and Solutions//

1. Effeminacy: manifestation of traits in a boy or man that are more often associated with feminine nature, behavior, mannerism, style, or gender roles.

Boorishness: uncouth in manners or appearance.

Manliness: possessing qualities, such as vigour or courage, generally regarded as appropriate to or typical of a man; masculine.

Hence, the correct option is (c).

2. Convulsion: a sudden, violent, irregular movement of the body, caused by involuntary contraction of muscles and associated especially with brain disorders such as epilepsy, the presence of certain toxins or other agents in the blood, or fever in children.

"toxic side effects like convulsions"

synonyms: fit, seizure, paroxysm, spasm.

Restful: having a quiet and soothing quality.

Cramp: painful involuntary contraction of a muscle or muscles, typically caused by fatigue or strain.

Shaking: tremble or vibrate.

Disaster: a sudden accident or a natural catastrophe that causes great damage or loss of life.

Hence, the correct option is (c).

3. Pejorative - expressing contempt or disapproval.
"permissiveness is used almost universally as a pejorative term".

Derogatory - showing a critical or disrespectful attitude. "she tells me I'm fat and is always making derogatory remarks".

Complimentary - expressing a compliment; praising or approving. "Jennie was very complimentary about Kath's riding".

Hence, the correct option is (c).

4. Barbarous - extremely brutal.

"Many early child-rearing practices were barbarous by modern standards".

Crude - in a natural or raw state; not yet processed or refined.

Civilized - polite and good-mannered.

"Such an affront to civilized behaviour will no longer be tolerated".

Hence, the correct option is (c).

5. The idiom 'Every inch a (something)' means 'Fully embodying a certain role, trait, or look.'

Example: He seemed every inch a gentleman into this project.

Hence, the correct option is (c).

6. The idiom 'gall and wormwood' means 'Strong feelings of bitterness and resentment.'

Example: I only feel gall and wormwood when I think of that colleague of mine.

Hence, the correct option is (b).

7. Triptan: a family of tryptamine-based drugs

Tripod: a three-legged stand for supporting a camera or other apparatus; a stool, table, or cauldron resting on three legs.

Thriver: To grow vigorously; flourish

Tricot: a fine knitted fabric made of a natural or man-made fibre.

Hence, the correct option is (b).

8. Anorexia: a serious mental illness where people are of low weight due to limiting their energy intake.

Anosmia: the loss of the sense of smell, either total or partial.

Aphasia: inability to comprehend or formulate language because of damage to specific brain regions.

Hypogeusia: a reduced ability to taste things (to taste sweet, sour, bitter, or salty substances).

Hence, the correct option is (c).

9. Let total work = LCM of 12 and 20 =60 units.

One day work of P = $\dfrac{60}{20}$ =3 units.

One day work of Q = $\dfrac{60}{12}$ = 5 units.

One day work of P, Q and R = $\dfrac{60}{5}$ =12 units.

One day work of R = 12 -3 - 5 =4 units.

Ratio of share of P, Q and R = 3: 5 : 4

Share of R = $\dfrac{4}{12}$ × 7200

= 2400

Hence, the correct option is (b).

10. Let $C.P. = x$
loss $= 5\%$
then $S.P. = \dfrac{100 - loss\%}{100} \times x$
$1900 = \dfrac{95}{100} \times x$
$x = \dfrac{1900 \times 100}{95} => 2000$
To gain $15\% = 2000 \times \dfrac{15}{100} = Rs.\,300$
New $S.P. = 2000 + 300 = $ Rs.2300

Hence, the correct option is (d).

11. Let the number be 5x and 11x

A.T.Q

$$\dfrac{5x+10}{11x+10} = \dfrac{7}{13}$$

65x +130 = 77x+70

12x =60

x=5

Then the number =25 and 55

Then the sum of number =25+55=80

Hence, the correct option is (d).

12. Let five consecutive positive integers are $x, x+1, x+2, x+3$ and $x+4$

According to questions,

$$x + x + 1 + x + 2 + x + 3 + x + 4 = 40$$
$$\Rightarrow 5x = 40 - 10$$
$$\Rightarrow x = 6$$

First Number $= 6$

Last number $= 10$

Average of first and last number $= \dfrac{6+10}{2} = \dfrac{16}{2} = 8$

Hence, the correct option is (b).

13. Speed of Suresh's car= 60 km/hr

Speed of Sanjay's car= $\dfrac{2}{3} \times 60 = 40$ km/hr

Required time taken to meet

$$= \dfrac{300}{60+40}$$

$= 3$ hr

Hence, the correct option is (d).

14. According to question:-

$$10CP = 15SP$$

So, $\dfrac{CP}{SP} = \dfrac{15}{10}$

Let CP and SP be $15x$ and $10x$ respectively.

Loss $\% = \dfrac{CP-SP}{CP} \times 100$

$$= \dfrac{15x-10x}{15x} \times 100$$

$$= \dfrac{1}{3} \times 100$$

$$= 33.33\%$$

Hence, the correct option is (c).

15. $CI = P\left[\left(1 + \dfrac{r}{100}\right)^n - 1\right]$

$$10176 = P\left[\left(1 + \dfrac{12}{100}\right)^2 - 1\right]$$

$$10176 = P\left[\left(\dfrac{112}{100}\right)^2 - 1\right]$$

$$10176 = P\dfrac{(12544-10000)}{10000}$$

$$10176 = \dfrac{2544P}{10000}$$

P = 40000

Hence, the correct option is (c).

16. Selling price = Marked price × (100-Discount1)% × (100-Discount2)%

ATQ,

221 = MP × (100-35)% × (100-15)%

MP = 211 × $\dfrac{100}{65}$ × $\dfrac{100}{85}$

So, MP = 400

Hence, the correct option is (a).

17. Dalton's law of multiple proportions is part of the basis for the modern atomic theory.

Law of multiple proportion statements that when two elements combine with each other to form more than one compound, the weights of one element that combine with a fixed weight of the other are in a ratio of small whole numbers.

Hence, the correct option is (a).

18. Vitamin K

The body needs vitamin K to produce prothrombin, a protein and clotting factor that is important in blood clotting and bone metabolism. Vitamin K belongs to a group of fat-soluble vitamins that play a role in blood clotting, bone metabolism, and regulating blood calcium levels.

Hence, the correct option is (b).

19. Chloroplasts found in plants and algae are responsible for capturing light energy to make sugar in photosynthesis.

Hence, the correct option is (b).

20. Photosynthesis is the process by which plants, some bacteria and some protistans use the energy from sunlight to produce glucose from carbon dioxide and water. This glucose can be converted into pyruvate which releases adenosine triphosphate (ATP) by cellular respiration. Oxygen is also formed.

Hence, the correct option is (b).

21. The Khajuraho monuments are located in the Indian state of Madhya Pradesh, in Chhatarpur district, about 620 kilometres (385 mi) southeast of New Delhi. The temples are located near a small town also known as Khajuraho, with a population of about 20,000 people.

Hence, the correct option is (c).

22. The Sundarbans is a mangrove area in the delta formed by the confluence of Ganges, Brahmaputra and Meghna Rivers in the Bay of Bengal. It spans from the Hooghly River in India's state of West Bengal to the Baleswar River in Bangladesh. Four protected areas in the Sundarbans are enlisted as UNESCO World Heritage Sites, viz Sundarbans National Park, Sundarbans West, Sundarbans South and Sundarbans East Wildlife Sanctuaries.

Hence, the correct option is (d).

23. A cashless society describes an economic state whereby financial transactions are not conducted with money in the form of physical banknotes or coins, but rather through the transfer of digital information (usually an electronic representation of money) between the transacting parties.

Sweden is the world's first cashless economy.

Swedes mainly use debit cards (PIN usually required, unlike in many countries) and our new favourite mobile payment apps.

Hence, the correct option is (b).

24. Parliament in April1993, passed the 73rd Constitutional Amendment Act. Through insertion of Article 243 to Part IX of Indian Constitution, the 73rd amendment provided a Constitutional status to the Panchayati Raj Institutions in India.

Hence, the correct option is (b).

25. Average amount of interest paid by the Company during the given period

$$= Rs. \left[\frac{23.4+32.5+41.6+36.4+49.4}{5}\right] lakhs$$

$$= Rs. \left[\frac{183.3}{5}\right] lakhs$$

= Rs. 36.66 lakhs.

Hence, the correct option is (d).

26. Required percentage = $\left[\frac{(3.00+2.52+3.84+3.68+3.96)}{(288+342+324+336+420)} \times 100\right]\%$

$$= \left[\frac{17}{1710} \times 100\right]\%$$

= 0.99415%

$\approx 1\%$

Hence, the correct option is (c).

27. Required percentage = $\left[\frac{(288+98+3.00+23.4+83)}{(420+142+3.96+49.4+98)} \times 100\right]\%$

$$= \left[\frac{495.4}{713.36} \times 100\right]\%$$

= 69.45%

Total expenditure on all these items in 1998 was approximately 69 percent of the total expenditure in 2002.

Hence, the correct option is (c).

28. Total expenditure of the Company during 2000

= Rs. (324 + 101 + 3.84 + 41.6 + 74)

= Rs. 544.44 lakhs.

Hence, the correct option is (a).

29. Let the amount of Royalty to be paid for these books be Rs. r.

Then, 20 : 15 = 30600 : r

$$=> r = Rs. \left(\frac{30600 \times 15}{20}\right)$$

= Rs. 22,950

Hence, the correct option is (c).

30. Central angle corresponding to Royalty = (15% of 360)°

$$= \frac{15}{100} \times 360°$$

= 54°

Hence, the correct option is (c).

31. Clearly, marked price of the book = 120% of C.P.

Also, cost of paper = 25% of C.P

Let the cost of paper for a single book be Rs. n.

Then, 120 : 25 = 180 : n

$$n = Rs. \left(\frac{25 \times 180}{120}\right)$$

= Rs. 37.50 .

Hence, the correct option is (b).

32. For the publisher to earn a profit of 25%, S.P. = 125% of C.P.

Also Transportation Cost = 10% of C.P.

Let the S.P. of 5500 books be Rs. x.

Then, 10 : 125 = 82500 : x

$$x = Rs. \left(\frac{125 \times 82500}{10}\right)$$

= Rs. 1031250

Therefore S.P. of one book = Rs. $\left(\frac{1031250}{5500}\right)$

= Rs. 187.50

Hence, the correct option is (a).

33. The Los Angeles Lakers defeated the Miami Heat to win the National Basketball Association (NBA) Championship 2020. This is the 17th NBA title win for LA Lakers and also there first since 2010, after late Kobe Bryant's fifth and final title a decade ago.

Hence, the correct option is (c).

34. There is little doubt that Lewis Hamilton is one of the best drivers that has sat behind the wheels of a Formula One car, but on Sunday, the British superstar took another step towards becoming the greatest ever. Lewis Hamilton won the Eifel Grand Prix on Sunday, and in the process equalled the great Michael Schumacher's record of 91 F1 race wins. Cricket legend Sachin Tendulkar, who was presented with a Ferrari by Michael Schumacher on behalf of Fiat in 2002, was all praise for Hamilton, saying he has always liked the Briton's "grit and balanced aggression while driving the @F1 car".

Hence, the correct option is (d).

35. The World Unani Day is observed every year on February 11. The day commemorates the birth anniversary of great Unani scholar and social reformer Hakim Ajmal Khan.

Hence, the correct option is (a).

36. Haryana's Chief Minister Manohar Lal Khattar launched Mukhyamantri Pariwar Smridhi scheme on the completion of 100 days of state government. The government will provide two thousand rupees to poor farmers in three installments in this scheme.

Hence, the correct option is (c).

37. Kerala's Finance Minister Thomas Isaac announced in the state budget that Kerala will ban the sale of both compact fluorescent lamp (CFL) and incandescent (filament) bulbs from November 2020. All street lights and bulbs in government offices will be replaced with LED lights.

Hence, the correct option is (d).

38. World Pulses Day is celebrated on February 10 every year around the world. World pulses day is celebrated by the United Nations to recognize the importance of pulses as a healthy food.

Hence, the correct option is (c).

39. India has been ranked 129 among 158 countries in the 2020 Commitment to Reducing Inequality (CRI) Index. The third edition of the index focuses on Fighting Inequality in the time of COVID-19. The 2020 CRI index has been topped by Norway. South Sudan is the lowest ranking country in the index at 158th position.

Hence, the correct option is (b).

40. Turkey announced on February 11, 2020 that it neutralized 101 Syrian regime soldiers following a bombardment that killed five Turkish soldiers in Syria's Idlib region on February 10. Syria's Idlib region is the last major rebel-held region.

Hence, the correct option is (a).

41. By interconnection of the elements one can obtain the maximum inductance of $L_1 + L_2 + 2M$.

By interconnection of the elements one can obtain the minimum inductance of $L_1 + L_2 - 2M$.

Hence, the correct option is (d).

42. The no-load power factor of a transformer is approximately 0.2 because at no load it only takes excitation current to excite the core and this current lag the no load voltage by an angle near to 90 hence power factor is low.

Hence, the correct option is (b).

43. By using source transformation technique, the given circuit reduces to,

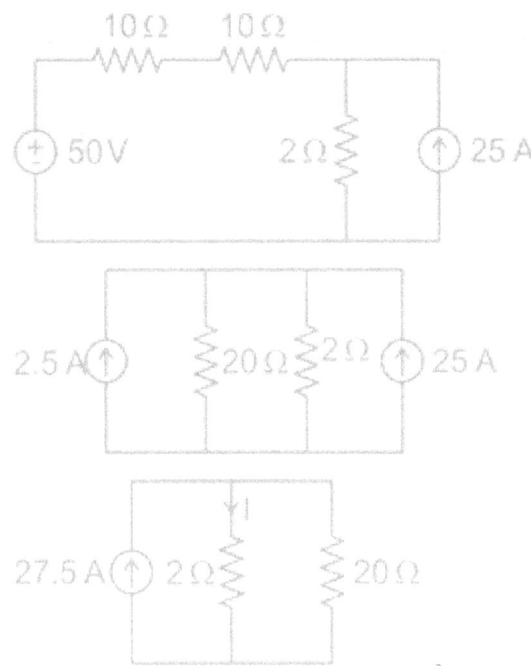

Let the current through 2 Ω resistance is I.

By using current division,

$$I = 27.5 \left(\frac{20}{2+20} \right)$$

$$= 27.5 \times \frac{20}{22}$$

$$= 25 \text{ A}$$

Hence, the correct option is (c).

44. The isentropic process is nothing but reversible adiabatic process since between the isothermal and adiabatic process the isothermal process has maximum area under P–V diagram the isothermal process will have maximum work done during expansion. Since the slope of p–v plot for adiabatic process is greater than isothermal process.

Hence, the correct option is (a).

45. Norton current is nothing but the short circuit current across the load terminal AB.

By applying superposition theorem

When only voltage source active and another source are inactive

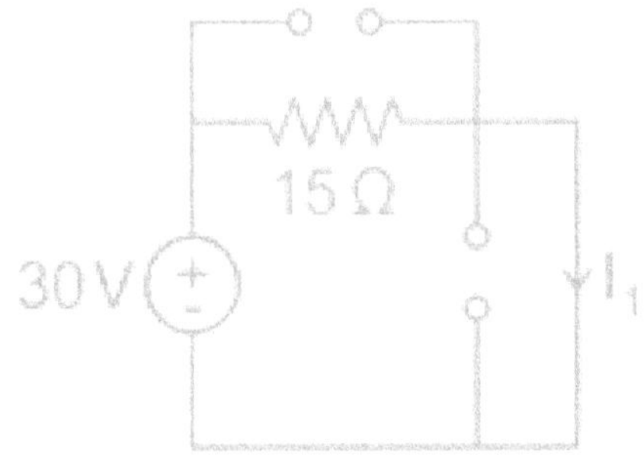

$$I_1 = \frac{30}{15} = 2A$$

Now consider 10 A current source

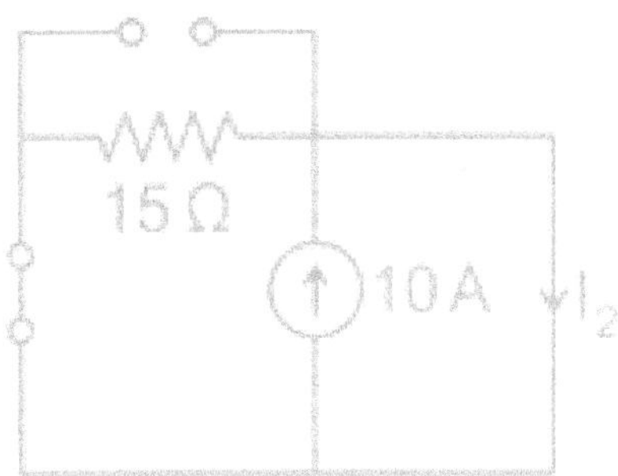

I_2 = 10 A

Now consider 5 A current source

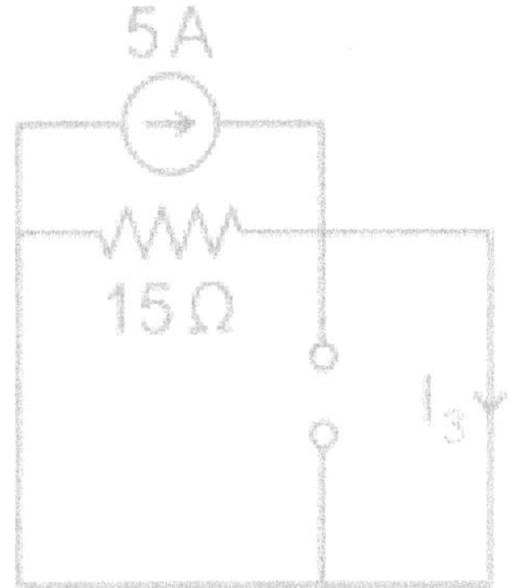

I_3 = 5 A

Norton current IN = I_1 + I_2 + I_3 = 2 + 10 + 5 = 17 A

Hence, the correct option is (b).

46. Being eco-friendly or environmentally friendly means having a lifestyle that is better for the environment. It involves taking small steps towards the proper maintenance Earth's environment for the present and future generations.

Some of the actions that can be taken to ensure that include;

1. Avoiding the use of plastic bags encouraging the use of biodegradable bags (cloth, paper etc.)

2. Reuse of the plastic bottles and tin cans.

3. Taking up the public transportation or walking instead of using a private vehicle.

4. Segregation of biodegradable and non-biodegradable wastes.

5. Switching off fans and lights when not in use.

Hence, the correct option is (D).

47. Synchronizing power is defined as the varying of the synchronous power P on varying in the load angle δ.

It is also called stiffness of coupling, stability or rigidity factor; It is represented as Psyn

A synchronous machine, when synchronised to infinite busbars has an inherent tendency to remain in synchronism.

At perfect synchronization, their synchronizing power is zero.

Hence, the correct option is (a).

48. The gate voltage in a JFET at which drain current becomes zero is called pinch-off voltage

Pinch off voltage:

It is the drain to source voltage after which the drain to source current becomes almost constant and JFET enters saturation region and is defined only when gate to source voltage is zero.

Hence, the correct option is (a).

49. The motor used in ceiling fan is capacitor run motor. Due to the high cost and proper maintenance of capacitor start motors, a fixed rated (generally 2.5μF to 3.5μF) capacitor is used permanently in motor (which is known as capacitor start capacitor run motors).

Hence, the correct option is (b).

50. Electrical Impedance (Z), is the total opposition that a circuit presents to alternating current. Impedance is measured in ohms and may include resistance (R), inductive reactance (X_L), and capacitive reactance (X_C)

$$\sqrt{R^2 + (X_L - X_C)^2}$$

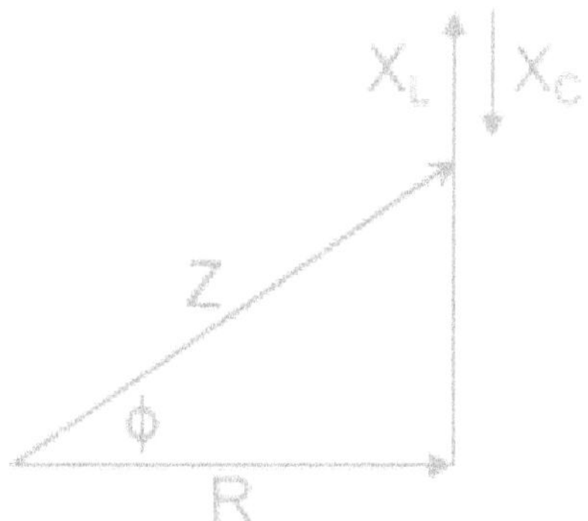

Hence, the correct option is (a).

51. Drawbacks of electric traction system:

Electric traction system involves high erection cost of power system.

Interference causes to the communication lines due to the overhead distribution networks.

The failure of power supply brings whole traction system to stand still.

In an electric traction system, the electrically operated vehicles must move only on the electrified routes.

Additional equipment should be needed for the provision of regenerative braking, it will increase the overall cost of installation.

Hence, the correct option is (d).

52. In series circuit, the current flowing through the circuit is same and the voltage is divided through all the elements in the circuit.

In parallel circuit, the voltage across each parallel branch is same and the current is divided between all the branches.

Thus, voltage divider is always a series circuit and current divider is always a parallel circuit.

Hence, the correct option is (c).

53. When we find Thevenin equivalent resistance we have independent current sources by open circuit and independent voltage source by short circuit.

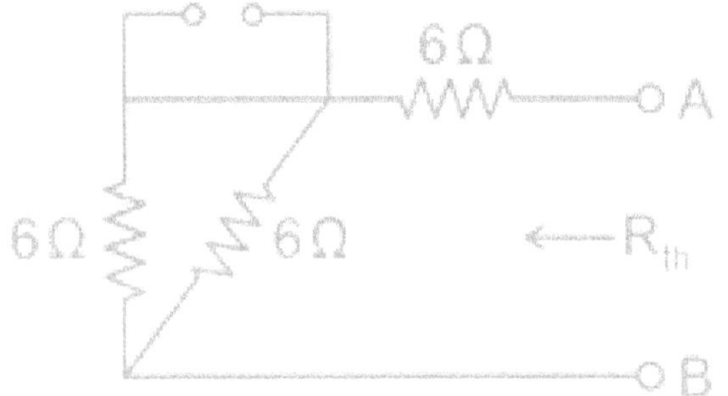

$$R_{th} = \frac{6 \times 6}{6+6} + 6$$

$$= 9\,\Omega$$

Hence, the correct option is (c).

54. The permissible temperature limit at which the insulators may be worked safely without deterioration depends upon the type and class of the insulation as detailed below.

Class Y - maximum temperature 90°C

Class A - maximum temperature 105°C

Class E - maximum temperature 120°C

Class B - Maximum temperature 130°C

Class F - maximum temperature 155°C

Class H - maximum temperature 180°C

Class C - maximum temperature above 180°C (limited stability up to 225°C)

Hence, the correct option is (d).

55. We know that

Leakage resistance is inversely proportional to the length

therefore R $\propto \dfrac{1}{L}$

$$\frac{R_1}{R_2} = \frac{L_2}{L_1}$$

$$R_2 = R_1 \times \frac{L_1}{L_2} = 1 \times \frac{100}{50}$$

$$= 2\ m\Omega$$

Hence, the correct option is (a).

56. Mathematically, it is equal to the ratio of input SNR to output SNR. For an ideal amplifier , when a signal passes through the system, then no noise is added to the signal and input SNR is equal to the output SNR and hence NF for ideal amplifier is 1 or 0 db.

Hence, the correct option is (a).

57. The transformer which changes the magnitude and phase angle at the certain point in the power system is known as the regulating transformer

It is mainly used for controlling the magnitude of bus voltage and for controlling the power flow, which is controlled by the phase angle of the transformer.

Important:

The regulating transformer is of two types. One is used for changing the magnitude of voltage which is called online tap changing transformer and the other is called phase shifting transformer. The regulating transformer compensates the fluctuation of voltage and current.

Hence, the correct option is (d).

58. The term "air core coil" describes an inductor that does not use a magnetic core made of a ferromagnetic material.

The coils are wound on plastic, ceramic, or other nonmagnetic forms that's by air core inductor has minimum eddy current loss and free from non-linearity.

Hence, the correct option is (c).

59. The best location of the power factor improving the device to be installed in the transmission line is at receiving end because the lagging load is connected at receiving end. The shunt capacitor is used to improve the power factor which is connected near to load.

Hence, the correct option is (a).

60. When a high voltage is applied across an air gap, the air in the gap gets ionized under the influence of electrostatic forces and becomes conducting medium.

Current flows in the form of a continuous spark, called the arc.

It is to be noted that a very high voltage is required to establish an arc across an air gap but to maintain an arc small voltage may be sufficient.

Hence, the correct option is (c).

61. Displacement of the particle executing SHM $x = A\sin wt$

Acceleration of the particle $a = \dfrac{d^2 x}{dt^2}$

$$\Rightarrow a = -Aw^2 \sin wt = Aw^2 \sin(\pi + wt)$$

Thus phase difference between displacement and acceleration of the particle is π radian.

Hence, the correct option is (c).

62. Given

I_m = Maximum value of current = 20 A, Frequency = 50 Hz

We know that

$I = I_m \sin \omega t$

$20 \sin \omega t = 10$

$\omega t = \sin^{-1}\left(\dfrac{1}{2}\right) = \dfrac{\pi}{6}$

$100t = \dfrac{1}{6}$

Time take the current to reach 10 A for the first time = $\dfrac{1}{600}$ s

Hence, the correct option is (b).

63. Brushless DC motors are similar to AC synchronous motors. The major difference is that synchronous motors develop a sinusoidal back EMF, as compared to a rectangular, or trapezoidal, back EMF for brushless DC motors. Both have stator created rotating magnetic fields producing torque in a magnetic rotor.

Hence, the correct option is (d).

64. Light load adjustment for induction type energy meter is usually done at 5% of full load current.

In order to recorded true energy by the energy meter during light load, a small shading loop is placed between the shunt magnet and the disc.

Hence, the correct option is (b).

65. Wattmeter reading in two wattmeter method are,

$W_1 = V_L I_L \cos(30 - \varphi)$

$W_2 = V_L I_L \cos(30 + \varphi)$

The active power will be = $W_1 + W_2 = 8.2 + 7.5 = 15.7$ W

Important:

$$tan\phi = \frac{\sqrt{3}(W_1 - W_2)}{(W_1 + W_2)}$$

Power factor = $\cos \varphi$

Hence, the correct option is (d).

66. Relative error is defined as the ratio of absolute error and true value.

The absolute error has the same units as the measurement. Relative error is defined as the absolute error relative to the size of the measurement, and it depends on both the absolute error and the measured value. The relative error is large when the measured value is small, or when the absolute error is large.

Hence, the correct option is (a).

67. Types of single-phase induction motor namely

Split phase induction motor.

Capacitor start inductor motor.

Capacitor start capacitor run induction motor.

Shaded pole induction motor.

Permanent split capacitor motor or single value capacitor motor.

Hence, the correct option is (d).

68. Advantages of AC power transmission:

The power can be generated at high voltages

The maintenance of a.c. sub-stations is easy and cheaper

The a.c. voltage can be stepped up or stepped down by transformers with ease and efficiency, this permits to transmit power at high voltages and distribute it at safe potentials.

Less loss of power during transmission

Disadvantages of AC power transmission:

An a.c. line requires more copper than a d.c. line

The construction of a.c. transmission line is more complicated than a d.c. transmission line.

Due to skin effect in the a.c. system, the effective resistance of the line is increased.

An a.c. line has capacitance. Therefore, there is a continuous loss of power due to charging current even when the line is open.

Hence, the correct option is (d).

69. As the temperature increases the energy gap between valence band and conduction band decreases and hence barrier potential may also decrease.

Hence, the correct option is (a).

70. Let the voltage across dependent current source = V_1

Now apply KVL in the loop we get

$V_1 = 20 + 15 = 35$ V

$\therefore$ Power delivered by current source = $35 \times \dfrac{20}{4}$

= 175 W

Hence, the correct option is (c).

71. Conductors are the substances through which a flow of current i.e. the flow of free electrons can be set up easily. The number of free electrons present in the substances decides its conductivity.

Properties of good conductor:

Low resistance.

Low specific resistance or resistivity.

Low specific gravity.

High conductivity.

Tensile strength is not a property of good conductor of electricity.

Hence, the correct option is (d).

72. When $R_L = 0$, $I = 3$ A

$\Rightarrow V/R = 3 \Rightarrow V = 3R$

When $R_L = 2$, $I = 1.5$

$$\Rightarrow \frac{V}{R+R_L} = 1.5$$

$$\Rightarrow \frac{3R}{R+2} = 1.5$$

$\Rightarrow R = 2\,\Omega$

When, $R_L = 1\,\Omega$

$$I = \frac{V}{R+R_L} = \frac{3R}{R+R_L} = \frac{3(2)}{2+1} = 2A$$

Hence, the correct option is (c).

73. The input sensitivity of many CROs is of the order of a few milli-volts per division and the voltage required for deflecting the electron beam varies from approximately 100 V (peak lo peak) to 500 V depending on the accelerating voltage and the construction of the tube. Thus, the vertical amplifier is required to provide this desired gain from milli-volt input to several hundred volts (peak to peak) output. The vertical amplifier should not distort the input waveform and should have good response for entire band of frequencies to be measured.

The deflection plates of CRO act as plates of a capacitor and when the input signal frequency exceeds over 1 MHz, the current required for charging and discharging of the capacitor formed by the deflection plates increases. So, the vertical amplifier should be capable of supplying current enough to charge und discharge the deflection plate capacitor.

Hence, the correct option is (a).

74. We know that, a current carrying conductor produces its own magnetic field, and this magnetic field affects the main magnetic field of the alternator.

It has two undesirable effects, either it distorts the main field, or it reduces the main field flux or both; They deteriorate the performance of the machine.

When the field gets distorted, it is known as a cross magnetizing effect; In this case, the output will be non-sinusoidal.

Cross-magnetizing effect can be reduced by shifting the brush positions.

Hence, the correct option is (a).

75. When two capacitors C_1 and C_2 are connected in series then

total capacitance $= \dfrac{C_1 \times C_2}{C_1 + C_2}$

$$C = \frac{10 \times 10}{20} = \frac{100}{20} = 5\mu F$$

Total charge $= Q = CV$

$= 5 \times 300$

$= 1500\ \mu C$

Hence, the correct option is (b).

76. In a series RLC circuit, the applied voltage is phasor sum of voltage existing across all these elements

let the total applied voltage is V and the voltage applied across R, L and C are V_R, V_L, and V_C respectively.

Now, $V = \sqrt{V_R^2 + (V_L - V_C)^2}$

Given that, V_R = 300 V, V_L = 100 V, V_C = 500 V

$$V = \sqrt{(300)^2 + (100 - 400)^2} = 500V$$

A is true, but R is false.

Hence, the correct option is (c).

77. Concept

When the LCR circuit is set to resonance, the resonant frequency is

$$F = \frac{1}{2\pi}\sqrt{\frac{L}{C}}$$

Quality factor is $\ Q = \dfrac{\omega_0 L}{R} = \dfrac{1}{R}\sqrt{\dfrac{L}{C}}$

At resonance current is Maximum i.e. I_0

$$I_0 = \frac{V_0}{R}$$

Calculation:

At resonance current is maximum i.e. I_0

$= \dfrac{200}{20}$

$= 10$ A

Hence, the correct option is (a).

78. Average energy = 720 MWh

Average power $= \dfrac{720 \times 10^6}{24} = 30MW$

$$Load\ factor = \frac{Averqage\ power}{Maximum\ demand}$$

Maximum demand $= \dfrac{30 \times 10^6}{0.6}$

$= 50$ MV

Hence, the correct option is (a).

79. An alternating (AC) quantity (voltage current or power) is defined as the one which changes its value as well as direction with respect to time.

It is important to note that a quantity is called as an AC quantity if and only if both its values as well as polarity changes with respect to time.

Hence, the correct option is (a).

80. The current flowing through armature of a Dc motor is AC.

In a DC generator, the current is induced from the rotation of the armature within the field magnetic flux; The commutator converts this to DC.

In a DC motor, the alternating current is produced by the rotation of the commutator.

Hence, the correct option is (c).

81. Purpose of Transposition:

Transmission lines are transposed to prevent interference with neighbouring telephone lines.

The transposition arrangement of high voltage lines helps to reduce the system power loss.

We have developed transposition system for Single circuit tower using same tension tower with reduced deviation angle.

Transposition arrangement of power line helps to reduce the effect of inductive coupling.

It is proved more economical Solution, in comparison of the conventional transposition system.

Important:

Transposition arrangement

The transposition arrangement of the conductor can simply show in the following the figure. The conductor in Position 1, Position 2 and Position 3 changes in a specific arrangement to reduce the effect of capacitance and the electrostatic unbalanced voltages.

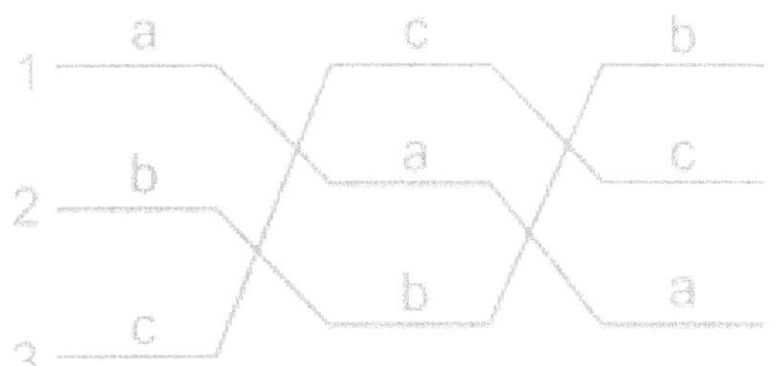

Hence, the correct option is (c).

82. Properties of voltage sources:

The terminal voltage remains constant irrespective of the load current by an ideal voltage source.

Voltage regulation low should be low as possible.

Terminal voltage decrease with increase in load current for a non-ideal voltage source.

The source resistance should be as small as possible.

Hence, the correct option is (d).

83. Positive sequence component: It represents three equal phasors with a phase displacement of 120° and has phase sequence same as the original phasors. It specifies that the current is flowing through source to load.

Negative sequence component: It represents three equal phasors with a phase displacement of 120° with each other and has phase sequence opposite to that of the original phasors. It specifies that current is flowing from load to source.

Zero sequence component: It represents three equal and parallel phasors with zero phase displacement. It specifies that current is flowing from source to ground.

In a balanced three phase system operating in normal condition, only positive sequence component exists and hence zero sequence currents are zero.

Hence, the correct option is (c).

84. A BJT is a current controlled device because its output characteristics are determined by the input current.

A FET is voltage-controlled device because its output characteristics are determined by the Field which depends on voltage applied.

Hence, the correct option is (c).

85. Interpoles are similar to the main field poles and located on the yoke between the main field poles.

They have windings in series with the armature winding. Interpoles in DC machine has basically two functions:-
Automatic neutralisation of cross magnetisation due to armature reaction.
To counter and cancel reactance voltage in the coil undergoing commutation.
Hence, the correct option is (d).

86. $V = L\dfrac{di}{dt}$

Where,

v = Instantaneous voltage across the inductor

L = Inductance in Henrys

Voltage across inductor = 2 × 4 = 8 V

Important:

$$i = C\dfrac{dv}{dt}$$

Where,

i = Instantaneous current through the capacitor

C = Capacitance in Farads

$\dfrac{d_v}{d_t}$= Instantaneous rate of voltage change (volts per second).

V = 2 ×4

V = 8 Volts

Hence, the correct option is (a).

87. Energy consumption refers to ALL the energy used to perform an action, manufacture something or simply inhabit a building. Let's look at a few examples: In a factory, total energy consumption can be measured by looking at how much energy a production process consumes, for example, by making car parts.

Hence, the correct option is (d).

88. ESCOs are usually companies that provide a complete energy project service, from assessment to design to construction or installation, along with engineering and project management services, and financing.

Hence, the correct option is (a).

89. Monitoring and verification is key to the successful involvement of an ESCO in performance contracting where energy cost savings are being guaranteed.

Hence, the correct option is (c).

90. The negative temperature coefficient of the resistance is only present in the insulators or the semiconductors. In these, the resistance decreases with increase in temperature.

Hence, the correct option is (b).

91. ESCO stands for Energy Service Company. The term Energy Savings Company is also used. It is a company or an entity that delivers energy services or other energy efficiency improvements in an energy user's premises, and accepts some degree of financial risk in doing so.

Hence, the correct option is (a).

92. Micro factors-Capital structure

sensitivity analysis-" what if"

Return on Investment expresses the-"annual return"

Cost Calculation-Depreciation

Hence, the correct option is (c).

93. Due to its high frequency, an ultra-high frequency (UHF) wave can not travel along the trajectory of the ground also it cannot get reflected by the ionosphere. The ultrahigh-frequency signals are propagated through line – of – sight communication, which is actually space wave propagation.

Hence, the correct option is (c).

94. Financing option for in-house energy management is by retaining a proportion of the savings achieved.

Hence, the correct option is (a).

95. It is essential to keep a careful watch on the organisation's maintenance policy and practices in order to protect any investment already made in reducing your organisation's energy consumption.

Hence, the correct option is (b).

96. ROI must always be higher than cost of money (interest rate); the greater the return on investment better is the investment.

Hence, the correct option is (c).

97. In line – of – sight communication, between the transmitter and the receiver there is no physical obstruction. So, there is no need for the transmitting and receiving antenna to be at the same height.

Height of the antenna, h = 81 m

Radius of earth, R = 6.4 x 10^6 m

d = 2Rh, for range

The service area of the antenna is given by the relation :

A = nd² = n(2Rh)

= 3.14 x 2 x 6.4 x 10^6 x 81

= 3255.55 x 10^6 m²

= 3255.55

= 3256 km²

Hence, the correct option is (a).

98. Number of turns in the solenoid, n = 800

Area of cross-section, A = $2.5 \times 10^{-4}\text{\:\,}m^{2}$

Current in the solenoid, I = 3.0 A

A current-carrying solenoid behaves like a bar magnet because a magnetic field develops along its axis, i.e., along with its length.

The magnetic moment associated with the given current-carrying solenoid is calculated as:

M = n I A

$$= 800 \times 3 \times 2.5 \times 10^{-4}$$

= $0.6\text{\:\,}JT^{-1}$

Hence, the correct option is (a).

99. The half-life of the radioactive isotope $= T$ years
N_0 is the actual amount of radioactive isotope.
After decay, the amount of the radioactive isotope $= N$
It is given that only 3.125% of N_0 remains after decay.
Hence, we can write:
$$\frac{N}{N_0} = 3.125\% = \frac{3.125}{100} = \frac{1}{32}$$
But, $\frac{N}{N_0} = e^{-\lambda t}$
Where, $\lambda =$ Decay
Constant $t =$ Time
$$e^{-\lambda t} = \frac{1}{32} - \lambda t = \ln 1 - \ln 32 - \lambda t = 0 - 3.4657$$
since, $-\lambda = \frac{0.693}{T}$
$$t = \frac{3.466}{\frac{0.693}{T}} \approx 5 \text{ T years.}$$

Hence, the isotope will take about $5T$ years to reduce to 3.125% of its original value.

Hence, the correct option is (c).

100. A Gantt chart is a type of bar chart that illustrates a project schedule, named after its inventor, Henry Gantt, who designed such a chart around the years 1910–1915. Modern Gantt charts also show the dependency relationships between activities and current schedule status.

Hence, the correct option is (d).

101. Initiating is the basic processes that should be performed to get the project started. This is where all projects begin. The value

of the project is determined, as well as its feasibility. Before the project is approved or rejected, these two documents are created to sell the work to stakeholders or sponsors:

Hence, the correct option is (c).

102. Mass m = 0.4 kg

Speed of the elevator = 8 m/s

Height h = 3 m

The potential energy gets converted into heat energy as the relative velocity is zero.

Heat produced = loss of potential energy

=> mgh = 0.4 x 9.8 x 3

= 11.76 J

Hence, the correct option is (d).

103. The current flowing in the wire is (I) = 8 A

The magnitude of the uniform magnetic field (B) is 0.15 T

The angle between the wire and the magnetic field, $\theta = 30°$

The magnetic force per unit length on the wire is given as F = $BIsin\theta$

$$= 0.15 \times 8 \times 1 \times sin30°$$

$= 0.6\text{\:\,}Nm^{-1}$

Hence, the magnetic force per unit length on the wire is $0.6\text{\:\,}Nm^{-1}$.

Hence, the correct option is (a).

104. A proactive report generated by project planner software can really help the project manager to know whether the tasks are progressing as per the plan.

Hence, the correct option is (b).

105. A finance manager's success is measured by the amount of cost optimisation done for a project.

Hence, the correct option is (c).

106. In the given problem,

the length of a side of the square coil (l) is 10 cm or 0.1 m

The magnitude of the current flowing in the coil (I) is 12 A

The number of turns on the coil (n) is 20

The angle made by the plane of the coil with B (Magnetic field), $\theta = 30°$

The strength of the magnetic field (B) is 0.8 T

The following relation gives the magnitude of the magnetic torque experienced by the coil in the magnetic field:

$\tau = n\text{\:\,}BIA\text{\:\,}sin\theta$

Where,

A = Area of the square coil

= 1 x 1 = 0.1 x 0.1 = 0.01 m²

So, $\tau = 20 \times 0.8 \times 12 \times 0.01 \times sin30°$

= 0.96 Nm

Hence, 0.96 Nm is the magnitude of the torque experienced by the coil.

Hence, the correct option is (d).

107. A critical feature of M&T is understanding the parameter that drives energy consumption, like production, hours of operation, weather, etc.

Hence, the correct option is (d).

108. Energy monitoring and targeting is primarily a management technique that uses energy information as a basis to eliminate waste, reduce and control current level of energy use and improve the existing operating procedures. It builds on the principle "you can't manage what you don't measure".

Hence, the correct option is (b).

109. Nuclear energy is not an example of a bio-mass energy source.
Bio-mass is obtained from the dead plants and animal wastes. In these dead plants and animals there is a chemical change as they react with water and sunlight. But nuclear energy is obtained by fusion and fission of atoms resulting in tremendous release of energy. Both nuclear fusion and fission can be carried out in the absence of the sunlight.
Wood is a part of plant, gobar-gas is obtained from the animal dung and coal is obtained by the dead remains of the plants and animals. Therefore, they are all bio-mass energy products.

Hence, the correct option is (c).

110. A better appreciation of variations is almost always obtained from a table of numbers, rather than from a visual presentation.

Hence, the correct option is (b).

111. We know that the potential difference between two points is given by the equation,
V = $\frac{W}{Q}$,

where,
W is the work done in moving the charge from one point to another
Q is the charge
From the above equation, we can find the energy given to each coulomb as follows:
W = V × Q
Substituting the values in the equation, we get
W = 6V × 1C = 6 J
6 J of energy is given to each coulomb of charge passing through a 6 V of battery.

Hence, the correct option is (a).

112. CUSUM means Cumulative sum.

Lower control limit, Plotted statistic, In statistical quality control, the CUSUM (or cumulative sum control chart) is a sequential analysis technique developed by E. S. Page of the University of Cambridge. It is typically used for monitoring change detection.

Hence, the correct option is (b).

113. A CUSUM graph therefore **follows a trend**, which represents the **random fluctuations of energy consumption and should oscillate** about zero.

Hence, the correct option is (d).

114. The amount of heat generated can be calculated using the Joule's law of heating, which is given by the equation
$H = VIt$
Substituting the values in the above equation, we get,
$H = 100 \times 5 \times 30$

$= 1.5 \times 10^4$ J
The amount of heat developed by the electric iron in 30 s is 1.5×10^4 J.

Hence, the correct option is (c).

115. The car starts from rest therefore the initial speed u = 0. Nothing is said about the initial position and we therefore assume it is equal to 0. Hence the position x is given by the equation $x = \left(\dfrac{1}{2}\right) \times a \times t^2$ where a is the acceleration (=8 m/s^2) and t is the period of time between initial and final positions
$x = \left(\dfrac{1}{2}\right) \times 8 \times (10)^2$

$= 400$ m

Hence, the correct option is (a).

116. Graphs generally provide an effective means of developing the energy-production relationships, Graph explain what is going on in the plant.

Hence, the correct option is (c).

117. India has launched a solar project with state-of-the-art technology to electrify a remote village in Egypt.

The Solar Electrification Project, an off-grid system that is ideal for remote locations, has been launched at Agaween village in the Western Desert in Matrouh Governorate, close to the Libyan border.

India provided all the solar panels and sub-systems, machinery, equipment and technical support, as well as training for technicians.

The Egyptian government provided the location for implementation of the project.

The project was inaugurated by India's Ambassador to Egypt Sanjay Bhattacharyya and Major General Alla Fathi Abou Zeid, Governor of Matrouh.

The project harnesses the sun and enriches the life of the villagers.

The project is a demonstration of India's technical capabilities, especially in renewable energy, and can be replicated at other locations in Egypt.

Hence, the correct option is (d).

118. A three-year Comprehensive Scheme for Powerloom Sector Development was launched by Union Textile Minister Smriti Zubin Irani at Bhiwandi on April 1, 2017 and simultaneously at 47 powerloom centres in the country.

It aims to boost common infrastructure and modernisation of the powerloom sector.

The scheme, with an outlay of INR 487 crore for three years from 2017-2018, has nine major components, including two new ones.

The two new schemes are: Pradhan Mantri Credit Scheme for powerloom weavers and solar energy scheme for powerlooms.

Existing powerloom units, new ones, and group enterprises in weaving will now get 20 % of project cost with a ceiling of INR 1 lakh as margin money subsidy and 6% interest subvention, both for working capital and term loan up to INR 10 lakh for a maximum period of five years.

Powerloom units with maximum eight looms each will be eligible for 50 % subsidy for going in for solar energy for captive use, be it on grid or off grid system.

Funds made available for upgradation of plain powerlooms, establishing yarn banks, and group workshed scheme have been increased and the minimum number of looms needed for group workshed scheme has been brought down to 24 from 48.

Hence, the correct option is (c).

119. The rate at which the heat develops in the heater can be calculated using the following formula

$P = I^2 R$

Substituting the values in the equation, we get

$P = (15A)^2 \times 8\ \Omega = 1800$ J/s

The electric heater produces heat at the rate of 1800 J/s.

Hence, the correct option is (a).

120. India is likely to export nearly one-fifth less cotton than previously estimated as pink bollworms are set to eat into the south Asian country's output which was expected to hit a record, industry officials told Reuters.

Lower exports from the world's biggest producer will help its rivals like the US, Brazil and Australia to raise their exports to Asian buyers like Pakistan, China and Bangladesh.

Hence, the correct option is (d).

Mock Test 09

Part - I

Q.1 Direction : In the following question, a sentence is divided into some parts. Find out which part of the sentence has an error. The number of that part is your answer. If there is no error, then choose (D) as your answer.
She shook her head, (A)/ once again amazed by (B)/ how awful pain was. (C)/ No error (D)

A. A   **B.** B   **C.** C   **D.** D

Q.2 Direction : In the following question, a sentence is divided into some parts. Find out which part of the sentence has an error. The number of that part is your answer. If there is no error, then choose (D) as your answer.
A balanced diet is one that provide (A)/ an adequate intake of energy and nutrients (B)/ for maintenance of the body and therefore good health. (C)/ No error (D)

A. A   **B.** B   **C.** C   **D.** D

Q.3 Direction : In the following questions, choose the word opposite in meaning to the given word.
Arraign

A. Accuse   **B.** Charge   **C.** Indict   **D.** Praise

Q.4 Direction : In the following questions, choose the word opposite in meaning to the given word.
Voluble

A. Reserved   **B.** Talkative
C. Fluent   **D.** Gabby

Q.5 Direction : In the following questions out of the four alternatives, choose the one which is best express the meaning of the given word.
Farcical

A. Serious   **B.** Absurd
C. Analytical   **D.** Lame

Q.6 Direction : In the following questions out of the four alternatives, choose the one which is best express the meaning of the given word.
Importune

A. Beseech   **B.** Important
C. Imply   **D.** Purchase

Q.7 Direction : In the following questions, out of the given alternatives, choose the one which can be substituted for the given words/sentence.
A small piece of burning or glowing coal or wood in a dying fire

A. Lumber   **B.** Copse   **C.** Grove   **D.** Ember

Q.8 Direction : In the following questions, out of the given alternatives, choose the one which can be substituted for the given words/sentence.
Revel in and make the most of something pleasing

A. Abhor   **B.** Bask   **C.** Fret   **D.** Edgy

Q.9 The 'noble tradition' was related to which of the following the dynasties?

A. Pal   **B.** Pratihara
C. Rashtrakuta   **D.** Sena

Q.10 Which of the following medieval rulers was called 'Jagat Guru'?

A. Ibrahim Qutbshah   **B.** Ibrahim Adilshah I
C. Akbar   **D.** Malik Ambar

Q.11 Who of the following operated the first regular trade union in India ?

A. M.N. Lokhande   **B.** B.P. Wadia
C. Shashipad Banerjee   **D.** N.M. Joshi

Q.12 The boundary of which of the following state/country does NOT touch with Arunachal Pradesh?

A. Assam   **B.** Nagaland
C. Bhutan   **D.** Manipur

Q.13 Pidurutalagala or Mount Pedro is the highest mountain peak of which of the following countries?

A. South Africa   **B.** Panama
C. Sri Lanka   **D.** Cambodia

Q.14 In India, which among the following can be amended by Special Majority of Parliament and Consent of States?
I. Election of President and its manner
II. Any of the lists in Seventh Schedule
III. Amendment in Fundamental Right

A. Only I   **B.** Only II
C. Only I and II   **D.** All I, II an d III

Q.15 In India, Financial Emergency can be extended for how much maximum duration?

A. Six months   **B.** Nine months
C. Two years   **D.** Indefinite period

Q.16 Which country topped the Global Climate Risk Index 2020?

A. Madagascar   **B.** Japan
C. Germany   **D.** Philippines

Q.17 Find the least number which should be added to 1456, So that it is divisible by 6,5 and 4 without leaving a remainder.

A. 6   **B.** 61   **C.** 44   **D.** 16

Q.18 Calculate the total numbers of prime factors in the expression.

$$(9)^{11} \times (5)^7 \times (7)^5 \times (3)^2 \times (17)^2$$

A. 35   **B.** 36   **C.** 37   **D.** 38

Q.19 Three numbers, first is twice the second and second is twice the third. The average of the three numbers is 21. Find the largest number of the three.

A. 36   **B.** 38   **C.** 47   **D.** 48

Q.20 What is the simplified value of $3 + \sqrt{3} + \dfrac{1}{(3-\sqrt{3})} + \dfrac{1}{(3+\sqrt{3})}$?

A. $2 + \sqrt{3}$ **B.** $2 - \sqrt{3}$ **C.** $4 - \sqrt{3}$ **D.** $4 + \sqrt{3}$

Q.21 In a bucket, paint and oil are in the ratio 7 : 5. 24 litres of mixture is drawn off and 24 litres of oil is added. If the ratio of paint and oil becomes 1 : 1, then how many litres of paint was contained in the bucket initially?

A. 49 **B.** 63 **C.** 84 **D.** 98

Q.22 The ratio of incomes of P and Q is 5 : 3. Ratio of income of Q and R is 5 : 2. If one-fourth of P's income is Rs 500 more than the R's income, then what is the income of Q?

A. Rs.7500 **B.** Rs.15000
C. Rs.30000 **D.** Rs.18000

Q.23 ABC is a triangle which is right angled at A and a perpendicular AD is drawn on the hypotenuse BC. If BC = 8 and AD =3, then what is the value of AB x AC ?

A. 12 **B.** 24 **C.** 32 **D.** 36

Q.24 If the ratio of the angle bisector segments of the two equiangular triangles are in the ratio of 3:2 then what is the ratio of the corresponding sides of the two triangles?

A. 2:3 **B.** 3:2 **C.** 6:4 **D.** 4:6

Ques (25-28): Study the following table and answer the questions.

Number of Candidates Appeared and Qualified in a Competitive Examination from Different States Over the Years.

| State | Year | | | | | | | | | |
| | 1997 | | 1998 | | 1999 | | 2000 | | 2001 | |
	Appr.	Qual.	Appr.	Qual.	Appr.	Qual.	Appr.	Qual.	Appr.	Qual.
M	5200	720	8500	980	7400	850	6800	775	9500	1125
N	7500	840	9200	1050	8450	920	9200	980	8800	1020
P	6400	780	8800	1020	7800	890	8750	1010	9750	1250
Q	8100	950	9500	1240	8700	980	9700	1200	8950	995
R	7800	870	7600	940	9800	1350	7600	945	7990	885

Q.25 Total number of candidates qualified from all the states together in 1997 is approximately what percentage of the total number of candidates qualified from all the states together in 1998?

A. 72% **B.** 77% **C.** 80% **D.** 83%

Q.26 What is the average candidates who appeared from State Q during the given years?

A. 8700 **B.** 8760 **C.** 8990 **D.** 8920

Q.27 In which of the given years the number of candidates appeared from State P has maximum percentage of qualified candidates?

A. 1997 **B.** 1998 **C.** 1999 **D.** 2001

Q.28 What is the percentage of candidates qualified from State N for all the years together, over the candidates appeared from State N during all the years together?

A. 12.36% **B.** 12.16% **C.** 11.47% **D.** 11.15%

Ques (29-30): In a school the periodical examination are held every second month. In a session during April 2001 - March 2002, a student of Class IX appeared for each of the periodical exams. The aggregate marks obtained by him in each perodical exam are represented in the line-graph given below.

Marks Obtained by student in Six Periodical Held in Every Two Months During the Year in the Session 2001 - 2002.

Maximum Total Marks in each Periodical Exam = 500

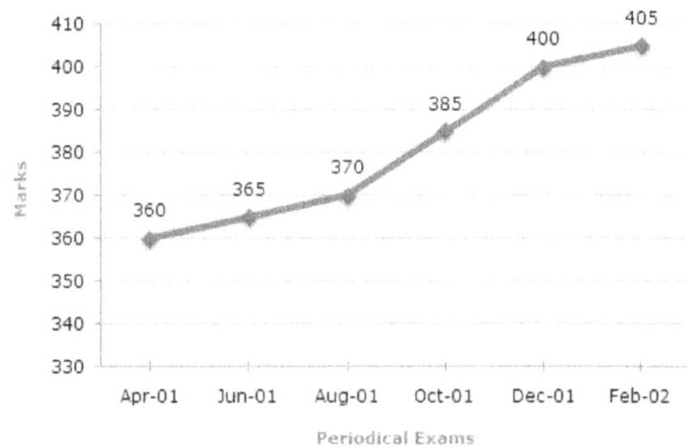

Q.29 In which periodical exams did the student obtain the highest percentage increase in marks over the previous periodical exams ?

A. June, 01 **B.** August, 01
C. Oct, 01 **D.** Dec, 01

Q.30 The total number of marks obtained in Feb. 02 is what percent of the total marks obtained in April 01 ?

A. 110% **B.** 112.5% **C.** 115% **D.** 116.5%

Q.31 What is the percentage of marks obtained by the student in the periodical exams of August, 01 and Oct, 01 taken together ?

A. 73.25% **B.** 75.5% **C.** 77% **D.** 78.75%

Q.32 What are the average marks obtained by the student in all the periodical exams during the last session ?

A. 373 **B.** 379 **C.** 381 **D.** 385

Q.33 What is the name of the trust that will be set up for the construction of the Ram Temple in Ayodhya?

A. Shri Ram Mandir Seva Trust
B. Shri Ram Janmabhoomi Teerth Kshetra
C. Shri Ram Sewa Samiti
D. Shri Ram Janmabhoomi Kalyan Kshetra

Q.34 Which international magazine has named RBI Governor Shaktikanta Das as the 'Central Banker of the Year-2020'?

A. Time **B.** The Economist
C. The Banker **D.** The Fortune

Q.35 Which among the following South-Asian countries recently developed a new classic swine fever vaccine?

A. Sri Lanka **B.** India
C. Bangladesh **D.** Afghanistan

Q.36 Which state has launched the Janasevaka scheme?

A. Telangana **B.** Maharashtra
C. Madhya Pradesh **D.** Karnataka

Q.37 Who has become the first Indian no.4 cricketer to hit a century outside India in four years?

A. Mayank Aggarwal **B.** Shardul Thakur
C. Rishab Pant **D.** Shreyas Iyer

Q.38 Which country recently introduced 'Sustainable Development Tax' for regional tourism?

A. Bhutan **B.** Myanmar
C. Nepal **D.** Tibet

Q.39 Daniel Arap Moi passed away on February 4, 2020. He was the longest-serving president of which nation?

A. Zambia **B.** Egypt
C. Kenya **D.** The Gambia

Q.40 According to the World Health Organisation, the cases of which disease can rise to 81 percent by 2040?

A. Tuberculosis **B.** Cancer
C. H1N1 **D.** HIV

Part - II

Q.41 The voltage wave $v = V_m \sin(\omega t - 150)$ volts is applied across in AC circuit. If the current leads the voltage by 10^0 and the maximum value of currents is I_m, then the equation of current is-

A. $i = I_m \sin(\omega t + 5^0)$amps
B. $i = I_m \sin(\omega t - 25^0)$amps
C. $i = I_m \sin(\omega t + 25^0)$amps
D. $i = I_m \sin(\omega t - 5^0)$amps

Q.42 Which one of the following is a valid value of the coefficient of coupling between two inductors?

A. 1.414 **B.** 0.9 **C.** 1.732 **D.** 17.32

Q.43 The emf induced in a coil is given by $e = -N\dfrac{20}{dt}$ where e is the emf induced, N is the number of turns and d φ is the instantaneous flux linkage with the coil in time dt-

A. Hans christain Oersted
B. Andre-Marie Ampere
C. Mechale Faraday
D. Emil Lenz

Q.44 The mutual inductance between two coils having self inductances 3 henry and 12 henry and coupling coefficient 0.85 is-

A. 12.75 henry **B.** 5.1 henry
C. 0.425 henry **D.** 1.7 henry

Q.45 Resistance temprature coefficient of copper at 20^0C at-

A. $0.0045/^0$C **B.** $0.0017/^0$C
C. $0.00393/^0$C **D.** $0.0038/^0$C

Q.46 The load characteristic of DC shunt generator is determined by-

A. the voltage drop in armature resistance

B. the voltage drop due to armature reaction, voltage drop due to decreased field current and voltage drop in armature resistance.

C. the voltage drop to armature reaction and voltage drop in armature resistance

D. the voltage drop due to armature reaction, voltage drop due to decreased field current and voltage drops in armature and field resistance

Q.47 How many watt-second are supplied by a motor developing 2 hp (British) for 5 hours-

A. 2.6856×10^7 watt-seconds
B. 4.476×10^5 watt-seconds
C. 2.646×10^7 watt-seconds
D. 6.3943×10^6 watt-seconds

Q.48 A 4-pole generator is running at 1200 rpm. The frequency and time period of the emf generated in its coils respectively.

A. 50 Hz, 0.02 sec
B. 40 Hz, 0.025 sec
C. 300 Hz, 0.00333 sec
D. 2400 Hz, $\frac{1}{2400}$ sec

Q.49 The single phase Induction Motor (IM) which does not have centrifugal switch is-

A. capacitor start single phase M
B. resistance split single phase IM
C. capacitor start capacitor run single phase M
D. Permanent capacitor run single phase IM

Q.50 When a multiplier is added to an exsiting voltmeter for extending its range, its electromagnetic damping-

A. remains unaffected
B. increases
C. decreases
D. changes by an amount depending on the controlling torque

Q.51 Phasor diagram of load voltage (V), current in pressure coil (I_P) and current in current coil (I_C) is shown in the figure when an electrodynamic wattmeter is used to measure power. The reading of the wattmeter will be proportional to-

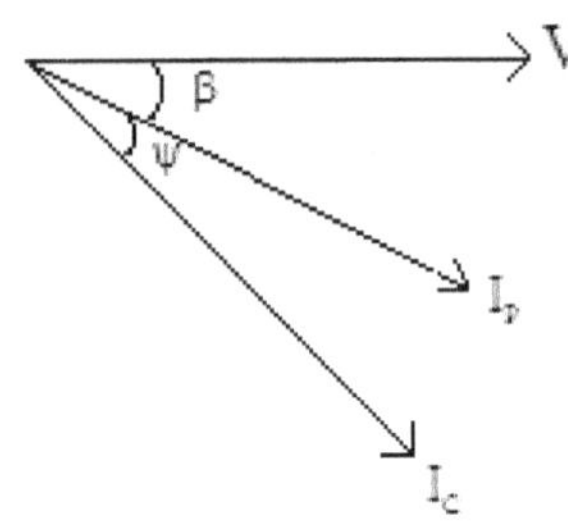

A. $\cos(\beta + \Psi)$

B. $\cos\Psi$

C. $\cos\beta \cos\Psi$

D. $\cos\beta \cos(\beta + \Psi)$

Q.52 Two parallel conductors carrying current in opposite directions will exert on each other-

A. an attractive forces

B. a repulsive force

C. an axial force

D. no force

Q.53 The unit of reluctance of magnetic circuit is-

A. AT/m

B. Weber/m

C. AT/weber

D. Weber/AT

Q.54 In indicating instruments the springs are mainly used to-

A. conduct the current to the coils

B. hold the pivot in position

C. control the pointer movement

D. reduce the vibration of the pointer

Q.55 A balanced 3-phase, 3-wire supply feeds balanced start connected resistors. If one of the resistors is disconnected, the the percentage reduction in load will be-

A. 33.33 **B.** 50 **C.** 66.67 **D.** 75

Q.56 The total flux at the end of a long permanent bar magnet is 100×10^{-6}. The end of this magnet is withdrawn through a 1000 turn coil in $\dfrac{1}{20}$ seconds. The induced e.m.f. in the coil is-

A. 20.0 V **B.** 2.0 V **C.** 0.2 V **D.** 0.02 V

Q.57 In reference to the figure, the voltage waveform v (t) is measured by a PMMC, a PMMC combined with bridge rectifier and a moving iron (MI) instrument. Two lists are prepared thereafter

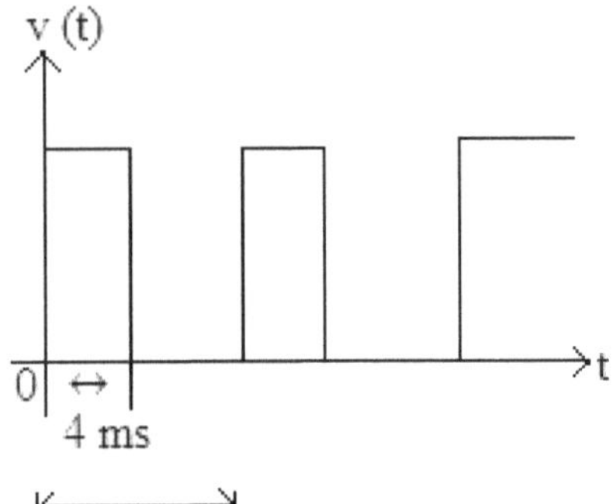

List-I (Instrument List)

a. PMMC

b. PMMC rectifier

List-II (List of instrument reading)

i. 5V

ii. 2.75

c. M.I

iii. 2.5 V

The correct option relation the instruments and their reading is-

A. a-i, b-ii, c-iii

B. a-iii, b-ii, c-i

C. a-ii, b-iii, c-i

D. a-iii, b-i, c-ii

Q.58 The switching transistor as shown, carries in the collector side an rms current of 8 mA. If the frequency of rectangular pulse train V_i is 50 Hz, then on-time of the transistor is-

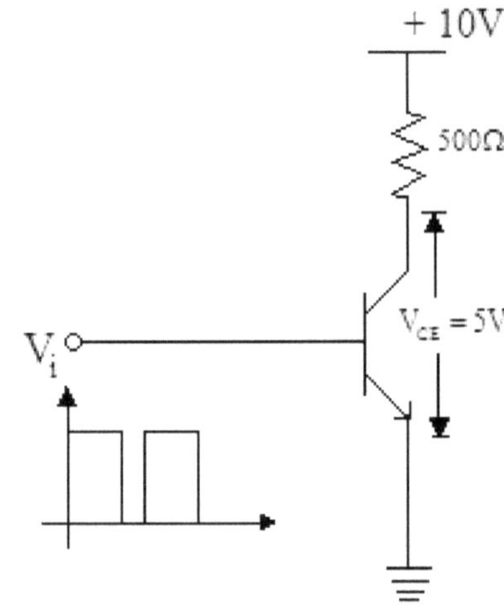

A. 2 ms **B.** 6.4 ms **C.** 12.8 ms **D.** 16 ms

Q.59 A ammeter of resistance R_m is placed an arrangement as shown in the figure . Material of R_m, R_{sh}, is copper whereas that of R_s, R_x, is manganin. The condition for which the meter performance is compensated against temperature, is-

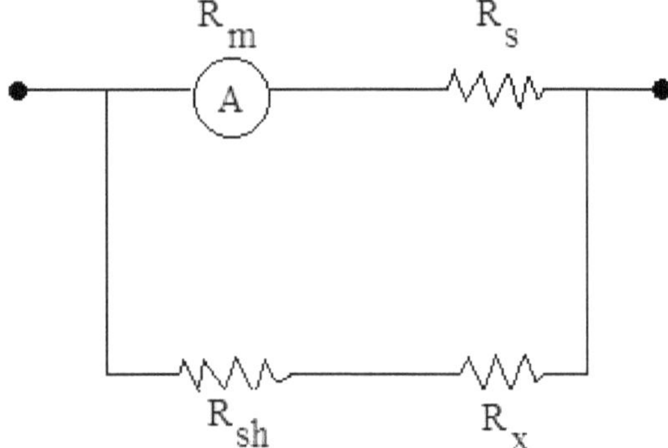

A. $\dfrac{1}{R_m} + \dfrac{1}{R_{sh}} = \dfrac{1}{R_S} + \dfrac{1}{R_x}$

B. $R_m R_s = R_{sh} . R_x$

C. $R_m + R_s = R_{sh} + R_x$

D. $\dfrac{R_m}{R_S} = \dfrac{R_{sh}}{R_x}$

Q.60 If a 110 V, 50 Hz is applied across a PMMC voltmeter of full-scale range 0-220 V and internal resistance of $10k\Omega$, reading of the voltmeter will be-

A. 0 V

B. 110 √2V

C. 78 V

D. 55 V

Q.61 To maximize the driving torque in an induction type instrument, flux produced by shunt coil and series coil should be-

A. In phase with each

B. In quadrature with each other

C. Displaced by with respect to each other

D. Out of phase with respect to each other

Q.62 To minimize the errors due to lead and contact resistances, low resistances used in electrical measurement work are provide with-

A. guard rings

B. four terminals

C. thick insulation

D. metal shields

Q.63 Examine the two statements 'A' and 'R' and select your answer

Statement A : Switching of a lamp in house produce noise in a radio.

Statement R : Switching operation produces are across separating contacts-

A. Both A and R are true and R is a correct explanation of A

B. Both A and R are true and R is not correct explanation of A

C. A is true but R is false

D. A is false but R is true

Q.64 The small pockets of air in the high voltage cable provide____relative permittivity___electric field and at these sites breakdown is likely to be initiated.

A. high, high

B. low, low

C. low, high

D. high, low

Q.65 The capacitance measured between any two cores of a 3-core cable with the sheated earthed is $3\mu F$. The capacitance per phase will be

A. $15\mu F$

B. $6\mu F$

C. $1\mu F$

D. None of the above

Q.66 In an insulated of cable having core diameter d and overall diameter D, the ratio of maximum to minimum dielectric stress is given by

A. $\left(\frac{D}{d}\right)^{\frac{1}{2}}$ **B.** $(\frac{D}{d})^2$ **C.** $\frac{D}{d}$ **D.** $\frac{d}{D}$

Q.67 Compared to the beaking capacity of a circuit breaker, its making capacity should be-

A. more

B. less

C. equal

D. the two are unrelated to each oth

Q.68 In electronic circuits, for blocking the DC component of a voltage signal, a/an_____is connected is series with the voltage source.

A. capacitor **B.** diode **C.** resistor **D.** inductor

Q.69 For n-type semiconductor, the doping material is-

A. tetravalent

B. pentavalent

C. trivalent

D. bivalent

Q.70 A attenuator probe as shown, is connected to an amplifier of input capacitance $0.1\mu F$. Value of C that must be connected across 100 k to make the overall gain independent of frequency, is-

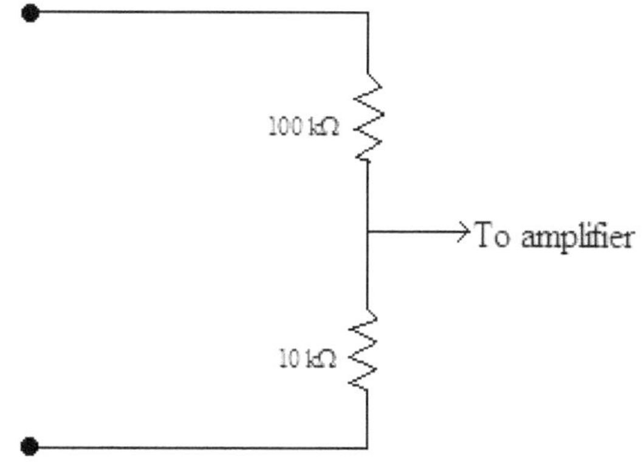

A. $0.01\mu F$

B. $0.1\mu F$

C. $1\mu F$

D. $10\mu F$

Q.71 Silicon content in iron lamination is kept within 5% as it-

A. makes the material brittle

B. reduces the curie point

C. increased bysteresis loss

D. increased cost

Q.72 A wattmeter is marked $\frac{15A}{30A}, \frac{300V}{600V}$ and its scale is marked up to 4500 watts. When the meter is connected for 30A, 600A, the point indicated 2000 watts. The actual power in the circuit is-

A. 2000 Watts

B. 4000 Watts

C. 6000 Watts

D. 8000 Watts

Q.73 Resistance switching is normally employed in-

A. bulk oil brakers

B. minimum oil breakers

C. air blast circuit breakers

D. all of (A) ,(B) and (C)

Q.74 If the angular frequency of an alternating voltage is ω, then the angular frequency of instantaneous real power absorbed in an ac circuit is-

A. 2ω **B.** ω **C.** 3ω **D.** $\frac{w}{2}$

Q.75 If the transistor having $V_{CE} = 5V$, $V_{EE} = 0.7$ has beta=45, value of R is-

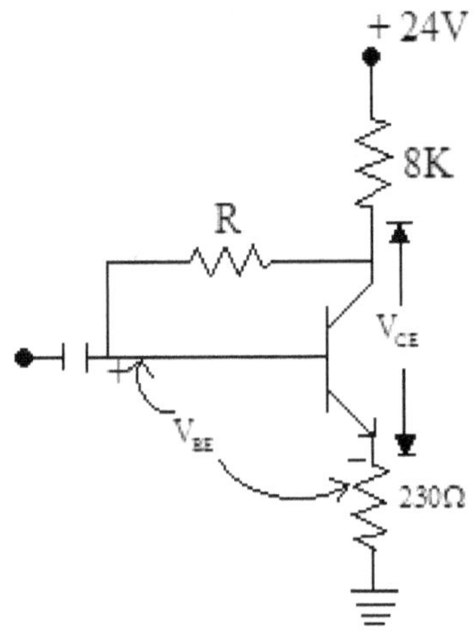

A. 85.64 k   **B.** 63.14 k   **C.** 72.15 k   **D.** 91.18 k

Q.76 In a balanced 3-phase circuit, the line current is 12A. When the power is measured by two wattmeter method, one meter reads 11kW while the other reads zero. Power factor of the load is-

A. 0   **B.** 0.5   **C.** 0.866   **D.** 1.0

Q.77 In case of frosted GLS lamps, frosting is done by-

A. Acid etching   **B.** Ammonia
C. Ozone   **D.** Salt water

Q.78 If the supply polarity to the armature terminals of a separately excited DC motor is reversed, the motor will run under-

A. Plugging condition
B. Regenerative braking condtion
C. Dynamic braking condition
D. Normal motoring condition

Q.79 For welding purpose, the secondary of transformer used should be capable of carrying-

A. high voltage, high current
B. high voltage, low current
C. low voltage, high current
D. low voltage, low current

Q.80 Which of the following is correct ?

A. Load factor = capacitor × utilisation factor
B. Utilisation factor = load factor × utilisation factor
C. Capacitor factor = load factor × utilisation factor
D. Load factor has no relation with capacity factor and utilisation factor

Q.81 What does the electromechanical contactor in a motor starter provide inherent protection against?

A. Over Circuit   **B.** Short Circuit
C. Single Circuit   **D.** Under Voltage

Q.82 In the circuit, V is the input voltage applied across the capacitor of 2F. Current through the capacitor is

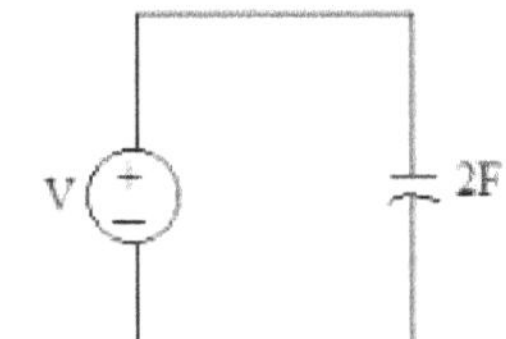

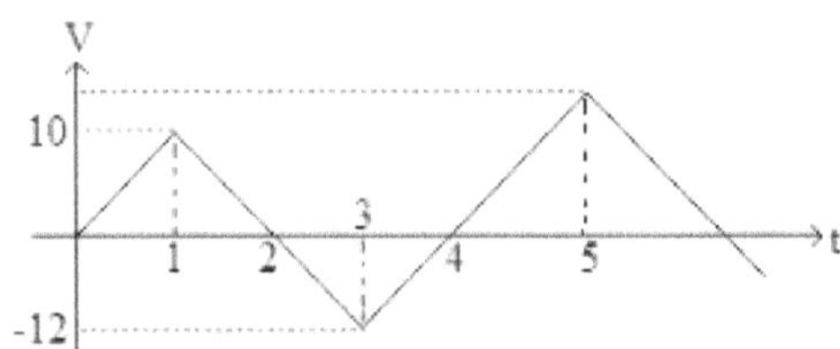

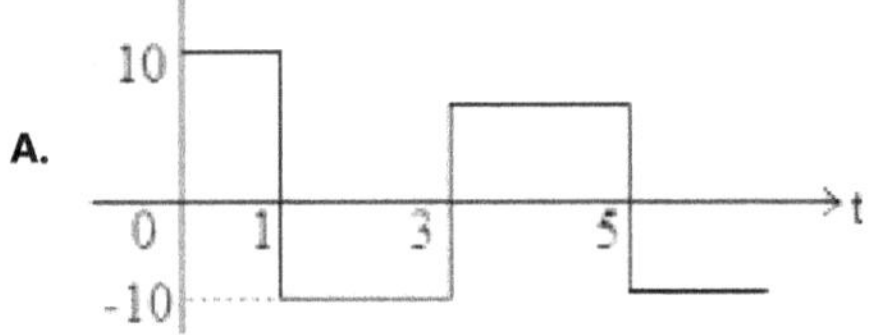

A.

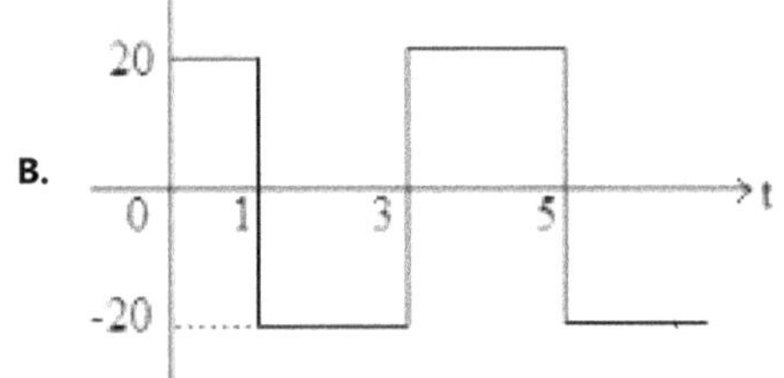

B.

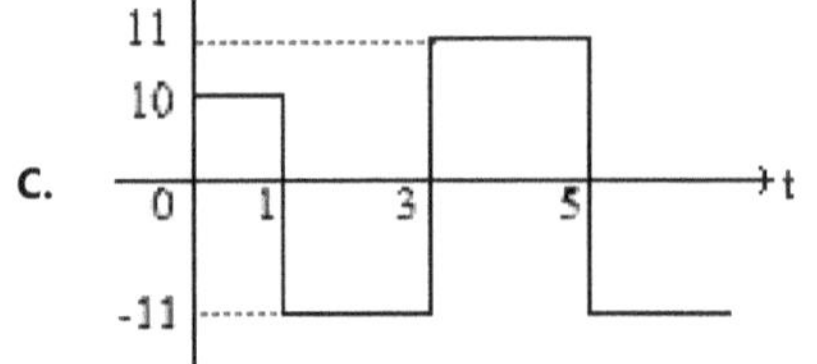

C.

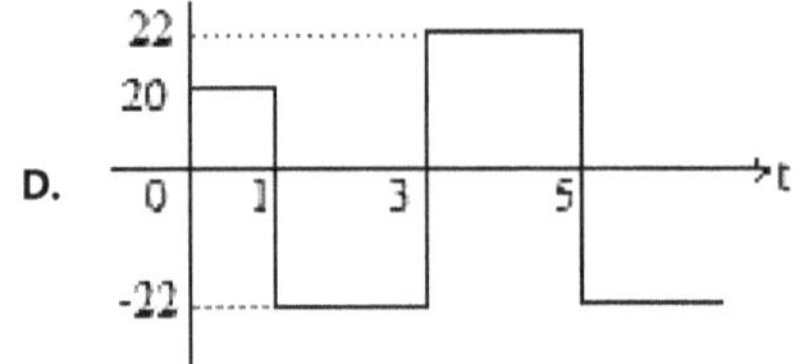

D.

Q.83 In a semiconductor, the resistivity-

A. depends on temperature
B. depends on voltage
C. depends on current through it
D. None of the above

Q.84 A geyser is operated from 230 V, 50 c/s mains. The frequency of instantaneous power consumed by the geyser is-

A. 25 c/s   **B.** 50 c/s   **C.** 100 c/s   **D.** 150 c/s

Q.85 Ampere -second is the unit of-

A. emf   **B.** power

C. electric charge   D. energy

Q.86 Two lossy capacitors with equal capacitance values and power factors of 0.01 and 0.02 are in parallel, and the combination is supplied from a sinusoidal voltage source. The power factor of the combination is-

A. 0.03   **B.** 0.015   **C.** 0.01   **D.** 0.0002

Q.87 A voltmeter when connected across a DC supply, reads 124 V. When a series combination of the voltmeter and an unknown resistance X is connected across the supply, the meter reads 4V. If the resistance of the voltmeter is . the value of X is-

A. 1550kΩ   **B.** 1600kΩ

C. 1.6kΩ   **D.** 1.5MΩ

Q.88 The purpose of providing a choke in the tube-light is-

A.   to eliminate the corona effects

B.   to avoid radio interference

C.   to improve power factor

D.   to limit current to appropriate factor

Q.89 In a 3-phase 400V, 4-wire system, two incandescent lamps, one having 230 V, 100 W specification and the other 230 V, 200 W are connected between R phase-neutral and Y phase-neutral respectively. If the neutral wire breaks

A.   100 W lamp will fuse first

B.   200 W lamp will fuse first

C.   both the lamps will fuse together

D.   both the lamps will glow

Q.90 A solenoid of inductance 250 mH and resistance is connected to a battary. The time taken for the magnetic energy to reach $\frac{1}{4}th$ of its maximum value is-

A. $\log_e(2)$ **B.** $10^{-3}\log_e(2)$

C. $25 \log_e(2)$ **D.** $\frac{1}{40}\log_e(2)$

Q.91 Energy is released from fossil fuels when they are______________

A. Pumped   **B.** Cooled

C. Burned   **D.** Pressurized

Q.92 The most nuclear fuel used in the world is______________

A. Thorium – 232   **B.** Uranium – 238

C. Uranium – 235   **D.** Plutonium – 239

Q.93 The blades in wind turbines are connected to______________

A. Nacelle   **B.** Tower

C. Foundations   **D.** String

Q.94 In the production of wave energy which form of energy is used?

A. Potential energy   **B.** Kinetic energy

C. Solar energy   **D.** Wind energy

Q.95 A tidal barrage is a barrier built over a______________

A. River bed   **B.** River estuary

C. River end   **D.** River starting

Q.96 In hydroelectricity power______________

A.   Kinetic energy is transferred to potential

B.   Potential energy is transferred to kinetic

C.   Solar energy is transferred to wind energy

D.   Wind energy is transferred to solar energy

Q.97 In order to produce solar energy during sunlight, where the energy is stored in the batteries?

A. Nickel Sulfur   **B.** Zinc Cadmium

C. Nickel Cadmium   **D.** Nickel Zinc

Q.98 How many forms of fossil fuels are there______________

A. One   **B.** Two   **C.** Three   **D.** Four

Q.99 According to WHO, how many premature deaths annually linked to air pollution causing by the burning of fossil fuels?

A. One million   **B.** Three million

C. Five million   **D.** Seven million

Q.100 Energy in the form of heat and light is obtained by______________

A. Biomass   **B.** Fossil fuels

C. Sun   **D.** Wind

Q.101 Energy sources that are available in the market for a definite price are known as ______________

A. primary   **B.** secondary

C. commercial   **D.** non-commercial

Q.102 ______________ is energy obtained from sources that are essentially inexhaustible.

A. Primary   **B.** Secondary

C. Non- commercial   **D.** Renewable

Q.103 One B.O.T unit is

A. 100 kWh   **B.** 10 kWh

C. 1 kWh   **D.** 0.1 kWh

Q.104 Which of the following is true?

A.   Geothermal energy is considered a renewable source of energy.

B.   Geothermal energy is considered a non- renewable source of energy.

C.   Geothermal energy is considered a commercial source of energy.

D.   Geothermal energy is considered a non-commercial source of energy.

Q.105 Which fuel is produced by fermentation of grains?

A. Ethanol   **B.** Butanol

C. Methanol   **D.** Pentanol

Q.106 The input resistance of a FET is of the order of

A. 100 Ω   **B.** 10 kΩ   **C.** 1 MΩ   **D.** 100 MΩ

Q.107 Match the following

1. Oldest form of energy	a. Photo synthesis
2. Climate change is also called	b. Primary energy
3. Bio Mass is related with	c. Global warming
4. Secondary energy is produced from	d. Bio-mass

A. 1-b, 2-c, 3-d, 4-a   **B.** 1-b, 2-,a 3-,d 4-c

C. 1-c, 2-d, 3-b, 4-a   **D.** 1-d, 2-c, 3-a, 4-b

Q.108 Match the following

1. Energy that are converted to steam and electricity	a. Primary Energy
Energy that are either found or stored in nature	b. Non-renewable Energy
3. Energy that is obtained from sources those are essentially inexhaustible.	c. Secondary Energy
4. Energy resources which are likely to deplete with time	d. Renewable Energy

A. 1-c, 2-a, 3-d, 4-b
B. 1-b, 2-d, 3-a, 4-c
C. 1-d, 2-c, 3-b, 4-a
D. 1-c, 2-d,3-b, 4-a

Q.109 _______________ is used as fuel to generate stem.

A. Methane   **B.** Bagasse   **C.** Ethane   **D.** Ethanol

Q.110 Power from wind is generated by _____________ turbines.

A. hydrogen   **B.** wind
C. water   **D.** nitrogen

Q.111 Match the following

1.It is the stored energy and the energy of position	a. Gravitational Energy
2. It is the energy stored in bonds of atoms and molecules	b. Nuclear Energy
3. It is the energy of place or position	c. Chemical Energy
4. It is the energy stored in the nucleus of an atom	d. Potential energy

A. 1-b, 2-a, 3-d, 4-c
B. 1-c, 2-d, 3-b, 4-a
C. 1-d, 2-c, 3-a, 4-b
D. 1-c, 2-a, 3-d, 4-b

Q.112 Match the following

1. Energy that deals with the movement of electrons	a.Thermal Energy
2. It is the internal energy in substances	b. Kinetic energy
3. It is the electromagnetic energy that travels in transverse waves	c. Electrical Energy
4. It is the energy in motion	d.Radiant energy

A. 1-b, 2-c, 3-a, 4-d
B. 1-d, 2-c, 3-b, 4-a
C. 1-b, 2-d, 3-a, 4-c
D. 1-c, 2-a, 3-d, 4-b

Q.113 ________________ is the movement of energy through substances in longitudinal waves.

A. Electrons   **B.** Photons
C. Sound   **D.** Solar Energy

Q.114 ________________ is the rate of flow of charge.

A. Volt   **B.** Ampere
C. Watt   **D.** Horse power

Q.115 Which of the following is false?

A. The unit of frequency is Hertz.
B. The unit of resistance is ohm.

C. kVA is the product of kilovolts and amperes.
D. kVAr is the apparent power.

Q.116 Which of the following is true?

A. Relation between kVA, kW and kVAr is $kVA = \sqrt{(kW)^2 + (kWAr)^2}$

B. Relation between kVA, kW and kVAr is $KVA = (kW)\sqrt{(kW)^2 + (kWAr)^2}$

C. Relation between kVA, kW and kVAr is $KVA = \dfrac{kWAr}{\sqrt{(kW)^2 + (kWAr)^2}}$

D. Relation between kVA, kW and kVAr is $kWAr = \dfrac{KVA}{\sqrt{(kW)^2 + (kWAr)^2}}$

Q.117 Which is the ratio between the active power(kW) and apparent power (kVA)

A. Single phase   **B.** Power factor
C. Electrical Tariff   **D.** Kilowatt-hour

Q.118 Which is a measure of the latent heat content of air-water vapour mixtures?

A. Dew Point
B. Dry bulb temperature
C. Wet bulb temperature
D. Dew point temperature

Q.119 The energy transferred is measured in _____________.

A. joules   **B.** calorific value
C. kilowatt   **D.** watt

Q.120 ________________ is the process by which radiation passes through a body.

A. Absorption   **B.** Evaporation
C. Condensation   **D.** Transmission

// Smart Answer Sheet //

Correct Indicates percentage of students who answered questions correctly.

Skipped Indicates percentage of students who skipped questions.

Q.	Ans.	Correct / Skipped	Q.	Ans.	Correct / Skipped	Q.	Ans.	Correct / Skipped	Q.	Ans.	Correct / Skipped	Q.	Ans.	Correct / Skipped
1	B	83.65 % / 15.34 %	17	C	79.67 % / 16.94 %	33	B	76.74 % / 12.07 %	49	D	85.47 % / 11.03 %	65	B	83.65 % / 10.62 %
2	A	80.16 % / 15.29 %	18	D	89.85 % / 10.11 %	34	C	88.33 % / 10.93 %	50	C	81.57 % / 17.95 %	66	C	88.09 % / 11.17 %
3	D	83.92 % / 11.11 %	19	A	79.26 % / 14.95 %	35	B	80.77 % / 12.37 %	51	C	77.39 % / 15.14 %	67	A	85.0 % / 10.23 %
4	A	83.19 % / 10.62 %	20	D	83.25 % / 15.03 %	36	D	82.15 % / 14.87 %	52	B	81.37 % / 18.46 %	68	A	88.22 % / 11.37 %
5	B	77.59 % / 14.39 %	21	D	81.86 % / 16.0 %	37	D	88.45 % / 11.03 %	53	C	84.1 % / 10.76 %	69	B	87.23 % / 11.69 %
6	A	85.92 % / 10.15 %	22	C	77.66 % / 21.47 %	38	A	83.84 % / 13.93 %	54	C	88.21 % / 10.26 %	70	A	80.15 % / 12.78 %
7	D	88.42 % / 11.45 %	23	B	82.69 % / 16.31 %	39	C	87.32 % / 12.48 %	55	B	76.84 % / 10.06 %	71	A	87.78 % / 11.03 %
8	B	82.9 % / 14.42 %	24	B	77.94 % / 14.94 %	40	B	89.93 % / 10.05 %	56	B	80.81 % / 13.67 %	72	D	88.9 % / 10.05 %
9	D	81.0 % / 14.57 %	25	C	80.07 % / 15.26 %	41	D	87.2 % / 11.62 %	57	B	82.04 % / 17.51 %	73	C	77.01 % / 13.29 %
10	B	78.73 % / 16.75 %	26	C	84.93 % / 12.31 %	42	B	81.77 % / 12.72 %	58	A	77.61 % / 19.43 %	74	B	78.72 % / 19.71 %
11	B	78.26 % / 17.97 %	27	D	76.48 % / 14.9 %	43	D	89.42 % / 10.48 %	59	D	79.6 % / 18.38 %	75	A	87.88 % / 11.14 %
12	D	76.24 % / 13.66 %	28	D	76.35 % / 17.8 %	44	B	76.17 % / 15.27 %	60	A	84.39 % / 13.89 %	76	B	87.56 % / 12.2 %
13	C	85.34 % / 11.55 %	29	C	87.8 % / 11.45 %	45	C	78.13 % / 21.27 %	61	B	81.34 % / 12.9 %	77	A	89.27 % / 10.18 %
14	C	82.95 % / 15.61 %	30	B	86.39 % / 13.46 %	46	B	81.3 % / 16.67 %	62	A	86.0 % / 11.87 %	78	A	88.32 % / 10.81 %
15	D	77.79 % / 20.04 %	31	B	79.47 % / 16.12 %	47	A	87.12 % / 12.3 %	63	A	81.61 % / 17.98 %	79	C	83.05 % / 11.08 %
16	B	89.86 % / 10.04 %	32	C	85.17 % / 14.68 %	48	B	89.21 % / 10.23 %	64	C	79.95 % / 12.66 %	80	C	79.51 % / 10.23 %

Q.	Ans.	Correct / Skipped	Q.	Ans.	Correct / Skipped	Q.	Ans.	Correct / Skipped	Q.	Ans.	Correct / Skipped	Q.	Ans.	Correct / Skipped
81	D	83.3 % / 11.55 %	89	A	78.73 % / 12.66 %	97	C	79.42 % / 18.06 %	105	A	87.4 % / 11.68 %	113	C	82.11 % / 11.37 %
82	D	88.0 % / 11.76 %	90	D	80.35 % / 14.98 %	98	C	89.48 % / 10.06 %	106	D	78.3 % / 13.83 %	114	B	86.6 % / 11.24 %
83	A	83.75 % / 13.03 %	91	C	85.17 % / 10.55 %	99	D	79.14 % / 19.92 %	107	D	88.8 % / 11.04 %	115	D	79.77 % / 10.52 %
84	C	81.82 % / 15.9 %	92	C	79.36 % / 13.0 %	100	C	89.74 % / 10.09 %	108	A	84.26 % / 10.06 %	116	A	81.82 % / 16.52 %
85	C	79.0 % / 14.65 %	93	A	78.58 % / 14.23 %	101	C	78.6 % / 16.41 %	109	B	77.09 % / 17.24 %	117	B	89.3 % / 10.15 %
86	B	77.49 % / 15.72 %	94	B	77.8 % / 17.44 %	102	D	87.45 % / 12.52 %	110	B	79.34 % / 13.99 %	118	D	83.55 % / 12.06 %
87	D	87.69 % / 11.89 %	95	B	82.1 % / 11.9 %	103	C	85.65 % / 12.23 %	111	C	87.09 % / 11.55 %	119	A	80.58 % / 12.13 %
88	D	88.72 % / 10.2 %	96	B	79.77 % / 13.03 %	104	A	78.22 % / 16.07 %	112	D	87.59 % / 11.17 %	120	C	84.88 % / 11.55 %

Performance Analysis

Avg. Score (%)	52.5%
Toppers Score (%)	70.0%
Your Score	

//Hints and Solutions//

1. The error is in the second part of the sentence.
The error is due to the incorrect usage of the preposition 'by' as it is used, usually after a passive verb, to show who or what does, creates or causes something.
We use the preposition 'at' with adjectives to show the cause of something. 'Amazed' being an adjective needs to be followed by 'at'.
Therefore, to make the sentence grammatically correct, 'by' must be replaced with 'at'.
Hence, the correct sentence is: She shook her head, once again amazed at how awful pain was.

Hence, the correct option is (b).

2. the subject 'a balanced diet' is singular and the sentence is Present Tense, therefore 'provides' must be used in place of 'provide'.

Hence, the correct option is (a).

3. Arraign - find fault with; censure.
"social workers were relieved it was not they who were arraigned in the tabloids"
Accuse - claim that (someone) has done something wrong.
"he was accused of favouritism"
Indict - formally accuse of or charge with a crime.
"his former manager was indicted for fraud"
Praise - express warm approval or admiration of.

Hence, the correct option is (d).

4. Voluble :(of a person) talking fluently, readily, or incessantly.
E.g."she was as voluble as her husband was silent"
synonyms: talkative, loquacious, garrulous, verbose, long-winded, wordy, chatty, chattery, gossipy
antonyms: taciturn, uncommunicative, mute
Reserved:slow to reveal emotion or opinions.
Talkative:fond of or given to talking.
Fluent:able to express oneself easily and articulately.
Gabby:excessively or annoyingly talkative.

Hence, the correct option is (a).

5. Farcical - relating to or resembling farce, especially because of absurd or ridiculous aspects. "he considered the whole idea farcical"
Absurd - wildly unreasonable, illogical, or inappropriate. "the allegations are patently absurd"
Analytical - relating to or using analysis or logical reasoning.
Lame - (of an explanation or excuse) unconvincingly feeble.

Hence, the correct option is (b).

6. Importune - harass (someone) persistently for or to do something.
"she importuned a waiter for profiteroles"
Beseech - ask (someone) urgently and fervently to do something; implore; entreat.
Imply - indicate the truth or existence of (something) by suggestion rather than explicit reference. "salesmen who use jargon to imply superior knowledge"

Hence, the correct option is (a).

7. A small piece of burning or glowing coal or wood in a dying fire – Ember
Something useless or cumbersome - Lumber
A thicket of small trees or shrubs - Copse
A group of trees planted and cultivated for the production of fruit or nuts – Grove

Hence, the correct option is (d).

8. Revel in and make the most of something pleasing – Bask
To regard with horror or loathing - Abhor
To be vexed or troubled - Fret
Nervous or irritable – Edgy

Hence, the correct option is (b).

9. The 'noble tradition' was related to Sena Dynasty. The Sena Empire was a Hindu dynasty during the Late Classical period on the Indian subcontinent that ruled from Bengal through the 11th and 12th centuries. The empire at its peak covered much of the north-eastern region of the Indian subcontinent.

Hence, the correct option is (d).

10. Ibrahim Adilshah I was called 'Jagat Guru'. Ibrahim Adil Shah I (1534–1558) was a Sultan and later Shah of the Indian kingdom of Bijapur. He succeeded his elder brother, Mallu Adil Shah, through the machinations of the Afaqi faction at the court.

Hence, the correct option is (b).

11. Bomanji Pestonji Wadia on 13 April 1918, along with V. Kalyanasundaram Mudaliar, founded the Madras Labour Union, one of India's first organised labour unions.

Hence, the correct option is (b).

12. Arunachal Pradesh borders the states of Assam and Nagaland to the south and shares international borders with Bhutan in the west, Myanmar in the east and is separated from China in the north by the disputed McMahon Line. Itanagar is the capital of the state.

Hence, the correct option is (d).

13. Pidurutalagala, or Mount Pedro, is an ultra prominent peak, and the tallest mountain in Sri Lanka, at 2,524 m. It's situated near the city of Nuwara Eliya.

Hence, the correct option is (c).

14. The federal structure of the polity related provisions of the Constitution can be amended by a special majority of the Parliament and also with the consent of half of the state legislatures by a simple majority. If one or some or all the remaining states take no action on the bill, it does not matter; the moment half of the states give their consent, the formality is completed; Like- Election of President and its manner, Any of the lists in Seventh Schedule, Extent of the executive power of the Union and the states, Supreme Court and high courts, Distribution of legislative powers between the Union and the states, Representation of states in Parliament and Power of Parliament to amend the Constitution and its procedure (Article 368 itself).

Hence, the correct option is (c).

15. In India, Financial Emergency can be extended for indefinite period. Financial Emergency is given under Article 360. If the President is satisfied that there is an economic situation in which the financial stability or credit of India is threatened, he or she can declare financial emergency. Such an emergency must be approved by the Parliament within two months.

Hence, the correct option is (d).

16. Japan topped the the Global Climate Risk Index 2020 as the most vulnerable of 181 countries to the effects of climate change, with its poorest being the most at risk.

Hence, the correct option is (b).

17. LCM of (6, 5, 4) = 60,

$$
\begin{array}{r}
60\,)\,1456\,(24 \\
120 \\
\hline
256 \\
240 \\
\hline
16
\end{array}
$$

Number to be added = (60-16) =44
So, 44 is the least number which should be added to 1456 So that it is divisible by 6, 5 and 4 without leaving a remainder.
Hence, the correct option is (c).

18. $(9)^{11} \times (5)^7 \times (7)^5 \times (3)^2 \times (17)^2$
$\Rightarrow (3)^{22} \times (5)^7 \times (7)^5 \times (3)^2 \times (17)^2$
Total no. of prime factors, $n = $ sum of powers
$\because n = 22 + 7 + 5 + 2 + 2$
$\because n = 38$

Hence, the correct option is (d).

19. Let IIIrd number $= x$
IInd number $= 2x$
Ist number $= 4x$
$x = 3 \times 3 = 9$
Largest number
$= 4 \times 9 = 36$

Hence, the correct option is (a).

20. $3 + \sqrt{3} + \dfrac{1}{(3-\sqrt{3})} + \dfrac{1}{(3+\sqrt{3})}$
$= 3 + \sqrt{3} + \dfrac{3+\sqrt{3}-\sqrt{3}}{9-3}$
$= 3 + \sqrt{3} + 1$
$= 4 + \sqrt{3}$

Hence, the correct option is (d).

21. Let in bucket, quantity of paint and oil be 7x and 5x respectively.
24 litres of mixture is drawn off and current ration of paint and oil is 7:5, so deduction will also be done in ratio of 7:5, therefore from paint 14 litres will be drawn off and from oil 10 litres will be drawn off.

So, new quantity of paint and oil will be (7x-14) and (5x-10) respectively.
Now, after adding 24 litre oil, ratio becomes

$$\frac{7x-14}{5x-10+24} = \frac{1}{1}$$
$7x - 14 = 5x + 14$
$2x = 28$
$So, x = 14$

Therefore, Initially bucket contains $7 \times 14 = 98$ litre of paint.

Hence, the correct option is (d).

22. Ratio of income of P and Q=5:3
And the ratio of Q and R=5:2
then the ratio of PQ and R = 5 : 3 x 5
5 : 2 x 3
= 25:15:6
let the income of P=25x
and the income of Q = 15x
and the income of R = 6x

A.T.Q.
$\dfrac{25x}{4} - 500 = 6x$
$\dfrac{25x}{4} - 6x = 500$
$\dfrac{x}{4} = 500$
$x = 2000$

then the income of $Q = 15 \times 2000 =$ Rs. 30000

Hence, the correct option is (c).

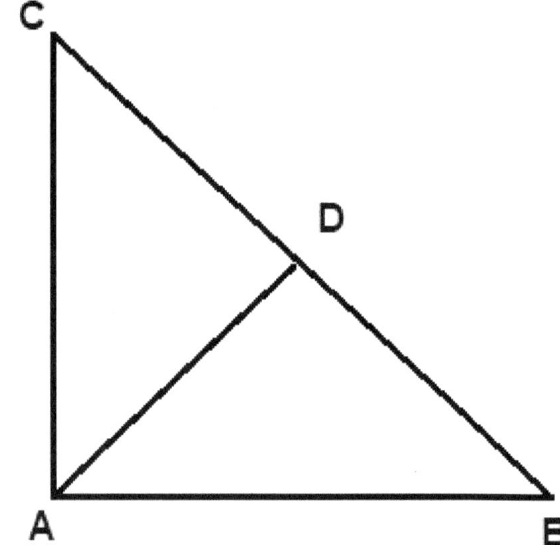

23.

Area of triangle $ABC = \dfrac{1}{2} \times AC \times AB = \dfrac{1}{2} \times AD \times BC$
$AC \times AB = 8 \times 3 = 24$

Hence, the correct option is (b).

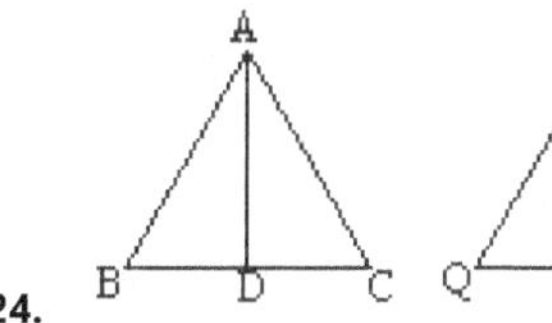

24.

As given,

$$\frac{AD}{PS} = \frac{3}{2}$$

and triangle are equiangular

So,

$$\angle A = \angle P$$
$$\angle B = \angle Q$$
$$\angle C = \angle R$$

Hence ΔABC and ΔPQR are similar triangle, due to which the ratio of their corresponding sides are equal.

Hence,

$$\frac{AB}{PQ} = \frac{BC}{QR} = \frac{CA}{RS} = \frac{AD}{PS} = \frac{3}{2}$$

Hence, the correct option is (b).

25. Required percentage = $\left[\frac{(720+840+780+950+870)}{(980+1050+1020+1240+940)} \times 100\right]\%$

$$= \left[\frac{4160}{5230} \times 100\right]\%$$

= 79.54% = 80%.

Hence, the correct option is (c).

26. Required average = $\frac{8100+9500+8700+9700+8950}{5}$

$$= \frac{44950}{5}$$

= 8990.

Hence, the correct option is (c).

27. The percentages of candidates qualified to candidates appeared from State P during different years are:

For 1997 $\left(\frac{780}{6400} \times 100\right)\% = 12.19\%$

For 1998 $\left(\frac{1020}{8800} \times 100\right)\% = 11.59\%$

For 1999 $\left(\frac{890}{7800} \times 100\right)\% = 11.41\%$

For 2000 $\left(\frac{1010}{8750} \times 100\right)\% = 11.54\%$

For 2001 $\left(\frac{1250}{9750} \times 100\right)\% = 12.82\%$

Maximum percentage is for the year 2001.

Hence, the correct option is (d).

28. Required percentage

$$= \left[\frac{(840+1050+920+980+1020)}{(7500+9200+8450+9200+8800)} \times 100\right]\%$$

$$= \left[\frac{4810}{43150} \times 100\right]\%$$

= 11.15%

Hence, the correct option is (d).

29. Percentage increase in marks in various periodical exams compared to the previous exams are:

For Jun 01 = $\left[\frac{(365-360)}{360} \times 100\right]\% = 1.39\%$

For Aug 01 = $\left[\frac{(370-365)}{365} \times 100\right]\% = 1.37\%$

For Oct 01 = $\left[\frac{(385-370)}{370} \times 100\right]\% = 4.05\%$

For Dec 01 = $\left[\frac{(400-385)}{385} \times 100\right]\% = 3.90\%$

For Feb 02 = $\left[\frac{(404-400)}{400} \times 100\right]\% = 1.25\%$

Clearly, highest percentage increase in marks is in Oct 01.

Hence, the correct option is (c).

30. Here it is clear from the graph that the student obtained 360, 365, 370, 385, 400 and 405 marks in periodical exams held in Apr 01, Jun 01, Aug 01, Oct 01, Dec 01 and Feb 02 respectively.

Required percentage = $\left(\frac{405}{360} \times 100\right)\% = 112.5\%$

Hence, the correct option is (b).

31. Required percentage = $\left[\frac{(370+385)}{(500+500)} \times 100\right]\% = \left(\frac{755}{1000} \times 100\right)\% = 75.5\%$

Hence, the correct option is (b).

32. Average marks obtained in all the periodical exam

$$= \frac{1}{6} \times [360 + 365 + 370 + 385 + 400 + 405]$$
$$= 380.83 \approx 381.$$

Hence, the correct option is (c).

33. The Union Cabinet on February 5, 2020 approved the setting up of Shri Ram Janmabhoomi Teerth Kshetra. The trust will be set up for the construction of the grand Ram temple in Ayodhya. PM Modi had made a statement regarding the same in the Lok Sabha on February 4, 2020.

Hence, the correct option is (b).

34. 'The Banker', a magazine run by the Financial Times of England, selected Reserve Bank of India Governor Shaktikanta Das as Banker of the Year-2020 for the Asia-Pacific region.

Hence, the correct option is (c).

35. The Indian Veterinary Research Institute (IVRI) of the Indian Council of Agricultural Research (ICAR) has developed a new vaccine to control 'classical swine fever'. Earlier, this vaccine was sourced from England.

Hence, the correct option is (b).

36. Karnataka has launched the doorstep delivery scheme- Janasevaka scheme to provide citizens with easy access to important government services such as the issuance of ration card, health card, senior citizen card, driver's licence and marriage registration certificate.

Hence, the correct option is (d).

37. Shreyas Iyer has become the first No. 4 player to hit a century outside India in four years. He scored 103 runs out off 107 balls during India's first ODI against host nation New Zealand on February 5, 2020.

Hence, the correct option is (d).

38. The Government of Bhutan recently passed the 'Sustainable Development Tax' Bill. It allows the government of Bhutan to impose a sustainable development tax on tourists arriving in the country.

Hence, the correct option is (a).

39. Daniel Arap Moi, longest-serving Kenyan President, passed away on February 4, 2020, at the age of 95 years. He had served as Kenya's President from 1978 to 2002 amid political repression, economic stagnation and corruption.

Hence, the correct option is (c).

40. Cancer cases can rise to 81 percent by 2040, as per a report published by the World Health Organisation on World Cancer Day (February 4, 2020).

Hence, the correct option is (b).

41. V =V$_m$ sin(ω t – 15^0)volts

If currents leads 10^0

I = I$_m$ sin(ω t – 15 + 10^0)

= I$_m$ sin(ω t – 50)

Hence, the correct option is (d).

42. The value of the coefficient of coupling is always greater than 0 and less than 1, or 0% and 100% respectively. A coefficient of coupling of 0 would represent no coupling, and 1 would represent perfect coupling.

Hence, the correct option is (b).

43. $e \ = \ N\dfrac{do}{dt}$

It is emil Len's law.

Hence, the correct option is (d).

44. $K \ = \ \dfrac{M}{\sqrt{L_1 L_2}}$

$M \ = \ K\sqrt{L_1 L_2} \ = 0.85\ \sqrt{3\times 12}$

$M \ = \ 5.1\ H$

Hence, the correct option is (b).

45. Resistance temperature coefficeint of copper at

20^{0}C is 0.00393/^{0}C.

Hence, the correct option is (c).

46. The load characteristic of DC shunt generator is determined by the voltage drop due to armature reaction, voltage drop due to decreased field current and voltage drop in armature resistance.

Hence, the correct option is (b).

47. 1hp = 765watt

In watt – seconds

= 765 × 2 × 5 × 3600

= 2.6856 × 10^7

Hence, the correct option is (a).

48. $N \ = \ \dfrac{120f}{p}$

$1200 \ = \ \dfrac{120\times f}{4}$

$f \ = \ \dfrac{1200\ \times 4}{120}$

$T \ = \dfrac{l}{f} \ = \dfrac{1}{40}$

$= 0.025 sec$

Hence, the correct option is (b).

49. The single phase induction motor (IM) which does not have centrifugal switch is permanent capacitor run single phase IM.

Hence, the correct option is (d).

50. Electromagnetic Damping :

- The movement of the coil in a magnetic field produces the eddy current in the metal former which further generates another magnetic field and interacts with the original magnetic field. Hence it produces torque that opposes the motion of conducting coil and plate. Thus the magnitude of the current and the damping torque is dependent on the resistance of the circuit.

Voltage Multiplier

- Multipliers are non-inductive high resistances connected in series with the voltmeter for the purpose of increasing the range of the voltmeter.

The resistance of Multiplier greatly exceeds the meter internal resistance hence it reduces the electromagnetic damping action on the meter movement. The electromagnetic damping can be improved by shunting the meter with a capacitor, but this method increases the meter's settling time.

Hence, the correct option is (c).

51. $P = VI\cos\beta \cdot I_c\cos\psi$

Where β is the angle by which I_p is lagging behind applied voltage V

ψ is the power factor of the load

Therefore the reading of wattmeter will be proportional to

$P \propto \cos\beta\cos\psi$

Hence, the correct option is (c).

52. If the current flowing in the same direction then the conductor attracts each other and if the current flowing in the opposite direction then the conductor generates a repulsive force.

Hence, the correct option is (b).

53. Reluctance is defined as

$\Re = \dfrac{F}{\Phi}$

F = magnetomotive force (MMF) in ampere-turns

Φ = the magnetic flux in webers.

Therefore the unit of Reluctance is ampere-turns per Weber (AT/Weber) (a unit that is equivalent to turns per Henry)

Hence, the correct option is (c).

54. Spring provides the controlling force in the measuring instrument if the controlling force is absent the pointer will not comes back to starting position i.e zero when the current is removed.

Hence, the correct option is (c).

55. Power in one resistor removed star removed from star connected load.

$P_1 = \dfrac{V_L^2}{2R}$

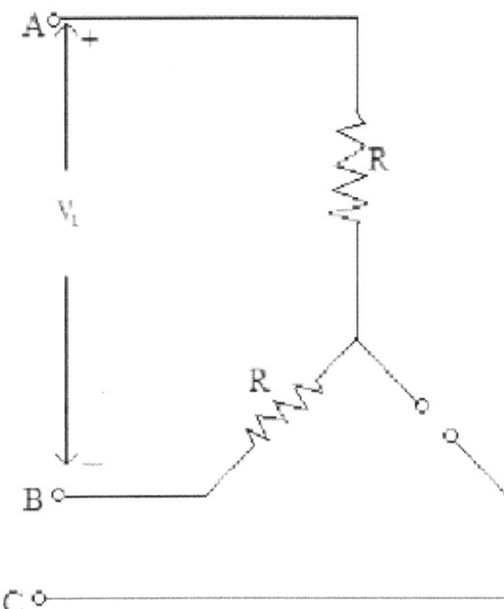

Power will be in all resistors

$P_2 = 3\left(\dfrac{V_L}{\sqrt{3}}\right)^2 \times \dfrac{1}{R} = \dfrac{V_L^2}{R}$

So, one of the resistor is disconnected, then the percentage reduction in load will be 50%

Hence, the correct option is (b).

56. Induced E.m.f. $= \dfrac{\Phi N}{t}$

$= \dfrac{100\times10^{-6}\times100}{\frac{1}{20}} = 2.0V$

Hence, the correct option is (b).

57.

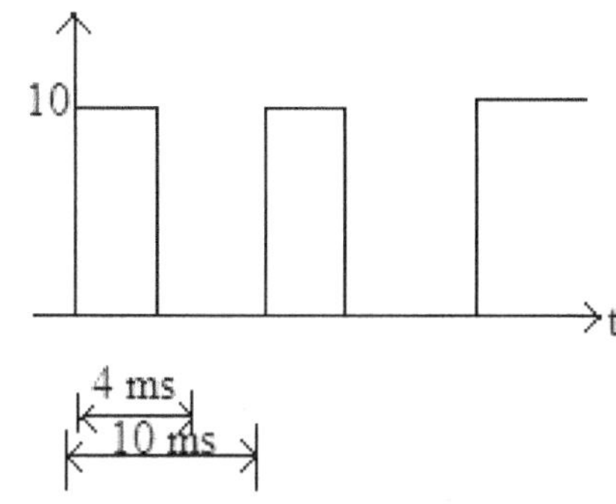

PMMC reads Average values

$= \dfrac{10}{4} = 2.5V$

PMMC rectifier

= 2.75V

M.I. reads $= \dfrac{10}{2} = 5V$

Hence, the correct option is (b).

58. Applying KVL in the output circuit-

10-500(Ic+Ib) - 5 = 0

$5 = 500 \times 0.008(1+ \dfrac{1}{beta})$

then, beta $= \dfrac{1}{9}$

so, alpha $= \dfrac{beta}{beta}+1 = 0.1$

Also, alpha $= \dfrac{Ton}{(Ton+Toff)}$

Ton+Toff $= \dfrac{1}{50} = 0.02$ sec

therefore, Ton = 0.1 $\times 0.02 = 2$ msec.

Hence, the correct option is (a).

59.

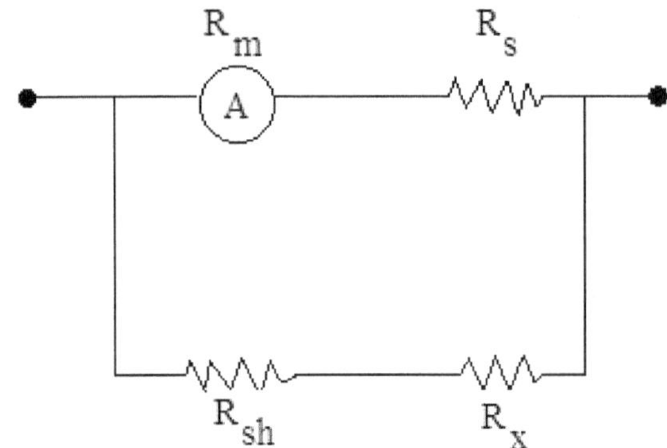

The condition for which the meter performance is compensated against the temperature will be when the resistance material is equally balanced

$$R_m R_x = R_{sh} R_x$$
$$\frac{R_m}{R_s} = \frac{R_{sh}}{R_x}$$

Hence, the correct option is (d).

60. For sinusoidal voltage, PMMC reads zero
PMMC type instrument uses two permanent magnets in order to create the stationary magnetic field. If we apply AC current to these types of instruments the direction of current will be reversed during the negative half cycle and hence the direction of torque will also be reversed which gives the average value of torque zero.
Also If a.c. supply given to these instruments, an alternating torque will be developed. Due to moment of inertia of the moving system, the pointer will not follow the rapidly changing, alternating torque and will fail to show an,y readings

Hence, the correct option is (a).

61. The Deflecting torque of Induction type Instrument is given as:

$$T_d = \Phi_1 \Phi_2 \sin\beta \cos\alpha$$

where $\Phi = $ flux

β & α are the phasor angle

- The torque in Induction type instrument is directly proportional to the cos\alpha. Therefore in order to maximize the torque, the angle " α^n should be near to zero.

- The torque in Induction type instrument is directly proportional to the $\sin\beta$. Therefore the angle β should be nearer to $90°$ in order to maximize the torque. The angle β is the angle between two shunt coil flux and series coil flux and quadrature means $90°$.

Hence, the correct option is (b).

62. Four-terminal sensing

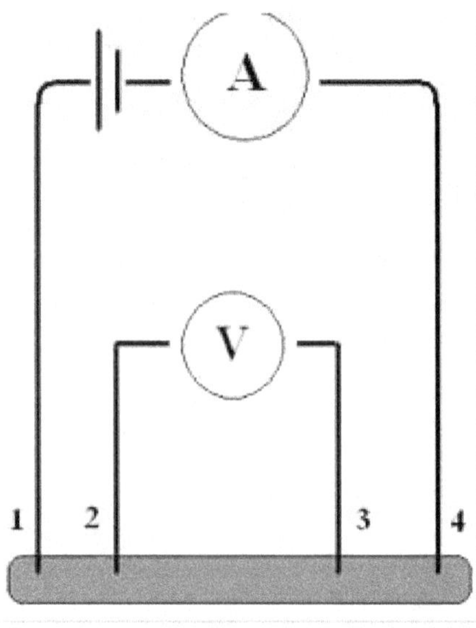

- Four-terminal sensing is also known as Kelvin sensing, which measures very low resistances using four-terminal sensing. Each two-wire connection can be called a **Kelvin connection.**

- When a Kelvin connection is used, current is supplied via a pair of source connections (current leads). These generate a voltage drop across the impedance to be measured according to Ohm's law V=IR.

- A pair of **sense** connections (voltage leads) are made immediately adjacent to the target impedance so that they do not include the voltage drop in the force leads or contacts.

- Since almost no current flows to the measuring instrument, the voltage drop in the sense leads is negligible hence accurate measurement can be obtained.

- It is usual to arrange the sense wires as the inside pair, while the force wires are the outside pair.

Hence, the correct option is (a).

63. Statement A:

- Usually, a radio will make a sharp 'pop' when another electrical item is switched off.

- The cause of the noise is the arc that momentarily bridges the contacts of the lamp's switch when it is opened (shut off).

- The arc produces radio-frequency energy, which nearby radios (especially AM, but sometimes also FM) detect.

- Since the radio can't differentiate between intended and unintended signals, it will reproduce whatever comes its way

Statement R:
During the opening of the contact, the medium between the contacts gets highly ionized therefore low resistive path is created between the contacts and current tends to flow through that path.

Hence both the statement are true and A is the correct explanation of Statement R.

Hence, the correct option is (a).

64.

- The relative permittivity of air is low(i.e about 1.0006) then the insulation material, therefore, they have higher voltage gradient then the surrounding insulation.
- The electric discharge is high enough to ionize the air and cause the corona discharge.

Hence, the correct option is (c).

65. The capacitance to neutral is twice the capacitance between conductors, that is,
$C_N = 2C_{AB} = 2 \times 3\mu F = 6\mu F$

Hence, the correct option is (b).

66. Dielectric stress $\alpha = \dfrac{1}{Diameter}$
The ratio of minimum and maximum stress in the insulation of the single-core cable is

$$\frac{Maximum\ dielectric\ strees}{Minimum\ dielectric\ stress} = \frac{D}{d}$$

Where D = Sheath Diameter
and d = Core Diameter
Note: The expression of the same will be explained in the theoretical section

Hence, the correct option is (c).

67. Making capacity used the peak value of current while breaking capacity work on the RMS value of current that's why making capacity is more than breaking capacity. Let's explain in detail.
Breaking capacity of Circuit Breaker When the breaker is closed and a fault occurs then it closes in the transient state(in transient state DC offset become zero) so the current capacity at this instant is only the RMS value of current(symmetrical component)in the transient state which is also called breaking capacity of the breaker.i.e
Breaking capacity=rms value of breaking current in the transient state.
Making Capacity Of Circuit Breaker Now when the breaker is going to be closed and at that time fault occurs then it will close sub-transient state and the current-carrying capacity at this instant contains RMS value of current (the symmetrical component in the transient state) and the DC offset current in the sub-transient state which is also
called Making capacity of the breaker at the sub-transient period amount of arc produce will be very high. Thus making capacity is very high. i.e
Making Capacity=DC offset current+rms value of breaking current in a transient state Thus **Making capacity >Breaking Capacity.**

Hence, the correct option is (a).

68. Why does a capacitor block DC but pass AC?

- A capacitor is nothing but 2 metal plates separated by an insulator. The insulator can be anything like paper, air, rubber, etc.
- When a capacitor is connected to a voltage source, positive charges from the positive terminal of the voltage source and negative charges(electrons) from the negative terminal of the voltage source, travel and GET ACCOMMODATED ON BOTH THE PLATES OF THE CAPACITOR.
- Once the capacitor gets fully charged it will now act as the insulator and it doesn't allow current to pass through it.
- Now as we know that the voltage value of DC remains constant for all the time the power supply is ON. Hence capacitor gets charged to its total limit and thus doesn't allow any current to flow hence **DC BLOCKED.**
- Talking about AC it is the time-varying Voltage i.e the polarity of AC changes from time T1 to T2, therefore, at time T1, the capacitor gets charged such that the positive charges are accommodated on the left plate.
- After time T1, the polarity changes (because the voltage source is AC) and now at the start of T2, voltage source V will attract the negative and positive charges from the respective plates to its terminals and current will flow in another direction. And because the capacitor is losing its charges hence the Capacitor is getting discharged.

Hence, the correct option is (a).

69.

- An N-Type semiconductor is created by adding pentavalent impurities like phosphorus (P), arsenic (As), or antimony (Sb), bismuth.
- A pentavalent impurity is called a donor because it is ready to give a free electron to a semiconductor. The impurities are called dopants.
- The purpose of doing this is to make more charge carriers, or electrons available in the material for conduction.
- In n-type semiconductors the number of electrons is more than the holes, so electrons are measured as majority charge carriers and holes are referred to as minority charge carriers.

Hence, the correct option is (b).

70. For overall gain to be independent of frequency, R1C1= R2C2

$100\ \times C1= 10\ \times 0.1$

C1= 0.01 micro farads

Hence, the correct option is (a).

71.

- Steel is used as a magnetic core in a transformer, it acts as a good conductor and whenever a time-varying flux passes through the core, circulating currents are produced and known as "Eddy currents".

- To reduce conductivity (eddy current losses) by not destroying magnetic properties, about 4 to 5% of silica impurity is added so that the conductivity of steel decreases.

- The high content of silica is not preferred the material becomes more brittle and it will destroy the mechanical properties.

Hence, the correct option is (a).

72. Power consumed by wattmeter = CT ratio $\times$ PT ratio $\times$ VIcos Φ........1

In the above question

Power consumed by wattmeter $= 2000$ watts

CT ratio $= \dfrac{15}{30}$

PT ratio $= \dfrac{300}{600}$

$VI = 600 \times 30$

Putting all the value in equation number 1 we get

$2000 = \left(\dfrac{15}{30}\right) \times \left(\dfrac{300}{600}\right) \times 600 \times 30 \times \cos\Phi$

$\cos\Phi = 0.4444$

Power $= VI\cos\Phi = 600 \times 30 \times 0.4444$

Power $= 7999.2 \cong 8000$ watts.

Hence, the correct option is (d).

73.

- A deliberate connection of resistance in parallel with the contact space (or arc) is called as the resistance switching.

- Resistance switching is employed in the circuit breaker having high post zero resistance of contact space (i.e air blast circuit breaker).

- High restriking voltage appears across the contacts because of current chopping. If these voltages are not allowed to discharge, they may cause break down of insulation of the circuit breaker or the neighboring equipment.

- The resistance discharges the heavy arc current through them this results in the decrease of arc current and an increase in the rate of deionization of the arc path.

- Thus the arc resistance increased leading to the further increase in current through the shunt resistance R.

- This build-up process continues until the current becomes so small that it fails to maintain the arc.

Hence, the correct option is (c).

74. Instantaneous power $\mathbf{p(t)}$ is defined as the product of instantaneous voltage $v(t)$ and instantaneous current $i(t)$. Assuming the sinusoids waveforms $\mathbf{v(t) = Vm\cos(\omega t + \theta v)}$ and $\mathbf{i(t) = Im\cos(\omega t + \theta i)}$ represent the voltage and current, then it can be shown:

$p(t) = P + P\cos2\omega t - Q\sin2\omega t$

where $P = \dfrac{1}{2} Vm\, Im\cos(\theta v - \theta i)$

and $Q = \dfrac{1}{2} Vm\, Im\sin(\theta v - \theta i)$

The term P is a constant and represents the average of the instantaneous power $p(t)$ (since the averages of $\cos2\omega t$ and $Q\sin2\omega t$ are both zero). The term $P + P\cos2\omega t$ represents the instantaneous real power (instantaneous active power). Q is called the reactive power and the term $Q\sin2\omega$ t represents the instantaneous imaginary power (instantaneous reactive power). The second term is a time-varying sinusoid whose frequency is equal to twice the angular frequency of the supply

Hence, the correct option is (b).

75. Using, Ie= Ic+Ib and Ic = (beta)Ib

Applying KVL in the output circuit-

$24 - (8000)(45)(Ib) - 5 - 230(1 + 45)(Ib) = 0$

so,

$Ib = 51.2 \times 10^{(-6)}$ Amps

Now,

Applying KVL in the input circuit-

$24 - 8000(1 + 45)Ib - RIb - 0.7 - 230 \times (1 + 45) Ib = 0$

putting the value of Ib in the above equation-

$23.3 = [(51.2 \times 10^{-6})(370580 + R)]$

so,

R = 84498.125 ohms or, 84.5 KOhms

Hence, the correct option is (a).

76. IL = 12A

WL = 11kW

W2 = 0

$\tan\varphi = \dfrac{\sqrt{3}(w_1 - w_2)}{(w_1 + w_2)}$

$\varphi = 60^0$

Power factor $= \cos60^0 = \dfrac{1}{2} = 0.5$

Hence, the correct option is (b).

77.

- GLS (general lighting service) lamps are the source of incandescent light.

- Acid etching creates a very smooth, glossy and satin finish; the acid-etched lamp is maintenance-free as it does not show dirt marks or fingerprints.

Hence, the correct option is (a).

78. Plugging in DC Motor

- Plugging of Dc motor is the method of reconnecting the motor to the line with reverse polarity hence now the motor will produce torque in the opposite direction to that of rotation.

- Plugging in DC motor means the reversing of either field or armature current. So either Eb or V gets reversed. Therefore, the voltage across the armature will be V+Eb which is almost twice the supply voltage.

- The rotor speed decreases until it becomes zero and then the rotor accelerates in the opposite direction. Therefore, the plugging is used to get a quick reversal and a rapid stop or Braking.

Hence, the correct option is (a).

79.

- Welding usually requires high current (over 80 amperes) and it can need above 12,000 amperes in spot welding.

- A transformer-style welding power supply converts the moderate voltage and moderate current electricity from the utility mains (typically 230 or 115 VAC) into a high current and low voltage supply, typically between 17 and 45 volts and 55 to 590 amperes.

Hence, the correct option is (c).

80. Plant Capacity Factor It is the product of load factor and the utilization factor.

Capacity factor = Load factor × Utilization factor Where load factor is the ratio of average demand and maximum demand And Utilization Factor is the ratio of kWh generated to the product of the plant capacity and the number of hours for which plant was in operation.

Hence, the correct option is (c).

81. An electrically held contactor is held closed by the same electrical supply that energizes the motor's stator windings. It has an inherent under voltage protection because the motor contactor opens once the motor's electrical supply dips below a certain threshold, typically 60-70% of the nominal voltage.

Hence, the correct option is (D).

82. The given triangle output can be changed into the square output

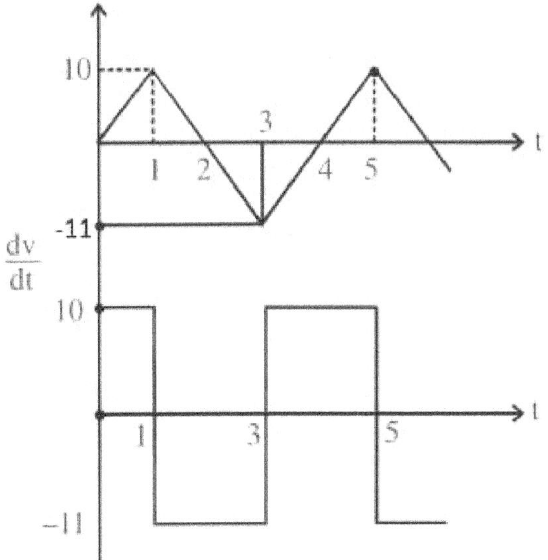

The instantaneous value of capacitor current is

$$i(t) = \frac{cdv}{dt}$$

where C is the capacitance in farad

$$\frac{dv}{dt} = \text{= instantaneous rate of voltage change(Volt/second)}$$

For charging rate of voltage change is 10 and for discharging rate of voltage change is -11 therefore

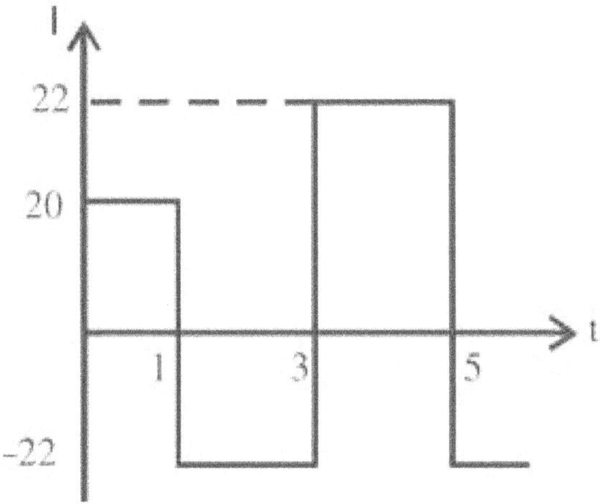

Hence, the correct option is (d).

83.

- In a semiconductor, there is a bandgap and at absolute zero temperature, all the electrons are below the gap, and thus not available for conduction.

- At finite temperature, some electrons are thermally excited into the conduction band, and thus you get conduction when an electric field is applied. As the temperature is increased covalent bonds breaks and more electron-hole pairs are available for conduction. Thus conductivity increases and resistivity, the reciprocal of conductivity decreases.

Hence, the correct option is (a).

84. Frequency of instantaneous power

= 2f = 2 × 50

= 100 c/s

Hence, the correct option is (c).

85. The SI unit of charge, the coulomb, "is the quantity of electricity carried in 1 second by a current of 1 ampere

Hence, the correct option is (c).

86.

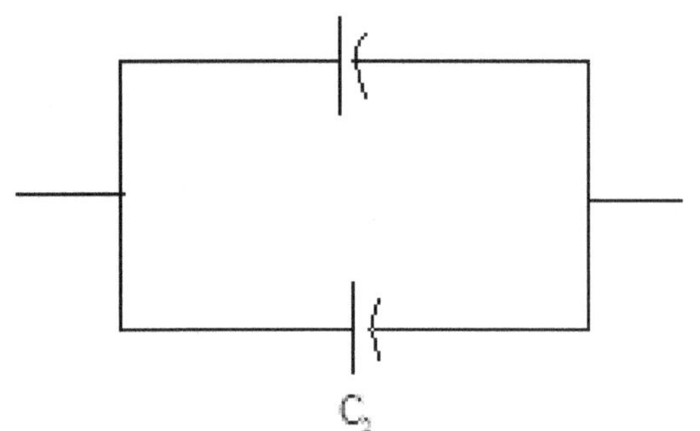

$$PF = \frac{p.f_{c1} + p.f_{c2}}{2}$$

$$= \frac{0.01 + 0.02}{2} = 0.015$$

Hence, the correct option is (b).

87. Current through voltmeter

$$Iv = \frac{V}{R} = \frac{4}{50000} = 8 \times 10^{-5} A$$

Dc supply voltage $Vdc = 120V$

Then the value of unknown resistance is given as

$$R = \frac{V}{I}$$

$$R = \frac{120}{8} \times 10^{-5} = 1.5 M\Omega$$

Hence, the correct option is (d).

88. There are mainly two functions of the choke coil

- Limit the current.
- Produce high voltage across the tube light.

Limit the current

- In a gas discharge, such as a fluorescent lamp, current causes resistance to decrease. This is because as more electrons and ions flow through a particular area, they bump into more atoms, which frees up electrons, creating more charged particles.

- In this way, the current will climb on its own in a gas discharge, as long as there is an adequate voltage (and household AC current has a lot of voltage).

- If the current in a fluorescent light isn't controlled, it can blow out the various electrical components.

Produces High voltage Across Tubelight

- Choke is nothing but the coil/ballast (inductor) which is used to induce the high voltage across it. as we know that inductor has a property to induce high voltage for the brief period of time, this high voltage is required to ionize the gases in the starter.

Hence, the correct option is (d).

89.

- The 100W lamp will fail first, Although the voltage across 100 w lamp will be higher (293V), it will fail

because of effective current (0.489A) which is more than the 100 w lamp normal current (0.4A).

- Increase in current cause more heat and heating element will fail.

Hence, the correct option is (a).

90.

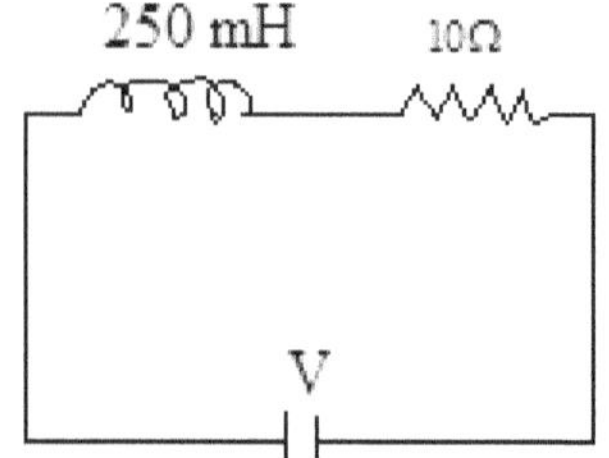

let at time t, magnetic energy reaches to $\frac{1}{4}$ of its maximum.

Energy, $E = \frac{1}{2}Li^2$

i.e. current that time should be $\frac{max}{2}$

$$\frac{1}{2} = e^{-tR/L}$$

$$In \frac{1}{2} = \frac{tR}{L}$$

$$\frac{tR}{L} = In2$$

$$t = \frac{L}{R}In2$$

$$= \frac{250 \times 10^{-3}}{10} In\, 2 = \frac{1}{40}\log_e 2$$

Hence, the correct option is (d).

91. Fossil fuels are fuels because they release heat energy when they are burned. They are fossil fuels because they were formed from the remains of living organisms billions of years ago. Some of the examples of fossil fuels are coal, oil and natural gas.

Hence, the correct option is (c).

92. The most used nuclear fuel is Uranium – 235. It is a radioactive metal. Nuclear fuels like Uranium do not burnt to release energy. Instead, the fuels are involved in nuclear reaction in nuclear reaction in the nuclear reactor.

Hence, the correct option is (c).

93. A nacelle is a cover housing that houses all of the generating components in a wind turbine. Wind turbines have huge blades mounted on a tall tower. The blades are connected to a nacelle. Thus the nacelle in wind turbines helps to work the wind turbines.

Hence, the correct option is (a).

94. The water in the sea rises and falls because of waves on the surface. Wave machines use the Kinetic energy in this movement to drive electricity generators. Wave energy also known as ocean energy. Wave energy is essentially power drawn from waves.

Hence, the correct option is (b).

95. A tidal barrage is a barrier built over a river estuary to make use of the kinetic energy in the moving water. Huge amounts of water move in and out of river mouths each day because of the tides. The barrage contains electricity generators.

Hence, the correct option is (b).

96. Hydroelectricity power stations use the kinetic energy in moving water. But the water comes from behind a dam built across a river valley. The water high up behind the dam contains potential energy.

Hence, the correct option is (b).

97. Nickel Cadmium cells offers along service life thereby ensuring a high degree of the economy. In the PV industry, Nickel Cadmium battery cells are majorly used for the energy storage technology from manufacturers and users of PV of grid systems.

Hence, the correct option is (c).

98. There are three major forms of fossil fuels they are coal, oil and natural gas. They formed from organic remains of plants and animals that were converted into coal, oil and natural gas by exposure to heat and the pressure of the earth's crust over millions of years.

Hence, the correct option is (c).

99. Fossil fuels are not environmental friendly. Burning of fossil fuels result in pollution and can cause serious environmental concerns. According to WHO, 7 million premature deaths annually linked to air pollution by the fossil fuels burning.

Hence, the correct option is (d).

100. Energy in the form of heat and light is obtained by sun. Sunlight contains a large amount of energy. The Sun's energy warms the planet's surface, powering titanic transfers of heat and pressure in weather patterns and ocean currents.

Hence, the correct option is (c).

101. The energy sources that are available in the market for a definite price are known as commercial energy. By far the most important forms of commercial energy are electricity, coal and refined petroleum products.

Hence, the correct option is (c).

102. Renewable energy comes from sources that are essentially inexhaustible such as the sun, the wind and the heat of the Earth, or from replaceable fuels such as plants.

Hence, the correct option is (d).

103. Board of Trade Unit (B.O.T) Board of Trade Unit (B.O.T) – a unit of energy equal to the work done by a power of 1000 watts operating for one hour
1 kWh = 1 BOT Unit

Hence, the correct option is (c).

104. Geothermal energy is a renewable energy source because heat is continuously produced inside the earth.
Geothermal energy is the heat produced deep in the Earth's core. Geothermal energy is a clean, renewable resource that can be

harnessed for use as heat and electricity. Geothermal energy is heat that is generated within the Earth. (Geo means "earth," and thermal means "heat" in Greek.)

Hence, the correct option is (a).

105. Ethanol can be fermented from many sources of starch, including corn, wheat, grain sorghum, barley, and potatoes, and from sugar crops such as sugar cane and sweet sorghum. Because there has been an abundant supply of corn, most of the ethanol made in the United States is from corn.

Hence, the correct option is (a).

106.

- The field-effect transistor (FET) is a transistor that uses an electric field to control the electrical behavior of the device. FETs are also known as unipolar transistors since they involve the single-carrier-type operation.

- FET has the high gate to main current resistance, on the order of 100 MΩ or more, thus providing a high degree of isolation between control and flow.

- FET has a negative temperature coefficient of resistance hence has better stability against the temperature.

Hence, the correct option is (d).

107. The oldest form of energy-Bio-mass

Climate change is also called-Global warming

BioMass is related to with-Photo synthesis

Secondary energy is produced from-Primary energy

Hence, the correct option is (d).

108. The energy that is converted to steam and electricity-Secondary Energy

The energy that is either found or stored in nature-Primary Energy

The energy that is obtained from sources that are essentially inexhaustible-Renewable Energy

Energy resources which are likely to deplete with time-Non-renewable Energy

Hence, the correct option is (a).

109. Bagasse is used as fuel to generate stem.
Bagasse (/bə'gæs/ bə-GAS) is the dry pulpy fibrous residue that remains after sugarcane or sorghum stalks are crushed to extract their juice. It is used as a biofuel for the production of heat, energy, and electricity, and in the manufacture of pulp and building materials.

Hence, the correct option is (b).

110. Power from wind is generated by wind turbines. Mountains, bodies of water, and vegetation all influence wind flow patterns,. Wind turbines convert the energy in wind to electricity by rotating propeller-like blades around a rotor. The rotor turns the driveshaft, which turns an electric generator.
Hence, the correct option is (b).

111. It is the stored energy and the energy of position-Potential energy

It is the energy stored in bonds of atoms and molecules-Chemical Energy

It is the energy of place or position-Gravitational Energy

It is the energy stored in the nucleus of an atom-Nuclear Energy

Hence, the correct option is (c).

112. Energy that deals with the movement of electrons-Electrical Energy

It is the internal energy in substances-Thermal Energy

It is the electromagnetic energy that travels in transverse waves-Radiant energy

It is the energy in motion-Kinetic energy

Hence, the correct option is (d).

113. Sound energy is the movement of energy through substances in longitudinal (compression/rarefaction) waves. Sound is produced when a force causes an object or substance to vibrate; the energy is transferred through the substance in a longitudinal wave.

Hence, the correct option is (c).

114. Ampere is the rate of flow of charge.

An electric current is a flow of electric charge. In electric circuits, this charge is often carried by moving electrons in a wire.

Hence, the correct option is (b).

115. kVAr is the apparent power.

While KVAR means Kilovolt-Ampere Reactive, kVA stands for Kilovolt amperes. For the most part, it is commonly referred to as Kilowatt or kW, which is the general term. It's the unit measurement used to rate most—if not all—of the electrical items you have at home.

Hence, the correct option is (d).

116. Relation between kVA, kW and kVAr is

$kVA = \sqrt{(kW)^2 + (kWAr)^2}$ is true.

To find out the results, it must be known what the value of Cosphi or the power factor of the installation or electrical device. For the value of cosphi = 1, then 1 KVA is equal to 1 KW. KVAr (Kilo Volt Ampere Reactive), or in smaller units usually uses units of VAr (Volt Ampere Reactive).

Hence, the correct option is (a).

117. The ratio between the active power(kW) and apparent power (kVA) is Power factor.

Hence, the correct option is (b).

118. The measure of the latent heat content of air-water vapour mixtures is Dew point temperature.
The dew point is the temperature to which air must be cooled to become saturated with water vapour. When cooled further, the airborne water vapour will condense to form liquid water (dew).

Hence, the correct option is (d).

119. The energy transferred is measured in joules.

Power is a measure of energy transfer rate. It is useful to talk about the rate at which energy is transferred from one system to another (energy per time). This rate is called power. One joule of energy transferred in one second is called a Watt (i.e., 1 joule/second = 1 Watt).

Hence, the correct option is (a).

120. Condensation is the process by which radiation passes through a body.

Condensation is the change of water from its gaseous form (water vapor) into liquid water. Condensation generally occurs in the atmosphere when warm air rises, cools and looses its capacity to hold water vapor. As a result, excess water vapor condenses to form cloud droplets.

Hence, the correct option is (c).

Part - I

Q.1 Direction : In the following questions, choose the word opposite in meaning to the given word.

Reckless

A. puzzling   **B.** preacher   **C.** spiritual   **D.** cautious

Q.2 Direction : In the following questions, choose the word opposite in meaning to the given word.

Babel

A. handsome   **B.** quiet

C. ignorant   **D.** careless

Q.3 In the following question, out of the four alternatives, select the word similar in meaning to the word given.

Insolent

A. impolite   **B.** dirty   **C.** feud   **D.** lucid

Q.4 In the following question, out of the four alternatives, select the word similar in meaning to the word given.

Sordid

A. unpleasant   **B.** variant

C. rigidity   **D.** tender

Q.5 Direction : In the following questions, four alternatives are given for the meaning of the given Idiom/Phrase. Choose the alternative which best express the meaning of the Idiom/Phrase.

To sow the dragon's teeth

A. To disturb the work

B. To suspect something foul

C. To take some action

D. To act foolishly

Q.6 Direction : In the following questions, four alternatives are given for the meaning of the given Idiom/Phrase. Choose the alternative which best express the meaning of the Idiom/Phrase.

Great minds think alike

A. When an evil plan is hatched criminals agree.

B. Said to those people who don't like each other to make them agree.

C. Said when two people have the same opinion or make the same choice.

D. Intelligent people will think of plans to which everybody will say yes.

Q.7 Select the correctly spelt word.

A. constituet   **B.** constetute

C. conctituet   **D.** constitute

Q.8 Select the correctly spelt word.

A. monopoly   **B.** manopaly

C. monnopoly   **D.** monnopolly

Q.9 Which one of the following is not an example of input computer device?

A. Mouse   **B.** Scanner

C. Speaker   **D.** Digital Camera

Q.10 Who discovered the nucleus for the first time in cell?

A. Leeuwenhoek   **B.** Schwann

C. Huffmaster   **D.** Robert Brown

Q.11 Which of the following diseases is caused by a virus?

A. Plague   **B.** Polio   **C.** Tetanus   **D.** Leprosy

Q.12 Forests are examples of _____.

A. Natural ecosystems

B. Artificial ecosystems

C. Virtual Environment

D. Synthetic Environment

Q.13 The covering of the lungs is called as.

A. Pericardium   **B.** Pleural membrane

C. Perichondrium   **D.** Peritoneum

Q.14 The exchange of gases in a mammal takes place in _____.

A. Trachea   **B.** Bronchioles

C. Bronchi   **D.** Alveoli

Q.15 An iron ball and a wooden ball of the same radius are released from a height H in a vacuum. The times taken by both of them to reach the ground are.

A. different   **B.** exactly equal

C. unequal   **D.** Exactly not equal

Q.16 Heavy water is _______________.

A. Rainwater   **B.** PH-7

C. Tritium Oxide   **D.** Deuterium Oxide

Q.17 Vijay is 10% more efficient than Vikas. If Vikas can complete a piece of work in 33 days, then Vijay can complete the same work in how many days?

A. 25   **B.** 27   **C.** 30   **D.** 36

Q.18 A trader sold an article at a gain of 20%. Had he purchased it for 40% more and sold for Rs 24 less, then he would have incurred a loss of 20%. What is the cost price of the article?

A. Rs.150   **B.** Rs.300   **C.** Rs.450   **D.** Rs.600

Q.19 A bag contains 10 rupees, 2 rupees and 1 rupee coins. The value of 10 rupees, 2 rupees and 1 rupee coins are in the ratio of 15 : 8 : 1 respectively. If total number of coins is 273, then what will be the total value (in Rs) of all coins?

A. 1008   **B.** 924   **C.** 1102   **D.** 1218

Q.20 The simple interest on a sum deposited at 8% p.a. for 8 years is Rs. 16,000. What will be the compound interest on the same sum at one-fourth of the above rate of interest for 2 years?

A. Rs.1020 **B.** Rs.980 **C.** Rs.1010 **D.** Rs.1015

Q.21 The average of 6 consecutive even numbers is 25. If the next even number is also considered, then what is the new average?

A. 27 **B.** 25 **C.** 26 **D.** 28

Q.22 A motorcyclist left $6\frac{6}{9}$ minutes later than the scheduled time but in order to reach its destination 21 km away in time, he had to increase his speed by 12 km/hr from the usual speed. What is usual speed (in km/hr) of the motorcyclist?

A. 28 **B.** 35 **C.** 42 **D.** 64

Q.23 A trader marks his a pair of shoes in such a way that after allowing a discount of 10%, he gains 15%. If an article costs him Rs. 720, his selling price if he sell him at 33.33% discount?

A. Rs.613.33 **B.** Rs.656.33
C. Rs.513.33 **D.** Rs.750.33

Q.24 Direction : What should come in place of question mark (?) in the following questions?

$$\sqrt{13924} + \sqrt[3]{238328} + 52\% \text{ of } 700 = 395 + ?$$

A. 138 **B.** 144 **C.** 149 **D.** 159

Ques (25-29): The following table gives the percentage of marks obtained by seven students in six different subjects in an examination.

The Numbers in the Brackets give the Maximum Marks in Each Subject.

Stud ent	Subject (Max. Marks)					
	Mat hs	Chemi stry	Phys ics	Geogra phy	Hist ory	Comp uter Scienc e
	(15 0)	(130)	(120)	(100)	(60)	(40)
Ayus h	90	50	90	60	70	80
Aman	100	80	80	40	80	70
Sajal	90	60	70	70	90	70
Rohit	80	65	80	80	60	60
Musk an	80	65	85	95	50	90
Tanvi	70	75	65	85	40	60
Tarun	65	35	50	77	80	80

Q.25 What are the average marks obtained by all the seven students in Physics? (rounded off to two digit after decimal)

A. 77.26 **B.** 89.14 **C.** 91.37 **D.** 96.11

Q.26
The number of students who obtained 60% and above marks in all subjects is?

A. 1 **B.** 2 **C.** 3 **D.** None

Q.27 What was the aggregate of marks obtained by Sajal in all six subjects?

A. 409 **B.** 419 **C.** 429 **D.** 449

Q.28
In which subject is the overall percentage the best?

A. Maths **B.** Chemistry
C. Physics **D.** History

Q.29
What is the overall percentage of Tarun?

A. 52.5% **B.** 55% **C.** 60% **D.** 63%

Ques (30-32): The following pie charts exhibit the distribution of the overseas tourist traffic from India. The two charts shows the tourist distribution by country and the age profiles of the tourists respectively.

Distribution of Overseas Tourist Traffic from India.

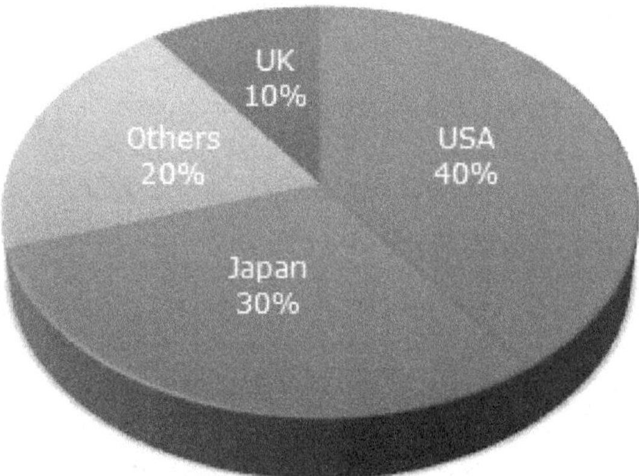

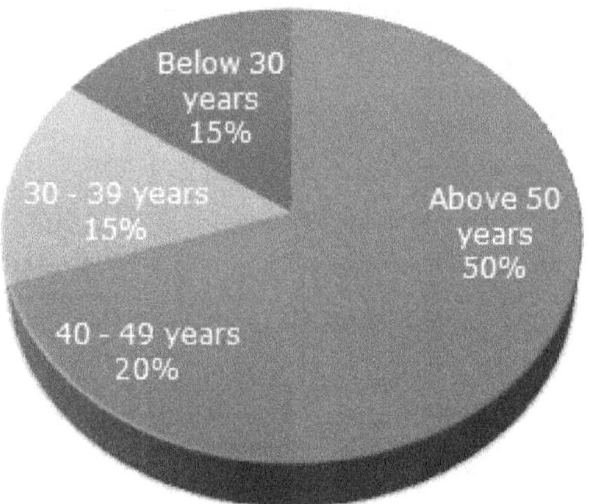

Q.30 What percentage of Indian tourist went to either USA or UK ?

A. 40 % **B.** 50 % **C.** 60 % **D.** 70 %

Q.31 The ratio of the number of Indian tourists that went to USA to the number of Indian tourists who were below 30 years of age is ?

A. 2:1
B. 8:3
C. 3:8
D. Cannot be determined

Q.32

If amongst other countries, Switzerland accounted for 25% of the Indian tourist traffic, and it is known from official Swiss records that a total of 25 lakh Indian tourists had gone to Switzerland during the year, then find the number of 30-39 year old Indian tourists who went abroad in that year ?

A. 18.75 lakh   **B.** 25 lakh
C. 50 lakh   **D.** 75 lakh

Q.33 The Indian Government signed a historic peace accord with which state's insurgent groups on January 27, 2020?

A. Jharkhand   **B.** Chattisgarh
C. Assam   **D.** Nagaland

Q.34 Which Indian city has the world's worst traffic, as per the Global Traffic Index?

A. New Delhi   **B.** Beijing
C. Tokyo   **D.** Bengaluru

Q.35 Which state or union territory's tableau was adjudged the best at the Republic Day Parade 2020?

A. Assam
B. Gujarat
C. Jammu and Kashmir
D. Meghalaya

Q.36 India's Gita Sabharwal has been appointed as the UN Resident Coordinator in which nation?

A. Maldives   **B.** Thailand
C. Vietnam   **D.** Kenya

Q.37 Who among the following actresses has been selected for the Padma Shri award 2020?

A. Deepika Padukone   **B.** Kangana Ranaut
C. Alia Bhatt   **D.** Katrina Kaif

Q.38 Which Indian theater personality has been selected for French honour of 'Knight of the Order of Arts and Letters'?

A. Priya Chauhan   **B.** Vani Tyagi
C. Sanjana Kapoor   **D.** Aarti Khanna

Q.39 The Supreme Court has allowed the National Tiger Conservation Authority to relocate which nation's cheetah to suitable habitat in India?

A. Iran   **B.** Malaysia   **C.** Australia   **D.** Namibia

Q.40 The Union Government has offered to sell its 100 per cent stake in which airlines?

A. Vistara   **B.** Air India
C. Air Asia   **D.** Indigo

Part - II

Q.41 The peak value of the output voltage of a half wave rectifier is 100V. The r.m.s value of the half-wave rectifier output voltage will be-

A. 100 V   **B.** 50 V   **C.** 70.7 V   **D.** 35.35 V

Q.42 The given circuit represents a-

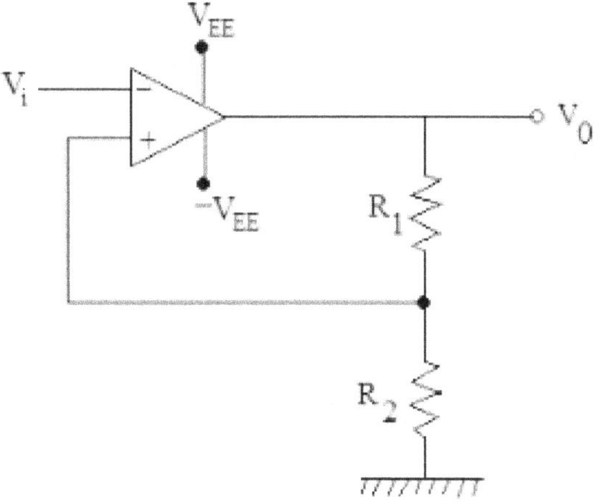

A. Monostable multivibrator
B. Astable multivibrator
C. Schmitt trigger
D. Bistable multivibrator

Q.43 The input resistance of a FET is of the order of-

A. 100Ω **B.** 10Ω **C.** 1Ω **D.** $100M\Omega$

Q.44 In a series R-L circuit supplied from an sinusoidal voltage source, voltage across R and L are 3 V and 4 V respectively. The supply voltage is then-

A. 7 V   **B.** 1 V   **C.** 3.5 V   **D.** 5 V

Q.45 If the insulation resistance of 2m long sample of a cable is $10M\Omega$, then a 8m long sample of the same will have an insulation resistance of-

A. $40M\Omega$ **B.** $2.5M\Omega$ **C.** $2M\Omega$ **D.** $5.5M\Omega$

Q.46 An inductor is supplied from a sinusoidal voltage source. The magnetic field energy in the inductor changes from peak value to minimum value 10 msec. The supply frequency is-

A. 50 Hz   **B.** 25 Hz   **C.** 1kHz   **D.** 100 Hz

Q.47 Two 2000Ω , 2 watt resistors are connected in parallel. Their combined resistance value and wattage rating are-

A. 1000Ω,2watt   **B.** 1000Ω,4watt
C. 2000Ω,4watt   **D.** 2000Ω,2watt

Q.48 We have three resistances each of value 1Ω , 2Ω and 3Ω . If all the three resistances are to be connected in a circuit, how many different values of equivalent resistance are possible ?

A. Five   **B.** Six   **C.** Seven   **D.** Eight

Q.49 The water hammer effect is expected in a

A. Draft tube   **B.** Penstock
C. Surge tank   **D.** Turbine casing

Q.50 An electric heater draws 1000 watts from a 250V source. The power drawn from a 200V source is-

A. 800 W   **B.** 640 W
C. 1000 W   **D.** 1562.5 W

Q.51 Three $3\mu F$ capacitors are in series. A 6 capacitor is in parallel with this series arrangement. The equivalent capacitance of this combination is-

A. 7µF   **B.** 15µF   **C.** 3.6µF   **D.** 1µF

Q.52 A DC series motor has an armature resistance of 0.06\Omega and series field resistance of 0.08\Omega . The motor is connected to a 400V supply. Thus line current is 20A when the speed of the machines is 1100 rpm. When the line current is 50 A and the excitation is increased by 30%, speed of the machine in rpm is-

A. 1100   **B.** 1003   **C.** 837   **D.** 938

Q.53 The voltage across R, L and C are 3V, 14 V, 10 V respectively as in the figure. If the voltage source is sinusoidal, then the input voltage (rms) is-

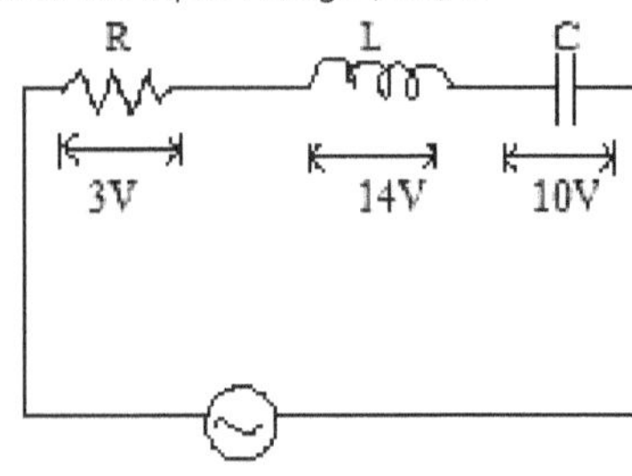

A. 10 V   **B.** 5 V   **C.** 2.5 V   **D.** 15 V

Q.54 In 1-phase series RL circuit fed by voltage source, the resistance and reactance values are 4 ohm each.

A. the current leads the voltage by 45^0
B. the current lags the voltage by 45^0
C. the current lags the voltage by 60^0
D. None of the above

Q.55 Super position theorem requires as many circuits to be solved as there are-

A. nodes   **B.** sources
C. loops   **D.** None of the above

Q.56 In squirrel cage induction motor, the rotor conductors are-

A. open circuited
B. short circuited via end rings
C. short circuited via external reactance
D. short circuited via external resistance

Q.57 A 3-phase synchronous motor is started by utilizing the torque developing in-

A. the high speed steam temperature
B. the damper winding on the rotor
C. the damper winding on the stator
D. the low speed water turbine

Q.58 If the frequency in input voltage of a transformer is increased keeping the magnitude of the voltage unchanged, then-

A. both hysteresis loss and eddy current loss in the core will increase.
B. hysteresis loss will increase but eddy current loss will decrease
C. hysteresis loss will increase but eddy current loss will remian unchanged.
D. hysteresis loss will decrease but eddy current loss will increase

Q.59 Two 1-phase AC motors A and B operate from a 1000V supply. A consumes 2kW at a powr factor of 0.8 (lagging) and B consumes 1 kW at a power factor of 0.5 (lagging). The total current drawn from the supply is approximately-

A. 4.5 A   **B.** 2.1 A   **C.** 4.41 A   **D.** 9 A

Q.60 The high voltage and low voltage winding resistances of a distribution transformer of 1000 KVA, 1100/220 equivalent resistances referred to high voltage side and low voltage side are respectively-

A. 2.504Ω and 0.2Ω
B. 0.2Ω and 0.008Ω
C. 0.10016Ω and 2.504Ω
D. 0.008Ω and 0.10016Ω

Q.61 A tank circuit consists of-

A. an inductor and a capacitor connected in series
B. an inductor and a capacitor connected in parallel
C. a pure inductane and a pure capacitance connected in series
D. a pure inductance and a pure capacitance connected in parallel

Q.62 The instantaneous power of a 1-phase series circuit supplying R-L load from a sinusoidal voltage source has in each cycle.

A. negative twice, zero four times
B. zero twice, negative once
C. negative four times, zero twice
D. negative twice, zero once

Q.63 In a series R-L-C circuit, the "Q-factor" is given by-

A. $Q = \frac{1}{R}\sqrt{\frac{L}{C}}$ **B.** $Q = R\sqrt{\frac{L}{C}}$

C. $Q = \frac{1}{R}\sqrt{\frac{C}{L}}$ **D.** $Q = R\sqrt{\frac{C}{L}}$

Q.64 In an ac circuit, V = (200 + j40) V and I = (30 − j 10) A. The active and reactive power of the circuit are respectively

A. 6400 W, 800 VAR capacive
B. 6400 W, 800 VAR inductive
C. 5600 W, 3200 VAR capacive
D. 5600 W, 3200 VAR inductive

Q.65 Application of Norton's theorem in a circuit results in-

A. A current source and an impedance in parallel
B. A voltage source and an impedance in series
C. An ideal voltage source
D. An ideal current source

Q.66 The voltage (v) vs current (i) curve of the circuit is shown below :

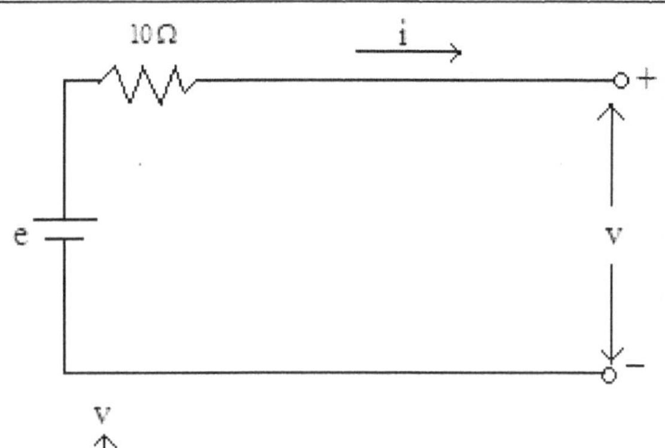

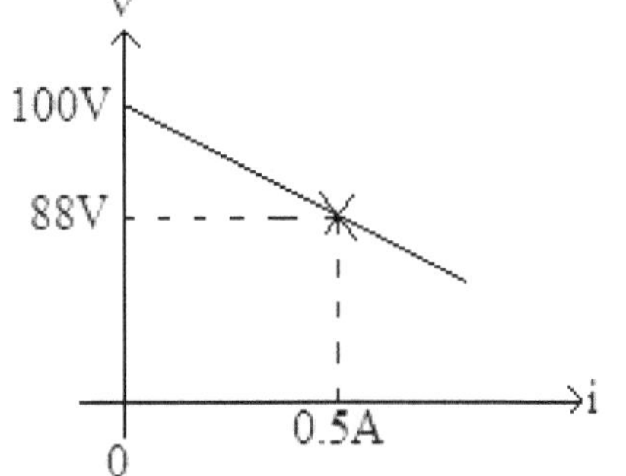

internal resistance of the source e is-

A. 24Ω **B.** 4Ω **C.** 10Ω **D.** 14Ω

Q.67 Value of the load impedance $\overline{Z}_L$ which for load consumes maximum power is-

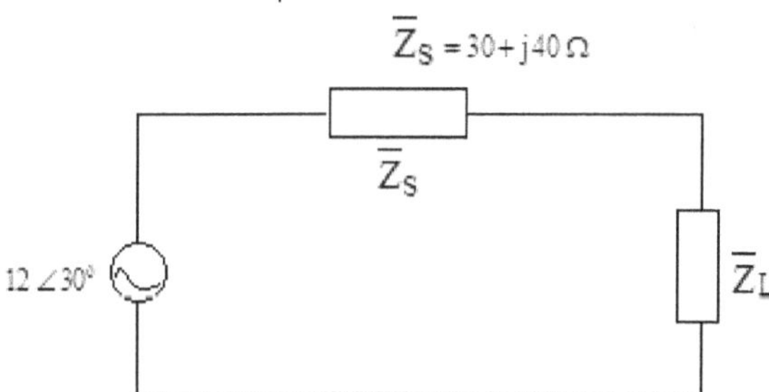

A. 50Ω at a power factor of 0.6 lead
B. 50Ω at a power factor of 0.6 lag
C. 30Ω at a power factor of unity
D. None of the above

Q.68 The speed-torque characteristics of a DC series motor operating from a constant voltage supply are-

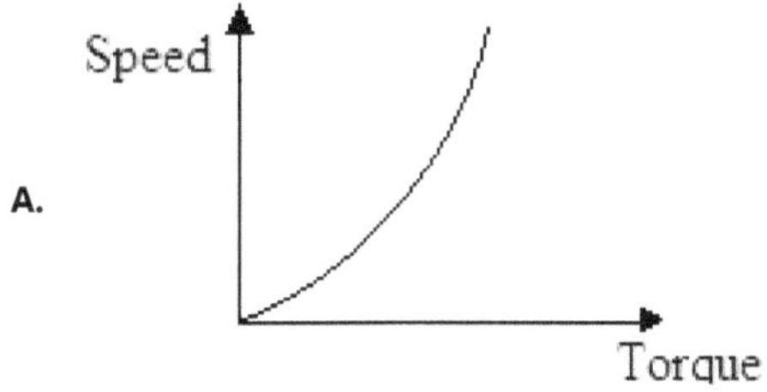

A.

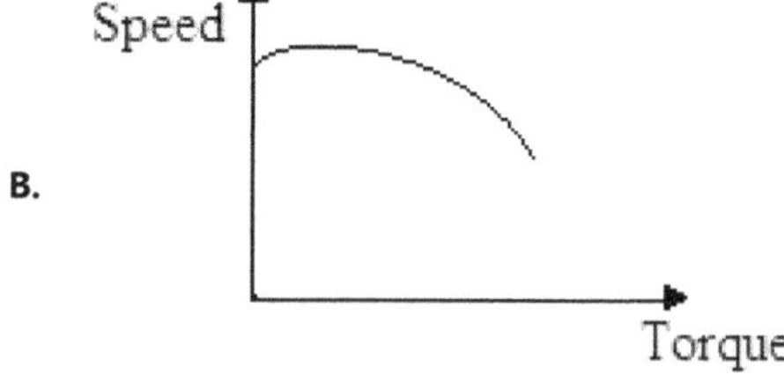

B.

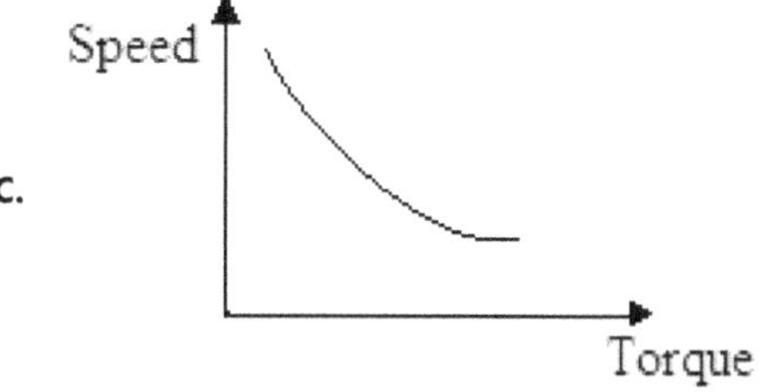

C.

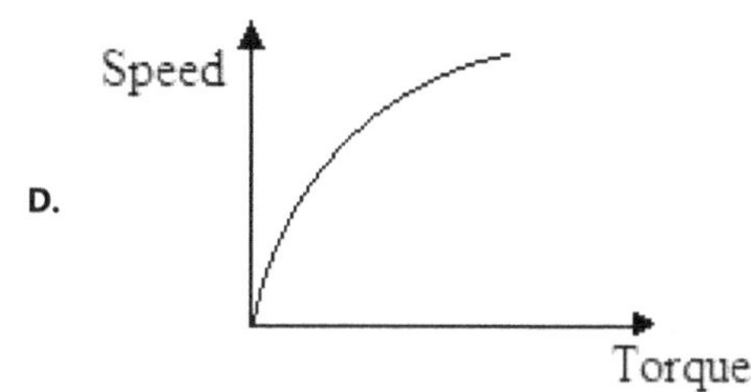

D.

Q.69 Match List I (Machin with List II (Graph) and select the appropriate response-

List I	List II
A. DC Motor	1. Circle diagram
B. DC Generator	2. V-Curve
C. Alternator	3. Open circuit characteristics
D. Induction motor	4. Speed-Torque characteristics

A. A-4, B-3, C-1, D-2 **B.** A- 3, B-4, C-2,D-1
C. A-4, B-3, C-2, D-1 **D.** A-3,B-4,C-2,D-1

Q.70 Three equal impedances are first connected in delta across a 3-phase balanced supply. If the same impedances are connected in star across the same supply

A. phase currents will be $\frac{1}{3}$ of the previous value
B. line currents will be $\frac{1}{3}$ of the previous value
C. power consumed will be $\frac{1}{3}$ of the previous value
D. power consumed will be 3 times the previous value

Q.71 The average value of the voltage wave V= 110 + 175 sin (314 t – 180°) volts is

A. 110 V **B.** 175 V
C. 165.57 V **D.** 206.7 V

Q.72 Two vehicles having masses m_1 and m_2 were moving in a circular path whose radii were r_1 and r_2 simultaneously. If they completed the circles at the same time, then what was the angular speed?

A. $\frac{m_1}{m_2}$ **B.** $\frac{r_1}{r_2}$ **C.** $\frac{m_1 r_1}{m_2 r_2}$ **D.** 1

Q.73 A universal motor is one which-

A. can run on any value of supply voltage

B. has infinity varying speed

C. can operate on ac as well as dc voltage

D. can work as single phase or three phase

Q.74 If the centrifugal switch of a single phase resistance split induction motor does not open after starting of motor, the motor-

A. will run above normal speed

B. will run below normal speed

C. will draw very small current

D. will draw high current and get over heated

Q.75 Alternators are usually designated to generate which type of AC voltage ?

A. with fixed frequency

B. with variable frequency

C. fixed current

D. fixed power factor

Q.76 Three inductors each of 60 mH are connected in delta. The value of inductance of each arm of the quivalent star connection is-

A. 10 mH   **B.** 15 mH   **C.** 20 mH   **D.** 30 mH

Q.77 The magnetic field energy in an inductor changes from maximum value to minimum vlaue in 5 msec when connected to an AC source. The frequency of the source in Hz is-

A. 500   **B.** 200   **C.** 50   **D.** 20

Q.78 A voltage source having an open-circuit voltage of 150 V and internal resistance of is equivalent to a current source of-

A. 2A is series with 75Ω

B. 2A in parallel with 37.5Ω

C. 2A in parallel with 75Ω

D. 1A in parallel with 150Ω

Q.79 A 300 kW alternator is driven by a prime mover of speed regulation 4% while the prime mover of another 200kW alternator has a peed regulation of 3%. When operating in parallel; the total load they can take without any of them being overloaded is-

A. 500kW   **B.** 567 kW   **C.** 425 kW   **D.** 257 kW

Q.80 The commutator in DC machine acts as-

A. a mechanical inverter

B. a mechanical rectifier

C. current controller

D. either (A) or (B)

Q.81 The purpose of using dummy coil in DC machine is to-

A. eliminate harmonics developed in the machine

B. eliminiate harmonics reaction

C. bring mechanical balance of the armature

D. bring mechanical balance of the body of the motor

Q.82 An inductor with a ferromagnetic core is supplied from a sinusoidal voltage source with frequency 'f'. The current drawn by the inductor will be-

A. sinusoidal with frequency 'f'

B. sinusoidal with frequency '2f'

C. a swatooth wave

D. non-sinusoidal with frequency 'f'

Q.83 For a 6-pole DC machine with wave wound armature, the number of brushes requires is-

A. 2   **B.** 4   **C.** 6   **D.** 12

Q.84 Function of interpoles in a DC machine is to-

A. reduce field winding heating

B. improve commutation

C. compensate for air gap variation

D. reduce losses

Q.85 The commulator segments of DC machines are made of-

A. tungsten   **B.** hard drawn copper

C. soft copper   **D.** electrolytic copper

Q.86 Which one of the following is a speed control method of there phase squirrel cage induction motor ?

A. Plugging method

B. Star-delta switch method

C. Pole changing method

D. Centrifugal clutch method

Q.87 Four relations have been given. Select the correct relation?

A. $MMF = \dfrac{Flux}{Reluctance}$ **B.** $Flux = \dfrac{MMF}{Permeance}$

C. $MMF = \dfrac{Flux}{Permeance}$ **D.** $MMF = \dfrac{Flux}{Reluctance}$

Q.88 Two coupled coills, connected in a series have and equivalent inductance of 16 mH or 8 mH depending on the connection. The mutual inductance between the coil is

A. 12 mH   **B.** $8\sqrt{2}$ mH   **C.** 4 mH   **D.** 2 mH

Q.89 Tesla is the unit of-

A. electric flux density

B. magnetic field intensity

C. electric field intensity

D. magnetic flux density

Q.90 Which one of the following is a valid value of coefficient of coupling between two inductors ?

A. 1.414   **B.** 0.9   **C.** 1.732   **D.** 17.32

Q.91 _______________ is the key to a systematic approach for decision-making in the area of energy management.

A. Audit Phase

B. Energy Audit

C. Pre audit phase

D. Conduct survey and monitoring

Q.92 _____________ is a Japanese concept which is widely adopted in many big industries.

A. TAIKEN   **B.** KAIZEN

C. TAWKEI   **D.** KAWKEN

Q.93 _____________ is used to determine the energy that would have been required to produce this year's production output if the plant had operated in the same way as it did in the reference year.

A. Plant energy factor
B. Power factor
C. Production factor
D. Reference year energy

Q.94 Reference year equivalent = Reference year energy use x_______________.

A. plant energy factor
B. power factor
C. production factor
D. reference year energy

Q.95 Which of the following is false?

A. There are two ways to reduce energy dependency; energy conservation and substitution.
B. Kerosene and Liquefied Petroleum Gas (LPG) have substituted soft coke in residential use.
C. The energy performance is the percentage of energy saved at the current rate of use compared to the reference year rate of use. The greater the improvement, the higher the number will be.
D. Detailed energy auditing is carried out in two phases.

Q.96 Which of the following is false?

A. A structured methodology to carry out an energy audit is necessary for efficient working.
B. An initial site visit may take one day and gives the Energy Auditor/Engineer an opportunity to meet the personnel concerned, to familiarize him with the site and to assess the procedures necessary to carry out the energy audit.
C. The audit report will include a description of energy inputs and product outputs by major department or by major processing function, and will evaluate the efficiency of each step of the manufacturing process.
D. Process analysis is not a useful tool for process integration measures.

Q.97 Match the following

I. Plant energy performance is related with	a. Reference year energy
2. Production factor is related with	b. LPG, Kerosene
3. Current years production is related with	c. Reference year's equivalent
4. Example of Fuel substitution is related with	d. Production factor

A. 1-c, 2-a, 3-d, 4-b
B. 1-b, 2-d, 3-a, 4-c
C. 1-d, 2-c, 3-b, 4-a
D. 1-d, 2-a, 3-b, 4-a

Q.98 Which gas can be used for preheating thick oil like furnace oil and LSHS?

A. Exhaust   B. Methane   C. Ethane   D. Butane

Q.99 Which is the key to a systematic approach for decision-making in the area of energy management?

A. Audit Phase
B. Energy Audit
C. pre audit phase
D. Conduct survey and monitoring

Q.100 Which is used to determine the energy that would have been required to produce this year's production output if the plant had operated in the same way as it did in the reference year?

A. Plant energy factor
B. Power factor
C. Production factor
D. Reference year energy

Q.101 The commutator segments of dc machine are made of

A. Tungsten   B. Hard-drawn copper
C. Soft copper   D. Electrolytic copper

Q.102 Which is the ratio of the number of moles of the solute to the total number of moles of all species present in the solution?

A. The mole fraction   B. The mole whole
C. The mole odd   D. The mole even

Q.103 ______________ heat is the heat required to change, at constant temperature, the physical state of materials from solid to liquid, liquid to gas, or solid to gas.

A. Mutant   B. Sensible   C. Latent   D. Photon

Q.104 ______________ heat is that heat which when added or subtracted from materials changes their temperature and thus can be sensed.

A. Mutant   B. Sensible   C. Latent   D. Photon

Q.105 Which of the following is false?

A. Boiler generates steam for heating and drying demand.
B. Fuels such as furnace oil, coal are purchased and then converted into steam or electricity.
C. Some plants generate their own electricity using DG sets or captive power plants.
D. For a complex production stream, it is not better to first draft the overall material and energy balance.

Q.106 Which of the following is false?

A. Material and energy balances can be worked out quantitatively knowing the amounts of materials entering into a process, and the nature of the process
B. Material and energy balances take the basic form.
C. Content of inputs = content of products + wastes/losses + changes in stored materials
D. Energy balances are often complicated because forms of energy can be inter converted, example mechanical energy to heat energy, but overall the quantities must balance

Q.107 Match the following

1. Continuity Equation	a. Fuel consumed Gross Calorific value
2. The law of conservation of mass leads to what is called a mass or a material balance.	b. $\dfrac{A_1 V_1}{V_1} = \dfrac{A_2 V_2}{V_2}$
3. n / V = ?	c. Mass In = Mass Out Mass Stored
4. Energy Supplied by Combustion:	d. p/RT

A. 1-b, 2-c, 3-d, 4-a
B. 1-d, 2-a, 3-b, 4-c
C. 1-c, 2-d, 3-a, 4-b
D. 1-b, 2-d, 3-a, 4-c

Q.108 Heat addition/rejection of a fluid is given by

A. $mC_p \Delta T + kWh$

B. $mC_p\Delta T + kWh * 860kcals$

C. $mC_p\Delta T + 860$ kcals

D. $mC_p\Delta T$

Q.109 Which diagram is a tool to represent an entire input and output energy flow in any energy equipment or system such as boiler generation?

A. Tankey   **B.** Sankey   **C.** Mankey   **D.** Lankey

Q.110 The __________ diagram is quite an old concept and is being used for several years, especially in thermal energy systems.

A. Tankey   **B.** Mankey   **C.** Sankey   **D.** Lankey

Q.111 __________ provides the foundation for setting performance goals and integrating energy management into an organisation's culture and operations.

A. Energy policy

B. Energy team

C. Energy manager

D. Shop manager

Q.112 What can motivate staff to support energy management efforts throughout the organisation?

A. plan and develop an audit strategy

B. review policies and procedures

C. communicating and posting goals

D. process or equipment

Q.113 Which of the following statement is true?

A. Goals are expressed as a function of increasing the energy intensity of a specific performance indicator, such as 5 kWh per unit of product.

B. Good communication does not require careful planning and implementation.

C. Successful organisations use a detailed action plan to ensure a disorganised process to implement energy performance measures.

D. Gaining the support and cooperation of key people at different levels within the organisation is an important factor for successful implementation of the action plan in many organisations.

Q.114 Which is a simple tool that can be used to gain additional insight about the change process to be pursued?

A. Efficiency improvement

B. Force field analysis

C. Benchmarking

D. Reviewing performance data

Q.115 Recognising the accomplishments of individuals and teams is a key to sustaining support and momentum for __________ initiatives.

A. review action plan

B. feedback

C. energy management

D. capital investments

Q.116 Which type of information systems provide a robust means for sharing information on best practices, technologies, and operational guidance?

A. Print-based

B. Computer-based

C. Audio-based

D. Video-based

Q.117 Setting goals helps the energy manager

A. To develop effective performance goals, determine scope, estimate potential for improvement and finally establish goals.

B. Review organisational policies and operating procedures to determine their impact on energy use.

C. Determine the starting point from which to measure progress

D. Energy policy provides the foundation for setting performance goals and integrating energy management into an organisation's culture and operations

Q.118 Which of the following is true?

A. Reporting and communicating allows comparing the energy performance of similar facilities or an established level of performance.

B. Energy team can encourage communication and the sharing of ideas with only one department in an organisation.

C. Providing and seeking recognition for energy management achievements is a proven step for sustaining momentum and support for the program.

D. Assesses the uselessness of the tracking system and other administrative tools to ensure better management and evaluation.

Q.119 __________ allows us to compare the energy performance of similar facilities or an established level of performance.

A. Track & Monitor

B. Get feedback

C. Measure results

D. Benchmarking

Q.120 Which of the following statement is false?

A. Recognition can strengthen the morale of everyone involved in energy management.

B. Providing and seeking recognition for energy management achievements is a proven step for sustaining momentum and support for the program

C. Assesses the uselessness of the tracking system and other administrative tools to ensure better management and evaluation

D. When setting goals, be sure to use the Energy Team's wide range of knowledge to help set aggressive, yet realistic goals.

// Smart Answer Sheet //

Correct — Indicates percentage of students who answered questions correctly.

Skipped — Indicates percentage of students who skipped questions.

Q.	Ans.	Correct	Skipped
1	D	76.76 %	10.34 %
2	B	87.16 %	11.91 %
3	A	79.36 %	18.36 %
4	A	82.35 %	15.22 %
5	C	81.88 %	15.88 %
6	C	76.6 %	11.97 %
7	D	86.88 %	10.89 %
8	A	87.39 %	10.35 %
9	C	76.33 %	14.53 %
10	D	86.8 %	11.51 %
11	B	87.55 %	11.82 %
12	A	78.61 %	15.71 %
13	B	78.85 %	20.22 %
14	D	81.6 %	17.84 %
15	B	77.36 %	19.38 %
16	D	79.44 %	13.21 %
17	C	84.49 %	12.24 %
18	B	87.27 %	11.67 %
19	A	87.43 %	11.63 %
20	C	84.28 %	10.58 %
21	C	81.52 %	18.46 %
22	C	77.88 %	20.12 %
23	A	77.46 %	14.16 %
24	C	78.03 %	17.84 %
25	B	84.49 %	12.18 %
26	B	77.22 %	15.97 %
27	D	82.98 %	11.42 %
28	A	79.48 %	14.46 %
29	C	88.13 %	11.24 %
30	B	87.28 %	11.86 %
31	B	82.56 %	10.29 %
32	D	76.67 %	19.53 %
33	C	80.66 %	13.74 %
34	D	81.54 %	17.33 %
35	A	76.73 %	16.92 %
36	B	79.56 %	16.92 %
37	B	79.64 %	12.98 %
38	C	80.2 %	14.86 %
39	D	84.03 %	11.76 %
40	B	89.03 %	10.58 %
41	B	88.5 %	10.42 %
42	C	82.39 %	17.18 %
43	D	89.08 %	10.13 %
44	D	87.46 %	10.97 %
45	B	84.25 %	14.35 %
46	A	87.05 %	10.16 %
47	B	80.0 %	10.25 %
48	D	84.5 %	11.14 %
49	B	89.48 %	10.05 %
50	B	76.44 %	16.39 %
51	A	79.24 %	15.48 %
52	C	79.61 %	16.34 %
53	B	87.94 %	10.96 %
54	B	88.51 %	11.32 %
55	B	79.27 %	13.0 %
56	B	83.99 %	13.69 %
57	B	78.19 %	15.23 %
58	C	77.74 %	18.22 %
59	A	79.0 %	20.57 %
60	B	82.03 %	11.87 %
61	D	89.55 %	10.21 %
62	A	76.26 %	12.02 %
63	A	84.66 %	11.1 %
64	A	89.69 %	10.13 %
65	A	79.53 %	13.73 %
66	D	87.03 %	11.09 %
67	A	86.15 %	11.07 %
68	C	85.43 %	14.17 %
69	C	81.85 %	15.58 %
70	C	89.87 %	10.04 %
71	A	87.9 %	10.89 %
72	D	88.51 %	10.01 %
73	C	79.89 %	14.96 %
74	D	80.98 %	12.64 %
75	A	81.04 %	13.25 %
76	C	76.1 %	20.14 %
77	C	82.9 %	15.95 %
78	C	86.18 %	13.22 %
79	C	83.31 %	15.91 %
80	D	86.48 %	12.99 %

Q.	Ans.	Correct / Skipped		Q.	Ans.	Correct / Skipped		Q.	Ans.	Correct / Skipped		Q.	Ans.	Correct / Skipped		Q.	Ans.	Correct / Skipped
81	C	88.37 % / 11.53 %		89	D	87.88 % / 11.66 %		97	A	81.61 % / 15.55 %		105	D	83.37 % / 13.73 %		113	D	87.03 % / 12.37 %
82	D	81.15 % / 13.13 %		90	B	82.42 % / 17.4 %		98	A	87.1 % / 10.63 %		106	D	86.38 % / 11.51 %		114	B	77.44 % / 12.32 %
83	A	81.63 % / 12.34 %		91	B	77.55 % / 11.16 %		99	B	77.8 % / 15.33 %		107	A	83.59 % / 11.62 %		115	C	85.41 % / 12.02 %
84	B	83.48 % / 14.87 %		92	B	85.77 % / 13.64 %		100	C	78.26 % / 13.14 %		108	D	76.91 % / 21.5 %		116	B	83.1 % / 16.86 %
85	B	79.82 % / 19.94 %		93	C	82.8 % / 16.78 %		101	B	83.32 % / 15.28 %		109	B	86.7 % / 11.16 %		117	A	83.48 % / 11.34 %
86	C	81.62 % / 15.39 %		94	C	79.48 % / 12.7 %		102	A	83.36 % / 15.87 %		110	C	84.51 % / 15.49 %		118	C	89.12 % / 10.65 %
87	D	76.49 % / 14.26 %		95	D	86.44 % / 12.24 %		103	C	88.43 % / 10.65 %		111	A	84.66 % / 13.18 %		119	D	80.58 % / 17.82 %
88	D	84.5 % / 10.46 %		96	D	87.1 % / 10.02 %		104	B	82.79 % / 10.45 %		112	C	86.66 % / 10.36 %		120	C	86.89 % / 12.27 %

Performance Analysis	
Avg. Score (%)	66.67%
Toppers Score (%)	73.33%
Your Score	

//Hints and Solutions//

1. Reckless means heedless of danger or the consequences of one's actions; rash or impetuous.

puzzling means causing one to be puzzled; perplexing.

preacher means a person who preaches, especially a minister of religion.

spiritual means relating to religion or religious belief.

cautious means careful .

Hence, the correct option is (d).

2. Babel means a confused noise made by a number of voices. Quiet means making little or no noise.
Ignorant means lacking knowledge or awareness in general; uneducated or unsophisticated.
careless means not giving sufficient attention or thought to avoiding harm or errors.

Hence, the correct option is (b).

3. insolent means showing a rude and arrogant lack of respect. Lucid means clear.
Feud means a prolonged and bitter quarrel or dispute.

Hence, the correct option is (a).

4. Sordid means dirty, unpleasant or squalid.

tender means showing gentleness, kindness, and affection

rigidity means inability to be too bent or be forced out of shape.

Hence, the correct option is (a).

5. Sow dragon's teeth means **to take some action** that is intended to prevent trouble, but which actually brings it about.

Hence, the correct option is (c).

6. Great minds think alike: Said when two people have the same opinion or make the same choice.
E.g. "looks like me and Jackie were posting simultaneously; great minds think alike!"

Hence, the correct option is (c).

7. The correctly spelt word is Constitute which refers to give legal or constitutional form to (an institution); establish by law.

Hence, the correct option is (d).

8. Monopoly: the exclusive possession or control of the supply of or trade in a commodity or service.

Hence, the correct option is (a).

9. ● In computing, an input device is a piece of computer hardware equipment used to provide data and control signals to an information processing system such as a computer or information appliance.

● Examples of input devices include keyboards, mouse, scanners, digital cameras and joysticks.

● Speaker is not an example of an input computer device.

Hence, the correct option is (c).

10. ● Robert Brown discovered the nucleus for the first time in cell.
● Brown was studying orchids under microscope when he observed an opaque area, which he called the "areola" or "nucleus", in the cells of the flower's outer layer.

Hence, the correct option is (d).

11. Poliomyelitis virus causes the crippling disease polio and it mainly affects children. Rest of the options are bacterial diseases.

Hence, the correct option is (b).

12. A forest ecosystem is a natural woodland unit consisting of all plants, animals and micro-organisms (Biotic components) in that area functioning together with all of the non-living physical (abiotic) factors of the environment. It's a natural ecosystem.

Hence, the correct option is (a).

13. The Pleura or Pleural membrane is thin, moist, slippery and has two layers. The outer or parietal, pleural lines the inside of the rib cage and the diaphragm while the inner, visceral or pulmonary layer covers the lungs. The pericardium covers the heart whereas peritoneum the internal organs

Hence, the correct option is (b).

14. Lung alveoli are the ends of the respiratory tree, branching from either alveolar sacs or alveolar ducts, which like alveoli are both sites of gas exchange with the blood as well. Alveoli are particular to mammalian lungs

Hence, the correct option is (d).

15. ● In this case, both the metal ball and the wooden ball will hit the ground at the same time!!!, irrespective of their shape, weights and sizes.

● The time required to hit the ground depends on the acceleration of the object, which in this case if 'g' (gravity) acting same on both the objects.

● In a vacuum, there is no resistance in form of air friction.

● The times taken by both of them to reach the ground are exactly equal.

Hence, the correct option is (b).

16. In heavy water, each hydrogen atom is indeed heavier, with a neutron as well as a proton in its nucleus. This isotope of hydrogen is called deuterium, and heavy water's more scientific name is deuterium oxide, abbreviated as D_2O.

Hence, the correct option is (d).

17. The efficiency of Vikas = 10 unit
The efficiency of Vijay = 11 unit
Total work $= 33 \times 10 = 330$ unit
Vijay can complete the same work $= \dfrac{330}{11} = 30$ days.

Hence, the correct option is (c).

18. Let the CP of article $= 100x$ unit
Gain $= 20\%$

SP of article $= 120x$ unit

New CP of article $= \frac{140}{100} \times 100x = 140x$ unit

ATQ,

$\frac{80x}{100} \times 140 = 120x - 24$

$112x = 120x - 24$

$x = 3$

CP of article $= 100x = 100 \times 3 = $ Rs.300

Hence, the correct option is (b).

19. Ratio of value of 10 rupees, 2 rupees and 1 rupees $=$ $15:8:1$

Multiplyby 2 Then the value of 10 rupees, 2 rupees and 1 rupees $= 30:16:2$

Number of 10 rupees coin $= \frac{30k}{10} = 3k$

And number of 2 rupees coin $= \frac{16k}{2} = 8k$

And the number of 1 rupees coin $= \frac{2k}{1} = 2k$

Now A.T.Q.

$3k + 8k + 2k = 273$

$K = 21$

Then total value of coin $= 48k = 48 \times 21 = 1008$

Hence, the correct option is (a).

20. Simple interest $= \frac{P \times R \times T}{100}$

ATQ,

$16000 = \frac{P \times 8 \times 8}{100}$

So, Sum or Principal = 25000

Now, Compound Interest $= P\left[1 + \frac{R}{100}\right]^T - P$

$= P\left(\left[1 + \frac{R}{100}\right]^T - 1\right)$

$= 25000\left(\left[1 + \frac{2}{100}\right]^2 - 1\right)$

$= 25000 \times \frac{101}{250}$

$= 1010$

So, Compound Interest is Rs. 1010.

Hence, the correct option is (c).

21. Let the number be $x, x+2, x+4 \dots \dots x+10$

A.T.Q.

$\frac{x+x+2+x+4\dots+x+10}{6} = 25$

$x + x + 2 + x + 4 + \cdots \dots \dots + x + 10 = 150$

$6x + 30 = 150$

$6x = 120$

$x = 20$

number will be $= 20,22,24,28,30$

and the next even number will be $= 32$,

then new average $= \frac{150+32}{7} = \frac{182}{7} = 26$

Hence, the correct option is (c).

22. Let the speed $= x \; km/hr$

A.T.Q.

$\frac{21}{x} - \frac{21}{x+12} = \frac{60}{9 \times 60}$

$\frac{21 \times 12}{x(x+12)} = \frac{1}{9}$

now from option if we take $x = 42$

$\frac{21 \times 12}{42 \times 54} = \frac{1}{9}$

$\frac{1}{9} = \frac{1}{9}$

So $x = 42$ satisfies the equation

Speed $= 42 \; km/hr$

Hence, the correct option is (c).

23. cost price $=$ Rs 720

Gain % $= 15\%$

Therefore,

selling price $= \left[\left\{\frac{100+gain\%}{100}\right\} \times CP\right]$

$= \left[\left\{\frac{100+15}{100}\right\} \times CP\right]$

$= \left\{\frac{(115)}{100}\right\} \times 720$

$= Rs. 828$

Let the maked price be x

Then, the discount $= 10\%$ of x

$= \left\{x \times \left(\frac{10}{100}\right)\right\}$

$= \frac{x}{10}$

Therefore,SP=(Marked price)-(discount)

$= \left(x - \frac{x}{10}\right)$

$\frac{9x}{10}$

But, the SP=Rs. 828

Therefore, $\frac{9x}{10} = 828$

$\Rightarrow x = \frac{828 \times 10}{9}$

$\Rightarrow x = Rs. 920$

Hence, the marked price is Rs 920.

His selling price if he sells it at a 33.33% discount

$SP = \frac{100-DISCOUNT}{100} \times M.P$

$SP = \frac{2}{3} \times 920 = Rs. 613.33$

Hence, the correct option is (a).

24. $\sqrt{13924} + \sqrt[3]{238328} + 52\%$ of $700 = 395 + ?$

$118 + 62 + \frac{52}{100} \times 700 = 395 + ?$

$180 + 364 - 395 = ?$

$? = 149$

Hence, the correct option is (c).

25. Average marks obtained in Physics by all the seven students

$= \frac{1}{7} \times (90\% \; of \; 120) + (80\% \; of \; 120) + (70\% \; of \; 120) + (80\% \; of \; 120) + (85\% \; of \; 120) + (65\% \; of \; 120) + (50\% \; of \; 120)$

$= \frac{1}{7} \times [(90 + 80 + 70 + 80 + 85 + 65 + 50)\% \; of \; 120]$

$= \frac{1}{7} \times [520\% \; of \; 120]$

$= \frac{624}{7}$

= 89.14.

Hence, the correct option is (b).

26. From the table it is clear that Sajal and Rohit have 60% or more marks in each of the six subjects.

Hence, the correct option is (b).

27. Aggregate marks obtained by Sajal-

= [(90% of 150) + (60% of 130) + (70% of 120)+ (70% of 100) + (90% of 60) + (70% of 40)]

= [135 + 78 + 84 + 70 + 54 + 28]

= 449

Hence, the correct option is (D).

28. We shall find the overall percentage (for all the seven students) with respect to each subject.

The overall percentage for any subject is equal to the average of percentages obtained by all the seven students since the maximum marks for any subject is the same for all the students.

Therefore, overall percentage for:

(i) Maths $= [\frac{1}{7} x (90 + 100 + 90 + 80 + 80 + 70 + 65)] \%$

$=[\frac{1}{7} x (575)] \%$

= 82.14%.

(ii) Chemistry $= [\frac{1}{7} x (50 + 80 + 60 + 65 + 65 + 75 + 35)] \%$

$=[\frac{1}{7} x (430)] \%$

(iii) Physics $= [\frac{1}{7} x (90 + 80 + 70 + 80 + 85 + 65 + 50)] \%$

$= \left[\frac{1}{7} \times (520) \right] \%$

= 74.29%.

(iv) Geography $= [\frac{1}{7} x (60 + 40 + 70 + 80 + 95 + 85 + 77)] \%$

$=[\frac{1}{7} x (507)] \%$

=72.43%.

(v) History $= [\frac{1}{7} x (70 + 80 + 90 + 60 + 50 + 40 + 80)] \%$

$= [\frac{1}{7} x (470)] \%$

= 67.14%.

(vi) Comp. Science $= [\frac{1}{7} x (80 + 70 + 70 + 60 + 90 + 60 + 80)] \%$

$=[\frac{1}{7} x (510)] \%$

= 72.86%.

Clearly, this percentage is highest for Maths.

Hence, the correct option is (a).

29. Aggregate marks obtained by Tarun

= [(65% of 150) + (35% of 130) + (50% of 120)+ ((77% of 100) + (80% of 60) + (80% of 40)]

= [97.5 + 45.5 + 60 + 77 + 48 + 32]

= 360.

The maximum marks (of all the six subjects)

= (150 + 130 + 120 + 100 + 60 + 40)

= 600.

Therefore Overall percentage of Tarun $= \left(\frac{360}{600} \times 100 \right) \% = 60\%$

Hence, the correct option is (c).

30. (40+10) = 50% (from first chart)

Hence, the correct option is (b).

31. The ratio of the number of Indian tourists that went to USA : the number of Indian tourists who were below 30 years of age = 40:15 = 8 : 3.
Hence, the correct option is (b).

32. Tourist traffic from other countries to Swiz is 20%.

Amongst this 20%, 25% of traffic from India.

So, 25% of 20% = 5% corresponds to the Indian traffic in Switzerland.

5 % corresponds to Switzerland's 25 lakh. Hence 15% will be 75 lakh.

Hence, the correct option is (d).

33. The Union Ministry of Home Affairs (MHA), the Assam Government and the Bodo Groups comprising the National Democratic Front of Bodoland (NDFB) and All Bodo Students Union (ABSU) signed a landmark agreement on January 27, 2020. The agreement aims to rename and redraw the Bodoland Territorial Area District (BTAD) in Assam.

Hence, the correct option is (c).

34. The city of Bengaluru was ranked at the top of Global Traffic Index, which was released recently by a Netherlands-based global provider of navigation.

Hence, the correct option is (d).

35. Assam's tableau was adjudged the best among all the 16 participating states and union territories at the Republic Day Parade 2020. The tableau was based on the theme 'Land of Unique Craftsmanship and Culture'.

Hence, the correct option is (a).

36. The United Nations appointed India's Gita Sabharwal as its resident coordinator in Thailand on January 29, 2020.The post is the highest-ranking in UN's country-level development system.

Hence, the correct option is (b).

37. Kangana Ranaut has been selected for Padma Shri award 2020. The full list of Padma Shri award 2020 winners was released on January 26, 2020, on the occasion of the Republic Day.

Hence, the correct option is (b).

38. Theatre artist Sanjana Kapoor has been selected for the prestigious French honour of ''Chevalier Dans Ordre des Arts et des Lettres (Knight of the Order of Arts and Letters).

Hence, the correct option is (c).

39. The Supreme Court on January 28, 2020, allowed relocation of African Cheetah from Namibia to suitable habitat in India.

Hence, the correct option is (d).

40. The Union Government recently offered to sell its full 100 per cent stake in Air India. The government has invited bids with March 17 as the deadline for the expression of interest (EOI) submissions.

Hence, the correct option is (b).

41. The ratio of RMS value to the average value of an alternating quantity is known as its form factor. RMS voltage of a half-wave rectifier, $V_{RMS} = \dfrac{V_m}{2}$ and Average Voltage $V_{AVG} = \dfrac{V_m}{\pi}$, V_m is the peak voltage.

$$V_{rms} = \frac{V_m}{2} = \frac{100}{2} = 50V$$

Hence, the correct option is (b).

42.

- Schmitt trigger is a device (or the input portion of a device) that has separate thresholds for a rising signal and a falling signal. It is a positive feedback circuit that holds the output level until the input sig the al to the comparator is higher than the threshold.

- The positive feedback is introduced by adding a part of the output voltage to the input voltage.

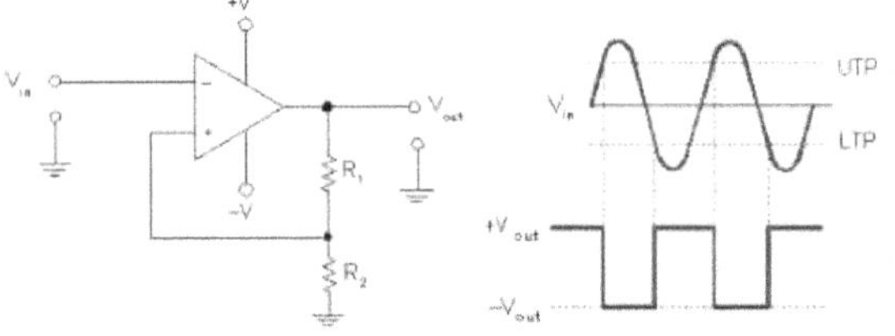

Hence, the correct option is (c).

43.

- The field-effect transistor (FET) is a transistor that uses an electric field to control the electrical behaviour of the device. FETs are also known as unipolar transistors since they involve the single-carrier-type operation.

- FET has the high gate to main current resistance, on the order of 100 MΩ or more, thus providing a high degree of isolation between control and flow.

- FET has a negative temperature coefficient of resistance hence has better stability against the temperature.

Hence, the correct option is (d).

44.

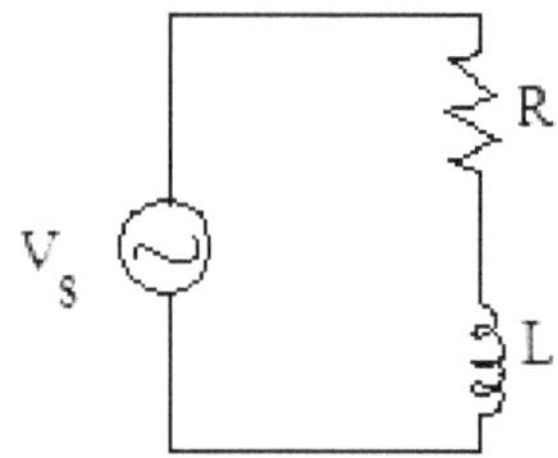

$$V_R = 3V$$

$$V_L = 4V$$

$$V_S = \sqrt{V_R{}^2 + V_L{}^2} = \sqrt{3^2 + 4^2}$$

$$V_S = 5V$$

Hence, the correct option is (d).

45. For insulation Resistance

$$R \ \alpha \ \frac{1}{1}$$

$$\frac{R_1}{R_2} = \frac{1_2}{1_1}$$

$$\frac{10}{R} = \frac{8}{2}$$

$$R = \frac{10 \times 2}{8} = 2.5 M\Omega$$

Hence, the correct option is (b).

46. For a quarter part of wave pulse energy going down to the maximum value to minimum value. i,e

$$\frac{T}{4} = 5 \times 10^{-3} s$$

$$T = 2 \times 10^2 s$$

or $v = \dfrac{1}{T} = \dfrac{1}{2} \times 10^2 = 50 Hz$

Hence, the correct option is (a).

47.

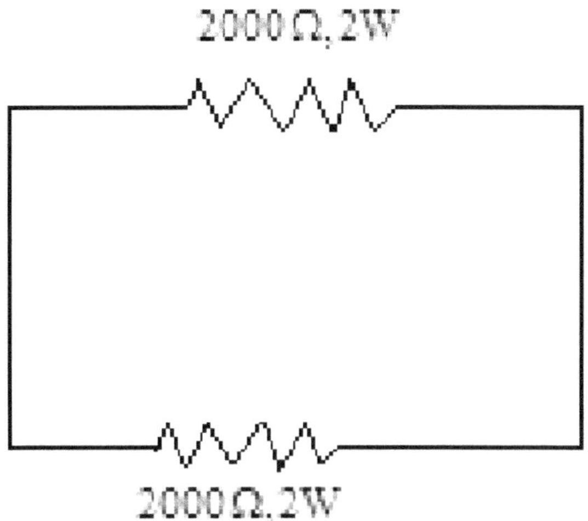

$$R_{eq}= \frac{(R1 \times R2)}{(R1 + R2)}$$

$$\frac{(2000 \times 2000)}{(2000 + 2000)}$$

$R_{eq}=1000Ω$

$P=P_1+P_2=2+2=4W$

The wattage of Resistor In Combination
The total wattage of a combination of resistance is always equal to the sum of the individual wattages of the resistor irrespective of whether the combination is series-connected or parallel connected. This is because the total physical size of the combination increases with the addition of the resistance. Therefore the total wattage for the above question will be 2W + 2W = 4W
Hence the answer will be 1000 ohm and 4 watts.

Hence, the correct option is (b).

48.

1.

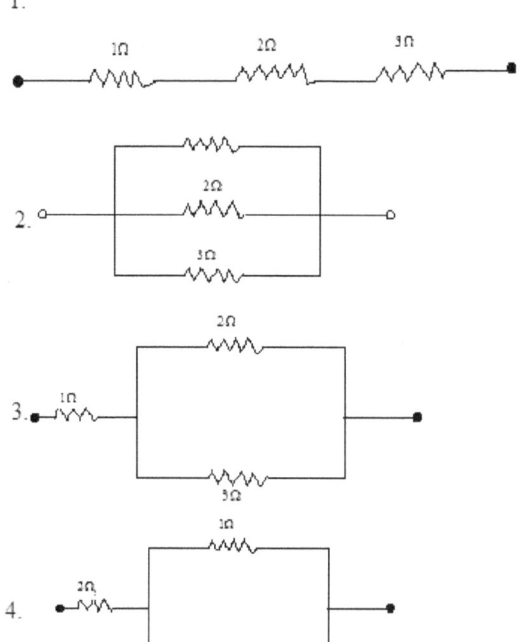

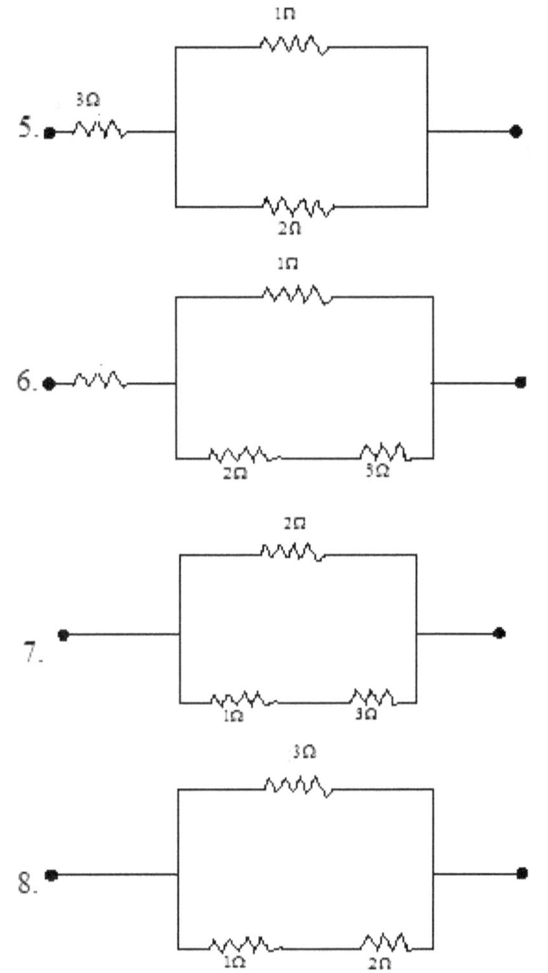

5.

6.

7.

8.

Hence, the correct option is (d).

49. When the generator of a water turbine is disconnected from a power network, the turbine speed starts to increase. Consequently, the turbine controller closes the inflow to the turbine, thus creating a water hammer in the penstock.

Water hammer effects in the penstock are created by any changes in discharge through the turbine, caused by changes in the connected power network. Sometimes, the entire system becomes unstable due to the mutual influence of a turbine equipped with a controller and to unsteady flow in the penstock. In such a case, even small variations in pressure in the penstock may increase steadily and perilously.

Hence, the correct option is (b).

50. $P = \dfrac{V_2}{R}$

$\dfrac{P_1}{P_2} = \dfrac{V_1{}^2}{V_2{}^2}$

$\dfrac{1000}{P} = \left(\dfrac{250}{200}\right)^2$

$P = \dfrac{1000}{25} \times 16 = 640W$

Hence, the correct option is (b).

51. The diagram of the above question will be

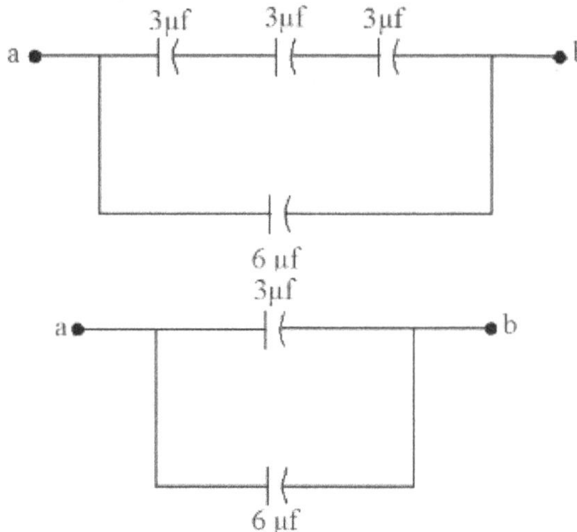

$C_{ab} = (1+e)\mu F = 7\mu F$.

Hence, the correct option is (a).

52. For 400 volts, 20A line current, emf E1 = 400-20(0.06+0.08) = 397.2 volts

Now, line current is 50 Amp and excitation is 1.3 times of initial flux.

E2 = 400- 50(0.08+0.06) = 393volts

Speed is directly proportional to emf and inversely proportional to excitation flux.

$\dfrac{1100}{speed} = \left(\dfrac{397}{393}\right)\left(\dfrac{1.3}{1}\right)$

$\dfrac{397}{393}$

So, speed at 50Amp is 837 rpm.

Hence, the correct option is (c).

53.

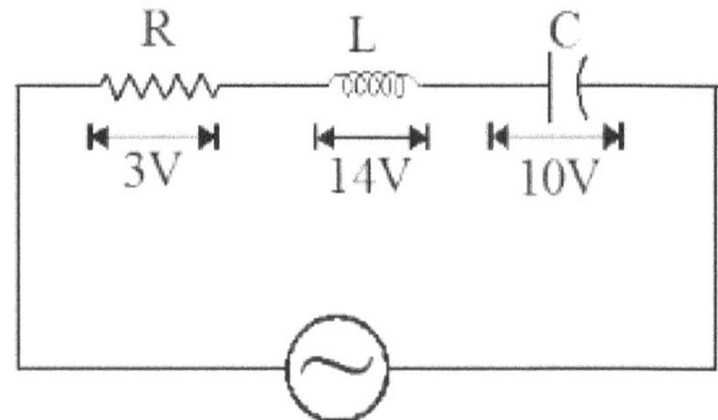

$V_s = \sqrt{V_R{}^2 + (V_L - V_C)^2}$

$= \sqrt{3^2 + (14 - 10)^2} = 5V$

Hence, the correct option is (b).

54. In 1-phase series RL circuit fed by voltage source. The resistance and reactance values are 4 ohm

Z=4+j4

tanθ=1

θ=45⁰

Current lags the voltage by 45⁰

Hence, the correct option is (b).

55.

- Superposition is used for circuit analysis methods when we have a circuit with multiple inputs or multiple power sources at least two sources are required which can be a voltage source or current source.

To solve the given circuit using superposition theorem the contribution of each individual source, all of the other sources first must be "turned off" (set to zero) by

- Replacing all other independent voltage sources with a short circuit (thereby eliminating the difference of potential i.e. V=0; internal impedance of the ideal voltage source is zero (short circuit)).

- Replacing all other independent current sources with an open circuit (thereby eliminating current i.e. I=0; internal impedance of the ideal current source is infinite (open circuit)).

Hence, the correct option is (b).

56.

- When 3 phase supply is given to the stator of a 3 phase induction motor, rotating stator flux will be produced, which will induce emf in rotor windings, according to Faraday's law of electromagnetic induction.

- Now if the rotor windings are kept open-circuited, no current will flow in these windings.

- Copper bars are short-circuited at both ends via end rings.

- Due to short-circuited rotor windings, short circuit rotor currents will flow in them, giving rise to their own magnetic field linking with the stator flux hence the motor start running.

Hence, the correct option is (b).

57.

- Damper windings are windings that are wound to the rotor poles of the machine (winding is similar to that of an induction machine) which helps in two ways.

- We all know that a synchronous machine is not self-starting. Thus providing damper windings help synchronous machines to act as an induction motor (only at starting). Which helps the machine to self-start.

- Hunting is a persistent phenomenon when it comes to synchronous machines.

- We can reduce hunting to a great extent by damping it. They don't let the motor to oscillate abruptly, they

damp the oscillations thus increasing the stability of the machine.

Hence, the correct option is (b).

58.

- Eddy Current Loss in the transformer is given as

$$P_e = K_e f^2 B^2 m$$

Where Ke = eddy current constant

Bm = Maximum flux density and Bm α $\dfrac{V}{f}$

- For any given voltage, if frequency decreases, Bm increases and if the frequency is increased Bm decreases correspondingly.

- Hence the eddy current loss Pe at any given voltage is independent of frequency.

For the fixed magnitude of applied voltage Hysteresis loss is given as

$$P_h = K_h V^{1.6} f^{0.6}$$

Hence from the above equation, it is clear that with the increase in the frequency Hysteresis losses will increase.

Hence, the correct option is (c).

59. $I_1 = \dfrac{P}{V\cos\theta_1} = \dfrac{2\times10000}{1000\times0.8} = 2.5A$

$I_1 = \dfrac{P}{V\cos\theta_2} = \dfrac{1000}{1000\times0.5} = 2A$

I=I₁+I₂=2.5+2

I=4.5A

Hence, the correct option is (a).

60. Resistance referred to high voltage side.

R₀₂=R₁+k²R₂

=0.1+(5)²+0.004

=0.1+0.1=0.2Ω

Resistance refered to low voltage side,

R₀₁= $\dfrac{R_1}{k^2}$+R₂

= $\dfrac{0.1}{25}$+0.004=0.008Ω

Hence, the correct option is (b).

61. Tank circuit

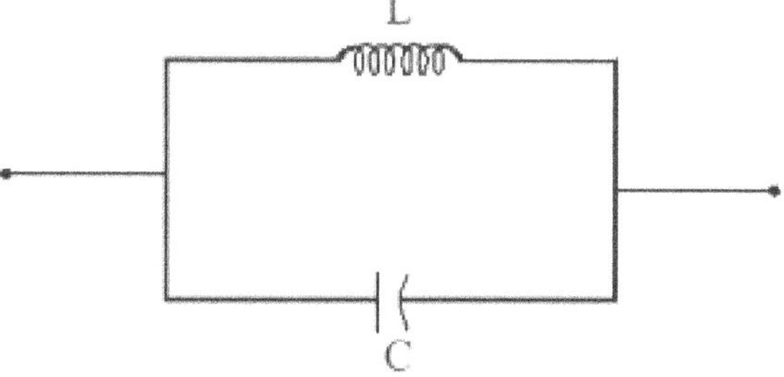

An LC circuit, also called a resonant circuit, tank circuit, or tuned circuit is an electric circuit consisting of an inductor, represented by the letter L, and a capacitor, represented by the letter C, connected together in Parallel.

Hence, the correct option is (d).

62. The instantaneous power of a 1-phase-series circuit supplying R-L load from a sinusoidal voltage souorce has in each cycle negative twice, and zero four times.

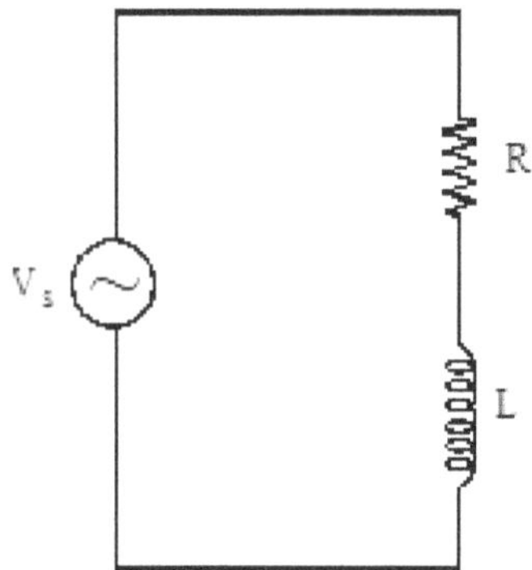

- Instantaneous power is the power of the object at any instant of time, in general, it is defined as p(t) = v(t) x i(t)

- In a single-phase ac circuit, the instantaneous power to a load is of pulsating nature. Even at unity power factor, the instantaneous power is always less than unity

- For a sinusoidal signal, the voltage swings through zero volts twice a cycle, so the instantaneous power is zero two times per cycle.

- If the load has both resistance and reactance, then the current, and voltage swings through zero twice a cycle, with different phase angle and thus the instantaneous power will swing through zero 4 times a cycle.

- Instantaneous power is positive for one part of the cycle and negative for another part of the cycle if there is both resistance and reactance in the circuit. then there will be one negative for voltage and one negative for current thus instantaneous power will have **two negative per cycle for single-phase R-L series circuit.**

Hence, the correct option is (a).

63.

- Q factor is a parameter that describes the resonance behaviour of an underdamped harmonic oscillator (resonator).

- In an ideal series RLC circuit, and in a tuned radio frequency receiver (TRF) the Q factor is: $\dfrac{1}{R}\sqrt{\dfrac{L}{C}}$

- The larger the series resistance, the lower the Q factor.

Hence, the correct option is (a).

64. Active power = 200 x 30 + 40 x10 =6400 W

Reactive Power = 200 x 10 – 40 x 30 = 800 VAR

Hence, the correct option is (a).

65.

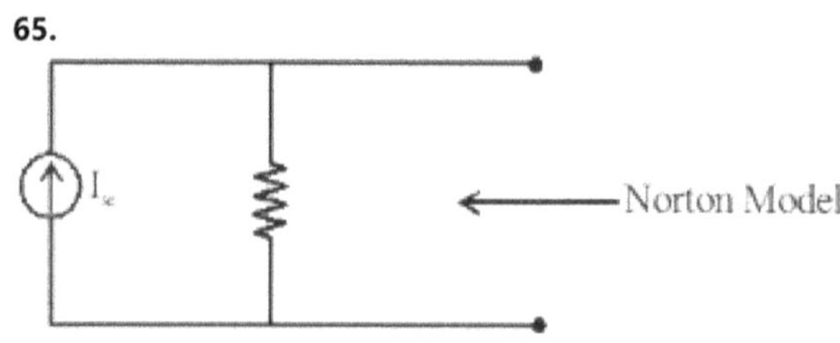

Norton's theorem illustrate that a network consists of several voltage sources, current sources and resistors with two terminals, which is electrically equivalent to an ideal current source " I_{NO}" and a single parallel resistor, R_{NO}.

Hence, the correct option is (a).

66.

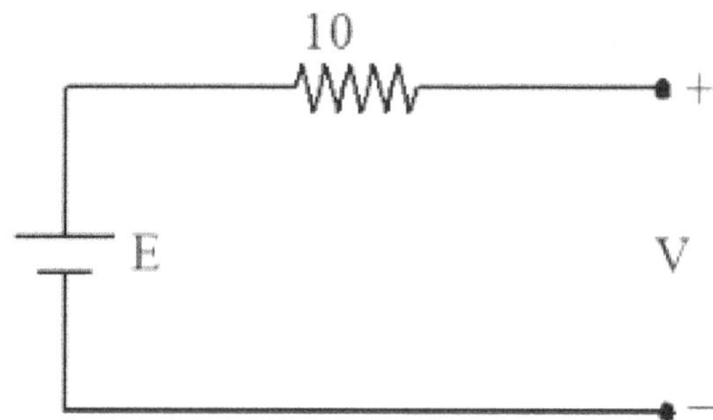

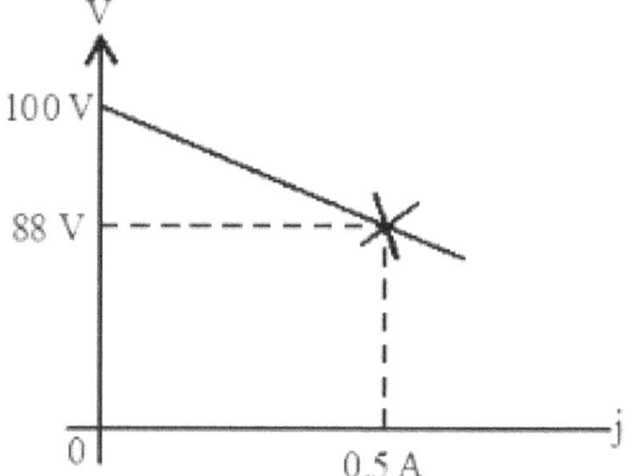

e=V-10i

$$dr= \dfrac{dv}{di}-10= \dfrac{12}{0.5}-10$$

$=24-10=14\Omega$

Hence, the correct option is (d).

67.

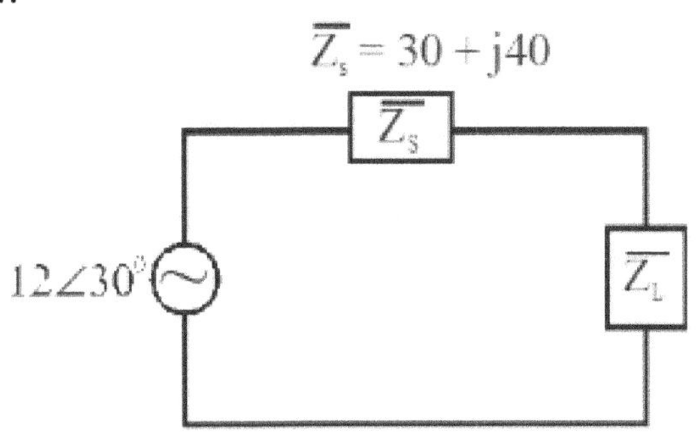

For maximum power transfer

$Z_L = Z_s^* = 30 - j40$

$|Z_L| = 50$

$Z_L = 50\,\Omega$ at power factor of 0.6 leading

Hence, the correct option is (a).

68. Speed torque characteristic

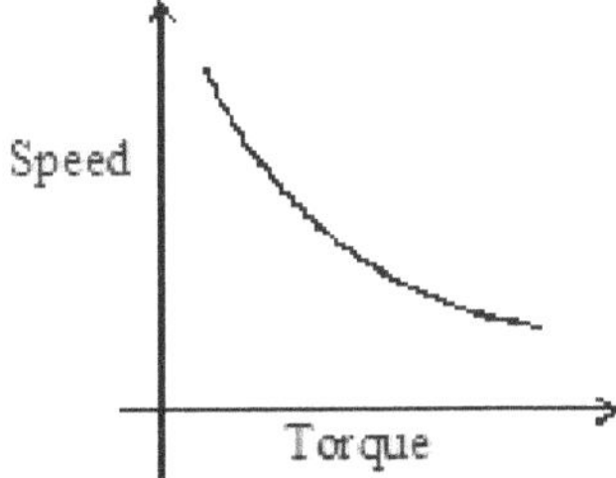

Speed torque characteristic is also called a mechanical characteristic. From the characteristics of the DC series motor, it can be found that when speed is high, torque is low and vice versa.

Hence, the correct option is (c).

69. DC motor $\rightarrow$ Spped – torque characteristic

DC generator $\rightarrow$ Open circuit characteristic

Alternator $\rightarrow$ V-cure

Induction Motor $\rightarrow$ Circle diagram

Hence, the correct option is (c).

70. Let us suppose Vs be the supply voltage per phase.
So the line voltage of the supply will be 3Vs.
Now assume any type of load; for simplicity, let's assume it a resistive load which is R per phase
For Delta connected load:
Calculation of per phase power; PD= I²R
Where I is load current (per phase)
And,

$I = \dfrac{\sqrt{3}Vs}{R}$ {as line voltage of the supply is directly applied to the phase of the delta load}

So,

Pd = $\left(\dfrac{\sqrt{3}Vs}{R}\right)^2 R = \dfrac{3Vs^2}{R}$ watts per phase.

For 3 phases:

P₃D = 3Pd = $\dfrac{3\times 3Vs^2}{R} = \dfrac{9Vs^2}{R}$ watts.

Now for Star connected load:

PS = I²R = $\left(\dfrac{Vs}{R}\right)^2 R = \dfrac{Vs^2}{R}$ watts

For 3 phases: P₃S = 3PS = 3 $\dfrac{Vs^2}{R}$ watts

Conclusion: $\dfrac{P_{3S}}{P_{3D}} = \dfrac{3Vs_2}{R} \div \dfrac{9Vs^2}{R} = \dfrac{1}{3}$

i.e The power ratio between Star to Delta is 1:3

Hence, the correct option is (c).

71. The average value of the second term is zero therefore answer is 110 V

Hence, the correct option is (a).

72. For one complete circle:

Time, $T = \dfrac{2\pi r}{v} = \dfrac{2\pi}{w}$

For vehicle having mass m_1,

$T_1 = \dfrac{2\pi}{\varpi_1}$

For vehicle having mass m_2,

$T_2 = \dfrac{2\pi}{\varpi_2}$

Given,

$T_1 = T_2$

So,

$\dfrac{2\pi}{\varpi_1} - \dfrac{2\pi}{\varpi_2}$

Therefore,

$\dfrac{\varpi_1}{\varpi_2} = 1$

Hence, the correct option is (D).

73.

- The universal motor is so named because it is a type of electric motor that can operate on AC or DC power.

- It is a commutated series-wound motor where the stator's field coils are connected in series with the rotor windings through a commutator.

- It is often referred to as an AC series motor. The universal motor is very similar to a DC series motor in construction but is modified slightly to allow the motor to operate properly on AC power.

- This type of electric motor can operate well on AC because the current in both the field coils and the armature (and the resultant magnetic fields) will alternate (reverse polarity) synchronously with the supply.

Hence, the correct option is (c).

74. If the centrifugal switch is failed to open then the starting winding will draw very high current and it may burn the winding

Hence, the correct option is (d).

75.

- n an alternating current electric power system, synchronization is the process of matching the speed and frequency of a generator or other source to a running network. An AC generator cannot deliver power to an electrical grid unless it is running at the same frequency as the network. If two segments of a grid are disconnected, they cannot exchange AC power again until they are brought back into exact synchronization.

- Hence alternators are usually designed with the fixed frequency of AC voltage.

Hence, the correct option is (a).

76.

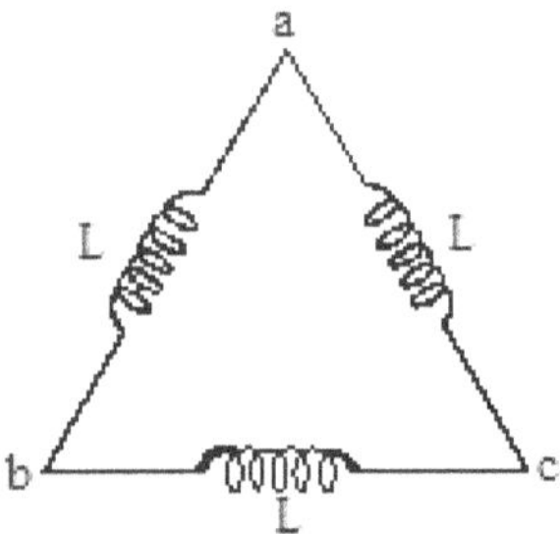

$$L_{ab}= \frac{L}{3}= \frac{60}{3}\times10^{-3}=20mH$$

Hence, the correct option is (c).

77. $\frac{T}{2}=2\times[5\times10^{-3}]$

$T=2\times10^{-2}sec$

$$f= \frac{1}{2\times10}=50Hz$$

Hence, the correct option is (c).

78. $V_{oc}=150V$

$R_{eq}=75\Omega$

$$I_{sc}= \frac{V_\alpha}{R_{eq}}=2A$$

$R_{eq}=75\Omega$

Hence, the correct option is (c).

79. Let load shared by two machinery are x kw and y kw

$$\left(\frac{4}{300}\right)x = \left(\frac{3y}{200}\right)$$

$$8x = 9y$$

$$x = 225\ kw.....(\because y = 200\ kw \text{ given })$$

$$\therefore \text{total load} = 225 + 200 = 425kw$$

Hence, the correct option is (c).

80.

- The commutator is a mechanical rectifier, so the commutator collects induced EMF or current developed in the armature.

- In a motor, the commutator applies an electric current to the windings. By reversing the current direction in the rotating windings each half turn, a steady rotating force (torque) is produced.

Therefore commutator work as the mechanical rectifier and current controller.

Hence, the correct option is (d).

81.

- Dummy coil is used with wave winding when the requirement of the winding is not met by the standard armature.

- Dummy coil is not connected to the commutator so they do not influence the electrical characteristics of the winding

- Dummy coil ends are cut short and taped.

- Their main use is to provide mechanical balance for the rotor because the rotor having some slots without winding would be out of balance mechanically.

Hence, the correct option is (c).

82. Inductors with ferromagnetic cores have additional energy losses due to hysteresis and eddy currents in the core, which increase with frequency. At high currents, iron core inductors also show a gradual departure from ideal behaviour due to nonlinearity caused by magnetic saturation of the core
If the current through a ferromagnetic core coil is high enough that the magnetic core saturates, the inductance will not remain constant but will change with the current during each half of the period to provide the maximum flux density, therefore, the inductor with ferromagnetic core end up having non-sinusoidal excitation current.

Hence, the correct option is (d).

83. In wave winding the number of brushes is always 2 irrespective of the number of poles.

Hence, the correct option is (a).

84.

- Interpol are small poles compared to main poles and placed in the Interpolar region between the main poles and they are connected in series with the armature winding.

- Their purpose is to counterbalance the armature reaction due to the flow of current in the armature winding.

- Interpol primary functions are

- It produces a counter flux on the coil which is undergoing commutation to nullify the REACTANCE VOLTAGE.

- It also nullifies the armature flux in the inter-polar region automatically.

Hence, the correct option is (b).

85. Commutators require periodic maintenance such as brush replacement, therefore, to reduce wear and tear commutator segment s of dc machines are made up of hard-drawn copper.

Hence, the correct option is (b).

86.

- The pole changing method is used in squirrel cage IM because like slip ring IM we can't add external resistance in the rotor to reduce speed.

- In this method, it is possible to have one or two speeds by changing the number of poles. This is possible by changing the connection of the stator winding with the help of simple switching.

Hence, the correct option is (c).

87. The amount of flux produced by the magnet indicates the strength of the magnet. The more the magnetizing force (MMF), the more is the flux produced. The more the opposition to the flux path (i.e., reluctance or magnetic resistance) less is the flux produced. This relationship is expressed as

$$\text{Flux} = \frac{MMF}{Reluctance}$$

Reluctance is the opposition offered by the material in the flux path to the establishment of the flux. The reluctance in a magnetic circuit is similar to the resistance in an electric circuit. Reluctance is the inverse of permeance.

$$MMF = \frac{Flux}{Permeance}$$

Hence, the correct option is (d).

88. The overall inductance of 2 coil L1 and L2 connected in series with mutual inductance aiding self-inductance L1 with mutual inductance opposing self-inductance L2 then the mutual inductance M is given as

$\frac{1}{2}$ (L1 − L2)

$\frac{1}{2}$ (16 − 8)

= 2mH

Hence, the correct option is (d).

89.

- The tesla (symbol T) is a derived unit of magnetic flux density (informally, magnetic field strength).

- One tesla is equal to one weber per square meter.

Hence, the correct option is (d).

90. The value of the coefficient of coupling is always greater than 0 and less than 1, or 0% and 100% respectively. A coefficient of coupling of 0 would represent no coupling, and 1 would represent perfect coupling.

Hence, the correct option is (b).

91. Energy Audit is the key to a systematic approach for decision-making in the area of energy management. It attempts to balance the total energy inputs with its use and serves to identify all the energy streams in a facility.

Hence, the correct option is (b).

92. KAIZEN is a Japanese concept which is widely adopted in many big industries.

Kaizen is a concept referring to business activities that continuously improve all functions and involve all employees from the CEO to the assembly line workers.

Hence, the correct option is (b).

93. Production factor is used to determine the energy that would have been required to produce this year's production output if the plant had operated in the same way as it did in the reference year.

Hence, the correct option is (c).

94. Reference year equivalent = Reference year energy use x production factor.

Hence, the correct option is (c).

95. Detailed energy auditing is carried out in two phases.

Detailed energy auditing is carried out in three phases: Phase I, II and III.

Hence, the correct option is (d).

96. Process analysis is not a useful tool for process integration measures.

Flow charts, process maps, Program Evaluation and Review Techniques (PERT), Critical Path Methods, Stem-and-Leaf Plots, Box plots, written procedures, and work instructions are tools used for process analysis and documentation.

Hence, the correct option is (d).

97. Plant energy performance is related with-Reference year's equivalent

Production factor is related with-Reference year energy

Current years production is related with-Production factor

Example of Fuel substitution is related with-LPG, Kerosene

Hence, the correct option is (a).

98. Exhaust gas can be used for preheating thick oil like furnace oil and lshs.

Hence, the correct option is (a).

99. Energy Audit is the key to a systematic approach for decision-making in the area of energy management.

An energy audit is an inspection survey and an analysis of energy flows for energy conservation in a building. It may include a process or system to reduce the amount of energy Input Into the system without negatively affecting the output.

Hence, the correct option is (b).

100. Production factor is used to determine the energy that would have been required to produce this year's production output if the plant had operated in the same way as it did in the reference year.

Hence, the correct option is (c).

101. Commutators require periodic maintenance such as brush replacement, therefore, to reduce wear and tear commutator segment s of dc machines are made up of hard-drawn copper.

Hence, the correct option is (b).

102. The mole fraction is the ratio of the number of moles of the solute to the total number of moles of all species present in the solution.

Hence, the correct option is (a).

103. Latent heat is the heat required to change, at constant temperature, the physical state of materials from solid to liquid, liquid to gas, or solid to gas.

Hence, the correct option is (c).

104. Sensible heat is that heat which when added or subtracted from materials changes their temperature and thus can be sensed.

Hence, the correct option is (b).

105. For a complex production stream, it is not better to first draft the overall material and energy balance is false.

Hence, the correct option is (d).

106. Energy balances are often complicated because forms of energy can be interconverted, example mechanical energy to heat energy, but overall the quantities must balance is false.

Hence, the correct option is (d).

107. Continuity Equation- $\dfrac{A_1 V_1}{V_1} = \dfrac{A_2 V_2}{V_2}$

The law of conservation of mass leads to what is called a mass or a material balance-Mass In = Mass Out Mass Stored

$$\frac{n}{V} = \frac{p}{RT}$$

Energy Supplied by Combustion-Fuel consumed Gross Calorific value.

Hence, the correct option is (a).

108. Heat addition/rejection of a fluid is given by $mC_p\Delta T$.

Hence, the correct option is (d).

109. Sankey diagrams are a type of flow diagram in which the width of the arrows is proportional to the flow rate. The illustration shows a Sankey diagram that represents all the primary energy that flows into a factory. The widths of the bands are linearly proportional to energy production, utilization and loss. Sankey diagram is a tool to represent an entire input and output energy flow in any energy equipment or system such as boiler generation.

Hence, the correct option is (b).

110. The Sankey diagram is quite an old concept and is being used for several years, especially in thermal energy systems.

Hence, the correct option is (c).

111. Energy policy provides the foundation for setting performance goals and integrating energy management into an organisation's culture and operations.

Energy Policy is a monthly peer-reviewed academic journal covering research on energy policy and energy supply. It is published by Elsevier.

Hence, the correct option is (a).

112. Communicating and posting goals can motivate staff to support energy management efforts throughout the organization. The Energy Manager in association with the energy team typically develops goals.

Hence, the correct option is (c).

113. Gaining the support and cooperation of key people at different levels within the organisation is an important factor for the successful implementation of the action plan in many organisations is true

Hence, the correct option is (d).

114. Force field analysis is a simple tool that can be used to gain additional insight about the change process to be pursued.

Force-field analysis is a development in social science. It provides a framework for looking at the factors that influence a situation, originally social situations.

Hence, the correct option is (b).

115. Energy management includes planning and operation of energy production and energy consumption units. Objectives are resource conservation, climate protection and cost savings, while the users have permanent access to the energy they need.

Hence, the correct option is (c).

116. Computer-based type of information systems provide a robust means for sharing information on best practices, technologies, and operational guidance.

Hence, the correct option is (b).

117. Setting goals helps the energy manager To develop effective performance goals, determine the scope, estimate the potential for improvement and finally establish goals.

To develop effective performance goals, determine scope, estimate potential for improvement and finally establish goals.

Hence, the correct option is (a).

118. Providing and seeking recognition for energy management achievements is a proven step for sustaining momentum and support for the program is true.

Hence, the correct option is (c).

119. Benchmarking allows us to compare the energy performance of similar facilities or an established level of performance.

Benchmarking is the practice of comparing business processes and performance metrics to industry bests and best practices from other companies. Dimensions typically measured are quality, time and cost.

Hence, the correct option is (d).

120. Assesses the uselessness of the tracking system and other administrative tools to ensure better management and evaluation is false.

Hence, the correct option is (c).

// Notes //

// Notes //